Enabling Praxis

PEDAGOGY, EDUCATION AND PRAXIS

Volume 1

The *Pedagogy, Education and Praxis* Series will foster a conversation of traditions in which different European and Anglo-American perspectives on 'pedagogy', 'education' and 'praxis' are problematised and explored. By opening constructive dialogue between different theoretical and intellectual traditions, the Series aims, in part, at recovering and extending the resources of these distinctive traditions for education in contemporary times. The Series aims to contribute to (1) theoretical developments in the fields of pedagogy, education and praxis; (2) the development of praxis in the pedagogical professions; and (3) the development of strategies capable of resisting and counteracting contemporary tendencies towards the technologisation, standardisation, bureaucratisation, commodification and de-moralisation of education.

Enabling Praxis
Challenges for Education

Stephen Kemmis and Tracey J. Smith (Eds.)
School of Education, Charles Sturt University, Wagga Wagga, Australia

SENSE PUBLISHERS
ROTTERDAM / TAIPEI

A C.I.P. record for this book is available from the Library of Congress.

ISBN 978-90-8790-253-7 (paperback)
ISBN 978-90-8790-254-4 (hardback)

Published by: Sense Publishers,
P.O. Box 21858, 3001 AW Rotterdam, The Netherlands
http://www.sensepublishers.com

Printed on acid-free paper

CONTENTS

STEPHEN KEMMIS, MATTS MATTSON, PETRA PONTE
AND KARIN RÖNNERMAN

SERIES INTRODUCTION

Pedagogy, Education and Praxis

The 'Pedagogy, Education and Praxis' series arose from shared concerns among educational researchers from Australia, the Netherlands, the Nordic countries and the United Kingdom about the relationships between different traditions of education and educational research that inform our work. The meanings of terms like 'pedagogy' and 'praxis' are contested *within* European research traditions and Anglo-American traditions and even more confusingly contested *across* or *between* traditions. These words, shared across languages and intellectual traditions, inhabit different spaces in different languages, with different characteristic ways of behaving in each. What 'pedagogy', 'education' and 'praxis' mean in Dutch or English or Swedish – where variants of these words occur – cannot be translated precisely and without remainder into another language. The Series aims to encourage a 'conversation of traditions' in which the voices of different traditions can be heard, and different perspectives can come into view. In this way, readers may glimpse beyond the English in which the conversation is conducted to the rich intellectual traditions presented by contributors to the Series We hope to use these key ideas – pedagogy, education and *praxis* – as windows through which we may see, even if darkly, into the rooms of other languages and traditions, and to learn what we can about those other traditions. The international collaborative project 'Pedagogy, Education and Praxis', of which this Series is an expression has three kinds of aims:

1. theoretical aims concerning the exploration and critical development of key concepts and associated understandings, from different educational and research traditions, of pedagogy, educational science and educational studies, and social and educational *praxis* and practice;
2. practical aims concerning the quality and transformation of educational *praxis* in settings including education, teacher education and the continuing professional development of teachers, in relation to a variety of contemporary educational problems and issues, as they emerge in a variety of educational contexts at different levels of education and in different national contexts; and
3. strategic aims of
   a. encouraging the dialogue between different traditions of theory, research and practice in education;

b. enhancing awareness about the origins and formation of our own (and others') presuppositions and understandings as participants in such dialogues; and

c. fostering collaboration and the development of networks between scholars interested in these problems and issues across traditions.

The volumes in the series are intended as contributions to this dialogue. Some aim to foster this dialogue by opening and exploring contemporary educational contexts, problems and issues within one country or tradition to readers from other countries and traditions. Other volumes aim to foster dialogue by bringing together, to address a common topic, authors and contributions from different countries and traditions. We believe that this endeavour will renew and revitalise some old conceptual resources, and make some, old or transformed, accessible as new resources for educational theory and practice in the international conversations, conferences and collaborations which constitute the globalised educational research communities of today.

Stephen Kemmis, Charles Sturt University, Australia
Matts Mattsson, Stockholm University, Sweden
Petra Ponte, Leiden University, The Netherlands
Karin Rönnerman, Goteborg University, Sweden

PETRA PONTE AND JAN AX

FOREWORD

On the first page of his book *Lessons of the Master* (Dutch translation, Amsterdam, *Bezige Bij*, 2004), Steiner argues that 'we are so immersed in the profusion of forms of education – primary, technical, scientific, humanistic, moral and philosophical – that we seldom just take the time to think about the wonder of transfer, the resourcefulness of deception, which I, pending a more precise and relevant definition, would like to call the mystery of what happens'.

This book has found the courage, at a time when the pursuit of the manageability of the human spirit is in the ascendancy, to pause and reflect on the 'mystery of what happens' in schools and on teacher education courses. It deals not only with the individual relationship between master and pupil, which was what concerned Steiner, but also with the context in which that relationship is formed.

We can ask ourselves why there is a need for this reflection now and, more than that, why any such attempt is relevant. After all, teaching is as old as humanity and much of our education still has characteristics of the education of centuries ago. At the same time we can see that educational needs have changed over time and that, in fact, teaching was always subject to pressure from social and societal developments. A significant example of this was the rise of education for the masses in the industrial age. Still it is possible to argue that right now we are also facing changes on an unprecedented scale due to our globalised information society, which present us more than ever before with global problems on the environment, intercultural relations, wealth and poverty, war and peace. These are issues that at the most profound level refer to the democratic quality of our global community. It seems obvious that there will be an attempt to reposition education in this new world order, so it is not surprising that the reflections in the book focus mainly on the moral responsibility of education and of those whose job it is to put it into practice – the teachers in schools and on teacher education courses. The book is concerned with analysing education as a morally informed endeavour, based on the responsibility to 'do good for oneself and humankind'.

The authors have tried in their analyses to capture the 'mystery of what happens' in a language borrowed from a concept that was formulated way back in antiquity, that is Aristotle's concept of praxis. Aristotle tried to answer the questions: What is wisdom? What is knowledge? What makes a person who has the capacity to act? He defined praxis as 'action', referring in a general sense to all intentional activities, by which people can reach a particular 'goal' through their own efforts. More specifically, the term referred to rational action based on a conscious choice and 'action' was defined as the product of observation, desires, and intellect or reason.

Kemmis, Stephen and Smith, Tracey J. (2008) Enabling praxis: Challenges for education.ix-xi

The praxis concept, as further developed over the centuries, offers an alternative to the dominant metaphors in present-day teaching which have been derived from domains of practice other than education. A striking example of this is the language used in connection with issues of total quality management (TQM): tailor-made teaching; client-oriented services; closed chains of information exchange; achievement-based reward and so forth. All of these notions have been developed in the world of industrial manufacturing and, more specifically, the domain of predictable technologies and closed production processes. A tendency to now perceive the teaching profession in terms of a combination of technological prediction, client orientation, efficiency and manageability can clearly be detected.

Clearly there is a world of difference between the language of praxis and the language of manageability. On page 253 of his book *Freedom Evolves* (Dutch translation, Amsterdam: Contact, 2004), Dennett described a fable to illustrate the misunderstandings that can arise from such a difference in language. In answer to the question as to whether things such as 'faith' and 'pain' are real, he wrote:

> The fable concerns people who speak a language in which they are talking about being overcome by 'fatigues' where you and I would simply say that we are 'tired' or 'exhausted'. When we come to them with our sophisticated science, they ask us which of the small bodies in the bloodstream are the fatigues. We wave the question aside, which then leads them to ask in disbelief: are you denying that fatigues are real?

Praxis can be compared with being tired. We all know that it exists, but it cannot be marked out as set rules, procedures and outcomes, just as fatigue cannot be marked out as 'small bodies in the bloodstream'. That makes communicating about praxis difficult and a dialectical mode of understanding would seem to be the obvious solution. That is why the book first presents some in-depth conceptual-theoretical views, placing the concept into an historical context. Then questions to do with how praxis manifests itself in empiricism today are fed into the debate: What are the characteristic features? What aspirations are there? What opportunities are seen and what problems are experienced in the practice of education as morally informed action? The comprehensive descriptions of practical experiences and empirical data are used in turn to enrich the conceptual and theoretical views. The advantage of this method of working is that it tends to open up and initiate fundamental debates about the essential tasks of education rather than closing down and warding off discussion.

Fundamental debates about the core tasks of education were initiated in the international context of the 'Pedagogy, Education and Praxis' project. The international reflections in the penultimate chapter are the product of these debates and they enabled the Australian study to be emulated in several forms. They also enabled the moral role of education to be debated proceeding from multiple conceptual usages. These discussions seemed to lead back time and time again to the question of the legitimacy of our practice, or as Steiner (ibid) put it: 'What gives a woman or a man the authority to teach another person? Where does the source of the power lie? How will those who are being taught respond?' These questions apply not only to the individual teacher, but also to the institutional power of governing bodies and authorities.

The authors of this book deserve genuine praise for the fact that as colleagues at the School of Education of Charles Sturt University they have been able to raise these issues together. They also deserve praise for the honest and thorough way they went about this.

Petra Ponte
Jan Ax

July 2007
Leiden/Amsterdam, The Netherlands

PART 1 THEORETICAL BACKGROUND

STEPHEN KEMMIS AND TRACEY J. SMITH

1. PRAXIS AND PRAXIS DEVELOPMENT

About this book

This volume aims to answer these questions: What is the nature of *praxis*? In what ways can a deeper understanding of *praxis* inform and guide the actions of educators? To what extent do the conditions of educational practice today, especially in institutionalised settings, enable, constrain or disable *praxis*? How best can *praxis* be developed in initial and continuing education? And finally, to what extent can *praxis* be safeguarded and preserved?

We have chosen to write a book about *praxis* because we believe there is too little of it in education today. From the outset, we would like to make clear that we are not presenting a 'how to' book or manual for *praxis* development. Instead, our book captures the collective work of a group of colleagues that have interrogated the notion of *praxis* from multiple perspectives over a sustained period of time. As educators, we think it is essential that we consistently ask the question "what *should* we do?" in relation to our practice. Perhaps an equally important question is "In whose interests are we acting?" This book foregrounds moral purpose in education and aims to examine *praxis* using a variety of lenses. Moral purpose is an aim for all professions that we would like to renew through the connected conversations threaded through the chapters in this book. In each of the chapters, our underlying assumption is that education and being an educator are inextricably linked to social and moral responsibility. Our hope is that we can reignite conversations about *praxis* for all professionals involved in the work and study of education.

As a community of inquirers, we have strategically examined the development of *praxis* in different fields of education, including the initial and continuing education of teachers for schools, vocational education and training, educational leadership, educational policy-making and community education. Collectively, our endeavours as writers and researchers have been to look more closely at the pattern and fabric of practice in diverse settings to discern those qualities of practice that embody *praxis*. We have engaged in open and sustained conversations about *praxis* and *praxis* development. One set of these conversations has been among the contributors to this volume in the university in which we work together as teachers and/or researchers. Another set of conversations has been with contributors to other volumes in this series – some from intellectual traditions rather different from our own. In addition to these conversations, of course, there is also the larger conversation we join as participants in the research fields and literatures of *praxis*, practice and pedagogy in education.

Kemmis, Stephen and Smith, Tracey J. (2008) Enabling praxis: Challenges for education.3-13

What is praxis?

Praxis is a particular kind of action. It is action that is *morally-committed, and oriented and informed by traditions in a field*. It is the kind of action people are engaged in when they think about what their action will mean *in the world*. *Praxis* is what people do when they take into account all the circumstances and exigencies that confront them at a particular moment and then, taking the broadest view they can of what it is *best* to do, they *act*.

Throughout this volume, we have italicised the word *'praxis'*, following the convention for foreign words. We have done this to emphasise the ancient Greek and Aristotelian usage and roots of the term. In doing so, we have taken a particular view of *praxis* which may or may not be taken in other languages and other theoretical traditions, where *praxis* sometimes means simply 'social practice' which, by virtue of its being social, necessarily implies a moral stance towards others involved in or affected by a particular practice.

Praxis means different things in different intellectual and cultural traditions. In some European traditions, for example, *praxis* is understood as any social action undertaken in the knowledge that one's actions affect the well-being and interests of others. In other traditions, notably Marxian traditions, *praxis* is the kind of action that makes transformations in the social world. In this book, we regard *praxis* as a kind of enlightened and 'elevated' action. From this perspective, we understand *praxis* to be a rather special kind of action undertaken in occupations and professions like education or social work or medicine or farming. In the specific setting of education, when an educator, through her or his practice, takes into account not only her or his own interests, but also the long-term interests of each individual student, and the long-term interests of society and the world at large – he or she is engaging in *praxis*.

One reason we take this particular view of *praxis* is that, in English, the word *'praxis'* is a specialist term. In everyday speech in English, people refer to 'practice' in contexts in which the term *'praxis'* might be used in German or Dutch, for example. We speak of 'practice' as something more shaped by intention, by social context and by tradition than mere 'action', 'acts' or 'behaviour'. Thus, for example, we speak of practices like chess or farming or medicine as socially-, culturally- and historically-formed, shaped and ordered. As far as we understand the way the term *'praxis'* is used in some other European languages, it seems to be used more or less the way the word 'practice' is used in English. In this book, we therefore reserve the term *'praxis'* to refer to those forms of practice that are enacted by those that are conscious and self-aware that their actions are "morally-committed, and oriented and informed by tradition" – like the traditions that orient the work, the being and the becoming of people practising a particular occupation or profession. By contrast, we will use the term 'practice' to refer to social practices more generally, when actors are not necessarily conscious or aware of the moral import and the social and historical consequences of their action.

Another important consideration for the authors in this book is that any understanding of *praxis* also needs to take into account that our actions as educators often involve in-the-moment decisions about complex and demanding situations. Acknowledging the messiness and day-to-day decision making related to being an educator must be part of any efforts to capture the nature of *praxis* and renew its place in education. There is no *praxis* utopia. Likewise, *praxis* does not refer only to an ideal. A proper understanding of *praxis* recognises that the person who is acting is doing so in response to the practicalities and particularities of a given situation – they do the best they could do on the day, the best they could do under the circumstances.

PRAXIS AS ENDANGERED: A FORGOTTEN TRADITION?

We believe *praxis* in education today is endangered. This concern has motivated us to write this book. In our view, *praxis* today risks being replaced by something else. We think this state of affairs has important and untoward consequences for students, teachers and the societies they serve. We think that *praxis* is slowly being edged aside in late modern times – what some think of as postmodern times – by that form of practice that amounts simply to *following rules*. While we do not consider rule-following to be generally or necessarily wrong or inappropriate, what we do consider important is that, as educators, we must regard the laws, policies, rules and procedures that impact on our actions critically, to explore whether, how and the extent to which they enable or constrain our educational *praxis* – our action when it is morally-committed, and oriented and informed by tradition.

What is at stake when practice becomes rule following is the *moral agency* of the educator. At some point, hemmed in by rules, the educator may become no more than the *operative* of some system – the organisation they work in. This distinction between being an agent and being an operative is at the heart of our concern for educational practice and *praxis*. Our capacity to live with, live by, interpret, extend and sometimes creatively trouble or avoid the rules of organisations is one of the things that give us our identities as educators. It is the thing that allows us to develop and enact *praxis*. In other words, *praxis* demands creative thinking, care, compassion and critical consciousness – thinking outside or beyond the rules. *Praxis* is not confined to education, of course: it is played out in a vast variety of settings including the actions of professional practitioners in all fields and occupations, in conscious acts of citizenship and frequently in social and political action.

We are not alone in our concern about *praxis* and its survival in contemporary educational practice. Joseph Dunne (2005) described practice as endangered in education and in other professions, building on arguments first advanced in his (1993) book *Back to the Rough Ground*:

> We speak of a species as endangered when, no longer responding adaptively to the imperatives of its environment, it fails to meet the implacable requirements of natural selection. Practices of course are not biological entities, nor can concern for their endangered status imply any wish that they find a place on some evolutionary superhighway. But for decades now the greatest dangers to living species have come from environmental changes

caused by human intervention and assault. And practices have their own similar ecology: they too are exposed to drastic changes in their human environments that threaten their continuing viability. 'Viability' here, however, is not a matter of mere survival; one can perhaps better speak of 'integrity' which introduces a necessary moral inflection and makes one look to other analogies, as, for example, when the integrity of a national territory is compromised by commercial pressures. While every analogy limps, I introduce 'practice' as the notion of something that can succeed or fail in being true to its own proper purposes, and that it can fail in this, even as it succeeds in accommodating powerful pressures from its environment (Dunne, 2005, p.367).

In our view, educational practice today sometimes does "fail in being true to its own proper purposes". It does so for different kinds of reasons which, we hope, will become clearer in the chapters that follow. Firstly, when educational practice is guided by theories not of education but of other kinds (for example, psychological theories or sociological theories) it can 'hand over' the practitioner's control of educational action to the authors of those 'external' theories. Secondly, when educational practice is guided solely by state or institutional policies and procedures that are not responsive to the needs of students and teachers and their communities, the practitioner similarly hands over control to the authors of those policies and procedures. At an extreme, curriculum, pedagogies and assessment may be governed by state and systemic policies and procedures to an extent that professional judgement and a practitioner's *praxis* are endangered. Thirdly, when educational practice is conducted in ways that are governed by the decisions of local school or organisational managers that exclude consideration of the needs of students, teachers and communities, then we can say that the practitioner becomes an operative of those decisions and not an agent.

In our view, too, a variety of trends and tendencies in recent educational literature offer responses to these dangers. For example, new developments in action research (see, for example, the Educational Action Research Journal) and self-study (Loughran, Hamilton, LaBoskey & Russell, 2004) aim to strengthen reflexive practice (Cole and Knowles, 2000). Similarly, developments in practice theory (Schatzki, 2002) also suggest that our concerns for the state, the development and even the survival of *praxis* in education are widely shared.

THEMES THAT STRUCTURE THIS BOOK

As will become clear, the book explores tensions between *praxis* and practice. As we have suggested, perhaps controversially, we see *'praxis'* as that particular kind of practice which is morally-committed, and oriented and informed by traditions. By contrast, we see the term *'practice'* as more general and encompassing, and as applying to a wide variety of actions and activities in social settings. In the book, we will encounter different kinds of theories of practice that explore its social, cultural and material formation. In a sense, then, the purpose of the book, insofar as it is addressed to educators as individuals, is to encourage *praxis* in the lived conditions of practice; insofar as it is addressed to those who create and shape the conditions under which educators work, it aims to encourage the formation and development of social, cultural and material conditions that make educational *praxis* possible.

A number of topics or themes recur in our conversations about the nature of *praxis* and reverberate through the chapters that follow:

1. agency, subjectivity, being, becoming, identity (and difference and otherness) and reflexivity;
2. particularity, concreteness and materiality;
3. connectedness, relatedness, order and arrangement;
4. history and biography;
5. morality and justice; and
6. praxis as doing (not just saying or intending).

These themes emerge in different ways in different chapters, not always explicitly, as we interrogate and reframe the notion and the development of *praxis*. An aspect of our reframing has been challenging ourselves to see beyond what we think we are doing to explore the consequences of our actions.

The first cluster of topics concerning the *agent* (a person with moral agency) is very significant. From the perspective of *praxis*, the actor is (perhaps intensely) aware of being watchful or conscious in order to 'steer' unfolding action and events towards a desirable state of affairs, not only in the best interests of participants in the action in the here and now, but also in terms of the good for humankind. The agent or actor rarely acts alone; she or he acts, in practice, in ways oriented by the actions of other persons. And perhaps most importantly: as we shall see, *praxis* is not just action in or on others and the world; it is also and always a process of becoming, of self-formation – the formation of the moral agency and the very identity of the actors *through their acts*.

The second cluster of topics, concerning *particularity*, recognises that all practice is located in concrete conditions of place, time and arrangement of objects. We discuss some of these by reference to cultural-discursive, social-political, material-economic and environmental dimensions and connections. Practices prefigure or frame action-possibilities in ways that are concrete and local, even if they are sometimes, and in some respects, abstract and general. This draws attention to difference and possibilities for recognition of difference. Each of us, in studying practice/*praxis*, enters particular relationships with particular people in the cases we are examining, particular ways of observing, particular times and places. This also influences our research methods and we need to be attentive to the particularity of these relationships in the cases we are reporting. The acts that make practice and *praxis* are always particular; they respond to particular circumstances and conditions; they are cases where we may act well or badly. This is at the heart of *praxis* – it concerns how well we did on the day, when we ourselves had to choose and to act (or not to act), when the consequences of our actions flowed on to others for better or for worse.

This last feature also distinguishes what is written in this book from other books about the quality of education. All too often, books about quality – in education and in other fields (like 'total quality management' or 'quality assurance' or even 'quality teaching') – are books about *external* criteria to which a process or an act must conform if it is to be regarded as of high quality. This is to regard quality impersonally, objectively and, in the end, we suggest, bureaucratically. To take that view of 'quality' is to take the actor out of the act, the person out of the unfolding events in which each of us does our best or aims to do as well as we can under the circumstances. A great deal of our contemporary experience of science, research and professional life is premised on this objectivising attitude – the notion that each of us, like all others, should strive to meet objective criteria of quality in our work. Although we do not reject that objectivising attitude out of hand, here we want to follow the poet W. B. Yeats (1965; from his 1928 poem 'Among school children'): "How can we know the dancer from the dance?" We want to insist that *praxis* is the action of people who act in the knowledge that their actions will have good and ill consequences for which they have sole or shared responsibility, and who, in that knowledge, want to act *for the good*. The book is thus addressed to those who want to develop not just 'quality' or 'quality outcomes', as 'quality' is seen by others, but the substance and excellence of *their own and others'* practice as *praxis*, and their virtue as practitioners in their own fields – in this book, the field of education. In short, the book is addressed to educational practitioners who want to judge their actions by their educational consequences, that is, the consequences of their actions for the particular students and communities with whom they work.

The third cluster concerns *connectedness*. Connectedness presupposes plurality. The actor exists in relation to, and in connection with, a variety of kinds of orders and arrangements: orders and arrangements of people, objects, words and ideas, and the natural orders and arrangements that form the living environment in which we exist. One might go so far as to say that the substance of practice and *praxis* is always enacted in each and all of these dimensions, enabled and constrained by pre-existing arrangements in each dimension. That is, we cannot conceive of practice or *praxis* other than in terms of its connectedness in each of these dimensions and, as we have seen, in the concrete particularity that situates it in real time, space and place.

The fourth topic is *history* – practice and *praxis* are always located in biographies, narratives, and histories and traditions of practice that prefigure practice/*praxis* in this particular time and this particular place. The way the world is interpreted depends on an understanding of history and one's own historicality. In *praxis* a person is conscious of themselves as acting in history, as making a world and a history through their action. The practitioner comes to a field of action that is always already structured by their own and others' ways of thinking and seeing the world, their ways of doing things, and their ways of relating to others. A critical consciousness in terms of history can help us find ways of thinking that, at least partially, allow us to escape the constraints that tradition has placed upon our thought, interpretations and perspectives and imagine our futures. Both in a broad sense in relation to traditions of practice and in the narrower sense of the situatedness of practice in this or that particular time or place, practice and *praxis* unfold in time, in a present that is shaped by the past that preceded it and rolling out into the uncertain future.

The fifth topic is *morality and justice* – aspects of *praxis* that presuppose an ethic of care which has a profound moral dimension that highlights an imperative to act responsively toward self and others and to sustain a moral relation with those in our care (Gilligan, 1982; Noddings, 1986). When a person's action is *praxis* they are striving to do something right, ethical, proper, the best that could be done under the circumstances, a right and principled thing to do. In such cases, people are not just following a rule, but aiming to act rightly and appropriately under these particular circumstances, in relation to these particular others, when these particular things are at stake. A sense of *praxis* also requires one to act fairly, honestly, and with integrity. Moreover, *praxis* demands a heightened awareness of, and a willingness to reflect on, the character, conduct and consequences of one's actions to determine if those actions are morally defensible and justifiable.

The sixth topic – *praxis as doing* is a crucial point, but so obvious as often to escape notice. Just as caring is something you engage in, an act of doing not just an attitude or something you are (Noddings, 1986), so too is *praxis*. The danger is that we describe as *praxis* things that are rules or principles or moral norms or virtues (things that are not in themselves *praxis*) instead of the acts or deeds that are themselves *praxis*. *Praxis* is the doing. It is an act done by an actor. The relationship between *praxis* as doing and *phronēsis* as the disposition towards acting rightly has been of particular interest. *Praxis* is a kind of action, not an external feature of action; a kind of practice, not an external feature of practice. In describing *praxis* and distinguishing it from practice, we have insisted that *praxis* is the action of an individual – what an individual person does or can do. At the same time, however, we do not want to exclude the possibility of *collective praxis*. In some of the case chapters in this book, we encounter groups of co-participants exploring their practice and *praxis* together: teacher educators, student teachers, people involved in professional development, in educational administration, and in social action addressing problems of global warming. In these cases, co-participants aim to act together in *collective praxis*.

THE ORGANISATION OF THE BOOK

The book is composed of three parts. Part One presents the theoretical background for the views of *praxis* and practice explored here. Part Two presents a number of cases that make use of the theoretical framework introduced in Part One to investigate features of *praxis* and practice in different kinds of settings. Part Three, 'Conversations and Conclusions', presents reflections from contributors to other volumes in this series (the 'conversations' part of the title), and conclusions from the editors of this volume.

In Part One, *Chapter Two*, Stephen Kemmis and Tracey Smith explore *praxis* and the development of *praxis* largely from the perspective of the individual. The underlying purpose of Chapter Two is to present an historical look at *praxis* development guided by the classical account of *praxis* put forward by Aristotle, and extended by the more critical perspectives of Habermas, Gadamer, McIntyre and Dunne.

In *Chapter Three*, Stephen Kemmis and Peter Grootenboer situate *praxis* in a wider context of social and other conditions that we describe as '*extra-individual*'. In this chapter we situate *praxis* within practice in cultural-discursive, social-political, and material-economic orders and arrangements. By doing this, our aim is to develop the notion of '*practice architectures*' or *metapractices* that must be changed and developed if *praxis* and practice within real settings is to change and develop. 'Practice architectures' to some extent prefigure, enable and constrain practices (and thus *praxis*). Our central argument in Chapter Three is that changing or developing *praxis* requires changing and developing the practice architectures within which particular practices occur.

In Part Two we encounter cases in which *praxis* and its development are explored and presented as a sequence of spheres of *praxis*. The chapters represent a shifting focus in terms of researchers working individually or collaboratively with participants to determine the nature of *praxis*. The sequence of cases begins with a focus on an individual teacher educator critically examining her own pedagogical practice and ends with a discussion of a *praxis of citizenship* in diverse communities.

In *Chapter Four*, Tracey Smith retrospectively analyses prospective teachers' reflective narratives sourced from her doctoral studies. Smith felt challenged to gain a deeper understanding of the subtle nuance between *phronēsis* and *praxis* and the extent to which reflective storying could enhance the development of a *praxis* stance. Smith was able to discern particular features of her practice, for example, the use of a *theory/practice/reflection cycle of inquiry* and the process of *noticing, naming and reframing* that fostered the development of a *praxis stance*. Smith argues that a *praxis* stance is a vital disposition that can be nurtured when a balance between support and challenge, and between theory and practice, is explicitly designed to occur within the practice architecture of teacher education programs.

Christine Edwards-Groves and Deana Gray present a cautionary case in *Chapter Five* that uncovers the complexities, the constraints and affordances of reflection and reflective practice to discover how prospective teachers understand the nature of reflection from their experiences of it in a particular university course. From the inner sphere of the perspectives of prospective teachers' themselves, Edwards Groves and Gray present a compelling case that urges all teacher educators to carefully re-examine their pedagogical intentions in light of the actual perceptions of those they teach. The chapter reveals that to be constructive and perceived as having value by prospective teachers, reflective practices need to be overt, explicit and developmentally embedded into the practice architectures of education courses.

In *Chapter Six*, Helen Russell and Peter Grootenboer present a case of their own critical reflection where they turn the *praxis* lens back onto their own tertiary teaching practice. The nature and context of their teaching situation was characterised by a number of unresolvable tensions – a condition that demanded an inward search for their own *praxis*. Indeed, they argue, it is the existence of tensions that 'call forth' *praxis* in a person's conduct. The chapter provides insight into a collective journey towards finding *praxis* from the perspective of a teacher educator. A feature of their journey was the use of a Blog as a reflective and analytical tool.

In *Chapter Seven*, we move from pre-service to in-service teacher education. Christine Edwards-Groves describes an alternative approach to professional learning that focuses on the moment-by-moment interactions of classroom teaching. She argues that models of professional learning that involve teachers in active and collaborative learning communities within the situated context of their schools can lead to the development of a *praxis*-oriented self. Pivotal features of *praxis* development identified in this chapter include opportunities for teachers to engage in action research, especially using transcriptions of classroom talk, that allows teachers to interrogate their own pedagogical practices.

In *Chapter Eight*, Ian Hardy provides insights into how teacher learning is influenced by broader policy contexts, and how these policies serve as metapractices or practice architectures that enable and constrain the teachers' professional development. In this chapter, we discover that policies and government programs are one powerful socio-political dimension in which practice architectures are constructed.

Jane Wilkinson explores the notion of educational leadership as *praxis* in *Chapter Nine*. She expands the *praxis* sphere by drawing on case studies of socio-economically and ethnically diverse senior female academics. The ways in which these women's practices contribute to diverse forms of leadership are examined. They feel themselves to be constrained in the forms of leadership they can provide in their universities by a prevailing culture of new managerialism in contemporary Australian universities. The chapter shows how institutional and organisational structures, social relationships and cultures are other dimensions in which practice architectures are constructed. The women Wilkinson studied resisted and challenged these practice architectures, not always successfully, but demonstrating how acting 'against the grain' expresses and realises these leaders' agency and their refusal to be no more than operatives of the administrative systems of the institutions in which they worked.

In *Chapter Ten,* Roslin Brennan Kemmis explores teacher preparation in the Vocational Education and Training (VET) sector. The history, virtues and characteristics of VET in Australia are examined in tension with the highly rationalised system of vocational education and training in Australia– the finely elaborated set of competencies, qualifications, accreditation mechanisms and regulations that are grounded in national legislation. The chapter shows how practice architectures in the dimension of curriculum – as it appears in the elaborate VET competency-based training arrangements – can constrain *praxis* but also, oddly and surprisingly, leave a space for agency for VET teachers and teacher educators. It appears that the Australian training system constrains but also enables *praxis*. The traditions of practice in the VET sector, grounded in the centuries-old apprenticeship tradition, provide an alternative source of enablement and constraint for VET teachers and teacher educators.

In *Chapter Eleven*, William Adlong takes us out of the sphere of formal education in schools, colleges and universities to the kind of informal education that occurs in every social movement – arguably, every social movement is an educational movement. Adlong suggests that our work as educators has the potential to open communicative spaces that can affect the solidarity, understandings and actions of persons in the civil sphere. By cultivating public spheres that reflect larger social movements, individuals become educators whose work changes the practices of a society to respond rationally to the risks we face with 'sustainability' issues such as climate change. This re-enlivening of politics in the Aristotelian sense provides a medium for the development of a *praxis of citizenship* which, in turn, may disembed a commitment to the status quo that can pervade our institutional practices and move towards a deeper understanding of *collective praxis* – indeed, to understand that all *praxis* is inherently social and political in nature. In this chapter, the social, economic and political structures of Western democracies are presented as practice architectures that shape the ways people use energy, for example, calling forth counter-movements that aim initially to resist and subvert established ways of providing energy, but also establishing alternative ways of living and using energy that offer more rational and sustainable alternatives. The chapter suggests that the transition from *poiēsis* to *praxis* – from technical action within the rules to agentic moral agency – may be parallelled at the social level by a shift from acting within a social order to acting within social movements that transform established orders.

In Part Three, 'Conversations and Conclusions', we bring in alternative perspectives to enrich our conversations and to conclude the book. The reflections in *Chapter Twelve* provide outside lenses that serve as a critique of the chapters in our book. As editors of the other books in the series, Jan Ax and Petra Ponte, Matts Mattsson, and then Karin Ronnerman present their thoughtful critiques of our chapters. Collectively, their interpretations of the chapters in this book highlight many points of interest, conceptual issues and empirical issues that foreground important questions that need to be addressed in the future.

In *Chapter Thirteen*, as co-editors we address some of the issues raised in Chapter Twelve and reconceptualise a way forward for developing professional praxis. A set of guiding questions is put forward as a frame of reference for all educators to more critically consider the underlying principles, and the impact, of the practice architectures that frame their programs. We conclude this chapter with an illustrative case of what it might look like for a teacher to embody *praxis* by 'living a certain kind of life'.

In *Chapter Fourteen*, Stephen Kemmis delivers an epilogue to suggest a radical proposal that would be required if the view of education we have reconceptualised in this book were to be put to work *in practice*. Educators, teacher educators, educational administrators and policy makers, and even educational institutions would need to reconsider the ways schooling is constructed and funded. This chapter suggests some of the ways in which education might need to be done differently if it is to be *education for praxis* – education for living rightly, and education that contributes to the good for humankind.

We invite you, as readers interested in education and *praxis*, to enter the collective conversations we have found so rewarding.

REFERENCES

Cole, A. L., & Knowles, J. G. (2000) *Researching teaching: Exploring teacher development through reflexive inquiry*. Needham Heights, MA: Allyn & Bacon.

Dunne, J. (2005) An intricate fabric: Understanding the rationality of practice. *Pedagogy, Culture and Society*, 13(3), 367-390.

Gilligan, J. (1982) In a different voice: Psychological theory and women's development (in italics). Mass: Harvard University Press.

Loughran, J. J., Hamilton, M. L., LaBoskey, V. K., & Russell, T. (Eds.) (2004) *International handbook of self-study of teaching and teacher education practices*. Dordrecht, The Netherlands: Kluwer.

Noddings, N. (1986) Caring: A feminine approach to ethics and moral education. Berkeley: University of California Press.

Schatzki, T. (2002) *The site of the social: A philosophical account of the constitution of social life and change*. University Park, Pennsylvania: University of Pennsylvania Press.

Yeats, W.B. (1965) *The collected poems of W. B. Yeats*. London: Macmillan.

AFFILIATIONS

Stephen Kemmis
School of Education
Charles Sturt University, Wagga Wagga, Australia

Tracey J. Smith
School of Education
Charles Sturt University, Wagga Wagga, Australia

13

STEPHEN KEMMIS AND TRACEY J. SMITH

2. PERSONAL PRAXIS

Learning through experience

PRAXIS

In Book VI of the *Ethics* (Folio Society Edition, 2003[1]), Aristotle (384-322 BC) distinguished three different kinds of reasoning – theoretical, technical and practical – each guided by a distinctive disposition, with its own *telos* or aim, and issuing in a distinctive form of action.

The first of these dispositions is *epistēmē* or the disposition to seek truth for its own sake, guided by the general aim (*telos*) of attaining truth. The distinctive form of action associated with *epistēmē* is *theoria* or contemplation, involving theoretical reasoning about the nature of things. Aristotle regarded this as the highest form of reasoning, associated with finding the truth about the nature of things – through philosophical and scientific contemplation in *theoria* as a branch of knowledge including such fields as "theology, metaphysics, astronomy, mathematics, biology, botany and meteorology" (Sinclair, 1962, p.10). In the case of a teacher, under the disposition of *epistēmē*, the contemplative action of *theoria* might include contemplating the nature and aims of education, or contemplating the nature and consequences of different forms of pedagogy as approaches to education.

The second disposition is *technē* or the disposition to act in a true and reasoned way according to the rules of a craft, guided by the general aim (*telos*) of making or producing something, where the thing produced is an object or outcome separate from the person producing it. The distinctive form of action associated with *technē* is *poiēsis* or 'making' action, involving means-ends or instrumental reasoning to make something which achieves a known objective or outcome (to make a pot or an object of art or a crop, for example). As 'making action' *poiēsis* is the production of any known product that can be produced by known means using known materials. This is, of course, an essential form of reasoning – it enables people to make things, to make them well, and to get things done. In the case of teaching, under the disposition of *technē*, the 'making action' of *poiēsis* might mean making a well-managed classroom, preparing a unit of work for students to learn, or producing pre-defined knowledge or skills in learners.

The third disposition is *phronēsis* which is the moral disposition to act wisely and prudently (with practical common sense[2]), with goals and means both always open to review. *Phronēsis* is guided by the general aim (*telos*) of wise and prudent judgement and informs good or right conduct – doing what is good, or 'the right thing'. 'Doing the right thing', in the case of *phronēsis* does not mean only

Kemmis, Stephen and Smith, Tracey J (2008) Enabling praxis: Challenges for education. 15-35 following a given rule or social norm or convention; it means something bigger – doing what will later be seen to have been good in the light of its historical consequences, and 'good' both for the individuals concerned and for the good of humankind. While Aristotle notes that *phronēsis* can be 'prudent' in the limited sense of acting for one's own good or the good of one's family, he argues that it also implies a commitment to acting for the good of humankind, which is the supreme good. The form of action distinctive to *phronēsis* is *praxis* or 'doing' action, involving practical reasoning about what it is wise and proper to do in a given situation[3]. It should be emphasised that *praxis* is not just thinking about action (which is to be guided by *phronēsis*), but a form of doing that constitutes right conduct (just as *poiēsis* is 'making action', guided by the disposition of *technē*)[4]. To do the right thing (*praxis*) in uncertain circumstances, when we are faced by perplexity or puzzles about what one should do in any particular circumstances, requires *deliberation* – consideration of what one is *really* doing in this situation, and what different kinds of consequences will follow for different people if one decides to do one thing rather than another.

One way to think about the difference between *technē* and *poiēsis*, on the one hand, and *phronēsis* and *praxis*, on the other, is that the first pair are concerned with the quality of the production of a] product or state of affairs external to the producer (doing a good job or making a good thing), while the second pair are concerned with doing what is right and proper (doing things in a way that demonstrates moral goodness in what is done, so that the consequences will be good for all the people involved and affected – the good for individuals and the good for humankind). *Technē* and *poiēsis* are about making things; *phronēsis* and *praxis* are about how people live in and through their actions – living rightly or properly.

In the case of teaching, *phronēsis* is the kind of reasoning that guides the teacher to think *educationally*, which means to be committed to the double task of the self-development of each individual learner in her or his own interests and, simultaneously, the development of the good for humankind. This commitment translates into action in the *praxis* of education, which is something bigger than teaching. Teaching can produce learning which may or may not be in the interests of the good for each individual and simultaneously the good for humankind. Educational *praxis* is purposive action – right educational conduct – which is guided by a moral purpose greater than the purpose of producing (just any) learning. Teaching which aims at no more than producing some particular piece of learning is not educational *praxis*; on the contrary, it is a species of *poiēsis* or 'making action', meaning that it is a form of action guided only by the intention to bring about a known end (a pre-given learning outcome) using known means.

To put it simply: *poiēsis* in teaching aims at no more than bringing about desired or required learning outcomes using known means while *praxis* has the greater moral purpose of also bringing about the self-development of each individual learner in her or his interests and for the good of humankind. The disposition that guides the teacher who is only teaching to achieve certain pre-given learning outcomes is *technē*; the disposition that guides the teacher who aims to act

16

educationally is *phronēsis*. The teacher who wants to act educationally may require *technē* as craft knowledge about how to bring about learning, but aims to do something more, namely, to *educate* the learner in their own interests and for the good of humankind. The teacher who wants to act educationally wants to model right conduct as a way of simultaneously living and demonstrating what is good for persons and good for humankind. In the European tradition of educational studies, this is the field of *pedagogy*, which concerns not just the 'how' of teaching (*technē*) but also the why. On the side of the good for each individual, the educator acts on the basis of *phronēsis*, the disposition to act wisely and prudently and with practical commonsense in response to the particular needs and interests of these particular students in these particular circumstances, as individual persons worthy of recognition and respect. On the side of the good for the humankind, the educator's action also recognises, that these students are, and that their circumstances are part of a wider history, and a wider community, society and world in which they live and will live well or badly, and in which their conduct will have consequences not only for themselves but also for others.

Education

Understood in this way, education is necessarily a moral activity. It requires that the teacher (in this case as an educator) has some idea of what might be in the interests of the self-development of each individual learner and for the good for humankind. It requires that the teacher knows more than how to get *this* particular learner to learn *this* particular piece of knowledge or to attain *this* particular learning outcome. It also requires having some idea of what is good for the self-development of learners and having some idea about what the good for humankind consists in. The educator cannot move in a moral vacuum, or take a 'value-free' or 'value-neutral' view of what learning outcomes are worth achieving. Someone who wants to be considered an educator – not only a teacher – must have some view of what constitutes 'the good' for individuals and the good for humankind.

Aristotle answers the question of what constitutes these goods in terms of 'happiness' – the happiness of people individually and collectively. He does not mean happiness in the short-term sense of being happy here and now, however; he means 'happiness' in the long term. The ancient Greeks said "call no man good until he dies" because we cannot know, even in the case of a person who *seems* good, that all of their actions will be the ones they would want to stand by as contributing to their long term happiness and the wider and long-term good for humankind. The ancient Greek word *eudaimonia* is usually translated as 'happiness', but it has a richer meaning. In his introduction to the Folio Society's (2003) edition of Aristotle's *Ethics*, Jonathon Barnes writes:

> ... happiness, as the term is used in ordinary English is a sort of mental or emotional state or condition; to call a man happy is (to put it very vaguely indeed) to say something about his general state of mind. *Eudaimonia*, on the other hand, is not simply a mental state; after setting out his analysis of

eudaimonia, Aristotle remarks that 'it agrees with our account that the *eudaimōn* lives well and acts well; for it [i.e. *eudaimonia*] has been pretty well defined as a sort of well-living and well-acting'. To call a man *eudaimōn* is to say something about how he lives and what he does. The notion of *eudaimonia* is closely tied, in a way in which the notion of happiness is not, to success: the *eudaimōn* is someone who makes a success of his life and actions, who realises his aims and ambitions as a man, who fulfils himself (p.xiii).

The ultimate success of the *eudaimōn* is to have lived well in ways that accord with others also living well – behaving in accordance with the law, contributing not only to one's own well-being but also to the well-being of one's family and the state. It is to live and act within a 'bigger picture', we might say, of how people ought to live and act.

On this view, the teacher as a (potential) *eudaimōn* who aspires to be an educator must thus act and live well according to principles about what constitutes the good for each individual and the good for humankind – not just for him- or herself, or even simply in the interests of each of his or her students, but for humankind as a whole. For the teacher or prospective teacher to learn *this* is to learn something more than about the science, art or craft of teaching. It means learning how to give an answer to the question of what *education* is for, and to be able to put some meat on the bones of saying what is in the interests of the self-development of each learner and for the good of humankind. An educator can be a *eudaimōn* if she or he lives and acts well, in the interests of individuals and the good of humankind, and is successful in living the sort of life that will allow people to say, when their life or career has ended, that she or he demonstrated a continuing commitment to those goods.

So: the educator needs to know something about *education* as well as about teaching (*technē*). The educator needs to develop *phronēsis* or the commitment to wisdom and prudence by knowing something about what education is and has been – something about the different forms education has taken in different places and times, and about what the consequences of these different traditions and approaches have been. In part, this requires studying education under the disposition of *epistēmē* through the contemplative mode of action of *theoria*. That is, it requires studying education as an object of contemplation in its own right. But this mode of preparation, guided by the disposition of *epistēmē*, is not necessarily a preparation for action. One could study education in the same way one could study philosophy, just for its own sake. To be 'translated' into action in 'doing' education, however, the educator must act (*praxis*), guided by the disposition to do what is wise and prudent, with practical common sense, under a given set of circumstances (*phronēsis*). When it comes to acting, the educator aims not merely to produce a given outcome or object, but to do so in a certain way – to act for the good of each individual and for the good of humankind. This is a difficult task. What it might be good to do in the interests of one student may be different from what would be in the interests of another. (Should I move on to the next topic because Jenny is bored, or wait until Johnny has understood clearly?) What might

18

be for the good of the class might not be what is for the good of humankind. (Should I shout at the class to demand their attention, like some kind of tyrant, or should I arrange the social relationships of the classroom so they require that everyone recognises and respects the others as persons, as one would hope for humankind as a whole?) As William Reid (1978) points out, these are "uncertain practical questions"[5].

These are the kinds of practical challenges and dilemmas that face teachers as educators, and they demonstrate their *educational* commitments in the way they respond to them. They 'rise above' the immediate concerns for getting things done and producing known outcomes (*technē, poiēsis*) to see their action against the broader perspective of a culture and society, and against the longer perspective of what the long-term historical consequences will be for each individual now present and the people who they will affect in their lives beyond this class and school, beyond this here and now.

To meet these challenges and dilemmas requires not only knowledge of educational traditions and theories, but also a capacity to see immediate circumstances against these wider and longer perspectives. It requires a capacity to *understand* and *interpret* what is going on in richer terms than the ones that might immediately present themselves. (This is not just an outbreak of unruliness which challenges the good order of the class; it is a form of bad behaviour which is unsustainable in the world because it denies recognition of and respect for others as persons.) It also demands that the educator act wisely and prudently and with practical commonsense (which, as Aristotle points out also involves the faculty of cleverness, *deinotēs*, about what one *can* do) which will show itself, in action, in a kind of *discretion* about what one chooses to respond to (and not to respond to).

Some of these capacities are not developed solely by gaining 'book knowledge'; they can only be developed by *experience* – the capacity to recognise what is more important and significant in the hurly-burly of the moment and to interpret things against the 'bigger picture'.

Experience

Aristotle thought that the young could not easily learn about ethics. They might be able to learn science or mathematics, which we might say 'have right answers', but they lacked the life experience to learn how to deal with ethical questions – especially since ethical dilemmas and problems require a kind of judgement about competing goals, competing principles and uncertain priorities among them. They also require that we *act* – even if we decide that the wisest course of action is to do nothing. They require that we face uncertainty about how a situation will unfold in different ways depending on how we (and others) act, because we cannot know with certainty how everything will turn out. And so we are obliged to *deliberate*, drawing on our knowledge and experience, before deciding what to do – and in the knowledge that things may turn out in ways other than we would wish.

The young, Aristotle thought, may not yet have the experience to study ethics because they are inclined to see it as a matter of learning moral or ethical principles

19

or rules that can be applied like laws of physics or mathematical formulae. They may not yet understand that a particular situation is many things at one time – for example, not just a learning situation but a situation in which people can do right or wrong; or not just a situation of choosing what is best for me or my family but also choosing in a way that means that the principles I use to inform my decision here and now are compatible with the principles all people ought to be able to use and choose. The young may not yet understand that the consequences of their actions will roll through time, and may 'come back to bite them', as the colloquial expression has it – or, worse, 'come back to bite' other people whom they did not mean to harm.

The young can gain some kind of information or knowledge that is the fruit of other people's experience, but they can only develop their own experience *through experience*. In his (1993) book *Back to the Rough Ground*, Irish philosopher of education Joseph Dunne draws on the work of German philosopher Hans Georg Gadamer and American social philosopher Hannah Arendt to consider the nature of experience in relation to *praxis*. He considers the kind of actions and events that are 'revealing', and distinguishes (p.130):

> between our established and routinised experience and a new experience that impresses itself on us (and finds expression in a phrase like "that really was an *experience*") precisely by interrupting our previous experience and therefore enriching it. There is a "reversal of consciousness" in the process of experience in that new experiences (if they are really new and not simply repetitions of 'old' ones) not only give us access to a new reality but also involve us in amending and reshaping our previous apprehensions of reality. And the experience of recurrently carrying through this reversal (i.e., the experience of experience itself) leads to a deepened self-awareness or self-presence in the truly experienced person; in becoming experienced, he has been involved not only in acquiring information but also, through this very acquiring, in a process of self-formation.

Quoting Gadamer, Dunne writes (p.131):

> We never really graduate from the school of experience to a university of higher knowledge: "the perfect form of what we call 'experienced' does not consist in the fact that someone already knows everything and knows better than anyone else ... the dialectic of experience has its own fulfilment not in definitive knowledge, but in that openness to experience that is encouraged by experience itself.

A little later, again quoting Gadamer and referring to an earlier discussion of Hannah Arendt, he writes (p.131):

> The truly experienced person is the one who has learned this lesson, "who knows that he is master neither of time nor the future," who has discovered "the limits of the power and the self-knowledge of his planning reason," and who has come to see that "all the expectations and planning of finite beings is

finite and limited." (What Gadamer is saying here is closely akin to what we have already seen in [Hannah] Arendt. The uncertainty and irreversibility which were so central in her account of action – and which underlay the need for promising and forgiving as remedies against an otherwise overwhelming hazardousness – find an exact parallel in Gadamer's insistence on "the limitedness of all prediction and the uncertainty of all plans" and on the fact that the experienced person has learned that "it proves to be an illusion that everything can be reversed." ...).

So: educators and prospective educators must also *become* experienced by learning from (their) experience. People cannot be prepared for *praxis* by 'book knowledge' alone, but by experiencing the irreversibility of their actions. On this, Aristotle (2003, p.120) quotes the Athenian poet Agathon (448-402 BC), friend of Euripedes and Plato:

For one thing is denied even to God:
To make what has been done undone again

In summary, then, how can prospective teachers learn to behave ethically and educationally? Not only by following rules but also by wise interpretation of the situations in which they find themselves, by deliberating wisely about the likely consequences of their actions, and by acting with the discretion borne of experience – knowing that, despite their best efforts, they may still not get it 'right' – just the best they could do under the circumstances.

A CRITICAL PERSPECTIVE

So far, we have considered the classical account of theoretical, technical and practical reasoning given by Aristotle. This classical view was extended by German philosopher Jürgen Habermas in his (1972) *Knowledge-Constitutive Interests* and (1974) *Theory and Practice*. Habermas argued that, in the light of philosophical developments since Aristotle, it was no longer reasonable to claim that the contemplative disposition *epistēmē* and the associated contemplative form of action *theoria* amounted to a kind of 'pure' contemplation – 'pure' in the sense that they stood above human interests in the creation of knowledge. While Aristotle's accounts of *technē* and *poiēsis*, and *phronēsis* and *praxis*, still gave a reasonable account of the dispositions and forms of action that gave rise to technical and practical knowledge and action, he argued that *epistēmē* and *theoria* could no longer be regarded, as once they were, as a 'disinterested' pursuit of knowledge for its own sake. Contemplative action in the modern era had become part of a scientific worldview in which no knowledge is pursued or created (constituted) without regard to human interests (hence the phrase "knowledge-constitutive interests").

In general, Habermas argued, much of the work of the natural and physical sciences is directed towards human control of nature, and is thus a species of *technē*, informing *poiēsis* as 'making action'. Similarly, history and aesthetics, and

21

some branches of the social, political and human sciences, in the general form of the interpretive sciences (or hermeneutics) are directed towards the aim of educating people about the nature and consequences of their actions, and are thus species of *phronēsis* informing *praxis* as right conduct.

The aspirations of 'pure' or contemplative reason, however, are no longer simply to contemplate the marvels of God's creation. If these aspirations have continued at all, they do so in the form of a science that aims to reach beyond the technical and the practical. The technical was always, and continues to be, governed by *technē* as an aspiration to control objects and outcomes. The practical was always, and continues to be, governed by *phronēsis* as an aspiration to educate people about how to act wisely and prudently. Given that *phronēsis* depends on interpreting the world in terms of *pre-given* traditions of thought (described by Gadamer, 1975, pp.267-269, as "prejudices" which are the interpretive categories given by tradition through which an interpreter interprets the world), however, there is a danger that interpretation will always be constrained by the interpretive categories the interpreter (or actor) happens to bring to the situation or thing to be interpreted.

Gadamer attempted to rise through this limit to interpretation by invoking a notion of "effective-historical consciousness" – the notion that the interpreter should aim simultaneously to reach an understanding of both an historical (or aesthetic) object and her or his own historicality (her or his own location in history, for example as the inheritor of the tradition to be interpreted) *vis-à-vis* the object. Habermas regarded this as an unsatisfactory resolution, leaving the interpreter as an inheritor of a tradition but unable to see its limits and to surpass them, even partially. Drawing on the theoretical tradition of critical theory (e.g., Horkheimer, 1972), Habermas argued that our interpretations of the world are always shaped by our location in processes of production (in terms of labour) and in political processes and structures (in terms of domination), and that by investigating how our interpretive categories have been shaped in structures, processes and histories of labour and domination we can find ways of thinking that, at least partially, allow us to escape the constraints that tradition has placed upon our thought, interpretations and perspectives (sedimented in the interpretive categories bequeathed to us by tradition).

Again in keeping with the tradition of critical theory, Habermas thus described a different kind of disposition (to use Aristotle's term, though Habermas now described these dispositions in terms of 'knowledge-constitutive interests – the *emancipatory* knowledge-constitutive interest). He proposed a *critical* disposition, which is pursued through a distinctive kind of action – *emancipatory* action aimed at overcoming the pre-given limitations of previous interpretive categories by developing new insights in the form of "*critical theorems*" which in turn support processes of the "*organisation of enlightenment*" through which people develop new ways of seeing things (especially new authentic insights into how their own circumstances are shaped and constrained by previous ways of seeing things). If these new insights seem to them authentic, and if it seems that the limitations exposed can be overcome through some new way of doing things, then these insights can lead to a *political struggle* to transform existing ways of seeing and doing things, and existing material and social-political structures. As Habermas acknowledges, this political struggle, guided by an idea about how a wrong might be righted, is a form of *praxis*[6].

Because the critical approach aims to reach beyond existing ways of seeing, doing and structuring social life, it offers a vantage point a little similar to the old *epistēmē* in the sense that it aims for a kind of contemplation on how things came to be (given ways of seeing, doing and structuring social life), but the critical approach is also different in a significant way. Instead of contemplation on the mystery and marvels of a Divine Creation, the critical perspective provokes contemplation on the possibility that existing ways of understanding things might be *irrational* (in the dimension of discourse or thought), that they might lead to *injustice* or *human suffering* (in the social dimension), that they might be *unproductive* or *destructive* (in the material dimension), and, one might add, that they might ultimately prove *unsustainable* (in the dimension of the conservation of the earth's resources). The critical approach thus emphasises not just how things are, but how they might be otherwise – not in the positive sense of pursuing some ideal form of rationality, justice or well-being, but in the negative (critical) sense of overcoming observed irrationality, injustice, suffering, unproductiveness and unsustainability.

Table 1: Four perspectives on dispositions and action

	Theoretical perspective	Technical perspective	Practical perspective	Critical-emancipatory perspective
Telos (Aim)	The attainment of knowledge or truth	The production of something	Wise and prudent judgement; acting rightly in the world	Overcoming irrationality, injustice, suffering, felt dissatisfactions
Disposition	*Epistēmē*: The disposition to seek the truth for its own sake	*Technē*: The disposition to act in a true and reasoned way according to the rules of a craft	*Phronēsis*: The moral disposition to act wisely, truly and justly; with goals and means both always open to review	Critical: The disposition towards emancipation from irrationality, injustice, suffering, felt dissatisfactions
Action	Theoria: Contemplation, involving theoretical reasoning about the nature of things)	*Poiēsis*: 'Making' action, involving means-ends or instrumental reasoning to achieve a known objective or outcome)	*Praxis*: 'Doing' action, involving practical reasoning about what it is wise, right and proper to do in a given situation)	Emancipatory: Collective critical reflection and action to overcome irrationality, injustice, suffering, harm, unproductiveness or unsustainability

While Habermas's account of knowledge-constitutive interests replaced *epistēmē* with the *emancipatory* knowledge-constitutive interest, we might

23

nevertheless, for argument's sake, retain *epistemē* in the following summary table of forms of reasoning and associated forms of action (Table 1).

Taking these four perspectives to the case of teacher education, the question then arises of how to develop these different dispositions, and how to teach these different ways of understanding the world and of acting in it. If each perspective does indeed have a legitimate place in the initial formation of teachers as educators, and in the transformation of practising teachers through continuing professional development, what place might each perspective find in curricula, pedagogies and modes of assessment for initial and continuing teacher education?

TEACHER EDUCATION AND PRAXIS DEVELOPMENT

It is initially plausible to think that there might be particular elements of a teacher education curriculum, of teacher education pedagogy, and of assessment and examination in teacher education where these four kinds of dispositions and action might be explicated, formed, developed and assessed. Table 2 suggests some of the kinds of topics within a teacher education course in which these different kinds of development might possibly be fostered.

This initially plausible conceptualisation may suggest that different subjects or units within a course might develop the different dispositions and forms of action presented in Table 1. On closer inspection, however, what seemed plausible begins to fall apart.

First, it is apparent that any one subject in the course might develop elements of each and all of the dispositions and forms of action listed in Tables 1 and 2. When we thought deeply about the Charles Sturt University (Wagga Wagga campus) *Bachelor of Education (Primary)* degree course subject *EEP 112 Education Studies 1: Education and Society*, for example, we began to see that even activities that aimed principally at developing theoretical ideas about education also involved the teaching and learning technical skills like those required for reading philosophical or theoretical texts. Similarly, an activity aimed at improving technical skills like skills of observing learners in the process of learning immediately raises practical and interpretive issues about who, what and when to observe, and how to grasp or interpret or understand a learner's own perspective when it appears to differ from one's own way of seeing things. In short, we came to understand that different elements of the *Education and Society* subject – different kinds of learning activities, for example – contributed in different ways to developing each of the dispositions and forms of action.

It appeared, then, that the teachers of this subject aim to develop all four kinds of reasoning, with their associated dispositions and forms of action. No doubt we are trying to develop one of them more than another at any particular moment, and students may be developing one more than another at any moment, but the differences between these things are not clear and observable in just one activity or episode or another. They are not the kinds of things that can be analytically separated in the dimensions of activity or time. They differ in terms of the meaning and purpose of what a person is doing, and they are intimately bound up, at different levels, in what anyone might be doing at a particular time. Moreover, one and the same activity can develop a range of different types of dispositions and forms of action.

Table 2: The four perspectives on dispositions and action in the case of teacher education

	Theoretical perspective	Technical perspective	Practical perspective	Critical-emancipatory perspective
Telos (Aim)	The attainment of knowledge or truth	The production of something	Wise and prudent judgement; acting rightly in the world	Overcoming irrationality, injustice, suffering, felt dissatisfactions
Disposition Example in teacher education	*Epistēmē*: Studying philosophy of education with the aim of developing a personal theory of education related to traditions of educational thought and action	*Technē*: Learning knowledge (like theories of learning, individual differences, motivation) and skills to teach a lesson, manage a class, assess learning	*Phronēsis*: Learning about the nature, traditions and purposes of education as a moral activity intrinsically involved with the formation of good persons and the good for humankind	Critical: Developing understanding of historical, discursive, social and material-economic circumstances which constrain students' and communities' capacities for self-expression, self-development and self-determination
Action Example in teacher education	*Theoria*: Development of logical thinking to use and develop educational theories and traditions – e.g., through writing a theoretical dissertation critiquing and extending the work of educational theorists, theories or traditions	*Poiēsis*: Development of lesson preparation skills, skills to teach a state curriculum, skills to assess students according to policy or rules – e.g., through supervised professional experience as part of a teacher education course	*Praxis*: Development of reflexive capacity to adapt immediate goals and means to changing circumstances in a class or school in light of educational values about the good for students and the good for humankind – e.g., through supervised professional experience	Emancipatory: Development of community action and education projects (and action research projects) to take collective action on educational and social issues confronted by a community – e.g., through project work as part of a teacher education course

It turns out that trying to understand any particular learning activity, or a subject or course as a whole, in terms of analytically separating activities from one another in terms of the distinctions between these forms of reasoning and associated forms of action is thus misguided. Reading philosophy of education is not only guided by the disposition of *epistēmē* in relation to the philosophical ideas being contemplated (*theoria*), for example. Reading philosophy of education is also a technical matter of reading or learning to read texts of this kind, and a practical matter of deciding whether to read this now or later or ever, or whether to take it

25

seriously in any case. And it may or may not help students critically to identify ideological distortions in the current structures of schooling that need to be overcome if schooling is to be more educational.

Moreover, all the subjects of the course, taken together, may or may not develop all of the dispositions and forms of action the teachers on the course hope for – or at least to the extent that, after completing the course, graduates will actually be guided by the desired dispositions, made manifest in the relevant forms of action. They may simply be unable to resist being socialised to the patterns of work of the schools they work in after they graduate.

It turns out, then, that developing *epistēmē, technē, phronēsis* and *critical* dispositions happens in ways that are profoundly connected to one another. At any time, one may be in the foreground, as it were, but the others may (or may not) accompany it in the background. So developing each requires attending to each as a specific disposition, and developing each associated form of action (respectively, *theoria, poiēsis, praxis* and *emancipatory action*) requires *making it explicit* that this is what it is intended to develop at any particular time. That is, it requires thinking about each as distinctive, and as a perspective on action guided by its own distinctive disposition. Part of the task of developing *praxis*, then, is to make it explicit that this is what is intended – to develop the learner's capacity to act on the disposition of *phronēsis*, to act wisely and prudently, using practical commonsense, and to be oriented by traditions (including relevant theory). The same might be said for developing theoretical perspectives (*theoria*), technical skill (*technē*), and critical capacities.

It makes *some* sense to see these different kinds of dispositions and actions as analytically distinct from one another, and to recognise that at any particular moment a teacher or student might be developing one of them more than another. Furthermore, it makes sense to try to clarify which of them a teacher might intend to develop in particular learning activities or at a particular moment in a subject or course. Nevertheless, we must conclude that these clarifications are no more than a guide to the teacher or the learner about *what to make explicit* if the teacher wants to nurture and strengthen each disposition, and to nurture and extend learners' capacities for the associated forms of action. To nurture and extend each of these dispositions and forms of action as distinctive, however, ordinarily requires reference to the greater aim or purpose intended: trying to think in the distinctive ways indicated by the *telos* (or aim) of each disposition, and trying to develop and do each of the associated forms of action. This, we shall see, requires that learners learn different ways of being.

Learning to live "a certain kind of life"

As Alasdair MacIntyre (1983) said of historians (and the practitioners of some other practices), the historian lives "a certain kind of life" – the life of a historian, dedicated to extending and developing history and the "internal goods" that can only be attained through 'doing history'. In MacIntyre and Dunne (2002, an account of a conversation between Dunne and MacIntyre), however, MacIntyre doubts whether teachers have "a certain kind of life" that marks them as teachers, since he regards teaching as a means to something else – for example, teaching mathematics in the service of the internal goods of mathematics as a practice. Dunne then (and without resolution) uses the arguments of MacIntyre's (1986) *After Virtue* to try to show that teachers do indeed have "a certain kind of life", that they are oriented in their work by educational *traditions*, that they are supported by *institutions* (that sometimes put at risk the very goods they aim to extend), and that teaching involves characteristic *virtues* (like care for students) – a number of the essential features in MacIntyre's (1986) account of practices. Put another way, MacIntyre had referred to "the narrative unity of a human life" which demonstrates commitment to the virtues and traditions and institutions of a practice, arguing that "a certain kind of life" will be one which shows, through a person's actions over the whole of their life or career, a lifelong dedication to the continuing development of the goods internal to the practice (like the goods of history, for example, or, we may argue, education) and the virtues appropriate to the practice (like the virtues of doing history or education well).

Kemmis (2005) argued that the conversation between Dunne and MacIntyre may have been inconclusive because it revolved around the question of whether *teaching* is a practice rather than *education*. Kemmis takes the view that education is a practice even though teaching may not be – not for the reason given by MacIntyre, but because teaching is the instrumental side of promoting learning, rather than the wider and deeper activity characterised by commitment to developing, through teaching or upbringing, the good for each individual and the good for humankind.

The task of education is always incomplete – for every teacher, every student, and for humankind. There is always more to (teach and) learn. What can be achieved in an initial teacher education course, then, may or may not be sufficient to support a beginning teacher in their teaching, and it may or may not be sufficient to support them to 'do' education through their teaching.

Perhaps the most important task of initial teacher education, then, is to equip beginning teachers to 'do' education – even if not as well as they may one day 'do' it, or as well as others now 'do' it. And this may mean equipping them to have all four of the dispositions and with at least some of the capabilities required for all four of the forms of action listed in Tables 1 and 2. The 'proof of the pudding' will be whether the beginning teacher remains dedicated to all of these throughout their working life, and to continuing to develop each and all of them.

DEVELOPING PRAXIS AS A SPECIFIC AIM

In many professions, including education, opportunities are provided for students preparing for the profession to develop their skills and capacities in work-place-based placements, clinical or practical experience settings. These opportunities are generally in the form of supervised practice, and they may range from shorter placements to longer, from observation of practice to doing it, and from closer supervision to less obvious monitoring.

Of course one principal task of this supervised practice is to allow students to develop *technical* skills in real or realistic contexts of use – in education, for example, learning to manage a class effectively or to plan and then implement and evaluate a lesson or a unit of classroom work. Most professional courses have further aims for supervised practice, however. One is to develop students' *theoretical* knowledge – their thirst for professional knowledge that might guide them further in their understanding of their work – for example, by developing professional knowledge of relevant theory and philosophy. Another is for students do develop *critical* understandings about the way professional practice is enabled and constrained in particular settings and arrangements – for example, to learn that the current forms of practice and structures regulating practice in the profession need to be continually revised and remade in the light of changing times and circumstances. And another aim is to develop students' *practical* abilities – in the sense of *praxis*. This last aim may or may not be well done. It is the task that many professional educators regard as the most 'sacred' and central – learning to *be* a professional, a practitioner who acts morally in the interests of each client and in the interests of the good for humankind, wisely and prudently in relation to unique needs and circumstances in particular places and times, and in a way that demonstrates *virtue* in the form of a commitment to the goods that are *internal* to the practice itself. As Alasdair MacIntyre (1983) argues, these virtues can only be developed by doing good history or education or medicine or farming, and by developing what history or education or farming means in ways that respond to the demands and opportunities of new times, new needs and changing circumstances.

This means that an educator, for example, needs to be 'inside' education as a practice not just as an individual but also as a member of the collective body that is the profession. The educator needs to be a knowledgeable interpreter of educational situations (in terms of what makes them educational), a knowledgeable actor whose educational practice is informed by educational ideas and ideals that have developed and are encoded in the traditions of the education profession, including relevant theoretical knowledge. It also means that the educator must understand themselves to be a bearer of these traditions, as someone whose practice has been formed within these traditions, and as someone who has moral and professional obligations to those traditions – obligations to be an excellent practitioner, to develop a deep understanding of what counts as excellence in the light of those traditions, and an obligation to develop shared ideas about what excellence consists in and what it might consist in the future. The latter is an obligation to develop the traditions of the profession by striving to develop not only one's own practice but also the practices of others in the profession – that is, it is a collective responsibility for the development of the profession itself, including its institutions, organisations and professional associations. All of this is true for every profession – substituting the relevant words, it is true in relation to the professions and practices of architecture, accountancy, farming, history, medicine, occupational therapy and social work, to give just some examples.

The task of developing *praxis*, at first in pre-service or initial professional education and later in in-service or continuing professional education and development, is to have the would-be professional or the developing professional understand themselves and their profession in the way described in the last paragraph.

In part, the development of *praxis* is achieved by developing the required *dispositions* in the educator – the disposition of *phronēsis*, to act morally, wisely, prudently and in ways informed by tradition. But dispositions are not enough. As we have seen, *praxis* is action, developed through action and reflection on the consequences of action. It is developed through experience – not just the 'raw' experience of having been consciously aware of what one was doing when one was doing it, but experience that has been thoughtfully reflected upon.

To what extent do initial and continuing professional education courses develop *praxis* of the kind described here? Many, but not all, professional education courses include opportunities for supervised practice. Many, but not all, create opportunities for thoughtful reflection on action and experience in the relevant practice settings, whether supervised or not.

The question that inevitably arises for the educators of professionals, in education and other professional fields, is whether *we* do this educational work of developing our students' or colleagues' *praxis* excellently, in the light of the best knowledge and traditions of our fields, critically exploring how practice has been formed and transformed, and enabled and constrained in different settings and changing circumstances. Do we give ample or even adequate opportunity for our students and colleagues to develop their professional *praxis* in the course of their studies or in their continuing professional education? Do we adequately assess the extent to which our students or colleagues are developing *praxis*? Do we adequately evaluate whether we have been effective and successful in developing our students' or colleagues' *praxis*?

Developing *praxis* requires opportunities for professional action and reflection on experience – although the term is hackneyed, it requires experiential learning. Do we provide adequate opportunities for action, experience and reflection? As we shall see in later chapters of this volume, one of the principal approaches used in teacher education to develop the *praxis* of student teachers is self-reflection. As in teacher education, many other professions have also adopted self-reflection in their professional education programs – both in initial professional education and in continuing professional education activities and settings.

Developing *praxis* also requires that learners are deliberately seeking to locate themselves in the professional field and traditions of their practice. It requires that learners identify themselves as educators or social workers or farmers who try to find and develop themselves, their knowledge and their practices as educators or social workers or farmers. In teacher education, we want to argue, this requires some engagement with the 400-year-old tradition of *pedagogy* – in continental Europe, initially a branch of philosophy that developed as a specialisation studying the field of *upbringing* in a variety of settings, not just the education of children or in the institutionalised settings of schools. The pedagogical tradition includes a variety of questions and answers about the proper relationships between the person being 'brought up', the person doing the upbringing (whether parent or teacher or youth worker) and the society and social context in which the upbringing occurs – questions differently explored by such thinkers as Jean-Jacques Rousseau (1712-1778), John Dewey (1859-1972) and Paolo Freire (1921-1997). A review of various educational thinkers of the last century who have contributed to this tradition can be found in W. F. Connell's (1981) *A History of Education in the Twentieth Century World*.

Developing *praxis* also requires engaging with and developing the traditions that inform the practice as an identifiable collective practice of a particular kind – whether education or social work or farming. It requires that learners and practitioners participate in the professional organisations and associations of their profession, to develop not only their own practices but also the professional practices of others. It requires acknowledging that one is a member of communities of practice, both locally in relation to others who are not members of the profession and generally in relation to others who are also, one might say, co-custodians (and, where necessary, co-transformers) of the virtues and the excellences encoded in the discourses and traditions of the practice and the profession (see MacIntyre, 1983).

THE PRACTICUM OR SUPERVISED PROFESSIONAL EXPERIENCE

The 'practicum' is a name frequently given in many Australian universities to preparatory supervised professional experience components of a teacher education course. Sometimes, the practicum is a 'block' of several weeks of supervised teaching in a classroom, but it may also be spread out over hours or days a week. In many Australian states, it is expected that, to be registrable as a teacher, a primary (or elementary) teacher education student will have had between 45 and 85 days of supervised professional experience, on the basis of which they will be assessed by supervising teachers and university teacher education staff as 'ready to teach' or 'not yet ready to teach' or 'unsatisfactory' in their performance. (Most employers would not consider appointing any applicants for positions who are not in the first category.)

The practicum experience is of course difficult and sometimes traumatic for teacher education students. They are inexperienced. They may have had many years of experience of being a student in a classroom, but they don't have the experience of being a teacher (Van Veen, forthcoming). They may make mistakes. They may miss important cues about the way a class is behaving and what the consequences of dissolving order are likely to be. They may be ill-equipped to accommodate the differing needs and interests of diverse students. They may not yet have an adequate grasp of the subject matter they are aiming to teach, of the technical skills of teaching, of the practical skills of making wise decisions about what it might be most prudent to do next, or of appropriate ways to assess student learning. And they may not have a critical grasp of questions like "To what extent is this particular form of schooling educational and to what extent is it a form of domestication to the existing social order?" or "Do these particular practices of schooling inevitably contribute to the injustices of domination and oppression[7] of students, and thus to the spread of these injustices through the world?".

One reason the practicum is so crucial, however, is that it is a vehicle for a student teacher to move from inexperience to experience, under the supervision of practising teachers (who may or may not be good models either as teachers or as educators). And student teachers may also learn that they are unsuited to teaching, or that teaching is unsuited to them. The practicum provides opportunities for exploring what it is to be a teacher, in terms of developing theoretical commitments, developing technical skills, developing practical wisdom and commonsense, and developing a critical perspective on the improvement of students and society through a developing professional commitment to the reform or transformation of schooling to make it more educational. It is an opportunity, also, to develop the *persona* of 'being' a teacher – to *become* a teacher, and preferably an educator. That is: to become a person who lives that "certain kind of life" which is characteristic of an educator.

In general, once Australian teachers have gained their initial teaching qualification, they do not undertake further supervised practice – like the practicum – in continuing professional development activities and courses. They may do projects, investigate their own practice, apply theoretical ideas learned in a short in-service course or a Master's degree program, but only in specialised cases will they undertake further supervised practice in teaching. (What may be supervised in a Master's degree course is a program of theoretical study or thesis research.) They may, of course, have one or other of various forms of induction or mentoring or coaching when they begin work as teachers, but generally they will be supervised as employees, once they start work, not as beginning professionals. As university graduates, they are regarded as professionally 'competent' and therefore regarded as not *requiring* further preparatory supervision; what they may need, however, is to see more deeply into the nature and consequences of their practice. In this they may find a kind of further developmental supervision by acting as 'critical friends' to other teachers, participating in collaborative action research projects with colleagues, and other such activities.

The point is that the pre-service teacher education supervised practicum and, to a lesser extent, 'practical' studies undertaken in in-service short courses and degree programs, are crucial moments at which *praxis* is or may be developed. Of course other things may be developed too – theoretical knowledge, technical skills and critical capacities – but it is likely that teachers and teacher educators will only be involved in the development of *praxis* through conscious, self-aware and self-critical investigation of their practice, their *experience* of their practice, and the *consequences* of their practice. The rest of *praxis* development will occur through opportunities to converse with and sometimes observe other teachers, through reading and some other kinds of professional development activities. And much of their continuing *praxis* development will occur through their own explicit efforts at self-development – for example, through investigating their own practices, understandings and situations in action research projects.

Mattson and Kemmis (2007) have pointed out that different criteria may be needed to evaluate conventional scientific research as opposed to *praxis-related research* – that is, research aimed at social change through transformative action.

31

They suggest that, among other things, conventional scientific research emphasises finding new knowledge while *praxis*-related research aims at transformation; conventional research aims to use accepted scientific methods while *praxis*-related research aims at empowerment of people to make a change; and conventional research aims at exploring an already-identified field of problems while *praxis*-related research aims at engaging and changing the life experiences of people in a situation. They argue that these two sets of criteria are not only relevant in evaluating research reports of conventional scientific research and reports of *praxis*-related research; they are also relevant in considering different kinds of examinations and assessments of students' work, for example in relation to assessment of students' developing theoretical knowledge as distinct from assessing their *praxis* in supervised professional experience settings like the practicum. On the view of Mattson and Kemmis, assessing students' *praxis* development requires attending to different criteria like those already indicated – whether student teachers produced transformations in the setting in which they worked (not just developing new knowledge about the settings), whether they were empowered by their experience and reflection on their experience (not just improving technical skills or knowledge), and whether they changed the life experience of people in the practice teaching setting (not just exploring already-identified fields of inquiry). Student teachers and other beginning professional practitioners develop wisdom through experience and reflection on their experience, and they aim to develop their own capacities in and for action *by acting* – by being personally-, morally- and socially-accountable for their actions in the supervised practice setting. Assessing the *action* – the *praxis* – of student teachers and other beginning professionals is more complex than assessing their knowledge. It requires assessing *their conduct and its consequences*, not just what they or others say about their conduct. This is a more complex task for teacher educators and other professional educators to consider, and it calls into play their (dispositions of) wisdom, prudence and discretion as well as their capacities for *praxis*, as revealed in the conduct (the *praxis*) of their teaching and assessment.

To summarise: initial *praxis* development and subsequent *transformations* of practice (pre-service and in-service *praxis* development) occur by 'doing' practice, and learning to see more richly and more far-sightedly into what its consequences are for students, their families and communities, and others.

Necessarily, this involves learning about one's own formation and continuing development and transformation as a teacher or educator *through practice*. As Dunne (p.130) says,

> the experience of recurrently carrying through this reversal (i.e., the experience of experience itself) leads to a deepened self-awareness or self-presence in the truly experienced person; in becoming experienced, he has been involved not only in acquiring information but also, through this very acquiring, in a process of self-formation.

The process of developing as a teacher (or educator), of which the initial teacher education supervised practicum is only the first part, is "a process of self-formation". It is part of the continuing process of learning and re-learning how to live "a certain kind of life" – the life of an educator.

What follows from this is that an initial teacher education student, and the teacher continuing their professional development, can be assisted by others who may give them advice or reading or access to the knowledge 'stored' in educational traditions, but teachers can only develop as teachers or as educators by *developing themselves through practice*. And this means: *learning to learn from one's own experience* as much as, if not more than, from relevant books, ideas, colleagues and others.

Praxis only comes from the disposition of *phronēsis* – the disposition to act wisely and prudently with practical commonsense, oriented by tradition including relevant theory. The disposition of *phronēsis* may be developed or honed by reading and contemplation, but *praxis* can only be developed through experience.

Through the explorations of the cases presented in subsequent chapters, we will find whether, or the extent to which, this is so.

NOTES

[1] The (2003) Folio Society edition of Aristotle's Ethics is based on J.A.K. Thompson's translation of 1953 as revised by Hugh Tredennick in 1976. Jonathon Barnes notes in his "Introduction" that this edition combines two of the thirty or so surviving treatises of Aristotle: the later treatise, the Nicomachean Ethics (so named because it was edited by Aristotle's son Nicomachus), and the earlier Eudemian Ethics (edited by Eudemus). The combined edition contains four books (or chapters) drawn from the Nicomachean Ethics, followed by three drawn from the Eudemian, followed by three drawn from the Nicomachean.

[2] In his (1976) "Notes" to the revised (2003) edition of Aristotle's Ethics, Hugh Tredennick writes: "Phronēsis … means 'practical common sense'" (p.279), also indicating that this has traditionally been rendered into English as 'prudence'.

[3] According to Jonathon Barnes, in his "Introduction" to the (2003) Folio Society edition of Aristotle's Ethics, "the aim of the Ethics is expressly practical: its philosophy aims at changing the world, not at interpreting it; and we should therefore expect it to advance a prescriptive 'should' rather than a descriptive psychological 'do'" (p.xli). The kind of practical 'doing' that Aristotle is concerned with in his discussion of praxis is thus 'doing the right thing' rather than just 'doing' anything at all.

[4] Joseph Dunne (1993), using the term poiesis where we have used poiēsis, remarks: "there was a form of activity with which Aristotle was familiar and which was under the firm control of an objective and impersonal 'method'. And yet when he came to formulate his concept of praxis his crucial move was precisely to distinguish it from this form of activity - which was called poiesis. The activity of poesis yielded a product or result which was quite separable from the one who produced it; and also separate - in the sense of being formulable and therefore at the disposal of anyone who might care to learn and use it - was the methodical knowledge or technē which governed this activity. Praxis, on the other hand, was always a realisation of the person himself, and the knowledge which guides it, i.e., phronēsis, was inseparable from the kind of person he had become (p.126).

[5] Of "uncertain practical questions", Reid writes: "First of all, they are questions that have to be answered - even if the answer is to decide to do nothing. In this, they differ from academic, or theoretic, questions which do not demand an answer at any particular time, or indeed any answer at all. Second, the grounds on which decisions should be made are uncertain. Nothing can tell us infallibly whose interests should be consulted, what evidence should be taken into account, or what kinds of arguments should be given precedence. Third, in answering practical questions, we always have to take some existing state of affairs into account. We are never in a position to make a

completely fresh start, free from the legacy of past history and present arrangements. Fourth, and following from this, each question is in some ways unique, belonging to a specific time and context, the particulars of which we can never exhaustively describe. Fifth, our question will certainly compel us to adjudicate between competing goals and values. We may choose a solution that maximises our satisfaction across a range of possible goals, but some will suffer at the expense of others. Sixth, we can never predict the outcome of the particular solution we choose, still less know what the outcome would have been had we made a different choice. Finally, the grounds on which we decide to answer a practical question in a particular way are not grounds that point to the desirability of the action chosen as an act in itself, but grounds that lead us to suppose that the action will result in some desirable state of affairs" (p.42).

[6] Habermas (1992, 1996, 2003) has criticised "praxis philosophy", which refers to the social philosophy that underpinned communist views about collectivities or "social macro-subjects" like a class or a state that aim to be self-regulating and to speak on behalf of, and to regulate, the actions of all members of the class or all citizens of the state (as a communist state might once have spoken on behalf of, or regulated, all of its citizens). His criticism of "praxis philosophy" is not directed at the notion of praxis as described in this chapter, but rather at the notion of "revolutionizing praxis" advanced by Marx in his (1845) Theses on Feuerbach but later taken up (and 'totalized') by later Marxists and communists as a substitute for democratic will-formation in totalitarian communist regimes.

[7] Philosopher Iris Marion Young (1990) argues that social structures and practices are unjust if they are characterised by domination (the unreasonable constraint on self-determination for individuals or groups) or oppression (the unreasonable constraint of self-expression and self-development). Oppression, she says, has five main types: exploitation, marginalization, powerlessness, cultural imperialism and violence.

REFERENCES

Aristotle (2003) *Ethics*, trans. [1953] J.A.K. Thompson, revised with notes and appendices [1976] Hugh Tredennick, with an introduction [1976, 2003] Jonathon Barnes, and preface [2003] A.C. Grayling. London: The Folio Society.

Connell, W.F. (1981) *A history of education in the twentieth century world*. Columbia: Teachers' College Press.

Dunne, J. (1993) *Back to the rough ground: 'Phronēsis' and 'technē' in modern philosophy and Aristotle*. Notre Dame, Indiana: University of Notre Dame Press.

Gadamer, H.-G. (1975) *Truth and method*. London: Sheed and Ward.

Habermas, J. (1972) *Knowledge and human interests*, trans. Jeremy J. Shapiro. London: Heinemann.

Habermas, J. (1974) *Theory and practice*, trans. John Viertel. London: Heinemann.

Habermas, J. (1992) *The philosophical discourse of modernity: Twelve lectures*, trans. Frederick G. Lawrence. Cambridge, Massachusetts: MIT Press.

Habermas, J. (1996) *Between facts and norms: Contributions to a discourse theory of law and democracy*, trans. William Rehg. Cambridge, Massachusetts: MIT Press.

Habermas, J. (2003) *Truth and justification*, ed. and trans. Barbara Fultner. Cambridge, Massachusetts: MIT Press.

Horkheimer, M. (1972) Traditional and critical theory, in Max Horkheimer, *Critical Theory*. New York: The Seabury Press.

Kemmis, S. (2005) Is Mathematics education a practice? Mathematics teaching? In M. Goos et al. (eds.) *Proceedings of the Mathematics Education and Society 4 Conference*. Brisbane: Centre for Learning Research, Griffith University.

MacIntyre, A. (1983) *After virtue: A study of moral theory*, 2nd edn. London: Duckworth.

MacIntyre, A. and Dunne, J. (2002) Alasdair MacIntyre on education, *Journal of Philosophy of Education*, *36*(1), 1-19.

Marx, K. (1845/1938) Theses on Feuerbach, in *The German ideology*. London: Lawrence and Wishart.

Reid, W.A. (1978) *Thinking about the curriculum: The nature and treatment of curriculum problems*. London: Routledge and Kegan Paul.

Sinclair, T.A. (1962) "Introduction" to *Aristotle: The politics*, trans. and introduction by T.A. Sinclair. Harmondsworth, Middlesex: Penguin.

van Veen, K. (forthcoming) Rethinking the teacher as professional: The case of Dutch high school teachers. In Jan Ax and Petra Ponte (eds.) *The teaching profession in dutch educational praxis*. Rotterdam: Sense Publishers.

Young, I.M. (1990) *Justice and the politics of difference*. Princeton, New Jersey: Princeton University Press.

AFFILIATIONS

Stephen Kemmis
School of Education
Charles Sturt University, Wagga Wagga, Australia

Tracey J. Smith
School of Education
Charles Sturt University, Wagga Wagga, Australia

STEPHEN KEMMIS AND PETER GROOTENBOER

3. SITUATING PRAXIS IN PRACTICE:

Practice architectures and the cultural, social and material conditions for practice

As we saw in Chapter Two, Aristotle's (2003) *Ethics* gives an account of action seen from the perspective of the actor – the virtuous person aiming to do what is good for humankind. Aristotle's virtuous person is not an isolated individual acting alone, however. The virtuous person acts in relation to others – family, friends, legislators and slaves in the city-state. She or he (but principally, for Aristotle, the latter, since he regards women and slaves as inferior by nature) is a law-abiding person. She or he aims to do what is good for her- or himself and also for others. To a degree that Aristotle does not make plain in the *Ethics*, the virtuous person is a cultured, socialised and politically-conscious person (a citizen and, in the case of men of a certain class, legislators), who is also part of the productive life of her or his society (as a farmer and a soldier, for example). He discusses the kind of states, constitutions and social orders proper for the good organisation of societies (polities) in his *Politics* (1962).

In this chapter, we will not follow Aristotle into the ancient world described in *The Politics*. His aim was to describe what makes a good society via its constitution – provisions concerning citizenship (for free, aristocratic men) and participation in discussions and the making of legislation, proper economic arrangements, military obligations, and the like. In this sense, he aimed to show how a well-constituted and well-ordered society might create what might nowadays be called a 'context' for the *praxis* of individual members of the society – viewing this context as a particular kind of background against which *praxis* might or might not occur. In this chapter, we will take a different approach to 'contextualising' practice, aiming to show that practice and *praxis* are not dependent solely on the experience, intentions and actions of individuals, but rather to show that they are also shaped and conditioned by arrangements, circumstances and conditions *beyond* each person as an individual agent or actor. We will call these *extra-individual conditions*. Unlike the approach taken by Aristotle we will not be contrasting the individual with the *group* or *polity*, but rather explore the ways in which the individual relates *intersubjectively* to any *other* – to other persons, whether individually or in groups. The distinction between these two oppositions – the individual and the group, on the one hand, and the self and other, on the other hand – is important philosophically, culturally, socially, psychologically and for practice theory.

Kemmis, Stephen and Smith, Tracey J. (2008) Enabling praxis: Challenges for education. 37-62
© 2008 Sense Publishers. All rights reserved.

In fact, we have much work to do to extract ourselves from widespread presuppositions about what it means to regard persons as individuals – as they tend to be understood in terms of the atomistic individualism which is a widespread, taken-for-granted self-understanding of people in the contemporary West (for a critique of atomistic individualism, see Charles Taylor, 1991). First, in relation to the opposition of the individual and the group or collectivity, we must understand that, as human beings, we are *social* beings – we are part of the societies that frame us and within which we have our social relations. In this dimension, the individual is not 'superior' (for example, as the bearer of human rights as if this could be the case without a society that confers those rights) to society or a group, and the society or group (including a culture or a class) is not a "social macrosubject" which can be 'superior' to individuals in the sense that it can compel people to understand the world in particular ways or coerce them into accepting whatever a state might want people to accept (see, for example, Habermas, 2003, p.282-3). The relationship between the individual and a state, society, culture or class is one of mutual constitution: each constitutes the other. Second, in relation to the opposition of the self and other, we must understand that, as human beings and especially as *persons* with *human agency*, we are constituted through our relationships with others – culturally, socially and economically. Those 'others' give us our selfhood through our *upbringing*, our education and our experience, and in this sense, those others are part of us and we are part of them. We become speakers of shared languages which allow us to understand ourselves, others and the world (through our 'sayings'). We become part of shared practices and activities through which our lives are constituted (through our 'doings'). And we become part of groups – families, neighbourhoods, occupations – through which we form identities and take roles in relation to others, and by means of which we find ourselves included and excluded from possible memberships and ways of belonging to those groups (through our 'relatings').

These 'sayings', 'doings' and 'relatings' are part of our lived relationships with others, and are so deeply sedimented in our experience that they may become invisible – taken for granted as 'the way things are'. But they are also supported by worlds of 'saying' and 'doing' and 'relating' that were, to a large degree, always already there as actualities or as possibilities before we came upon the scene. It is as if (but only as if) the cultural, discursive, social and material world anticipated our being in it, or at least has shapes and structures – and cultural, discursive and social practices – that prefigure ways we can live in the world. We grow and develop to fit some of these shapes of being, and in ways that make us 'unfit' for others (particular ways of being that are *other* ways of being, or *others'* ways of being).

We will not, in this chapter, follow Aristotle from his *Ethics* into his *Politics* because we will take a different view about the relationship of individual to the group and of selves to others than the view that Aristotle took two millennia ago. The initial account of *praxis* given in Chapter Two appears to suggest that the good for each individual and the good for humankind is pursued through each individual acting rightly. As we have begun to see, however, this is only partly true. The account of *praxis* in Chapter Two might be read to suggest that each person, because of or despite their virtuous intentions, is either a hero or a victim who rises above, or falls victim to, the circumstances in which they find themselves.

The good teacher – the educator – depicted in Chapter Two is a person who

- is well-informed about educational traditions (with the disposition *epistēmē* put into practice through the contemplative action called *theoria*),
- has the technical skill to achieve educational aims using appropriate means (with the disposition of *technē* put into practice through the technical action called *poiēsis*),
- aims to act rightly (with the disposition of *phronēsis* put into practice through the practical action called *praxis*), and, as suggested in Chapter Two,
- has a *critical* disposition to overcome irrationality, injustice and suffering through *critical* reflection and *emancipatory* action in concert with others who arrive at critical insights about how irrationality, injustice and suffering might be overcome.

Such an educator does not develop 'naturally', nor solely through having these good intentions and acting on them. As Karl Marx famously put it in the third of his *Theses on Feuerbach* (1845/1938), the educator is formed through her or his own education and experience[1]:

> The materialist doctrine that men are products of circumstances and upbringing, and that, therefore, changed men are products of changed circumstances and changed upbringing, forgets that it is men who change circumstances and that the educator must himself be educated.

If we should not forget that educators are products of their education, circumstances and experience, then what *'makes'* this product? In this chapter, we will consider some of the conditions that produce education and educators, including not only their dispositions and the forms of action they can take, but also – a category not made explicit in Aristotle's account of different forms of action – the kinds of social connections they have with others. As we shall see, *the educator's practices are also the product of other practices* – they are shaped and conditioned by circumstances and prior histories, and by the situations in which she or he acts, not entirely by the action of the practitioner alone. Many of these circumstances and prior histories are themselves the products of the prior practices of others, for example educators of earlier times who laid down particular educational traditions, or educational planners and administrators who have made particular kinds of resources available for teachers to use in a school or college. Some (but not all) of these prior practices can be described as *meta-practices* – practices, like policy practices and some theoretical practices, which are constructed with a view to producing (for example, regulating, informing, enabling or constraining) the content and conduct of other practices like particular practices of teaching for example. Others are not meta-practices in the sense of being *intended* to shape other practices, but they still influence what kind of practice is possible (the possibilities of practice) before any particular case of practice or *praxis* actually occurs.

THE SHAPING OF DISPOSITIONS

As we saw in Chapter Two, Aristotle describes the disposition of *epistēmē*, guided by the *telos* (aim) of attaining knowledge or truth; the disposition of *technē*, guided by the *telos* of producing something; and the disposition of *phronēsis,* guided by the *telos* of wise and prudent action or acting rightly in the world. To these, following Habermas (1972, 1974), we added a fourth: the *critical* disposition (or knowledge-constitutive interest) guided by the *telos* of overcoming irrationality, injustice, suffering and felt dissatisfactions by *emancipatory* action. These dispositions do not arise 'naturally'; they are formed and informed by an education in what it means to care for and aim for these things. In the case of the education of an educator, this is the gaining of knowledge about what it means to aim for or to attain truth or ideas that count as justified true beliefs about education; gaining relevant technical knowledge and skill in teaching; gaining wisdom, prudence and practical commonsense about how to act in educational situations (among others); and developing the commitment to overcome irrationality, injustice and suffering as they occur in and as a result of education or the particular actions of teaching and learning. The relevant content knowledge for a range of other professions and occupations could be similarly related to these dispositions.

While these kinds of knowledge, skills, capacities and commitments appear, from the perspective of an individual person, to be 'properties' of the individual, they do not arise from the individual person alone. They are also *extra-individual* in the sense that they are part of the collective knowledge of groups (including professions, occupational groups, and many other kinds of groups), codified in the form of theories and traditions. They are carried in the *culture* and *discourses* of these groups, from local to global levels.

The cultural and discursive formation of dispositions

In the case of the education of an educator, the disposition of *epistēmē* – aimed at attaining truth – is formed and developed through engaging with, and coming to one's own conclusions about, the different knowledge and traditions that have shaped and formed education in the past, and the perspectives of different educational theorists that inform different approaches to education today. The educator's disposition of *technē* is formed and developed through engaging with, and developing some skill in the use of, knowledge of the different kinds of educational aims and 'methods' that have characterised education in the past, and about the aims and methods available today. The educator's disposition of *phronēsis* – aimed at wise and prudent action – is formed and developed through engaging with, and making judgements about, what is most morally right and appropriate in the light of past and contemporary views about morality, ethics, social justice and politics, and ideas about the most pressing problems to be addressed by rising generations of people today. The educator's *critical* disposition is formed and developed through critical thinking and reflection about topics, themes and issues that have fuelled the debates and actions of social movements of the past, about the consequences of those debates and actions, and about pressing issues of irrationality, injustice and suffering that face education and the world today.

To develop these dispositions, the educator must engage in learning, discussion and debate, acquiring knowledge and understanding from others who have gone before (for example, through reading in the history and philosophy of education and in many other fields) and from others in their local and professional communities – other teachers, students and local community members, as well as the many other people they encounter through the media (for example, in debates about current affairs, the arts, science and other fields). The educator is continuously made and remade through these encounters, through her or his own experience and through learning from the experience of others.

Developing these four dispositions can thus be seen as occurring in a sea of language – a sea of *discourse*. The teacher and the student teacher are 'offered' the world in the pre-given codifications of everyday language, in the specialised discourses of different fields (like education and science), and in conventional ways of understanding things or accepted wisdom. What it means to understand the field of education is thus partially (pre-) given by *culture* and *discourses* – knowledge 'handed down' or otherwise acquired by the educator's participation in conversations with people or texts. Part of the process of becoming an educator is to acquire relevant educational knowledge and to learn to participate in educational conversation and debates about educational matters which are frequently conducted in educational discourses, informed by particular ideas about education. Part of what it means to be an excellent educator is to use these discourses with facility, to be able to use them to inform discussions with non-specialists ('translating' them, as it were, so they can be understood by others), and to use the discourses critically, to press knowledge beyond existing limits as people address new problems, or as they address old problems in new ways.

The dispositions of *epistēmē*, *technē*, *phronēsis* and towards *emancipation* are thus acquired and developed in processes of cultural and discursive formation. They are formed through reading and writing, listening and speaking – that is, by participating in *practices of communication*. Insofar as the educator is developing *as an educator*, this generally also means that they are formed through practices of communication *with other educators* and specialists and professionals in the field of education and in various related fields (for example philosophy, sociology or psychology, or curriculum theory or educational administration).

To say that the educators' dispositions are *culturally-* and *discursively-formed* is to say that at any time, the teacher or student teacher is swimming in a sea of discourse about contemporary and immediate problems, issues, ideas, confronting conflict, contradictions and contestation about what is true, right and productive, bringing to bear knowledge and theories handed down from traditions, acquired from debates, and from the educator's own and others' experience. How he or she

KEMMIS & GROOTENBOER

will participate in practices of communication – for example, through discussion and debate – will depend, in part, on his or her own experience in the use of the relevant discourses, but it will also depend, in part, on the language and discourses used *by others* to address particular educational issues.

Participating in practices of communication is always to enter an *intersubjective* space in which others also control the direction and content of the conversation. As Jürgen Habermas (2003a) put it:

> As historical and social beings we find ourselves always already in a linguistically structured lifeworld. In the forms of communication through which we reach an understanding with one another about something in the world and about ourselves, we encounter a transcending power. Language is not a kind of private property. No one possesses exclusive rights over the common medium of the communicative practices we must intersubjectively share. No single participant can control the structure, or even the course, of processes of reaching understanding and self-understanding. How speakers and hearers make use of their communicative freedom to take yes- or no-positions is not a matter of their subjective discretion. For they are free only in virtue of the binding force of the justifiable claims they raise towards one another. The logos of language embodies the power of the intersubjective, which precedes and grounds the subjectivity of speakers.
>
> …. The *logos* of language escapes our control, and yet we are the ones, the subjects capable of speech and action, who reach an understanding with one another in this medium. It remains 'our' language. The unconditionedness of truth and freedom is a necessary presupposition of our practices, but beyond the constituents of 'our' form of life they lack any ontological guarantee. Similarly, the 'right' ethical self-understanding is neither revealed nor 'given' in some other way. It can only be won in common endeavour. From this perspective, what makes our being-ourselves possible appears more as a transsubjective power than an absolute one (pp.10-11).

To say that dispositions are acquired and adopted intersubjectively is to say that they are not solely the property of the people who have them – they are shaped by the *practices of communication* they have participated in – whether reading or writing, listening or speaking. It is also to say that they are formed *intertextually* – by the transfer of ideas through texts and utterances from readers who are also writers to other readers, and from listeners who are also speakers to other listeners. Educators' *understandings* of education and the world – and the good for each individual and the good for humankind – are culturally – and discursively-shaped and formed in these practices of communication. Their dispositions are partly *prefigured* by their own *and others'* participation in these practices, so that particular educators will tend to 'see' this particular situation as a situation of this or that *type*, and to think of this or that feature of the situation as more relevant, pertinent or important, if only at this particular moment. And their dispositions

42

(and the action they take in the situation) will reflect longer (historically) and wider (contemporary) concerns about the most important things they should be doing in their work as teachers or educators – whether the enactment of a particular approach to pedagogy (like 'progressive' or 'productive' pedagogy) or following a particular policy (for example, a particular policy about the education of boys and men, or a policy about testing, or about officially-sanctioned approaches to literacy development).

Finally, the *content* of the cultures and discourses that the teacher or educator participate in – what they know and understand – also suggests which of the dispositions will be primary at any particular moment. Moment by moment, the teacher is confronted by situations which can be and will be *understood and interpreted* in different ways, on the basis of their experience and knowledge. Is this something I need to think more deeply about – disposing me towards *epistēmē* and *theoria*? Is this something I need to do skilfully to produce my intended outcome – disposing me towards *technē* and *poiēsis*? Is this a case where I must pay special attention to acting rightly and properly – disposing me towards *phronēsis* and *praxis*? Is this something I must take a critical view about, to overcome an existing irrationality, injustice or suffering – disposing me towards the *critical* disposition and *critical* reflection and *emancipatory* action?

Which of the dispositions will be primary at any moment is partly determined by knowledge and experience and by the exigencies of the current situation, but it is also partly *prefigured* by previous practice – the 'givens' of the practices in which people have previously participated. For example, if we are in a professional development seminar, hearing about the speaker's theory of learning, the setting will suggest that *epistēmē* is the appropriate disposition. If we are in the classroom, teaching how to perform a statistical test, the setting may suggest that *technē* is the appropriate disposition. If there is a fight going on outside the classroom, the situation may suggest that *phronēsis* would be the appropriate disposition. If we have discovered that the boys are taking a disproportionate share of the time available for students to use the classroom computers, so the girls can't get their work done the situation may suggest that it would be appropriate to have a *critical* disposition. There are no fixed *rules* for determining which disposition is appropriate at any time, or in any situation (though we may have some rules of thumb to guide us); which one the individual adopts is partly determined by experience and judgement. Which disposition comes to the fore, becoming foreground while others are in the background, will also be partly determined by the kind of situation it is – a form partly given by social and material circumstances, and by traditions and conventions of thinking about and understanding situations – in cultural and discursive terms that are *extra-individual*, and in some ways *prefigured* by the situation and setting.

The social formation of dispositions

Developing these four kinds of dispositions is not only a matter of cultural or discursive knowledge. It also occurs in a social world of connections with other people. The educator's parents, friends, community, teachers, professional colleagues and many others influence the content of the different dispositions, as the educator understands them, and also influences the educator's view of the significance of each disposition in general and in different kinds of situations. Where the educator is located in such webs of social connections to some extent determines their access to ideas, the value and importance attached to them, and the degree to which they are likely to be regarded as legitimate.

Dispositions are socially-formed in a second sense. As we have seen, the social situations and settings the educator inhabits also provide 'prompts' for what will be regarded as significant at any moment. Conflict in the classroom may suggest that the situation calls for wise and prudent action (*praxis*), but it may also call for *technē* in the form of conducting a structured mediation process. Through experience, the educator learns when different dispositions will be primary, and which will be secondary. Other people are part of the social conditions of being in a situation for the educator, and their words and actions and their relationships with the educator influence, and can even direct, what disposition will be primary for the educator at this particular moment in this particular place.

The life experience of the educator is partly a life experience of social connections, influencing what the educator values, the groups to which she or he belongs or wants to belong, the kinds and strengths of solidarities she or he feels with others, what he or she will regard as morally-right and appropriate, and what she or he will regard as legitimate. If dispositions are formed and adopted in a sea of discourse, then they are also formed in a sea of *relationships*.

The material-economic formation of dispositions

Similarly, material conditions, like the physical properties of objects and relations between them shape the formation of dispositions. Distance means that only some people will have access to this or that teacher or text, for example. And economic factors – like cost – also influence who will have access to what educational opportunities and thus to this or that idea.

It is obvious that physical conditions (like the configuration of a classroom or the distance between people) and economic conditions (like salaries, and different kinds of roles in processes of production and consumption) shape what an educator can do. Like the sea of discourse and the sea of relationships, these physical and economic conditions create 'webs' of possibility for practice, both in general and at particular moments. The child who is too far away to hear a shout of caution, or the child arriving at school too hungry to learn obviously shape the conditions of practice for the teacher. The educator encounters learners, families and communities under physical and economic circumstances and conditions that have their own histories that shape how the educator can and should act at any particular time, and the educator's disposition to act in a particular way at a particular time. Just as cultural conditions (like teaching in an Indigenous community) or social conditions (like teaching a class that includes newly-arrived immigrants or refugees) shape the educator's dispositions in general or at any particular time, so physical and material conditions shape her or his dispositions to act in different ways.

In a community confronting environmental crises like lack of water, salinity problems or loss of biodiversity, a newly-arrived teacher may respond with the disposition of *epistēmē*, and spend time reading and reflecting (*theoria*) on the nature of the problems. She or he may work with a group of students to revegetate a stream bank or manage school energy use and waste, adopting the disposition of *technē* and working skilfully (*poiēsis*) to deal with identified problems. She or he may adopt the disposition of *phronēsis* while considering how to act appropriately (*praxis*) towards students whose families are polluting a stream alongside students whose families must drink the polluted water. She or he may adopt a *critical* disposition and encourage critical reflection and emancipatory action on the issues with students and their families.

The same kinds of dispositions and responses similarly come into play in relation to economic issues. The educator responding to students whose lives and life opportunities are constrained by poverty will at different times adopt each of these four dispositions. And similarly, the educator will respond at different moments with each of these dispositions in relation to issues about production and consumption, both in the economy of the community (perhaps seeing these in relation to global economic issues) and in the school itself – in terms of what he or she 'produces' and 'consumes' as a teacher, in relation to the processes of production and consumption she or he creates as the work of the class, and in relation to the accumulation and use of the economic and material 'goods' students variously achieve in relation to one another.

Material conditions like the different kinds and quality of resources available to different schools or universities, and economic conditions like questions about what students must pay and how much teachers are paid, prefigure practice by creating conditions that enable or constrain different kinds of practice. They also prefigure what dispositions the educator will adopt in general and at particular moments. Knowing that these children or this community live in poverty or ill-health, or that they have been traumatised by violence or war, or that they cannot leave the community for further study, shapes the dispositions of the educator. These material and economic conditions prefigure possibilities for practice and thus what the educator will think about as she or he works out how to respond to the circumstances of students, their families, their community and the place of all in the wider world – environmentally or economically, for example. In this sense, material and economic circumstances and conditions also prefigure the dispositions of the educator.

THE SHAPING OF FORMS OF ACTION

We can conclude, then, that dispositions are shaped culturally and discursively, so that situations are understood in different kinds of ways, as different kinds of situations calling for different ways of responding to them. In the same way, forms of action are shaped through previous actions and interactions, previous experience, and the ways situations themselves are arranged.

In this section, we want to emphasise that action itself is culturally-discursively, socially-politically and materially-economically shaped *in the doing of the action itself.* As we hope to show, meaningful, significant action more or less always occurs in these three dimensions simultaneously, as 'bundles' of interrelated 'sayings', 'doings' and 'relatings'. *Praxis*, and 'practice' in any significant sense, is always composed in words, and oriented and accompanied by 'sayings' that are shaped within worlds of culture and discourses; it occurs in 'doings' that are shaped against backgrounds of previous actions and interactions and that unfold through new actions; and it occurs in 'relatings' that occur as moments in unfolding histories of relationships between people and groups, as well as in relation to organisations and institutions.

In Chapter Two, four types of action corresponding to the dispositions just discussed were considered: *theoria* or contemplation, *poiēsis* or 'making action', *praxis* or right conduct, and *critical* reflection and collaborative action to address irrational ways of understanding things in the world, unjust outcomes, and suffering. Each of these forms of action or practice is also structured by people's prior experience and the way situations are *prefigured* for particular kinds of action. The capacity of *theoria*, contemplation, is developed through learning and participating in discussions with others with the aim of understanding the world clearly. The skills needed in *poiēsis* are developed by practising making the things to be made, using the appropriate materials, tools and procedures, and producing, better and better one hopes, the things that are to be made. The capacities needed for *praxis* are similarly developed, as we saw in Chapter Two, through experience in 'reading' situations more wisely and in acting with greater prudence and good sense. And the capacities needed for *critical* reflection and *emancipatory* action are similarly developed through experience in developing critical insights (what Habermas, 1974, pp.32-34, called "the formation and extension of critical theorems"), enlightening oneself and others about problems or issues (what Habermas called "the organisation of enlightenment"), and collaborative action to overcome such problems (what Habermas called "the conduct of political struggle").

The cultural-discursive formation of action

In relation to each form of action, some relevant knowledge is required. Thus, as in the case of dispositions, each form of action is partly formed by culture and discourses that *inform* or *guide* it. But skill and capacity in each form of action is also partly formed by *doing it* – through action and, one might add, by reflection on the outcomes of each. In developing *theoria* or contemplative action, a person asks themselves whether in fact they did reach a deeper understanding or new knowledge (even if only new for them, but not for others). In developing technical skills for 'making action' or *poiēsis*, a person asks themselves about how their use of the materials, their application of their skills, and their use of the appropriate tools has contributed (or failed adequately to contribute) to the quality or success of the thing to be made – whether it is a watercolour painting, a child capable of reading, or winning in football. In developing wise and prudent action or *praxis*, the person asks themselves about whether the short- and long-term consequences of their action were indeed things that could be said to be 'the good for each individual' and 'the good for humankind'. In developing *critical* capacities, a person asks themselves about whether their collective action did indeed lead to overcoming an irrational way of understanding something, overcoming an injustice, or reducing suffering.

Some of these things can only be learned through experience, by actually doing these different kinds of action, because of the irreversibility of action discussed in Chapter Two: it is only possible to see whether one has done what one intended after it has been done. Only then can it be seen how well or badly it was done. And, though reflection on the experience, one may consider how it could have been done better.

Complex forms of action like the practice of education are always culturally- and discursively-formed in a more general sense. Whether in the form of *theoria*, *poiēsis*, *praxis*, or *emancipatory* action, a complex practice like education involves knowledge and understandings not just in *anticipation* of or *preparation* for practice, but also in the *doing* of the practice itself. Practices of any complexity are the 'living out' of traditions and theory; they ordinarily involve *communication* with others, and they are partly conducted through 'sayings' as well as 'doings' and 'relatings'. The teacher and the doctor and the social worker speak, ask questions, answer questions and make comments to others they are working with. Part of the work of the practice – part of the action of doing the practice – is to foreground topics and concerns relevant to that kind of practice – about learning or about the subject-matter of a lesson or about rules or policies relevant in conducting the practice, in the case of education, or about symptoms, illnesses, their causes and relevant therapies in the case of health. To conduct a practice is to evoke the world of knowledge relevant to it, naming and speaking (those aspects of) the world the practice addresses. It is to use a specialised language of upbringing in the case of education, a specialist language of caring for nurses, a specialist language of 'occupation' (enabling people to do the different activities that make up their lives) for occupational therapists.

As we have seen, then, the four forms of action we have discussed are partly shaped by cultures and discourses, both, in preparation for action, by the knowledge that shapes the way we understand a situation and, in the conduct of the practice, by thematising and guiding our communication with others while we act. Practices are *enacted in* and composed of communication and discourses. This is one dimension of the shaping of action.

The social formation of action

Action is also *socially* shaped and formed. In the present, or on the basis of the past, the actor always acts in ways shaped by connections with others – family, friends, teachers, students, a community or others. Every action, and especially every interaction that involves others, involves *social connections* and *relationships* that spread out around the actor towards previous or present social orders and arrangements. It involves relationships of *belonging* or *not belonging*, *inclusion* or *exclusion*, *solidarity* or *opposition/resistance*, *harmony* or *conflict*, *social integration* or *fragmentation*. It involves acting within or outside established or accepted *social orders*, it strengthens or erodes *solidarities*, it happens in accordance with or against accepted and legitimate *social norms*.

Thus, for example, a teacher acts within or outside the accepted modes of conduct for the education profession, strengthening or eroding the solidarity of students in the class, and appropriately or inappropriately towards students or their families or peers in the profession. She or he always acts in a way that is partly shaped by a history of relationships that have shaped her or him. Past actions and interactions with others shape the way the teacher acts and interacts in newly-arising situations.

What a person will do in a new situation is thus *socially-formed* as well as culturally- and discursively-formed, but not only in relation to her or his own history. All of the people involved in and affected by a particular setting or situation bring similar histories of action and interaction to bear. If the situation is a very familiar kind of setting, like a classroom, then what people can do will be very greatly shaped by a history of what is done in classrooms – who does what, who takes what roles, who commands and who submits (or rebels), and in relation to others outside the setting who will be affected by what happens (for example, a student's family or friends, the teacher's peers, the school principal). In this way, forms of action and social practices are also *socially prefigured*. New action and interaction takes place against a web of social relationships that stretch beyond those immediately present to people in the past and people who will learn about what happens in the future.

As in the case of the cultural-discursive formation of action, the conduct of a complex practice like education is not only socially-formed by a *history* of relationships that precede the conduct of the practice on a particular occasion, it is also socially-formed in *the way it is conducted*. Practices like education are conducted in and through relationships with others – indeed, they form (or enhance or sometimes damage) relationships between teachers and students, between students, between teachers, between teachers and school principals, between teachers and students' families, between a teacher and the local community, and so on. Professions may encourage, regulate and proscribe particular kinds of relationships between members of the profession and 'clients' – as education authorities may encourage, regulate or proscribe particular kinds of relationships between teachers and students, particularly at school level. For example, professional bodies in education and educational employers are likely to encourage recognition and respect for people of other cultures, non-discrimination against minority groups, and fairness in assessment; school-level educational authorities may regulate attendance at staff meetings and 'professional' relationships among colleagues; and educational authorities and community norms proscribe sexual relationships between school teachers and their students. The practice and those responsible for conducting the practice recognise that it is *enacted in* and composed of 'relatings' as well as 'doings' and 'sayings'.

The material-economic formation of action

A third dimension in which action and interaction are shaped is the *material-economic* dimension. This is the world of objects and things, natural and made, that enable and constrain what people can do. Part of this is *material* and obvious – most of us live under the force of gravity, must eat and breathe, and cannot walk through walls, for example. Part of it is also determined by a mixture of the social and the material in the form of the *economic* realm – we produce and consume things, buy and sell goods and services, pay or are paid for services we receive or give.

Forms of action are thus also *materially-economically-formed*. What people can do will be shaped, in material terms, by arrangements of things – 'set-ups' which may be dense like a particular classroom or elaborate and extended like a railway system. And what they can do will be shaped by economies that enable and constrain particular kinds of production and consumption, that are arranged to enable and constrain particular kinds of work and activity that are paid or unpaid, bought or not bought.

As in the cases of the cultural-discursive and social formation of action, so, too, the action in a complex practice like education is also materially- and economically-formed not only in anticipation but also in the doing. The school buildings and many of the resources made available for the practice of education anticipate the practice of teaching and learning in this particular place. But the 'doing' of education also occurs in interactions with the material world, and in economic transactions that are sometimes more or and sometimes less apparent to teachers and students. The embodiment of teachers and learners, their physicality, their senses of space and place and the location of a school attest to the materiality of educational encounters. The payment of salaries, the payment of school fees, the cost of resources and the price of excursions attest to the economic dimension of the practice. And the practice involves a range of processes of production – production of units of work by teachers, production of assignments or answers to questions or tests by students – and processes of consumption – use of energy to light and heat or cool the classroom, the use, maintenance and decay of computers, paper, pencils and all the other resources of the school. And the practice of education takes place against a background of the political economies at work within and beyond the school – a background of producing and consuming student grades, social statuses, roles in the hierarchy of positions in the school staff, and in the positions available to parents on school committees.

Each of the four forms of action we have discussed – *theoria, poiēsis, praxis* and *emancipatory* reflection and action – takes place in a matrix of material and economic transactions, under local circumstances and conditions, in the form of bodily action in and on the world, with nourishing and sustaining or corrosive and hurtful consequences for the health, well-being, interests and self-interests of the people involved. Professional practices like education are not just cultural or social or cognitive work, they involve physical activity and physical work, too – and emotional work with long-term consequences for both students and teachers. The practice of education is *enacted in* material-economic 'doings' as well as 'sayings' and 'relatings'.

Individual and extra-individual formation of dispositions and action

We can thus conclude that dispositions and actions are not formed entirely by individuals in their own right. They say what they say in conversations in ways shaped by cultural-discursive conditions and possibilities that existed before them and extend beyond them – in a history and contemporary sea of discourse. They do what they do in ways shaped by material-economic conditions that existed before them and extend beyond them in the material world. They relate to others in ways shaped by social conditions that existed before them and extend beyond them in webs of social relationships and connections.

This is to say that, in each of these dimensions, *extra-individual* conditions shape dispositions and actions, both in the educator's general response to a particular situation or setting, and in relation to their particular responses at particular moments.

The relationships between individual and extra-individual formation and shaping of practice in each of these dimensions or realms of *culture* and *discourses*, *sociality* (or *society*), and the *material-economic* are abstractly depicted in Table 1.

Table 1: Four perspectives on dispositions and action

Dispositions	Action	Shaped by the intentions and actions of the individual	Shaped by extra-individual structures and processes		
			Cultural-discursive	Social-political	Material-economic
Epistēmē	*Theoria*				
Technē	*Poiēsis*				
Phronēsis	*Praxis*				
Critical	*Emancipatory*				

To understand practices as culturally-discursively-, socially- and materially-economically-shaped and formed is to see them always as *situated*. Of course they are always situated in the sense that they happen in some particular place and at some particular time – but to see practices as situated means more than that. It is also to see that the form a practice takes will be shaped partly by the circumstances and conditions of the particular concrete location where it occurs, but also as situated in *time* and *history*. How a practice turns out will also be shaped by the history and experience of the people involved, but also against *cultural histories* (how discourses have been shaped in usage over time for particular groups and in particular places), *social histories* (the histories of different groups and societies, shaped by relationships of inclusion and exclusion, identity and difference, solidarity and conflict) and *material-economic histories* (how objects and things in the natural and physical world and economic processes and relations have changed over time). Practices must thus be seen as dynamic and evolving, being *reproduced* and *transformed* over time as they meet changing needs and demands in different places at different times.

Table 2 below aims to suggest how the 'realms' of the individual and the social or societal (cultures, societies, material-economic conditions) shape one another over time through the *generic practices* of communication, social connection and production-consumption. On this view, individuals as *agents* (persons with agency) shape cultural, social and material-economic structures, and cultural, social and material-economic practices dialectically and reciprocally shape individuals over time, *through practice*.

Table 2: Individual and extra-individual realms mutually-constituted through practice

INDIVIDUAL Knowledge and identity	Mediated through generic practices	In collectively-shaped social media	EXTRA-INDIVIDUAL Structures
Understandings and self-understandings	*Communication* *('Sayings')*	*Language*	Cultural-discursive (languages, discourses)
Skills, capacities	*Production* *('Doings')*	*Work*	Material-economic (physical, natural worlds)
Solidarities, values, emotions	*Social connection* *('Relatings')*	*Power*	Social-political (lifeworlds, systems)

'Practice' in the sense in which it was used in the last paragraph has a different meaning from the way 'practice' has been spoken of earlier in this (and other) chapters. The *generic practices of communication, production-consumption and social connection* refer, crudely speaking, to 'saying', 'doing' and 'relating' in general. In fact, however, all three usually occur as *bundles* of sayings, doings and relatings. What makes a complex practice like *education* or *medicine* distinctive is the *content* of sayings, doings and relatings characteristic of the practice, and *the way sayings, doings and relatings are bundled together* in the conduct of these different professions – just as sayings, doings and relatings are distinctively bundled in other occupations and activities.

Think of an empty classroom at night. It contains many of the resources needed to enact the practice of education in the morning. Curricula and lessons have been planned. Policies are in place about how people should relate to one another in the setting. The people who will take their roles as students and teachers are particular known people, though they are elsewhere for the moment. With the new school day, they will come into the classroom and put in motion not exactly what was planned, or only what the resources enable and constrain them to do, but something that can be envisaged in general on the basis of the extra-individual features that prefigure a practice like education in this place and time. At various levels of analysis, from the school year to the school day to a single lesson, the empty classroom and its resources to some extent *prefigure* the practice to be enacted by the students and teacher when the school day begins.

SCHATZKI AND PRACTICE AS 'PREFIGURED'

Theodore Schatzki (1996, 2002) describes practices as 'prefigured' in this way. He identifies several key features of practices to show how they are not just the property of individuals but also "sites of the social". Some social practices, like asking questions or walking, are what Schatzki (2002) calls *"dispersed practices"* – they appear in many different kinds of 'higher-order' practices. Schatzki contrasts dispersed practices with other social practices that he describes as *"integrative practices"*. Integrative practices involve many dispersed practices and other activities arranged in larger patterns. Education, and teaching or learning, are integrative practices according to Schatzki's notion of practices. Schatzki describes integrative practices as being organised, as *"hanging together"*, and as having four principal constituent features:

> … practices are organized nexuses of actions. This means that the doings and sayings composing them hang together. More specifically, the doings and sayings that compose a given practice are linked through (1) practical understandings, (2) rules, (3) a teleoaffective structure, and (4) general understandings.

> By "practical understandings", I mean certain abilities that pertain to the actions composing a practice (p.77).

> By "rules", I mean explicit formulations, principles, precepts, and instructions that enjoin, direct, or remonstrate [with] people to perform specific actions (p.79).

> A "teleoaffective structure" is a range of normativized and hierarchically ordered ends, projects and tasks, to varying degrees allied with normativized emotions and even moods. By "normativity," I mean, first oughtness and, beyond this, acceptability (p.80).

And Schatzki describes "general understandings" in terms of features like these:
> – "a variety of the doings and sayings that compose … practices" jointly express a common orientation among people to the meaning and significance of what they are doing, and/or
> – people share a "sense of common enterprise, [or] concern", and/or
> – participants share the same kind of understanding of the significance of what is being done, and/or

– they share a common manner of doing things, which are "expressed in the manner in which people carry out projects and tasks" (p.80).

Schatzki (1996, 2001, 2002) arrived at his view of practices by following clues in Ludwig Wittgenstein's (1953) view of language as comprehensible only through the playing (as it were) of *language games* in which people are oriented to one another and to the world in the 'game' of language such that they can reach agreements with one another. Their agreements are not just in words, however. Wittgenstein says that to reach agreement also requires that people can be similarly oriented to the topic that they are discussing, and that this requires agreement not just in the words they use but in *forms of life*. That is, they must have sufficiently common background knowledge to be able to agree about something *in words*. Any conversation, then, calls into play a shared background knowledge of the world, made through the way people experience the world by sharing (or not sharing) similar forms of life. What lies beyond the specific words being spoken, called into play like the harmonics that run above the specific notes of a melody, is a *poetics* of knowledge and experience that orients people more or less similarly to the world or to a particular topic of conversation[2].

Schatzki's view of practice as "the site of the social" aims to give a more concrete and material form to Wittgenstein's notion of forms of life and to the notion of a poetics of practice. It gives shape and substance to the particulars of forms of life in the shape and substance of people's doings and sayings and relatings and the way they are bundled together in particular practices and settings, to the extent that they become characteristic of what people do and say and how they relate to one another in particular (integrative) practices like education or medicine, or in particular places (settings) and times. (Schatzki illustrates much of his characterisation of practices in *The Site of the Social* by referring to the herbal medicine production practices of the Shaker religious sect at New Lebanon, New York, pointing to the way the buildings, the separate housing arrangements for men and women, and the equipment and facilities for different Shaker enterprises and meetings for religious observance were arranged spatially and temporally in relation to one another and in relation to different members of the Shaker community.)

Schatzki's move to 'substantialise' or 'materialise' practice in this way, by reference to particular arrangements of sayings (words), doings and relatings, and their bundling together in particular settings and in particular kinds of integrative practices, is similar to the argumentative move taken by Marx in relation to Hegel. Marx took Hegel's idealist view of history as moving towards Absolute Knowledge (at which point we would simultaneously know the truth about the world and about ourselves in it), and made it material in actual history – to see the history of changing forms of human societies, for example, as unfolding in the real history of people and groups, not as a progress of ideas alone.[3]

COMMUNITIES OF PRACTICE

Similar moves to 'socialise' learning and the development of knowledge and identities have been taken by Lave (1988), Lave and Wenger (1991) and Wenger (1998) in the formation and development of the notion of "*communities of practice*". The first step was to notice that learning takes place in a cultural context which shapes the ideas learners can form; the next was to notice that these ideas pass from person to person in social networks composed of actual people who have particular kinds of relationships with one another in any setting; and the third was to notice that the learning taking place in the setting occurs through "legitimate peripheral participation" in which novices or outsiders to a practice gradually become "old hands" in a "*community of practice*".

> A community of practice is a set of relations among persons, activity and the world, over time and in relation with other tangential and overlapping communities of practice. A community of practice is an intrinsic condition for the existence of knowledge, not least because it provides the interpretive support necessary for making sense of its heritage. Thus, participation in the cultural practice in which any knowledge exists is an epistemological principle of learning. The social structure of this practice, its power relations, and its conditions for legitimacy define possibilities for learning (i.e., for legitimate peripheral participation) (p.98).

> To begin with, newcomers' legitimate peripherality provides them with more than an 'observational' lookout post: It crucially involves *participation* as a way of learning – of both absorbing and being absorbed in – the 'culture of practice'. An extended period of legitimate peripherality provides learners with the opportunity to make the culture theirs (Lave and Wenger, 1991, p.95; emphases in original).

> Knowledge within a community of practice and ways of perceiving and manipulating objects are encoded in artefacts... (Lave and Wenger, 1991, p.102).

Lave and Wenger distinguish "talking about" and "talking within" a practice:

> Talking within itself includes both talking within (e.g., exchanging information necessary to the progress of ongoing activities) and talking about (e.g., stories, community lore). Inside the shared practice, both forms of talk fulfil specific functions: engaging, focusing, and shifting attention, bringing about coordination, etc., on the one hand; and supporting communal forms of memory and reflection, as well as signalling membership, on the other. (And, similarly, talking about includes both forms of talk once it becomes part of a practice of its own, usually sequestered in some respects.) For newcomers then the purpose is not to learn *from* talk as a substitute for legitimate peripheral participation; it is to learn *to* talk as a key to legitimate peripheral participation (p.109).

These quotations from Lave and Wenger sketch the trajectory of becoming a full participant in a community of practice, and indicate that communities of practice are themselves reproduced and transformed over time. In their conclusion to *Situated Learning*, they write about how the concept of situated learning has been transformed:

> *Situated learning activity* has been transformed into legitimate peripheral participation in communities of practice. Legitimate peripheral participation moves in a centripetal direction, motivated by its location in a field of mature practice. It is motivated by the growing use value of participation, and by newcomers' desires to become full practitioners. Communities of practice have histories and developmental cycles, and reproduce themselves in such a way that the transformation of newcomers into old-timers becomes unremarkably integral to the practice.

> *Knowing* is inherent in the growth and transformation of identities and it is located in relations among practitioners, their practice, the artefacts of that practice, and the social organisation and political economy of communities of practice. For newcomers, their shifting location as they move centripetally through a complex form of practice creates possibilities for understanding the world as experienced (pp.122-3).

THE INDIVIDUAL AND THE SOCIAL:
A RELATIONSHIP MEDIATED *IN* AND *BY* PRACTICES

What we see in Lave and Wenger, and again in Wenger (1998) is a *situating* of *both* learning and practice in cultural, social and material forms. In Lave and Wenger, however, the emphasis is markedly on the side of the *individual* – the individual's developing knowledge and identity in the practice. As psychologists, their interest is in how people can learn a practice, and their answers are couched in terms of legitimate peripheral participation and communities of practice.

What we saw in Schatzki, by contrast, was an attempt to find the *social* 'in its own terms', as it were, in the form of a social realm of social practices that prefigure and thus enable and constrain practices even before a particular practitioner arrives on the scene. On both sides of this dialectic of the individual and the social, we see efforts reaching out to embrace the other – from the individual to the social, in the case of Lave and Wenger, and from the social to the individual, in the case of Schatzki. Table 2, presented earlier in this chapter, aims to represent the two as dialectically-related; that is, as mutually-constituted, so, on the one side, the knowledge and identities – the (self) understandings, values and skills of individuals – are constituted through engaging with, on the other side, the culture and discourses, social structures and material-economic arrangements of the worlds they inhabit, for example, in communities of practice. These relationships are not to be understood passively or deterministically, as if the social world 'writes itself' onto individual persons as objects or victims; people are active *agents* in 'writing themselves into' these cultural-discursive, social and material-economic arrangements. As Lave and Wenger's account makes clear, people achieve knowledge of a practice by *participation* and by their *activity* – by learning to talk, for example, rather than learning from talk, and we would add, learning *to do* and learning *to relate* rather than from just *observing* others doing and relating. This is why, in the theoretical scheme depicted in Table 2, the relationships between the individual and social realms are conceived as occurring through *practice* – the generic practices of communication, social connection and production-consumption (sayings, relatings and doings). Both individual persons and social settings are constructed *in* and *by* practices; the relationships between them are mediated *in* and *by* practices.

Kemmis (forthcoming 2007) describes some of the relationships between the *individual* and *extra-individual* (cultural-discursive, social-political and material-economic) features of practice using an elaborated version of Table 3 below. The rows in the Table are aspects of the individual and extra-individual features of practice which are theoretical foci for a range of different theorists of practice.

Table 3: Individual and extra-individual features of practice

| | (1) Individual features | (2) Extra-individual features of practice | | |
		(a) Cultural-discursive	(b) Social-political	(c) Material-economic
A. Meaning and purpose	Meaning, intention	Linguistic grounding	Values, norms	Purposive action
B. Structured	Subjectivity, habitus	Cultural fields	Social fields	Economic fields
C. Situated	Embodiment, identity	Localised discourses	Social integration	Material exchange
D. Temporally-located	Narrative	Tradition	Historicity	Action in space-time
E. Systemic	Roles, professions	Discursive regulation	Institutions	Economies
F. Reflexivity	Reflexive identities	Cultural change	Social change	Economic change
G. Forms of reasoning	Practical	Aesthetic-expressive	Critical	Technical

Thus, to give just a few examples, Michel Foucault (for example, 1990) focuses on practices as located in *history* and *discourses*; Pierre Bourdieu (for example, 1998) focuses on *habitus* (an individual's dispositions) in relation to the structure of cultural, social and economic *fields*; Alasdair MacIntyre (1983) focuses on the role of traditions (including traditions of the virtues) and institutions in the conduct of practices and how these are revealed in the "narrative unity of a human life"; post-Vygotskian activity theorists like Yrjo Engeström (2000) focus on the material conduct of activity in various kinds of object-subject relations in their accounts of practice; and, in his *Theory of Communicative Action*, Jürgen Habermas (1984,

1987) focuses on relationships between system and lifeworld that are mediated in practices like strategic action and communicative action.

Different theorists of practice have focused on different aspects of practice in their inquiries into and investigations of practice, drawing on different traditions in philosophy and theory. Similarly, practice has been approached differently from the perspectives of different disciplines (for example psychology versus sociology versus history versus social and political theory). The discussion of Lave and Wenger, and of Schatzki, earlier in this chapter suggests that there is a growing recognition that many theorists of practice are reaching out from taken-for-granted disciplinary foundations and philosophical traditions to avail themselves of other resources. The title of the (2001) edited volume by Schatzki, Knorr Cetina and von Savigny – *The Practice Turn in Contemporary Theory* – reflects a new opening of theoretical space around the concept of practice.

One of the tasks of this volume is to describe some of the ways in which different theoretical resources throw other lights on *praxis* and practice – as illustrated by the theoretical resources used by different authors describing cases of *praxis* development in the following chapters.

Another task for this volume is to show that *praxis* development cannot and does not occur in a vacuum. Lave and Wenger (1991) show how learning a practice occurs through legitimate peripheral participation in communities of practice; Wenger (1998) suggests some of the ways in which organisations (can) create "learning architectures" to enhance (or inhibit) learning. We would go further, however. It is not just whether organisations (like a school, an education system, a medical practice or a professional body) create *learning* architectures that is at stake in the development of *praxis* and practice; it is that their architectures enable and constrain practices *themselves*. And they do so in such pervasive ways that they may even suffocate the very practices they aim to nurture – as Alasdair MacIntyre (1983) says of institutions that can, by their concern with goods external to a practice (like preoccupations with money and power), threaten the conduct of the practices they aim to engender and sustain. Thus, for example, a medical centre focusing too sharply on profitability may threaten the good conduct of medicine (if physicians are pressed to see too many patients in a day), or a university focusing too single-mindedly on publication rates as evidence of its research success may threaten the practices of philosophy or history if these are deemed as producing too few publications per year by comparison with publication rates in the physical or natural sciences.

PRACTICE ARCHITECTURES

To take Lave and Wenger's point about 'learning architectures' a step further, organisations, institutions and settings, and the people in them, create *practice architectures* which prefigure practices, enabling and constraining particular kinds of sayings, doings and relatings among people within them, and in relation to others outside them. The way these practice architectures are constructed shapes practice in its cultural-discursive, social-political and material-economic dimensions, giving substance and form to what is and can be actually said and done, by, with and for whom.

These practice architectures are, in general, *constructed* by people inside and outside an organisation, institution or setting. People within a school – teachers and students, for example – may construct the practice of a particular unit of work, in terms of the cultural-discursive, social-political and material-economic resources that will be called in to play in teaching and learning the particular material to be presented in the unit. People outside the school – curriculum developers, text-book writers, educational planners and policy-makers – may have played significant roles in shaping what kinds of units of work will be done, how pedagogy is to be conducted, the kinds of relationships between teachers and learners that are and are not permissible, and even whether the school is to stay open or be closed next year.

The notion of 'practice architectures' invites us to think of practice settings like schools and classrooms as *designed* – even if only partly so, and even if the designs cannot anticipate or account for the actual world of learning and teaching that will take place in a particular school, college, university or other learning setting. Among the practices of design by which they are envisaged and constructed are *meta-practices* – as suggested earlier, practices that shape (for example, by regulating, informing or otherwise enabling and constraining) the content and conduct of other practices. Meta-practices of *educational policy-making and administration* shape practices of teaching and learning through planning facilities, equipment, resources, staffing and a wide range of policies and regulations that support and regulate the conduct of educational practices in schools and elsewhere. Meta-practices of *curriculum development* shape ideas about what will be taught and learned – not only in specific curricula for specific subject-areas, but also shaping the aims and goals of education in this or that institution. Meta-practices of *teacher education* shape what and how teachers will teach, and extend beyond initial teacher education into the continuing professional development of teachers. Meta-practices of *educational research and evaluation* investigate and review the consequences of all kinds of forms of education in all kinds of educational institutions – and reflexively inform the *reconstruction* or transformation of education through bringing pressure to bear through each of the other kinds of meta-practices mentioned thus far.

The most important meta-practice, however, is the one being shaped by the ones mentioned so far: the practice of *teaching and learning* actually enacted through the *curriculum* and *pedagogy* of schools and other educational institutions, and actually experienced by the people involved in teaching and learning. The realisation of curriculum and pedagogy in schools may appear, from the point of view of some people outside schools, to be the point at which the goods of education, or the service of education, are actually 'delivered', as if the work were then done. Well, yes, it may have been done, and, as we saw in Chapter Two, what was done cannot be undone. In being done, it has become part of the great irreversibility of time and experience that requires of everyone the capacities to forgive and to make promises about the future. On closer inspection, however, observers of schools who think in terms of the 'delivery' of education will also concede that the moment of 'delivery' is not the most important moment in understanding an education, or the work of a school, or the work of a student twenty years later. There are many, many 'points of delivery' in an education, some of which make contradictory and competing claims on the future lives and conduct of students, teachers, and others involved in the construction of the education and the construction of the society in which the education occurs. The unfolding stream of an education actually experienced by any person is not just the transmission and accumulation of particular content, or the development of particular values or skills. These things are not static; they interact with dynamic effects and life-changing consequences for the students and teachers involved. The practice of education is also a meta-practice – it shapes (regulates, informs, enables and constrains) the practice of living a life, especially for students but also for teachers.

To speak of an educational design, then, is not only to speak of the 'making' disposition of *technē* and the 'making' action of *poiēsis*. One might be tempted to judge the quality of an educational design simply by looking at the planned curriculum or the intended pedagogy, but it soon becomes apparent that what has been planned may have unexpected, unanticipated or untoward short- or long-term effects that would cause a reasonable person to do things differently *next time*. Learning from experience, the wise educational designer brings more to the design task than *technē* and *poiēsis*; she or he also brings *phronēsis* and *praxis* – the disposition to act wisely and prudently, and the action that is right conduct for the circumstances. The experienced educational designer also knows that the effects of the intended curriculum or pedagogy will be different for different people, and may serve the interests and self-interests of some groups at the expense of others – and thus also bring the *critical* disposition to act against irrationality, injustice and suffering into play in *critical* reflection and *emancipatory* action aimed at averting or overcoming such untoward effects and consequences. And the wise educational designer will not approach the task of design entirely as a positive task of producing new futures – via the formation of new kinds of people, knowledge, social solidarities and skills – but also as a task of using present and past knowledge as resources for understanding more richly and deeply what the tasks of education must be for *these* particular times and *this* particular place. She or he will thus approach the work of design with the contemplative disposition of *epistēmē* and the reflective, theorising action of *theoria*.

Educational design is not just a technical task, then, it is also a task requiring knowledge, skills, wisdom and a capacity for critical reflection and emancipatory action. It is a task of constructing learning architectures and practice architectures that enable and constrain the work and the lives of students and teachers inside and outside schools, colleges and universities, with effects that ripple out into the lives of others in communities and societies and the planet we all share.

Like the educator in the school or university, the people responsible for the design of education and educational institutions have their shares in the responsibility of making futures through education – the education of children, young people and adults, and the continuing professional education of educators.

Just as the practice of education is a meta-practice shaping the future practices of learners, so the meta-practices of educational policy-makers, administrators, curriculum developers and teacher educators shape the conditions under which education can be carried out. They, too, and not just teachers, can fail in their responsibilities to students and the good for humankind. We depend, then, not just on their aims and objectives and their *poiēsis* in doing their jobs in providing resources, but also on their *praxis*, their *critical* reflection, and their *epistēmē*. In the words of Marx's (1938) *Third Thesis on Feuerbach*, "...the educator must himself be educated". We need informed and enlightened educational policy-makers, administrators, curriculum developers and teacher educators, not just ones who want to produce particular outcomes and effects that may seem important at any particular historical moment, in the context of particular political issues of the day. They, too, must be held to account for their work in the construction of the practice architectures of schools and colleges and universities.

To conclude: improving practices like the practice of education may require improving the *praxis* of individual practitioners but it also requires creating the institutional and social conditions that will support improved or other forms of practice. Professional practitioners like professional educators cannot and should not be made victims of the pursuit of improved 'quality' or 'best practice' as it is defined solely in terms of immediate, current resources and demands. While improved teacher education and continuing professional development, including by legitimate peripheral participation, may be needed to improve or strengthen educational practice, there is an equally-pressing claim for improved *conditions of practice*. Better educational practice requires not just better educators but also better schools, colleges and universities, better resources, better funding and better support and regard. Equally, better health care requires not just better doctors and health professionals, but also better facilities, equipment and technologies. In times of reduced public expenditure in fields like education and health, pinning our hopes for improved education and health care solely on the initial and continuing education of the relevant professionals is insufficient. Similarly, if government and professional regulatory bodies take the view that the overall quality of professional practice is less than it could be because some practitioners are not following guidelines about best practice, increasing the regulation and accountability of professional practitioners can, by itself, undermine and subvert good practice whenever the administrative burden of compliance is transferred to practitioners, reducing the time they have to conduct the practice which is their primary concern.

The 'case' chapters in Part 2 of this volume aim to throw light on the connection between the work and development of *praxis* in various educational settings, and how these conditions *enable and constrain praxis* for teachers, students, administrators and policy-makers in education. In particular, we will discover the influence of meta-practices like teacher education (in Tracey Smith, Chapter Four; Christine Edwards-Groves and Deana Gray, Chapter Five; and Helen Russell and Peter Grootenboer, Chapter Six), the continuing professional development of teachers (Christine Edwards-Groves, Chapter Seven; and Ian Hardy, Chapter Eight), educational policy-making (Ian Hardy, Chapter Eight), educational administration and organisation (Jane Wilkinson, Chapter Nine), curriculum specification (Roslin Brennan Kemmis, Chapter Ten) and broader cultural and social-political structures in societies (William Adlong, Chapter Eleven). In each case, we discover how *working conditions* function as practice architectures or metapractices that enable and constrain practice culturally and discursively, socially and politically, and materially and economically. Understanding how practices are constructed, enabled and constrained in these different dimensions may suggest ways of improving and developing *praxis* and practice that require action not only by practitioners acting alone, on their own behalf and on behalf of their students and communities, but also by those who fund and manage the organisations and institutions in which the practice of education is conducted and constructed. They, too, are the architects of practice architectures, and thus of practices.

NOTES

[1] For a powerful re-thinking of Marx's *Theses on Feuerbach* for contemporary times, see Alasdair Macintyre's (1998) 'The *Theses on Feuerbach*: A road not taken'.

[2] Post-Wittgensteinian practice theorist John Shotter makes extensive use of the notion of a poetics of practice; see Shotter (1996, 1999, 2000) and Katz and Shotter (1996).

[3] The move is also similar to Jürgen Habermas's [1972, 2003b] view that questions of truth should not be treated solely as questions of epistemology but also of a kind of 'anthropology' – that is, an anthropology of actual processes of communication between people, in which there are different kinds of relationships of speakers and listeners to one another, and different kinds relationships between these people, their ideas and the world which are characteristic of different kinds of communication – like technical or strategic communication aimed at controlling or regulating things versus practical or hermeneutical-interpretive communication aimed at reaching educated understandings versus critical forms of communication – communicative action – aimed at intersubjective agreement, mutual understanding and uncoerced consensus about what to do in a particular situation.

REFERENCES

Aristotle (2003) *Ethics*, trans. [1953] J.A.K. Thompson, revised with notes and appendices [1976] Hugh Tredennick, with an introduction [1976, 2003] Jonathon Barnes, and preface [2003] A.C. Grayling. London: The Folio Society.

Aristotle (1962) *The politics*, trans. J. A. Sinclair. Harmondsworth, Middlesex: Penguin Classics.

Bourdieu, P. (1998) *Practical reason: On the theory of action*, trans. Randal Johnson and others. Cambridge: Polity Press.

Engeström, Y. (2000) Activity theory as a framework for analysing and redefining work. *Ergonomics*, *43*(7), pp.367-390.

Foucault, M. (1990) *The history of sexuality, Volume 1: Introduction*, trans. R. Hurley. New York: Vintage.

Habermas, J. (1972) *Knowledge and human interests*, trans. Jeremy J. Shapiro. London: Heinemann

Habermas, J. (1974) *Theory and practice*, trans. John Viertel. London: Heinemann.

Habermas, J. (1984) *Theory of communicative action, Volume One: Reason and the rationalisation of society*, trans. Thomas McCarthy. Boston: Beacon.

Habermas, J. (1987) *Theory of communicative action, Volume Two: Lifeworld and system: A critique of functionalist reason*, trans. Thomas McCarthy. Boston: Beacon.

Habermas, J. (2003a) *The future of human nature*, trans William Rehg, Max Pensky and Hella Beister. Cambridge: Polity.

Habermas, J. (2003b) *Truth and justification*, ed. and trans. Barbara Fultner. Cambridge, Massachusetts: MIT Press.

Katz, A.M. and Shotter, J. (1996) Resonances from within the practice: Social poetics in a mentorship program, *Concepts and Transformation 1*, (2/3), pp.239-247.

Kemmis, S. (forthcoming 2006) What is professional practice?, in Clive Kanes (ed.) *Developing professional practice*. New York: Springer.

Lave, J. (1988) *Cognition in practice: Mind, mathematics, and culture in everyday life*. Cambridge: Cambridge University Press.

Lave, J. and Wenger, E. (1991) *Situated learning: Legitimate peripheral participation*. Cambridge: Cambridge University Press.

MacIntyre, A. (1983) *After virtue: A study in moral theory*, 2nd edn. London: Duckworth

MacIntyre, A. (1998) The t*heses on Feuerbach*: A road not taken, in Kelvin Knight (ed.) *The MacIntyre Reader*. Notre Dame, Indiana: University of Notre Dame Press.

Marx, K. (1938) Theses on Feuerbach, in *The German ideology*. London: Lawrence and Wishart (originally published in German, 1845).

Schatzki, T. (1996) *Social practices: A Wittgensteinian approach to human activity and the social*. New York: Cambridge University Press.

Schatzki, T.R. (2001) Introduction: Practice theory, in Theodore R. Schatzki, Karin Knorr Cetina and Eike von Savigny (2001) *The practice turn in contemporary theory*. London: Routledge.

Schatzki, T. (2002) *The site of the social: A philosophical account of the constitution of social life and change*. University Park, Pennsylvania: University of Pennsylvania Press.

Shotter, J. (1996) Living in a Wittgensteinian world: Beyond theory to a poetics of practices, *Journal for the theory of Social Behaviour, 26*(3), 293-311.

Shotter, J. (1999) 'Living moments' in dialogic exchanges, *Human Systems, 9*, pp 81-93.

Shotter, J. (2000) From within our lives together: Wittgenstein, Bakhtin, Voloshinov and the shift to a participatory stance in understanding understanding. In L. Holzman and J. Morss (eds.) *Postmodern psychologies, societal practice and political life*. New York: Routledge.

Taylor, C. (1991) *The malaise of modernity*. Concord, Ontario: Anansi Press.

Wenger, E. (1998) *Communities of practice: Learning, meaning and identity*. Cambridge: Cambridge University Press.

Wittgenstein, L. (1953) *Philosophical investigations*, trans. G.E.M. Anscombe. Oxford: Basil Blackwell.

AFFILIATIONS

Stephen Kemmis
School of Education
Charles Sturt University, Wagga Wagga, Australia

Peter Grootenboer
School of Education,
Charles Sturt University, Wagga Wagga, Australia

PART 2 CASES

TRACEY J. SMITH

4. FOSTERING A PRAXIS STANCE IN PRE-SERVICE TEACHER EDUCATION

In this chapter I present a retrospective analysis of the insights gained from a self-study of pre-service teacher education pedagogy. Initially, I describe a case of practice from the study that presents a collage of one prospective teacher's experiences, as evidenced through her written and oral narratives. The case illustrates how narrative practices can dramatically increase the potential for learning from experience in a teacher preparation program. The construction of narrative texts by prospective teachers enabled them to engage with, and make judgements about, the contradictions and complexities that emerged from their experiences as inquirers into their own practice. The case of practice is then theorised in terms of a 'theory/practice/reflection cycle of inquiry' that might be described as an enabling practice architecture (see Chapter Three) for teacher education. The process of 'noticing, naming and reframing' learning is identified as an influential aspect of narrative practice that nurtures an inquiry stance and has the potential to foster what is here described as a *praxis* stance – a vital disposition for the development of *praxis* in teacher education programs.

As a teacher educator, I have tried for many years to make sense of the relationship between practice and *praxis*. The term practice has become a natural component of our educational discourse that generally refers to one's actions and ways of being as a teacher. However, over the years, descriptive qualifiers such as "reflective", "reflexive", "professional", "critical", "moral" and "thoughtful" have emerged and demanded attention in the teacher education literature to more richly capture the nature of a particular type of practice that transcends basic rules and procedures and goes beyond technical/rational actions (see, for example, Bleakley, 1999; Cole & Knowles, 2000; Day, 1999; Hansen, 2001; Kemmis & Grootenboer, this volume; Schön, 1983; van Manen, 1990). Similarly, Eisner's (2002) description of the 'crafting' of action, teacher as 'connoisseur' and teaching as 'artistry' emphasise distinctive conditions of being an educator that require the ability to make sensitive and wise judgements and act "on the sense of rightness" (p. 383). This chapter is written with the underlying assumption that these types of practice and conceptualisations of teaching, no matter what their nomenclature, can all be understood as forms of enacting *praxis* – acting wisely and carefully in a particular situation.

At my university, the subtle nuances between implementing a practice and carrying out a practice in an informed and reasoned way have consistently remained a topic of intellectual and collegial debate. Could it be that the term *praxis* captures a more heightened form of practice that reflects practical reasoning

Kemmis, Stephen and Smith, Tracey J.(2008) Enabling praxis: Challenges for education.65-84

and a personal commitment to acting truly and justly? If so, can *praxis* be fostered in teacher education programs and is it possible to map a transition from practice to *praxis*? Rather than beginning to address these questions by turning to theoretical perspectives, I first of all present Molly's story to situate and illustrate the nature and conditions of the practice architecture that emerged when undertaking this self-study. In light of Molly's case, I then interrogate existing theories that inform teacher education in order to theorise my own practice. A retrospective analysis of my self-study in terms of the presence of *praxis* and the opportunities for fostering a *praxis* stance through the use of narrative practices is then discussed.

Setting the scene

Self-study describes the focus of an inquiry rather than a method. Self-study is situated under the conceptual umbrella of practitioner research that is informed by the 'teacher research movement' that emerged from a number of intellectual traditions. The literature related to teacher education, professional development, school reform, action research, 'participatory' action research, and practical inquiry (Cochran-Smith & Lytle, 1999; Kemmis & McTaggart, 2000; Zeichner & Noffke, 2001) has informed self-study research. To undertake a self-study is to learn from experience by planning a critical examination of pedagogical practice in order to improve it (Loughran, Hamilton, LaBoskey & Russell, 2004). Paradoxically, one of the most important aspects of a *self*-study is to rigorously pursue, and engage with, alternative perspectives that can inform and guide future practice. A unique feature of this self-study was that there were two concomitant layers of practitioner research – my own research and the action research undertaken by prospective teachers that provided an additional perspective for examining my practice.

The contextual boundary for the self-study was a year-long assessment and mathematics curriculum subject in which I was the sole teacher. The fifty-six prospective teachers enrolled in this subject were in their fourth, and final, year of a Bachelor of Education (Primary) program in my rural Australian university. The learning experiences designed for the subject required prospective teachers to become researchers of their own practice and authors of their own narratives of learning as they constructed case stories about their experiences undertaking action research in two school-based settings. A guiding principle of the program was to enhance the development of the prospective teachers as critically reflective practitioners. Fostering *praxis* was not foregrounded as a guiding principle when I carried out my initial research. It would be if I were to do it now.

Case stories as a narrative pedagogical practice

The use of case methods has been increasing since the early nineties as a valued pedagogy in inquiry-based teacher education programs. Before writing case stories, the prospective teachers in this study had to personally undertake case investigations or action research into their own practice in two separate school-based settings. Case investigations were adapted from a model used by LaBoskey (1992, 1994). For this study, case investigations required prospective teachers to carry out a modified version of case-study research that incorporated aspects of action research – a cycle of plan, act, observe, reflect, and re-plan (Kemmis & McTaggart, 1988). This required prospective teachers' participation in: *planning* an investigation by identifying an educational concern or issue of interest, reviewing the relevant literature and outlining methods for addressing their concern or issue; *acting* out the plan by collecting data in school settings; *observing* the impact of those actions; and *reflecting* on actions and observations by analysing the data and producing a case write-up. Case investigations were planned by the prospective teachers utilising peer and teacher educator support in the university setting before being carried out in two different school settings and reported on using written reflections in the form of case stories.

My background as a classroom teacher and experienced action researcher meant that I held a deep conviction about the empowering nature of the action research process for learning about teaching. As a teacher educator, I designed the first case investigation to be completed in stages over one semester (February – June). It required prospective teachers to write a case proposal that detailed both an assessment strategy in mathematics they chose to explore during an extended school-based practicum (ten weeks) and the related literature that guided their thinking. At the end of this process prospective teachers had to submit a case story that documented their learning during the investigation. The second case investigation occurred in the second semester (August – November) during five separate one-hour visits to a cooperating school. Prospective teachers worked with one school student to assess and diagnose the student's strengths and areas in need of development in terms of mathematical understanding. During this experience, prospective teachers had the opportunity to revisit and reframe the experiences they had on their earlier practicum and to address issues that may have emerged in the first case story.

In essence, every prospective teacher in the study produced unique case stories that reflected their personal learning journeys. Molly has been chosen not because she was necessarily typical of the other cases. Instead, Molly's collective experience provided an information-rich case (Patton, 1990) that was especially enlightening, but not considered unusual or extreme, in comparison to other prospective teachers' stories. I have incorporated Molly's voice into the chapter by using direct quotes presented in *italics* throughout the case to enhance authenticity and fluency.

MOLLY'S STORY: A CASE OF PRACTICE

To introduce Molly, I first of all draw on excerpts from her initial personal theories[1] written at the beginning of our year together. As a mature-age student, Molly's personal stance towards teaching and learning had not only been shaped by her thirteen years as a school student, but also by her ten years as a nanny or *au pair* and child care worker prior to coming to the university to study. Molly made explicit reference to her prior experiences that had taught her *the importance of developing personal and positive relationships with students* and *having a good rapport with [her] class*. She believed that *learning occurs most effectively if the class has direction, guidance, and the teacher is actively involved and interested in their learning.* Molly used explicit terms like *scaffolding, problem-solving* and *open-ended tasks* to describe strategies she had employed in past practicums *to help children help themselves, encourage discussion and help children develop their metacognitive skills.* When it came to thinking about assessment, Molly wrote: *I will be honest about assessment – it scares me to death...I so much want to be good at it but I know how poor I am in this area...Hopefully through this subject...I will gain the skills, confidence and information I need to succeed in this area.*

Like many of her peers, Molly mentioned the importance of realising that everyone *makes mistakes – both students and their teachers...I don't see any harm in letting your class be aware of this...it could remind the class that we as teachers are also human.* By her own admission, Molly was extremely passionate and took her studies very seriously. She wrote that: my studies will help shape me into what I hope will one day be a good teacher. Molly had experienced both positive and negative experiences during her own schooling but believed that the negative experiences had taught her just as much as the positive ones. Having experienced teachers who treated me like an individual and pushed me beyond what I believed I was capable of, Molly now felt that these expectations are something important in the classroom as long as they are realistic. Molly also articulated her belief that family values, surroundings, the learning environment and social situations can affect learning.

In her case proposal for the first case story, Molly described her inquiry focus as exploring the use of student journal keeping as a self-assessment strategy and the use of observation grids to record student progress in mathematics. While her proposal reflected a clear vision of practice based on her personal theories, Molly provided a chain of reflections that articulated an understanding that her proposal does not come with 100% guarantee of success...considering the huge number of factors that must be considered along with the diversity in the classroom. She elaborated on this point when she wrote that: unless *I provide lessons that are meaningful, motivating, and conducive to the environment and personalities within the classroom context, my approach cannot be considered valid.*

It is worth noting that prior to Molly's ten-week internship (extended school-based practicum) she had experienced two very successful practicums (one of two weeks duration and one of five weeks duration). All her previous maths experiences *had been wonderful – you could see the learning and feel the learning take place and hear the wonderful language used which demonstrated learning and understanding.* However, the reality of Molly's internship classroom setting shook her confidence and considerably blurred the vision of practice that she had developed in her case proposal prior to arriving at her school. Because of this, Molly and I had a number of phone conversations during the early stages of her internship. Her school was in a remote rural centre and the students were predominantly from low socio-economic and diverse cultural backgrounds. The new principal, who arrived at the school the same time as Molly, had placed a strong focus on discipline and behaviour management because they had not been a priority before she arrived.

Molly's first case story was written honestly, with a deep sense of critical awareness that reflected the realities of classroom life. She began her case story by saying that she *could have made up a happy story*, but she *did not have the energy left*. Through the conversational tone of her case story, Molly warned me that *you may be very disappointed with the lack of data collected and the lack of information which is to follow*. On the contrary, Molly's honest and descriptive case story caused me to critically reflect on my own practices as a teacher educator more deliberately.

Molly wrote about *kids who did not care about school...kids who did not care about learning...kids who were not interested in the relevance that mathematics had to their lives and their future because they did not seem to care about their life and their future.* She viewed her efforts to provide exciting, motivating, hands-on, student-centred activities that would allow students to construct their own knowledge as a total waste of time. In Molly's classroom, using manipulating materials for many was no more than an exercise in developing gross and fine motor skills...and [she] was sick of things being broken, used for weapons and stolen. Molly had persisted with this practice, along with group work and open-ended tasks, for the first three weeks of her internship not because that was what worked, but because that is what we are told at university works best in the classroom.

As mentioned earlier, Molly took her studies seriously and she clearly wanted to enact her image of a good teacher that she had formed as a result of her university experiences and other practicum placements. Unfortunately, Molly documented in her first case story that the *tables seemed to turn* when she made the decision to *seek employment in some other career* after her internship. As a result, the remainder of the practicum was going to be conducted *just how [she] liked it* because there was no pressure to *worry about [her] case study*.

One of the saddest features of Molly's turnaround was her belief that she was still not meeting the expectations of the university, even though her story turned to one of resilience. During one of her lessons, Molly demonstrated out the front of the classroom during a unit on volume. She described her lesson in the following way:

I came in early one day and put the tables in rows. The lessons were not hands-on. I began by reading the Archimedes bath time book and then discussed the concept. Then we decided together on a suitable definition that I could write on the board and the class could write the same in their books. I then conducted an experiment out the front of the class by measuring the overflow collected after placing an object in the water (displacement). I drew a picture of the experiment on the board and asked the class to do the same in their books. I then invited the children to write their own description of the experiment.

Perhaps the most revealing message in Molly's reflections was that she felt this scenario *could not be described as the ideal learning environment* and to some extent her first case story still resonated with a sense of failure.

At the beginning of her second case story, Molly wrote that:

...my internship experience now seems to have a degree of relevance to everything I do in some way or another...I think of it often and now know that as a result I have a different view of teaching and have different hopes and aspirations for both my future and the way in which I will conduct myself in a classroom.

The impact that these reflections had on Molly's identity as she went into the first school visit for the second case story seemed influential. Molly reflected that: *I went to my first school visit feeling subdued and depressed about my ability as a teacher...I thought my time at university had all been in vain and my attempts at classroom praxis were a failure.* Molly's sense of failure in the first case story was clearly still present at the beginning of her school visits for the second case story.

However, Molly's second case story revealed that Kate, the Grade One student she was partnered with, had a very positive attitude toward mathematics...by nature she was very determined...she had a strong character and did not appear shy or uncomfortable at any stage...she freely shared the information that she knew about specific areas of maths. The cathartic nature of this experience was exemplified when Molly revealed: because I went in believing I knew a very limited amount, I have come out feeling informed, fresh, overwhelmed and completely renewed. Because Molly believed that mathematics in general has never been a strength... and the whole notion of assessment overwhelmed me, I did a great deal of research on the topic...to be prepared and informed for any situation that may arise. Consequently, Molly began to make connections between assessment and instruction so that she could now design lessons which [she] felt appropriate to assess. She now had a grasp on this once sickening and overwhelming aspect of teaching.

In another revealing reflection, Molly wrote: *I was forced to stand back and look at what I have done in the past, what I do now and how these experiences are shaping my work for the future. When critically reflecting and personally evaluating all aspects of yourself as a teacher and as a learner you also have to face your strengths and weaknesses which for me is not an easy or enjoyable thing.* Molly believed that as a teacher she would be *continually engaged in personal reflection, evaluation, assessment, communication and questioning... If we walk around with our eyes shut we will learn nothing, however, if we take a little time to look and listen we will go home at the end of the day with a little more insight than what we left home with.*

In terms of reflecting on her developing personal theories of teaching and learning at the end of her second case story, Molly found it *easier to organise...thoughts and processes in point form.* Her list of developing personal theories included:

- *learn to take each day as it comes;*
- *do not take everything personally;*

- *classroom management is not easy – our strategies that work one day may not work the next;*
- *respect every child;*
- *no matter how prepared and organised we are, sometimes a lesson is not going to work – we must always consider the outside influences which the children bring to school with them as these impact hugely upon the classroom;* and
- *it only takes one person to make a difference.*

Perhaps the most important point that Molly made, in terms of her developing sense of authority and identity as a teacher, was that *you have to believe in what you do and the decisions you make.*

Along with almost all of her peers, Molly experienced a strong sense of success in the micro-teaching context for the second case story. She wrote: *given my past experiences in the classroom* [documented in the first case story], *I now feel more relaxed – and I can't say whether that is a good thing or bad thing!* The school visits had allowed Molly to become involved with a student on a personal level, therefore, observing the learning processes of individuals and the impact that assessment has for their future learning. Molly concluded her second case story by writing that: *although we are so close to finishing our teaching degree, I still don't consider myself as a teacher! I still think of myself as someone at uni trying to work towards their desired goals in life.*

Upon reflection, reading and analysing multiple case stories such as the one illustrated in Molly's story presented me with a deeper understanding of the importance of continually revisiting and reframing beliefs, images of teaching and the realities of practice. The writing of case stories required prospective teachers to undergo a process of "interrogating aspects of teaching and learning by *storying experience*" (Lyons & LaBoskey, 2002 p. 21, emphasis added). The production of case stories was a powerful way of helping prospective teachers to understand how their world works and for becoming more aware of the conditions that contribute to, and shape their experiences as beginning teachers. An in-depth analysis of narratives like Molly's enabled me to critically reflect on aspects of pedagogical practice that appeared to enhance this process.

THEORISING PRACTICE

Opportunities for timely and productive connections between theory and practice are not always evident in teacher education programs (Feiman-Nemser, 2001; Wideen, Mayer-Smith & Moon, 1998). This absence has often led to a lack of coherence and conceptual understanding for prospective teachers. In contrast, imagining teacher education in terms of participation in inquiry-based cycles such as case investigations describes a *practice architecture* that concomitantly connects theory and practice. The case of practice described earlier illustrates that together, the use of action research methods and narrative practices can create a productive relationship between theory and practice through reflection.

71

Connecting theory, practice and reflection

The relationship between theory, practice and reflection that narrative practices can produce is represented as a cycle of inquiry in Figure 1 to emphasise the fusion of borders between the fields that is necessary to create an inquiry landscape for learning. The two-way arrows indicate the cyclic and interdependent nature of learning within an inquiry-based program. The triangular border represents the contextual and situated nature of learning to show how practice is located in concrete conditions such as discourses, cultures and social relationships that may prefigure or constrain action possibilities (Kemmis & Smith, this volume).

The field of theory

In terms of the field of *theory*, a crucial feature of the inquiry cycle developed in my self-study was the way in which it accommodated both personal and public theories as mutually informing and interdependent sources. From the perspective of structuring experience through case stories, a vital consideration was that prospective teachers' beliefs, as articulated in their personal theories, served as filters for making sense of the experiences they encountered while learning to teach. Put another way, prospective teachers bring with them to the teacher education context a set of prefigured practices. Thus, many teacher education programs have acknowledged that one of the central tasks of teacher preparation is to assist prospective teachers to identify and analyse their existing beliefs in order to form new visions of practice for the future (Beattie, 2001; Bullough & Gitlin, 2001; Cole & Knowles, 2000; Feiman-Nemser, 2001; Korthagen & Kessels, 1999). The development of personal theories and case stories as narrative practices provided opportunities for prospective teachers like Molly to frame and reframe their developing understandings and beliefs about teaching and learning based on their experiences as researchers of their own practice. In turn, it is essential that teacher educators ensure that prospective teachers also engage with more public educational theories (for example, socio-cultural learning theory, practice theory, critical theory) so that their personal theories can be informed, guided and supported using these alternative perspectives.

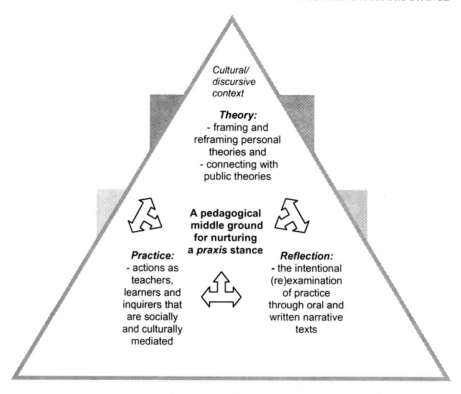

Figure 1: An inquiry-based cycle: a pedagogical middle ground for nurturing a praxis stance

The field of practice

The field of *practice* particularly refers to the cultural/discursive and social practices that condition the process of learning about teaching. Practice and learning are inseparable actions within this inquiry cycle. The narrative practices I used in the study represent a practice of communication that occurs in an intersubjective space (Habermas, 2003). As Molly's story has highlighted, such a space enables and constrains particular kinds of *sayings, doings* and *relatings* among the people within those spaces and in relation to others outside them (see Kemmis & Grootenboer, Chapter Three).

The writing of case stories also required what van Manen (1990) refers to as the "ability to bring to language our insights" (p. 156). From this perspective, narrative practices are seen as enabling practices, but, as many have argued, the need to frame experience into language, to be able to give voice to our thoughts and feelings, is not unproblematic. Voice has the capacity to affect who we are as teachers because it can set us apart from or connect us to the social world (Olson, 1995) as we attempt to write ourselves into a practice in order to understand that practice more wisely. According to Elbaz (1991), voice can be both political and epistemological and "implies that one has a language in which to give expression to one's authentic concerns, that one is able to recognize those concerns, and further that there is an audience of significant others who will listen" (p. 10). However, Elbaz (1991) also reminds us that the language available for teachers to talk about teaching has long been inadequate because the academic and professional discourses available have always been influenced by assumptions that all problems have solutions and that understanding teaching can be described as a sequential set of steps. And, voice is always an issue simply because, as one starts to say something about the situation in which one finds oneself, one does so in a voice shaped by experiences in other situations. What one says is always partly prefigured by one's own prior experience of speaking, of giving voice to one's ideas. Our own previous speaking 'speaks us'; the 'I' who speaks is already presupposed as in some measure continuous with the 'I' who spoke before.

One's voice in teaching necessarily speaks from moral, caring, and critical standpoints that affect those who listen as well as the teller (Elbaz, 1991). The relationship between the listener and the teller always occurs in anticipation. Our backgrounds, our commitments and our implicit beliefs impact on what we hear and what we say and in many ways prefigure our practice as educators. For me, one of the most poignant comments made by Molly in her first case story was that: *although the literature written about how children learn best must be true, I don't remember learning about the students who don't want to construct their own knowledge and the students who don't want to have to learn through hands on, and this is where I felt I was being let down.* The dissonance highlighted in this excerpt was between Molly's image of teaching and the realities of practice. Molly's comments compelled me to think critically about the kind of messages I was sending to prospective teachers through the practices I was enacting and requiring them to enact.

What tends to attract the attention of self-study researchers is that which does not work as anticipated (Loughran, 2004). I seemed to be living out Loughran's suggestion that exposing one's own shortcomings, doubts and concerns left self-study researchers confronted with their own vulnerability. What was very disconcerting for me was that the analysis of Molly's case story contributed to the realisation that this time, the loudest silence was coming from my own practice and I had contributed to the dissonance that Molly was experiencing. In this instance, Molly and her peers' honest portrayals provided me with a timely reminder that no matter how implicitly it had occurred, I was sending silent messages about my beliefs and values to prospective teachers. It is worth noting that at no stage in our time together did I consciously advocate the idea that group work, hands-on learning or open-ended tasks were the best or only approaches to the teaching and learning of mathematics. However, by omission, and perhaps through my own passionate persuasions, I believe that I inadvertently sent silent messages to Molly and her peers about the 'correct' or ideal way of doing things and that perhaps there was no other 'acceptable' way of teaching and learning mathematics. As Molly's story illustrated so cogently, these silent messages can compel prospective teachers, who wish to act truly and justly, to implement counter-intuitive pedagogical practices that do not develop or enhance their sense of identity and agency as agentic teachers.

Another way to think of the impact of the dissonance between university and school learning is that when prospective teachers put into practice something other than what they have been exposed to as part of their university learning, their belief that there is a 'gap' between theory and practice is compounded. Moreover, in Molly's case, a sense of failure seemed to develop because she so desperately sought to enact the visions of practice that her university experience had suggested were 'best' practice. At the end of her first case story I wrote that "your story has made me reflect on what we are doing here at university both explicitly and implicitly". Similarly, after one of Molly's phone calls in May, 2001, I recorded in a journal entry my "unwitting support of false dichotomies between transmissive and transformative approaches to teaching and learning" and how this may have contributed to Molly's apparent sense of failure.

In terms of the practice architecture of teacher education programs, is there an ethical limit for the extent to which we only present what is considered 'best' practice? What about preparing prospective teachers like Molly and her peers to work with schools and the current practices that already exist – is that a moral imperative as well? I came to the realisation that, as a teacher educator, one of my moral responsibilities should always be to create opportunities for developing prospective teachers' authority and agency in terms of their ability to make wise and prudent decisions that will lead to a sense of personal agency and a disposition to act wisely and rightly. In turn, this would enhance the agency that prospective teachers like Molly so desperately need to make appropriate decisions that promote resonance instead of dissonance. Rather than adopting other people's positions or best practices that are decontextualised and often inconsistent with prefigured beliefs and practices, Molly needed to notice, and listen to, the significant indicators within her own personal context and then make educated decisions that were deemed appropriate. This would mean the melding of personal and more public theories that would make sense of past practices and inform future practice.

Reflecting on Molly's response to the apparent failure of constructivist and hands-on approaches in her first case story, it could be argued that she had indeed successfully done exactly that. Molly had adopted another approach, against her ideas, but in accordance with what she believed would work in the knowledge that it might be just 'the best she could do on the day', 'the best she could do under the circumstances'. Molly *chose* and she chose to do the best she could. She had chosen to be a teacher of a different kind to the one she hoped to be, but she was choosing to be a teacher and to teach nonetheless. She had not abandoned the role, the task, the responsibility or the care that bound her to her students as *their teacher*. This tenacity suggests a moral commitment entirely congruent with her chosen career, even though it seemed dissonant from an ideal of constructivist teaching that would 'work' with 'constructivist learners' – the learners who might share her commitment to their learning, their lives and their futures; she did not fail, she adapted.

The field of reflection

The field of *reflection* refers to a mediating process that accentuates learning from experience because it intentionally connects and contextualises the other two fields of theory and practice so they can be more closely examined and re-examined in order to learn from them. In the teacher education literature, it is generally acknowledged that defining reflection is problematic (Hatton & Smith, 1995; Rodgers, 2002). The definition of reflection adopted in this self-study is: *reflection is a meaning-making process that involves participation in a systematic inquiry that contributes to the interpretation of experience in order to learn from that experience.* In our teacher education programs at Charles Sturt University, we believe that sustained and supported participation in the process of reflection leads to the development of a reflective disposition. A reflective storying approach supports recent research on learning to teach focusing on the need to create opportunities to make explicit, and build on, prospective teachers' existing knowledge, beliefs and attitudes about teaching and learning because "what has to be learned is intimately connected to what is already known" (Beattie, 2000, p. 19).

By their very nature, narrative practices such as the writing of case stories celebrate open-endedness, complexity and creativity. Through reflective writing, the goal is to gather and represent truthfulness about one's insights into practice in a trustworthy way rather than to speak or find 'The Truth'. This narrative turn can be directly linked to a move away from positivist views of objective truth and reality that tend to "squeeze the life out of teaching and to silence the voices of those who know most about teaching phenomena, namely, teachers themselves" (Doyle, 1997, p. 94). As a way of knowing, narrative is subjectively created, and is in a constant state of change as stories are framed and reframed. Such a reflective practice supports the idea that humans make meaning of their lives by "endlessly telling and retelling stories about themselves that both refigure the past and create purpose in the future" (Connelly & Clandinin, 1990, p. 24). In short, narrative forms of reflection are a legitimate form of reasoned knowing (Bruner, 1986).

Cases as storied knowledge, written by prospective teachers themselves, provide insights into the interpretive structures they use to organise and make sense of their experience as researchers of their own practice. A deep analysis of case stories confirmed for me that our actions are significantly oriented and influenced by others and that practice is socially constructed in our 'sayings, doings and relatings' in a variety of contexts (see Chapter Three, this volume). Learning to teach is contextually dependent and highly influenced by the social frames or practice architectures present in the contexts in which prospective teachers find themselves.

The writing process is a key feature of the theory/practice/reflection cycle because it creates the intellectual and emotional space for reconciling and connecting ideals and the realities of practice, as well as bridging university learning and school-based learning. I identified the notion of 'noticing, naming and reframing' in an attempt to shape this reflective process into a pedagogical construct that might be useful for other teacher educators to implement in their programs.

Noticing, naming and reframing learning

The continual back and forthing (Clandinin & Connelly, 2000) that characterises narrative practices such as the construction of case stories is complex and messy. Even so, I have come to think of it as a vital and generative meaning-making process. The idea of noticing and naming first emerged from a learning journal entry written after I had graded prospective teachers' first case stories (August 4, 2001). I noted that "the idea of 'naming' needs to be explored – by naming a concern, practice or personal theory we are taking ownership for it…that is we have made sense of the idea through the naming process by bringing it into words". Another journal entry written later on the same day documented my ideas for the next workshop conversation. I noted that for the second case story, prospective teachers should be reminded to "listen to their inner voice and to other people's conversations (public theories) and 'notice' what resonates with them as a learner and prospective teacher, then 'name' that resonating moment so it becomes a part of their personal theories for the future".

Choosing to describe this process as noticing and naming was influenced by the notion of 'noticing and marking' described by Mason (1998). My change of phrase from 'marking' to 'naming' is deliberate. Rather than marking an observation that has been noticed, heard or experienced, I prefer the term 'naming' which highlights my belief about the important role that language plays in making sense of our teaching experiences. However, what I also noticed about the case story process was the way in which revisiting and re-examining lived experience enhanced prospective teachers' ability to learn from their experience. Put another way, the process of reframing seemed a vital addition to the already identified processes of noticing and naming.

The process of undertaking action research and inquiry-based practice helped to focus the prospective teachers' 'noticing'. Essentially, the writing process was a 'naming' process that required them to frame their thoughts in language. Thus, naming implies a type of initial framing. On the other hand, 'reframing' what has been named implies a type of sustained and iterative examination that leads to restructuring and reinvention. Noticing and naming a life experience brings it forth and frames it for closer examination, but what has been noticed and named needs to undergo a process of reframing, or "carefully cultivated thoughtfulness" (van Manen, 1990, p. 131) if the person is to learn from it and become personally committed to it. From this perspective, reframing what one knows is a process of recontextualising one's understanding, making conceptual connections so that practice can be understood theoretically and representing such understanding in a public form (the case story) so that it can be shared and critiqued. It is this reframing process that provides the intellectual and emotional space where a *praxis* stance can be nurtured – a point taken up in the next section.

The connective process of noticing, naming and reframing turned experience into text and was a transformative and influential one for Molly and the majority of her peers. Molly commented that *the most valuable part of my comprehension of assessment has been this proposal...the writing down of ideas... [it] helped me sort through all my information and material to construct logic and understanding.* She continued her chain of reflective thoughts by adding that *writing the proposal had a positive effect on my outlook, as I have been provided with a heightened awareness through communicating ideas with lecturers, teachers and peers and also through valid research and reading.* These excerpts illuminate how the noticing, naming and reframing process provided the intellectual space for reflective thought that produced a nexus between personal and public theories.

How the prospective teachers choose to name and reframe what they notice about their action research experiences provides insights into their developing beliefs and commitments. The process of noticing, naming and reframing learning experiences, using a discourse that is conversational and personally meaningful, can enhance conceptual connections between theory and practice. Such a connective tool empowers inquirers to author their own learning and generate their own personally meaningful and justifiable stance towards teaching. An implication for teacher educators is that the process of noticing, naming and reframing, when made explicit, can become a pedagogical strategy that supports and enhances the reflexive and critical nature of teacher thinking. The noticing, naming and reframing process describes how the theory/practice/reflection cycle of learning can be implemented in a teacher education program, but to what extent can this cycle foster *praxis*?

What became clearly evident during the retrospective analysis of the self-study findings was that case stories like Molly's do not necessarily give evidence of *praxis*. *Praxis* is evident only in our actions, not in the telling of stories about them (see Chapter One). However, what Molly's story does highlight so cogently is how the narrative writing process can provide an opportunity for developing practical reasoning and articulating principles about what is true, right and productive in particular contexts – what I suggest is the development of a *praxis* stance. As Kemmis and Smith have illustrated in Chapter Two, many educators have gone back to Aristotle to understand *praxis* development in terms of fostering a particular disposition that moves beyond the technical (techne) to describe a more moral disposition (*phronesis*) to *act* wisely, truly and justly (*praxis*) as an educator. In terms of theorising my practice, my attention turned to establishing a deeper understanding of the distinction between *praxis* and *phronesis* – between 'right conduct' and the disposition to act morally and justly.

Defining a praxis stance

One of the most powerful insights I gained during my self-study was the realisation that a disposition towards inquiry – an inquiry stance – is an essential attribute for effective teaching (Smith, 2004). When writing about the development of an inquiry stance, Cochran-Smith (2003) suggests that the term stance "is intended to capture the ways we stand, the ways we see, and the lenses we see through" (p. 8) and an inquiry stance is characterised as "a way of questioning, making sense of, and connecting one's day-to-day work to the work of others" (p. 21). From this perspective, a person who has developed an inquiry stance is deliberative and reflective. The nature of the practice architecture described earlier in this chapter as a theory/practice/reflection cycle of inquiry aims to nurture such a stance.

What I have also come to realise is that the notion of an inquiry stance, while still essential, does not foreground the moral and emotional aspects of teaching that are embedded in the everyday lives of teachers. In my view, educators need to go one step further and recognise that an inquiry stance is an essential element in developing a *praxis* stance. A *praxis* stance can be thought of as maintaining an ethical and caring way of being in the world; it is enhanced by and stimulates reflective thinking and inquiry. The three personal qualities of character outlined by Dewey (1933) can offer further insights into the nature of a *praxis* stance. He suggested that to convert action into intelligent action we need to possess the qualities of: open-mindedness - an attitude of freedom from prejudice that would require an active and positive desire to listen to more sides than one and a willingness to give full attention to alternative possibilities; whole-heartedness - an attitude of absorption in an activity that would require a vigorous and energetic commitment; and responsibility - the need to be intellectually responsible by considering the consequences of a possible action.

An inquiry-based cycle of theory/practice/reflection, as described in this chapter, created fertile ground for exploring aspects and consequences of practice that mattered the most to the pre-service teachers themselves. It would be difficult to argue that Molly's case stories did not demonstrate her open-mindedness, whole-heartedness and responsibility to some extent. While Molly's story demonstrated evidence of moral considerations in terms of the students she taught, I did not explicitly encourage prospective teachers to move beyond the personal. The case stories I analysed were relatively silent in terms of an explicit concern for "otherness" and "difference" (Bleakely, 1999, p. 328). If we are to support the enactment of morally defensible practices that are true and just, teacher educators need to address these aspects more explicitly in their pedagogical planning.

Further guidance in my quest to articulate a *praxis* stance more clearly, and develop it more explicitly in my programs, was found in the dispositional theory of thinking outlined by Perkins, Jay and Tishman (1993). If we accept that *praxis* is a thoughtful and moral mode of action, then developing *praxis* requires a *praxis* stance (*phronesis*) that has three qualities adapted from Perkins et al. (1993). To develop a *praxis* stance, a practitioner would need to have: the 'inclination', or felt tendency to think about his/her practice in morally caring ways; a 'sensitivity' or heightened awareness to occasions or opportunities when moral decisions are warranted, and the 'ability' or know-how to undertake practical reasoning in order to develop a future commitment to practices that are informed and morally defensible. Such dispositional qualities highlight the need to recognise that developing *praxis* does not just require the ability, or skill building to reason about and reflect on practice but also requires the more personal dispositions of sensitivity and inclination or willingness to act in caring and morally defensible ways. The *praxis* stance is a willingness and readiness to act in the mode of *praxis* (not just *poiesis* as described in Chapter Two); the *praxis* is the action itself.

A *praxis* stance is present when a person is being intellectually responsible and acting with integrity, which creates a "consistency and harmony in belief" (Dewey, 1933, p. 32). I argue that a practice architecture that incorporates narrative inquiry practices has the potential to nurture the capacities needed for *praxis* such as 'reading' situations more wisely and acting with greater prudence and good sense in new situations (see Chapter Three on the shaping of forms of action). The development of a *praxis* stance is enhanced when the practice architecture of teacher education programs establishes opportunities for transforming action into informed, committed action; that is, when the design of teacher education programs cultivates the dispositions characteristic of a *praxis* stance in the university (and other settings) and the opportunities to enact *praxis* in teaching settings. As I have argued, creating opportunities for *praxis* means creating opportunities for inquiry into a prospective teacher's practice – a grounding in experience that fosters learning to act rightly.

A narrative inquiry landscape can provide a natural and supportive space for developing a *praxis* stance because such a landscape invites and nurtures reflection and connectedness. The notion of *praxis* as "informed action which, by reflection on its character and consequences, reflexively changes the 'knowledge-base' which informs it" (Carr & Kemmis, 1986, p. 33) highlights the appropriateness of capturing and describing the overarching potential of an inquiry-based approach to teacher education as creating multiple opportunities to foster a *praxis* stance. Thus, the development of a *praxis* stance relies heavily upon prospective teachers' capacity and willingness to make professional judgements by reconciling sources of authority from different contexts. Molly's story was rich with interpretive echoes that provided insights into how narrative practices can begin to nurture a *praxis* stance.

CLOSING THOUGHTS…

In this chapter, I have argued that case stories, as a narrative pedagogical practice, provide a rich landscape for learning and for fostering the capacities necessary to develop a *praxis* stance. In terms of my own developing *praxis*, I have been able to notice, name and reframe aspects of a practice architecture that have the potential to more explicitly address the development of a *praxis* stance. The insights gained from the retrospective analysis of case stories enabled me to understand more deeply, and then make explicit, some of the characteristics of a practice architecture that could nurture a *praxis* stance. Molly's story helped identify and map the process of transforming practice into a heightened form that can be considered thoughtful, informed and justifiable. Thus, *praxis* always originates in practice but is a more developed form of practice that reflects a willingness and personal commitment to think deeply about what is true and right. As prospective teachers framed and reframed their images and beliefs about teaching in their case stories they were able to identify and critically examine the factors that shaped their practice. As they connected their inquiry experience in a school context (case story one) and school-based visits (case story two) with their university-based understandings, they were able to critically analyse their practice and begin to generate a *praxis* stance – a habit of mind that would ensure careful consideration about how they would act more wisely when faced with similar circumstances in the future. The complexities that prospective teachers wrote about in their narrative practices helped them to understand that their *praxis* stance would always be in a dynamic and evolving state.

It seems vital that teacher educators design multiple opportunities for prospective teachers to come to terms with who they are as teachers and not just who they think they should be according to other sources of authority. By participating in iterative cycles of inquiry that were supported by narrative documentation, the prospective teachers in this study were able to develop habits of analysis and reflection over time that led to opportunities for developing a way of knowing and being that would give them confidence to make wise and just decisions as teachers. Prospective teachers need to feel they have permission to imagine themselves as life-long learners rather than impending experts who will know all the answers before they begin their teaching careers. I have argued that including iterative cycles of inquiry in a teacher education program increases the likelihood that such habits will be sustainable and that a *praxis* stance can be nurtured and developed.

Narrative practices such as case stories, undertaken over a sustained period of time, can afford opportunities for examining the consequences of action systematically through a "critical revival of practice" (Carr & Kemmis, 1986, p. 190). The timing of these revivals of practice is crucial. This chapter has revealed how one site for learning (such as a university setting) can complement or contradict another (such as a school-based setting) depending on the extent to which they can be meaningfully aligned, connected and supported through prospective teachers' reflective work. The cycle of inquiry depicted in Figure 1 highlights the importance of continuously revisiting and reconstructing understanding in light of new experiences and other authorities which are gained from external sources. The explication of such a cycle provides a tangible point of reference for teacher educators to use as a reflective lens on their own practice. In this way, teacher educators can evaluate the extent to which they, and not just their students are nurturing generative connections between theory and practice that are both timely and contextualised.

A developing sense of *praxis* needs to take into account the complex and uncertain nature of teaching and capture aspects of teaching like emotions, beliefs, images of teaching and contextual realities. The message for teacher educators is that the architecture of our programs needs to provide a balance between support and challenge and between theory and practice. Our programs must provide the social, emotional and intellectual space for foregrounding and enabling *praxis*. When we get these balances right, we will assist prospective teachers to enact progressive pedagogical approaches, experience positive and negative consequences, and then slow teaching down as they notice, name and reframe their experiences. In this way, prospective teachers can talk and write themselves into *praxis*.

NOTES

1 While not addressed in this chapter, personal theories (Griffiths & Tann, 1992, Cole & Knowles, 2000) were another narrative practice developed in this study. Initial personal theories were submitted in February as a non-assessable task. Reframed personal theories were submitted in November at the conclusion of the subject as an assessable task.

REFERENCES

Beattie, M. (2001). *The art of learning to teach: Preservice teacher narratives.* Upper Saddle River, NJ: Prentice-Hall.

Bleakley, A. (1999). From reflective practice to holistic reflexivity. *Studies in Higher Education, 24*(3), 315-330.

Bruner, J. (1986). *Actual minds, possible worlds.* Cambridge, MA: Harvard University Press.

Bullough, R. V., & Gitlin, A. D. (2001). *Becoming a student of teaching: Linking knowledge production and practice* (2nd Ed.). New York: Routledge Falmer.

Carr, W., & Kemmis, S. (1986). *Becoming critical: Education, knowledge, and action research.* London: Falmer Press.

Carter, K., & Anders, D. (1996). Program pedagogy. In F. B. Murray (Ed.), *The teacher educator's handbook: Building a knowledge base for the preparation of teachers* (pp. 557-592). San Francisco, CA: Jossey Bass.

Clandinin, D. J., & Connelly, F. M. (1999). Storying and restorying ourselves: Narrative and reflection. In A. Chen & J. Van Maanen (Eds.), *The reflective spin: Case studies of teachers in higher education transforming action* (pp. 16-23). Singapore: World Scientific.

Clandinin, D. J., & Connelly, F. M. (2000). *Narrative inquiry: Experience and story in qualitative research.* San Francisco, CA: Jossey-Bass.

Cochran-Smith, M. (2003). Learning and unlearning: The education of teacher educators. *Teaching and Teacher Education, 19*(1), 5-28.

Cochran-Smith, M., & Lytle, S. L. (1999). The teacher research movement: A decade later. *Educational Researcher, 28*(7), 15-25.

Cole, A. L., & Knowles, J. G. (2000). *Researching teaching: Exploring teacher development through reflexive inquiry.* Needham Heights, MA: Allyn & Bacon.

Connelly, F. M., & Clandinin, D. J. (1990). Stories of experience and narrative inquiry. *Educational Researcher, 19*(5), 2-14.

Day, C. (1999). Researching teaching through reflective practice. In J. Loughran, (Ed.), *Researching teaching: Methodologies and practices for understanding pedagogy.* London: Falmer Press.

Dewey, J. (1933). *How we think.* New York, NY: Heath & Co.

Doyle, W. (1997). Heard any really good stories lately? A critique of the critics of narrative in educational research. *Teaching and Teacher Education, 13*(1), 93-99.

Elbaz, F. (1991). Research on teachers' knowledge: The evolution of a discourse. *Journal of Curriculum Studies, 23*(1), 1-19.

Eisner, E. W. (2002). From episteme to phronesis to artistry in the study and improvement of teaching. *Teaching and Teacher Education, 18*(4), 375-385.

Feiman-Nemser, S. (2001). From preparation to practice: Designing a continuum to strengthen and sustain teaching. *Teachers College Record, 103*(6), 1013-1055.

Griffiths, M., & Tann, S. (1992). Using reflective practice to link personal and public theories. *Journal of Education for Teaching, 18*(1), 69-84.

Habermas, J. (2003). *The Future of Human Nature.* Cambridge: Polity Press, 2003.

Hansen, D. T. (2001). Teaching as a moral activity. In V. Richardson (Ed.), *Handbook of research on teaching* (pp. 826-857). Washington D.C: American Educational Research Association.

Hatton, N., & Smith, D. (1995). Reflection in teacher education: Towards definition and implementation. *Teaching and Teacher Education, 11*(1), 23-32.

Hunter, J., & Hatton, N. (1998). Approaches to the writing of cases: Experiences with pre-service Master of Teaching students. *Asia-Pacific Journal of Teacher Education, 26*(3), 235-245.

Kemmis, S., & McTaggart, R. (Eds.) (1988). *The action research planner* (3rd Ed). Melbourne, VIC: Deakin University Press.

Kemmis, S., & McTaggart, R. (2000). Participatory action research. In N. K. Denzin, & Y. S. Lincoln (Eds.), *Handbook of qualitative research* 2nd Ed. (pp. 567-605).Thousand Oaks, CA: Sage.

Korthagen, F. A. J., & Kessels, J. P. A. M. (1999). Linking theory with practice: Changing the pedagogy of teacher education. *Educational Researcher, 28*(4), 4-17.

LaBoskey, V. K. (1992) Case investigations: Pre-service teacher research as an aid to reflection. In J. H. Shulman (Ed.), *Case methods in teacher education* (pp. 175-193). New York, NY: Teachers College Press.

LaBoskey, V. K. (1994). *Development of reflective practice: A study of prospective teachers.* New York, NY: Teachers College Press.

Loughran, J. J., Hamilton, M. L., LaBoskey, V. K., & Russell, T. (Eds) (2004). *International handbook of self-study of teaching and teacher education practices.* Dordrecht, The Netherlands: Kluwer.

Loughran, J. J. (2004). A history of context of self-study of teaching and teacher education. In J. J. Loughran, M. L. Hamilton, V. K. LaBoskey, & T. Russell (Eds.), *International handbook of self-study of teaching and teacher education practices* (pp. 7-39). Dordrecht, The Netherlands: Kluwer.

Lyons, N., & LaBoskey, V. K. (Eds) (2002). Why narrative inquiry or exemplars for a scholarship of teaching? In N. Lyons & V. K. LaBoskey (Eds.), *Narrative inquiry in practice: Advancing the knowledge of teaching* (pp. 11-27). New York: Teachers College Press.

Mason, J. (1998). Researching from the inside in mathematics education. In A. Sierpinska & J. Kilpatrick (Eds.), *Mathematics education as a research domain: A search for identity* (pp. 357-377). Dordrecht, Netherlands: Kluwer Publications.

Olson, M. R. (1995). Conceptualizing narrative authority: Implications for teacher education. *Teaching and Teacher Education, 11*(2), 119-135.

Patton, M. (1990). *Qualitative evaluation and research methods.* Newbury Park, CA: Sage.

Perkins, D. N., Jay, E., & Tishman, S. (1993). Beyond abilities: A dispositional theory of thinking. *Merrill-Palmer Quarterly, 39*(1), 1-21.

Rodgers, C. (2002). Defining reflection: Another look at John Dewey and reflective thinking. *Teachers College Record, 104*(4), 842-866.

Schon, D. A. (1983). *The reflective practitioner.* London: Temple Smith.

Schon, D. A. (1987). *Educating the reflective practitioner: Toward a new design for teaching and learning in the professions.* San Francisco, CA: Jossey-Bass.

Smith, T. J. (2004). Learning in a community of inquirers: Developing an inquiry stance. In I. Putt, R. Faragher & M. McLean (Eds.), *Mathematics education for the third millenium: Towards 2010,* (Proceedings of the twenty-seventh annual conference of the Mathematics Education Research Group of Australasia, pp. 525-532). Townsville, QLD: MERGA.

van Manen, M. (1990). *Researching lived experience: Human science for an action sensitive pedagogy.* Cobourg, ON: Althouse Press.

Wideen, M., Mayer-Smith, J., & Moon, B. (1998). A critical analysis of the research on learning to teach: Making the case for an ecological perspective on inquiry. *Review of Educational Research, 68*(2), 130-178.

Zeichner, K. M. & Noffke, S. (2001). Practitioner research. In V. Richardson (Ed.), *Handbook of research on teaching* (pp 238-330). Washington D.C: American Educational Research Association.

AFFILIATION

Tracey J. Smith
School of Education,
Charles Sturt University, Wagga Wagga, Australia

CHRISTINE EDWARDS-GROVES AND DEANA GRAY

5. DEVELOPING PRAXIS AND REFLECTIVE PRACTICE IN PRE-SERVICE TEACHER EDUCATION

Affordances and constraints reported by prospective teachers

INTRODUCTION

Pre-service teachers enter the professional world of teaching by participating in social communities of practice, both in the context of the university and in the school settings they work in, to meet professional experience requirements of their courses (in Australia this involves so-called practicum placements in schools for blocks of one to six weeks or longer on internships). These communities of learning are defined by and cohere around the shared goal of engaging in and developing 'educationally right practice'; that is, *praxis*. Developing these shared goals and understandings over time involves both mutuality and reciprocity through a range of participatory modes of action such as focused observation, interaction with people and texts, and 'practising teaching' through presenting, performing and trialling, substantive dialogue and reflection.

Developing a *praxis* stance is the most highly desired outcome the university hopes to achieve for its students. It hopes they will learn to act not just with technical skill but also with moral and ethical integrity. A praxis stance also involves pre-service teachers developing sustainable ways to remain informed about their teaching and their profession. In the knowledge that they can only develop this orientation to a high degree through experience (see also Chapter Two, this volume) the university encourages pre-service teachers to develop this *praxis* orientation by engaging in ongoing, focused reflection. This not only serves to enable pre-service teachers to continuously think about and reframe their professional self throughout their career, but to reframe the questions and issues their profession needs to address in changing times and circumstances. Therefore, a main role of the university is to provide meaningful opportunities for pre-service teachers to learn the profession through participation in teaching actions and interactions that will move them towards a *praxis* orientation. One such *praxis* action is reflective practice, the focus of this chapter.

Reflective practice has long been advocated by educationalists as a crucial characteristic of a 'quality teacher' (Dewey, 1933; Porter & Brophy, 1988). It is viewed as a tool for understanding and mediating teaching practice; that is, for shaping and informing future actions. What is posited is that to learn to be an effective teacher pre-service teachers need to learn to engage in reflective practice;

Kemmis, Stephen and Smith, Tracey J. (2008) Enabling praxis: Challenges for education.85-107

that is, to become 'reflective'. Reflection, therefore, has come to occupy an important position in the life of university students in teacher education courses, as well as in many other courses aimed at preparing students for professional practice in a variety of professions. Given the centrality of 'reflection' and 'reflective practice' in education for the professions, we need to ask critical questions like: Who and what does reflection serve in the university sector? How is it perceived by the students? What is its role in learning to teach and learning about teaching? What counts as 'reflection' within the university sector? And, what does it afford in the development of reflective practitioners with a *praxis* orientation, and what does it constrain?

The case presented in this chapter explores these important questions by investigating the experience of pre-service teachers beginning their own journey of learning within a profession that explicitly calls for its members to be 'critically reflective'. The chapter largely draws on a recent research study which elicited perspectives from 194 pre-service teachers across each of the four years of the Bachelor of Education (Primary) degree offered at one university – Charles Sturt University in regional Australia. The study involved collecting survey data from the 194 participants; and then interviewing a sub-sample of 15 students from the larger cohort. The study aimed to capture pre-service teachers' perceptions about the relevance of reflection to the professional work of teachers in what these students see as 'the real world' of teaching. This is important especially in light of their own professional experience placements in which pre-service teachers were obliged to reflect on their own practice, and as a first-hand experience where they could encounter classroom teachers reflecting (more or less explicitly) on their own practice.

The significance of reflection can be understood by what is accomplished by it. Arguably, how these students come to view reflection will generate information about what is truly accomplished by reflection. Further it will determine not only its effectiveness in their future lives and work as teachers, but will configure in its utility, sustainability and portability across contexts (and, especially, when after graduation they begin to teach). Consequently, the particular structured practices of reflection – described here as 'technologies for reflection' – built into the practice architecture (see Chapter Three, this volume) of this university course are also examined. The chapter aims to uncover the complexities, the constraints and affordances of *reflection* to discover how pre-service teachers understand the nature of reflection from their experiences of it in this particular course.

Throughout the course, in many different subjects, pre-service teachers are invited to *reflect* and to *do* reflective practice. As their teachers, university lecturers are deeply committed to developing what some describe as *sustainable reflexivity*; that is, productive and constructive reflection that will be an ongoing and organic professional activity for graduates. One that aims to help them adopt what is described as *a praxis stance* in their teaching [see also Chapter Four, this volume]. A vast body of literature supports this commitment to developing reflective practice in students and graduates suggesting that reflection has a capacity to construct knowledge of the profession and to assist pre-service teachers to move towards *praxis* – defined in this book as *morally-committed educational action, oriented and informed by (educational) theories and traditions* (see Chapter Two, this volume). In these aspirations, and with this continuing emphasis on reflection and reflective practice, this course is like many other teacher education courses around the world. But the very dominance of this widespread view aroused suspicion: what if reflective practice has become no more than an ideology? What if the ways of teaching reflective practice are in fact counter-productive, technicising, side-tracking and in the end distorting and demeaning reflection?

Listening to the students' voices as they articulate their experiences of, and perspectives on, reflection is important as their experiences and perspectives were shaped, in practice, by the technologies for reflection they encountered in this particular undergraduate teacher education course. To anticipate a main finding of this study: there are indeed grounds for our suspicion: the student voices presented in this chapter actively challenge the university's ideal for pre-service teachers developing a *praxis* stance. For some of our students, at least, reflection and reflective practice become activities or artefacts significant only within the work required for university subjects, rather than a useful life-long endeavour with its merits grounded in a desire to continually improve in the profession.

UNDERSTANDING REFLECTION AND ITS CONNECTION TO *PRAXIS*

Praxis, in this chapter, is taken to be more than the *disposition* or desire to act in a morally-committed way developed through public discourse in public spheres (*phronesis*- see Chapters Two and Three, this volume, for discussion of the distinction); it is 'right' educational action that has been shaped and re-shaped as a result of focused thinking and reflection, experience and on-going learning about one's own teaching and circumstances. It is *right conduct* by people acting for the good of the profession to do what is collectively regarded as wise, prudent, sensible and appropriate for the circumstances. The connection between reflection and *praxis* emerges at this point, when *reflection as action* forms, informs and transforms one's practices of teaching. *Praxis*-oriented teachers purposely and consciously act on the assembly of information afforded by reflective practice. They act as responsive problem solvers who are constantly adjusting and learning from their practice and reconceptualisations of their practice; that is, they are *praxis-oriented professionals* constantly learning from, and responding to, new situations and experiences.

Praxis does not form in a vacuum, but rather within a climate which enables thinking and action to merge explicitly. Reflection, although not a solitary criterion for *praxis*, can create a space that assembles the individual and collective thinking required to reframe and progress teaching action in an educationally sound and morally-right manner. Along with focused and substantive dialogue, reflection provides a vehicle for *praxis development* as teachers and pre-service teachers are supported in the development of their ability to explicate, describe, reframe and adjust classroom actions and interactions. Reflection also enables teachers and pre-service teachers to write about their teaching in a focused and critically analytic way so they can interpret and learn from their own teaching. Therefore, teachers have an opportunity, through reflection, to develop the capacity to develop *praxis* as they interact with their own cognitions to change what they do. In this way, *praxis* and reflection and learning are inextricably linked. The question then arises about how universities encourage the development of this *praxis stance*, or way of being a teaching professional, through the opportunities they provide for pre-service teachers (see Chapter Four, this volume for one example of how a praxis stance may be developed). The case study presented here offers some insights into this question.

Conceptualising and contextualising teaching through focused reflection

The term 'reflection' and the way it is understood are contested issues in contemporary educational literature. Given that 'reflection' is currently enjoying a renewed status in national and international research on the qualities of effective teachers, the term now comes loaded with a variety of contending political agendas and interpretations. However, it is not the intention of this chapter to review the extensive literature on reflection or policies advocating reflection and reflective teaching. We will present only a brief indication of the relevant literature in this chapter – enough, we hope, to sharpen the tension or contradiction between the aims of university teacher education courses that aspire to develop reflective practice in their graduates (aims we have in our course), and the perspectives of some pre-service teachers on reflection – views that will determine whether, and to what extent, these graduates are likely to adopt a *praxis* orientation in their own careers.

Reflective teaching or the 'active, persistent and careful consideration of action, belief or knowledge' (Dewey, 1933) has long played an important part in the lifeworld of the teaching professional. Reflection has been attributed to enabling teachers to conceptualise and contextualise their teaching circumstance; that is, it enables teachers to generate information that assists in knowing about teaching and to locate their thinking about teaching within its context. Reflective teaching can be described as informative and constructive action that connects the thinking about teaching to practical action. Taken to the critical level, reflective teachers look back on pedagogical events, analyse them, make judgments about them and transform teaching behaviours in light of the realities of their own context, current research and ethically informed knowledge (Edwards-Groves, 1998; 2003; Valli, 1997). Not surprisingly therefore, reflection now plays a central role in the "learning architecture" (Wenger, 1998) or "practice architecture" (see Chapter Three, this volume) of many pre-service teacher education courses both as a systematic requirement of university assessment plans and as an activity (often an assessable activity) to be completed during pre-service teachers' professional experience placements in schools.

From the perspective of educational *praxis*, reflection is an ongoing, dynamic process of social renewal whereby teachers continuously consider their actions and problematise, question and analyse them in a purposeful, conscious and deliberate way. Reflection *is* for action (Schön, 1983) as critical thinking about teaching informs future actions. Reflection too, is essential for *praxis* and ongoing teacher learning because it is not possible for teachers to improve their practices, if those practices are not made the object of focused thought and transformation (Hart, 1992). Reflective thinking, in fact, takes place across different temporal dimensions with different pragmatic purposes as shown in Table 5.1.

Table 5.1: Temporal dynamics of reflection for action

Temporal dynamics of reflection for action		
Pragmatic dimension	**Temporal dimension**	**Characteristics and Outcomes**
Descriptive or technical reflection A practice orientation	*Thinking is concerned with the here and now within the immediacy of the situation.* *Reflection-[with]in-Action and considers Reflection-on-Action* Includes both acting in the present and considering what has been in order to act differently in the immediate future. It is momentary and regular thinking to consider and/or regulate various courses of action. May include consideration of possible events and circumstances before they take place.	Reflection at the *descriptive or technical level* is regulatory thinking. On the one hand, it enables teachers to consider current courses of action and make spontaneous adjustments within the teaching event. On the other hand, this level is also formative 'thinking back', enables teachers to recount and deconstruct a teaching event to consider what happened, what worked well and how the participants were affected. It may include making 'on-the-run' formative assessments and judgements about student learning which may or may not be accounted for in future teaching. The ethical dimension is implicit and understood but not the object of explicit thought.
Dialogic Reflection Towards a *praxis* orientation	*Thinking and/or professional dialogue is concerned with the immediate or short term future action.* *Reflection-on-Action* Considers past action, may include practical but deliberate thinking focusing on the explication and clarification of underlying assumptions, practices and their consequences. Meanings are not absolute, but embedded. Systematic approach to reflection that is focused around a particular issue, usually related to one's own teaching. Teaching is conceptualised.	*Dialogic reflection*, by contrast, requires a going beyond situated practice to consider a deeper level of thought and deliberation. It may mean consulting other people, contexts, texts and/or ideologies to consider present action and the consequences of future action. In dialogic reflection, teachers consider the particularities of past action and the interactive participants in the classroom in a focused way, with the explicit aim of making covert actions overt and changing practice. Here teachers may also be engaged professional learning experiences that ask teachers, often as a collective, to consider new pathways and approaches in light of current circumstance. Teachers are engaged in reflective practices that work towards a *praxis* orientation.
Critical analytic reflection A *praxis* orientation demonstrating sustainable reflexivity	*Thinking and/or professional dialogue is concerned with long term committed action and change over time.* *Reflection-for-future-Action and Reflection-on-Action considering ongoing deep analysis, research, reframing and re-theorising over time (months or even years)*	Reflection at the *critically analytic level* is highly consultative and based on ethical inquiry which considers carefully assembled evidence from multiple texts, contexts, perspectives and ideologies. Critique focuses on future consequences of present actions for different people and groups. As a *praxis* activity reflection at this level enables teachers to set up ethical problems, questions and issues they encounter in a way that is

	Thinking and questioning in relation to self, ideologies and context. Information is collected about one's own teaching and may include an examination of a teacher's personal theories or their teaching practices in relation to the wider profession. High degree of intellectual engagement as teaching is reconceptualised.	directly tied to future 'right' action, and positions their actions in relation to the wider profession. By posing questions, interrogating their own and other's practices, challenging assumptions, and engaging in constructive dialogue with peers, it is believed teachers have the opportunity to transform teaching. Reflective activity is sustained over time.

Synthesis of work adapted from Edwards-Groves, 1998; Griffiths & Tann, 1992; Hatton & Smith,1994; Valli, 1997; van Manen, 1997; Schön, 1983;1987

Reflective practices at university predominantly aim to enable pre-service teachers to conceptualise teaching; that is to take a critical view of their own teaching in order to understand and learn from it, and about teaching more generally. However, Valli (1997) cautions that no one should take it for granted that student teachers will become reflective practitioners with time in the field. Nor should it be assumed, that even if students are provided with the approaches or 'technologies' of reflection that they will use these tools explicitly or consciously as part of their professional lives when they begin to teach. In our view, for reflexivity to be an enduring, portable and sustainable feature of life as a teacher, it needs to be learned and practiced, and that the artefacts of reflection need to be shared with peers, deconstructed and critiqued. So too, do the issues and discoveries arising from reflections require collegial professional scrutiny and response.

Although there is a great deal of conjecture about pre-service teachers' ability to reach the higher levels of critical reflection during their time at university (Griffiths, 2000), this is understandable given that the critical reflective dimension required of *praxis*-oriented teachers develops and is sustained throughout their careers. The focus must then turn to how universities support pre-service teachers in adopting a *praxis* stance so that they can productively connect reflective practices to future *praxis* actions. Therefore, exploring the views of pre-service teachers about reflection and reflective practice is crucial if we are to learn more about the efficacy of the kinds of communicative spaces teacher education courses provide. Answers may lead to considering and reconsidering the types of opportunities universities provide for students to engage in substantive dialogue and develop the capacity for critical analysis necessary for developing a *praxis* stance in teaching.

For reflection to be a constructive, authentic and sustainable activity which offers relevant information to its participants it is important to consider the kinds of reflective opportunities universities offer pre-service teachers. For example, it would be helpful to know more about the range of modes, purposes and outcomes of reflective practice activities student teachers actually encounter, and whether these clearly connect reflective practice to learning, action and re-framing of existing practices and beliefs. Equally, it might be asked whether reflective activities actually assist pre-service teachers and teachers in service to act rightly – morally and educationally speaking (that is, for their actions to be recognisably *praxis*). It has been suggested that individual and collaborative reflection tasks requiring multi-modal responses to teaching and learning about teaching are necessary to encourage and support both cognitive and task-oriented competencies and affective and attitudinal development (Grushka, McLeod and Reynolds, 2005). To be sustainable, it might also be the case that approaches to reflection need to encompass a broad range of temporal (when), process (how) and content (what) practices which are taken to further increasingly complex and critical levels of thinking (Schon, 1983; 1987).

The focus of the study

The study reported here aimed to gather data to provide information about the beliefs, attitudes and values of pre-service teachers towards reflective practices developed as a result of their participation in their teacher education course. The data focus on these students' understandings and perspectives about reflection in terms of its perceived utility, connectedness and relevance. It seems likely that the experiences and perspectives of the participants in 'doing' various forms of reflective practice will influence their perceptions of the relevance of reflection to 'real world' teaching practice and their personal connectedness to the reflection activities they experience. As we shall see, their personal accounts give substance to the way these perspectives fashion their reflective responses and suggest that there is a need for much closer examination of the detail and the structure of reflective practices in the university teacher education programs.

This chapter mainly draws on interview data gathered in the study which focused on the nature and use of reflective practices by students as they experienced 'reflection' in their studies. These interviews called for in-depth comment about the utility, sustainability and portability of reflective practices across professional experiences and learning contexts. Participants considered a range of technologies for reflection like those presented below in Table 5.2:

Table 5.2 Technologies for reflection documented in the course requirements of the Bachelor of Education (Primary) degree

The multi-faceted nature of reflective teaching practices is exemplified by the scope and diversity of approaches shown here. In different ways, the following 'reflective' practices invite students to consider (reflect upon) a range of texts, contexts and teaching and learning experiences:
reflective journals or diaries to write recounts and record impressions of events; anecdotal notes; use of metaphors; concepts maps; think-alouds; focused dialogue and observation; reading-logs; case stories; case studies; critical incident analysis; reflective narratives; conversational communities and critical friends; action research; reading summaries; on-going annotated evaluations of practicum experiences; thinking and recording; reflective essay; reviewing lecture notes; recording self (tape, video); reading text books

It is evident that within the learning or practice architecture of this teacher education course, pre-service teachers are expected to engage in a range of reflection modes and approaches across the duration of their degree, including a range of written, verbal, visual, textual and cognitive approaches. How these pre-service teachers engage with and interpret these experiences of 'reflection' is the critical point that will impact on the sustainability of reflective practice over time. These interpretations and perceptions will be taken up in the next section.

REFLECTION PRACTICES WITHIN THE LEARNING ARCHITECTURE OF TEACHER EDUCATION

Reflective practices form a central part of the learning or practice architecture of many subjects in teacher education courses. The challenge for pre-service teachers is to learn to use their reflections as a productive way to conceptualise teaching as a profession while they are learning to teach and while they are *practising* teaching in professional experience placements in schools. In addition to these reflective activities, student teachers are likely to be required to make analyses of their reflections to critique and interpret their own teaching in relation to theories and practices which shape the profession and professional work in contemporary circumstances.

Situating the practices of professional teachers with practical, logical and reasonable connectivity requires that these pre-service teachers engage with a range of educational texts and contexts. As suggested by Smith (Chapter Four, this volume), the process of reflection can create an intellectual and emotional space to balance and bring coherence between practice and theory. Ideally reflective activities can strengthen pre-service teachers' conceptualisation of the teaching profession as their individual professional knowledge evolves. Understanding the perspectives of pre-service teachers and their perceptions about the reflective activities they are required to use may help teacher educators to understand what, in fact, is accomplished by various kinds of reflective practice exercises. Such an understanding is necessary if reflection is to be viewed as an intellectually rigorous professional activity with a long-term, sustainable connection to the lifeworlds of teachers.

Learning to reflect: opportunities and understandings

Pre-services teachers require assistance to conceptualise and contextualise teaching through focused reflection. Our findings, like others (Hart, 1992), suggest that reflection needs to be learned and practised. The following quotations from the pre-service teachers in this study suggest that they employ a wide range of definitions of reflection[1]. This range leads us to wonder how reflection is, or was, portrayed to these pre-service teachers. According to some of the pre-service teachers in this study, reflection is:

...looking back at a particular situation in the classroom to give an insight into what you need to change for the future.

...consider[ing] what you have done and how you can improve on it for the future.

...thinking about something which you have been a part of, or just done. Establishing parts you liked or disliked, that worked or failed and then thinking about how to improve it for next time...

...a buzz word...and I really think it is a fancy word for what people do all day – think!

Thinking is just thinking, where reflection is taking it a step further; it is following it through more.

...more linear, thinking is more scattered...reflection is more focused than thinking.

...cause and effect. Something happens and something has to change as a response. Something comes from reflection, where sometimes nothing may come from thinking.

These definitions are simply descriptive (see above table), but they invite us to consider the issue of consistency about what this group of students were offered as definitions of reflection in their course (recognising, too, that they may have encountered different definitions of reflection in different subjects in their course). Although some of the definitions of reflection given by the pre-service students themselves show that some consider that there is a relationship between reflection and future action, others of the responses suggest that reflection is about thinking in a rather superficial sense. As indicated earlier, merely thinking about teaching may not be enough to affect practice and assist pre-service teachers to understand and critique their teaching in an intellectually rigorous and informed way; if this is so, then pre-service teachers need to understand how reflection is to be understood (in a particular course) and what it is expected to mean for their actions as teachers when they consider how to conduct themselves in their day-to-day working lives as teachers in classrooms. The definitions of reflection the students actually gave, some of which are listed above, suggest that they have not been given clear definitions and conceptions of reflection by their teachers. The pre-service teachers' views suggest a lack of clarity about what 'reflection' is and how it can be defined. Some, indeed, called for *'a more refined definition of reflection'*. The next set of excerpts (mainly from fourth year pre-service teachers) highlight a compelling point that even in this final year of their course they are very unclear about what reflective practice is, its purpose and its definition:

...I am wondering, is thinking about it still reflection? Or have we got this idea in our heads that reflecting has to be written down for it to be valid? Is it enough for us to have a casual five-minute conversation with someone or think about it as we are going to sleep at night?

...I always have the sense that I am missing something big [when I reflect]...

These responses are surprising given that they are from fourth year pre-service teachers. One would expect final year students, who are about to enter the profession as beginning teachers, to be able to provide a more substantive account of reflection. This finding suggests that within our university course, the processes for, and purposes of, reflection do not just lack clarity but also lack a sense of the explicit support required for students to engage in reflection; as indicated in this statement: *we are still learning, we have insecurities about our abilities to do things. We want to be able to do it well but we need help.* The lack of clarity expressed here suggests that, in our course at least, we need to be clearer about what we perceive to be the meaning and value of reflection. Given that most of the teachers on the course believe they place a high value on reflection and reflective practice, and that we emphasise its utility in the work of all teachers, this finding was surprising. Consider, too, these comments from students:

> *...I think I understand the theory of reflection; I think that I understand that it is good and that we need it, but I don't enjoy it because I am trying to learn how to do it – the process and the content... the learning skills required* [for reflection]...

> *...we need the thinking skills you use to reflect, we are told to reflect, and sometimes we get told what reflection is – to look at a past experience and to use references, but we don't get taught how to think that through, we don't get taught how to make the mental connections – our schema says reflection is... but we haven't been taught about the connections...*

> *...more needs to be taught about the actual process of reflection – the process that you need to go through...we need a 'how to' manual,*

> *...we need to complete modelled, guided and then independent examples of reflection in class.*

In the interviews, students made suggestions about how the university could scaffold their learning and practice of reflection. They recommended that it would be useful to engage in pedagogical approaches such as *open dialogue with lecturers, mentor systems, deconstructing lessons* and even *reflecting on videos of teaching as a group* about the substance of the reflections they make. These suggestions indicate that pre-service teachers need explicit support as they engage in and learn about reflective practice, adding significance to the point that reflection needs to be learned and practice.

In their accounts, most pre-service teachers heralded its usefulness to teaching, but they acknowledged that they do not simply produce 'good' reflections about teaching by instinct. They question what counts as a good reflection. Interestingly, in their thinking and public accounts of what they take reflection to be, they are beginning to espouse a *praxis* orientation by locating it as 'right educational practice', in the sense that they clearly articulate the benefits of reflection for the good of their future action. This would seem to imply that pre-service teachers need to have opportunities for focused, substantive dialogue and critical analysis which will help them to reach the critical domain of reflection, where reflection provides a basis for critique of existing conditions of teaching practice. In the end, we believe, arriving at this critical level of reflection is necessary if our students are to be able to reframe their experiences as a process of life-long learning in the profession.

Understandings about reflection are highly dependent on which lecturer students are doing their reflecting for. According to the students, *'[reflection] means different things to different lecturers'* and *'you write your reflection based on who you are writing it for and what subject you are writing it for'*. This finding is significant. Apparently students believe that they are left with misconceptions about what reflection is and what it is for. Without a coordinated and coherent understanding of reflection and reflective practice across subjects in a course, learning to reflect may be no more than a vacuous activity. The danger is that reflection will not have a constructive impact on pre-service teachers' thinking or their future actions in classrooms. Indeed, it is possible that *not* reaching a course-wide agreement on how reflection is to be understood and practised may undermine the intention of encouraging pre-service teachers to develop a *praxis* stance.

The students' views of reflection listed earlier also suggest that they may remain preoccupied with the *techne* of reflection (using only the technologies of reflection and recounting experiences) if they are not explicitly supported to understand the purposes, processes and *praxis* of reflection as part of *praxis* in teaching itself. In our view, this suggests that teacher educators need to be explicit in making a distinction between the *technē* of reflection (using known means to produce known products like pieces of ' reflective writing') and the *praxis* of reflection – reflection undertaken as part of the task of 'right conduct' or 'doing the best one can do under the circumstances'. In the latter case, one puts one's actions to the test retrospectively through reflecting on the character, conduct and consequences of one's action as part of a continuing process of understanding oneself as a *professional* teacher aiming to do the best work possible. This is what it means to have a *praxis* stance. If pre-service teachers do not have a sense of control over and knowledge about the nature and purpose of reflection and the part reflection plays in allowing them to evaluate and transform their work as professionals, then it will not become sustainable as a hallmark of their practice as professionals. In fact, the movement towards educational *praxis* may be compromised by modes of teaching and teaching about reflection that turn it into an instrumental technique for (technical) 'improvement' of a pre-service -teacher's practice without drawing attention to the way reflection contributes to developing their knowledge, attitudes and skills of teaching and their capacities to act in morally-defensible ways.

Reflection as authentic texts through writing, thinking or dialogue

The views presented so far indicate that these pre-service teachers took 'reflective practice' mostly to mean recounting what happened. These recounts take the form of either written or verbal texts; although writing seemed to be privileged as a dominant technology of reflection in this university course. In fact, journal writing is one of the most commonly used strategies to promote 'critical' reflection among pre-service teachers (Hatton & Smith, 1994). However, when these journals become an object for assessment, students often adapt or alter their journal responses to accommodate the requirements of the subject or the assignment to meet the readers' [lecturers] perceived expectations (Hatton & Smith, 1994). One student wrote:

> *...I write it down because that is what the lecturers want – that is the uni thing...*

Requiring reflective writing for an assessment or classroom task does not mean pre-service teachers will engage with more critical levels of reflection. These pre-service teachers' responses indicate that these 'reflective' texts seem to invite them to recount events rather than to develop the capacity to be critically reflective of, and learn from, their own actions (and the details of the action), to take judicious risks and sustain a broader view of professional issues. How the 'critical' element enters the reflective domain of pre-service teachers remains a question for further consideration. Although one student acknowledged that *'writing is a very clarifying thing. It is almost like through the act of writing, other stuff seems to come out of your pen that you didn't think was there'*, the student did not elaborate on how writing connected to future action in any critical way.

The pre-service teachers' comments in this study throw doubt on the extent to which teacher educators should regard their written reflective texts as authentic expressions of self-examination:

> *...reflection is about playing the game* [at university]*...*

> *...there is danger in reflecting because often you are reflecting for someone else...and so you censor yourself...and there is concern over how genuine reflections really are.*

> *...A girl who is doing one of our courses did not go on prac and was told that she would have to pretend how a child would react and reflect on that. Now if that's not saying there's a certain line of what they* [lecturers] *want then I don't know what it's saying....It shows that it doesn't make any difference...*

> *...you write your reflection based on who you are writing it for and what subject you are writing it for..... written reflections are more about how you wrote rather than what you wrote...*

> *You can still get a good mark even if it hasn't happened, even if you haven't reflected...I have found that even if something hasn't happened, put it in anyway, make it up because it looks good...even if you haven't developed, or you haven't learnt you just say you have...OR...even if it hasn't happened.make it up because it looks good... OR ...just give them what they want...AND THIS...fudge it...*

What is surprising across this collection of comments is that reflection is not taken to be an authentic or genuine activity by at least some of these pre-service teachers, despite our expectation that they will take the practice of reflection into their careers in a meaningful, serious way. Some of their comments suggest that they were simply unclear about the rationale for reflecting; they did not know what its benefits were meant to be for their own learning in the here and now of university nor for their ongoing development in the profession as an effective teacher. Some comments suggest they were simply not engaged with their reflective texts in any meaningful way. The comment above that a student might as well *make up* reflective comments to satisfy a particular university requirement, without engaging with an experienced social reality and their position in that reality, must surely undercut the claim that reflection enables pre-service teachers to conceptualise and reconceptualise their teaching on the basis of their lived experience and their reflection on that lived experience.

While not necessarily representing the whole range of these pre-service teachers' views about reflection, the comments above suggests that at least some of them perceive reflection to be a highly questionable activity at university, with little relevance for their development as thinkers about education or as practitioners of education. For some at least – maybe a substantial minority –it appears that pre-service teachers do not connect 'reflection' to their own or others' professional practice in an authentic way. It is reasonable to conclude that for some of these pre-service teachers at least, this perception will have an impact on their estimates of the likely utility of reflection when they enter their own professional lives and careers as teachers

Reflection 'as assessment': compliant and constructive action

These pre-service teachers frequently encountered reflection and reflective activities in the context of assessment. Written texts reporting (real or fabricated) reflection were often required as an assessment device in their course. This was the source of some dissonance and disquiet for. Whilst the intention of individual subjects and teacher educators may well be that, by embedding reflection activities into the assessment programs, pre-service teachers, will be afforded multiple ways to enter the reflective space required of them to develop as reflective *praxis*-oriented practitioners in the future. Our data suggests, however, that contrary effects may be produced. Although the main aim of reflective activities may have been to contextualise teaching, and learning about teaching, requiring that reflective activities be undertaken for assessment was met with strong antipathy among the pre-service teachers in this study, as illustrated in the following accounts which typify the views expressed:

> *...I hate being forced to reflect...*

> *...I don't want lecturers judging me on my thoughts...*

These comments suggest that these pre-service teachers regard themselves as relatively powerless, despite their lecturers' expectations that reflection will allow them to fully engage with their learning about teaching in a positive way. It is well known that a powerful formula for influencing one's capacity to learn is through positive experiences with learning. That some of these pre-service teachers make such strong criticisms of reflection (also evidenced in the comments below) suggests that some of the reflective activities they encounter in the course may be 'inoculating' them *against* reflection. Those who experience reflective activities as intrusive and negative will be unlikely to carry reflective activities (or at least *these* reflective activities) with them into their careers, as part of a sustainable practice of reflection connected to their professional learning from their own experience. Such negativity was prominent in the views of a number of these pre-service teachers who repeatedly expressed disillusionment in comments such as they '*are sick of reflection*' or '*all reflected out*' – views also mirrored in the following comments:

> *...so for us it has become too overdone. It gets to the point where you think, if I have to write another reflection I am going to scream*

> *The abuse that we have had here; it* [reflection] *is so repetitive and boring. When we get there* [schools] *we will be, 'I'm not reflecting anymore because I have done it so many ( ) times that I just don't want to do it anymore!' It is like giving a kid worksheet after worksheet after worksheet.*

> [reflection] *is like Pavlov's theory of classical conditioning... it is like a certain subject that I have had a bad experience with... I really don't feel like teaching this subject... purely because of the fact that it was a horrible experience at university.*

These strong views are directly attributed to these pre-service teachers' experiences of 'reflection' at our university, in one of our teacher education programs. Other teacher education and professional education programs in other universities may also have these effects. We had not expected that the views we have reported here would be so prevalent; on the contrary, we believed our emphasis on reflection and reflective practice accorded with best practice in teacher and professional education. Close scrutiny of these students' comments, however, causes us to believe that, despite our intentions, our use of reflective activities in our course may be doing less well than we imagined at developing the reflective capacities that we believe to be crucial in fostering a *praxis* stance among our students – and graduates. The strength of the convictions of some of these pre-service teachers on the matter of reflection was unexpected and, for those of us committed to reflection and reflective practice, a little overwhelming.

The responses reported here demonstrate that some students at least perceive reflection in terms of a *task orientation* (doing reflection activities) rather than a *relational orientation* (making authentic connections between thinking, reflective practices, multiple ideologies and viewpoints and future practical action). Indeed, these *tasks* are designed and built into the learning or practice architectures of our teacher education course. If students see reflective activities as a matter of 'production of work' or 'producing reflective texts' rather than as tasks with a deeper purpose of enabling them to see relationships between their ideas, their practices and their situations, we may to some extent be disabling rather than enabling authentic opportunities for pre-service teachers to adopt a *praxis* stance.

When reflection as a mere activity or task becomes the object, rather than the interrelationships between 'thinkings, sayings, doings and relatings' that constitute (reflective, *praxis*-oriented) teaching practice, our aspirations for fostering a *praxis*-stance are jeopardised. One student, for example, stated that *'on practicum we don't reflect if it is not an assignment requirement'*. Such a comment suggests that reflection is not uniformly regarded as a genuine contribution to the development of pre-service teachers' practice (let alone *praxis*). It throws doubt on the extent to which reflection will become a sustained and sustainable element in the everyday life experience of teachers in the classroom context - particularly if pre-service teachers only engage in reflective practices as a matter of compliance. When reflection is a matter of compliance, teachers may actually be drawn away from engaging in the formative professional thinking we hope will be characteristic of their work and lives. It may lead them away from acting positively to become teaching professionals with an orientation to continuously reframe themselves and their profession.

If the intention of reflective activities in teacher education programs is to move pre-service teachers beyond simply making rhetorical statements in their reflections, then perhaps we need to take further considered action to help students progress towards a higher degree of connectivity with their reflections, with the actions they reflect on, and the consequent courses of action resulting from their critique. It is simply not clear that the reflections made by students challenge and lead them to think deeply about and reframe future practices in a deliberate and conscious way; that is, their thinking is not being nourished nor is their teaching experience being critiqued through substantive, analytic dialogue with their colleagues, their lecturers and the teachers with whom they work in schools. To the extent that this is so, the reflective practices they experience at university may remain peripheral to meaningful professional learning after they graduate, limiting the 'sustainable reflexivity', and, perhaps, their *praxis* development that we hope for.

Oddly, teacher educators in our teacher education program seem to have initiated and sustained little systematic or developmental discussion about our use of reflective practice activities across the whole of our course. We quickly adopted reflection and reflective practice as crucial ideas to be developed in our programs, and we were unprepared for the findings of this study – especially that the variety of our approaches to teaching reflection might be experienced as confusing or boring by our students, or that we might even be teaching them to abandon reflection once they graduate. We had not been as careful or as systematic as we could have been in identifying and interrogating the use of reflection in the teaching and assessment arrangements of university subjects across the duration of the four year course. We had not adequately differentiated our expectations about the nature and conduct of reflection at different levels in the course (from novice or first year to more experienced fourth year students). Nor had we adequately developed a systematic approach to scaffolding reflection in terms of the support and explicit orientation we provided to students about its purposes and processes, and about the specific practices we employed with students at different stages in the course, as well as in different subjects where reflection might serve different specialised purposes and take appropriately specialised forms. If reflection is an ideal, and an essential feature of *praxis* development, and if it needs to be learned and practiced in a systematic way, then the results of this study suggest that learning about reflection should be located within a developmentally appropriate and supportive program. Pre-service teachers seemed to be constrained by the *ad hoc* arrangement of reflection experiences they encountered in our program.

Making reflection part of the university assessment agenda may in fact have turned its value toward the disposition of a *techne* disposition where reflection is an activity to be 'done' rather than a more desirable disposition of *praxis* where reflection takes on a moral character as an integral foundation stone for informing future action. Although reflection, as a feature of *praxis* in the teaching profession, may contribute to forging ongoing critical dialogue about the classroom learning experiences, our data suggest that reflection at university may not be taken to the metacognitive or critically analytic level we hope for. Our practices may have inadvertently replaced *praxis* with the *poiēsis* of engaging with reflective technologies – simply 'doing' reflection (and, what is worth, merely 'getting it over and done with'). Ideally, pre-service teachers should have opportunities to make public their ideologies and cognitions about their experiences through reflective dialogue and journaling in a way which is deemed developmentally supportive. Ideally, they should be able to do this in a collegial way – with their peers as well as with their lecturers and with the teachers they work with in schools – in a way that anticipates their joining the communicative spaces of a critical and self-critical teaching profession. This study suggests that we are not yet attaining these ideals through our practice as teacher educators.

We have come to understand that the production of reflection pieces *for assessment* has a significant potential impact on the sustainability of reflective practice. Across the corpus of the data reported here, students were unable to connect reflective practice with a committed change in future action. Written reflections are linguistic evidence that a certain type of practitioner is a desirable thing; but the assessment of these reflections may not help students to resolve the tensions and issues raised. Under such conditions, we can understand how student teachers might regard reflection as a 'game' – as an exercise or a methodical activity, rather than a part of the mediation of action required by *praxis*. We understand that this may be so when they receive a grade as a result of their reflection rather than a resolution of tensions or issues they identify as important or even critical to their continuing development as professional practitioners. Under such conditions, we can see that reflection might well lose its significance and relevance to the lifeworld of these pre-service teachers.

Reflection as public discourse in public domains

In the study reported here, there appeared to be a strong resonance with the value of learning through public discourse in public domains (Hatton & Smith; 1994); that is, talking about teaching experiences with others. The comments below suggest that pre-service teachers may prefer verbal forms of reflection as opposed to written tasks:

> *...I hate assignments where you are asked to reflect. I have learnt so much more [talking] than sitting down and writing. I struggle having to put down on paper what I think. I can verbalise it, but I can't always write it down...*

Reflection is presented here as communicative action (Kemmis and McTaggart, 2005). Although this pre-service teacher, like others, expressed a view about the merits of engaging in public discourse, what is absent is the critical dimension. Many pre-service teacher comments simply referred to the serendipitous nature of peer discussions. Our reading of these views suggests that many students in the study do not have a clear understanding of the value of reflection beyond recounting events or simply debriefing with peers. The relationship of reflection to conceptualising and contextualising teaching through focused observation and substantive dialogue is overlooked.

It seems that many pre-service teachers in the sample confused unplanned or incidental 'conversations' with peers with engaging in reflection, indicating that they had reached only a descriptive level of reflection. They reported tensions when they were expected to make public the connections between learning theories and their own learning. One second year student indicated: *"we need to use theory and practice and all that, but a lot of that is just opinions and I hate to back up my own opinions and make a statement about who else has said what I think in order for a reflection to be seen as valid"*. These participants generally valued verbal engagements as long as they were able to exercise control over the topics discussed and tailor the topics to be relevant to their own personal situations and requirements, as the following comment shows:

> *....I learn more about reflecting, more about myself as a teacher by going down to the Rivcoll [student café and common room] and having a yak [a conversation]...I have learnt so much more there than sitting down and writing...*

This view of reflection, as an end in itself, is at the descriptive level of reflection [see Table 5.1]. While it might be unreasonable to query the benefits of descriptive interactions, the danger is that pre-service teachers' attention is diverted from the chief educational and critical task to use reflection to transform future actions. They may settle for looking only superficially at their work. What is overlooked is the importance of substantive dialogue for future classroom action. To be communicative action in any significant sense – what Kemmis and McTaggart (2005) describe as communication oriented towards intersubjective agreement, mutual understanding and unforced consensus about what to do – their interactions

101

must begin (at least) to unravel the complexity of 'teaching' in a systematic and theoretical yet formative way.

According to the accounts of many of the preservice teachers in this study, the quality of reflection is not taken to be contingent on what critical, formative action takes place as a result of the experience of reflection. Reflection requires some reframing to ensure students count reflection as an interactive tool for critique and as a deliberate, planned opportunity to formulate and extend understandings and practices. Although pre-service teachers indicate the benefits of *'learning as a collective, not in isolation'*, and that it *'is a good way of confirming things'*, that *'you get other peoples' opinions and you can see other angles that you hadn't thought about and then you think about that as well, on top of what you had already thought about'*, and *'you can talk about applying it'*, their perceptions only loosely relate to a critical level of intellectual rigour as there is no assurance that their discussions will transform future teaching.

What counts as meaningful reflection is a point of conjecture raised by the results of this study. Many students do not view reflection as an important way to engage in deep learning about complex situations. They had not yet placed value on learning to connect theory with practical action in a critically analytic way. If these pre-service teachers only talk about what is already known without challenging and extending their ideas and knowledge, then their reflection will have little impact on their classroom action in the future. Peer dialogue will remain at the surface level.

These findings also suggest that perhaps the time at university is not, in and of itself, long enough to enable pre-service teachers to develop a *praxis* stance which requires critically analytic reflection with a realistic connection to one's practice and to the teaching profession. As indicated earlier, there is also a need for reflection practices to be aligned and/or co-ordinated consistently, coherently and developmentally across the teacher education course. Communicative space for interpretative discourse is required. This would provide an opportunity to explicate the principles of reflective teaching as part of the professional work and continuing professional development of members of the teaching profession.

Connectivity of reflective practice to the lifeworld of classroom teachers

The profile of the connectivity between pre-service teachers' reflections and developing and improving productive pedagogies needs to be raised along with explicating the links to the lifeworld of classroom teachers who engage in reflective practice as an ongoing and valid activity. It requires design and purpose. Meaningful reflection can only be accomplished if it explicitly links to what pre-service teachers are learning about in their practicum experiences and in their education course at university. Some of the pre-service teachers in this study recognised this point as they grappled with the concepts, the rationales, the meta-language and the processes for reflecting on teaching and learning:

...[we] *need opportunities to 'talk though reflections at the end of the practicum, allowing for open dialogue, perhaps the use of reflection mentors* [would be useful]..*

..the things that they [lecturers] *have taught us about reflection at uni. really have helped me when I am teaching...I know that I can write things down at the end of the day and it helps me to see what has happened and sometimes why it has happened. But sometimes I am left with a pile of notes that are just retelling what has happened in the day which doesn't help me accomplish anything. I don't have the thinking skills I need to be able to do that. I think we need an emphasis on the thinking skills that you use to reflect with on prac. I sometimes wonder if more time should be spent before prac. Discussing how you think when you are reflecting, like critical questioning, how to get to higher levels of thinking so that you can start to solve your own problems a bit better.*

It was evident that these pre-service teachers engaged in reflective practices at some level or another. Although it was reported that many participants *'reflected all the time'*, reflection was not perceived as being connected to the lifeworld of classroom teaching. The following excerpt also illustrates the distance placed between the professional action of teachers and the utility of reflection.

They [lecturers] *give us this idea at uni that teachers out in the 'real' world are writing these big long passages after each lesson and reflecting, when we know clearly that they aren't.*

For this group of pre-service teachers, reflection was often perceived as an act of complicity to satisfy university requirements and this did not always lead them to use 'reflection' as a tool for engaging in understanding the profession. It was not viewed as an activity or learning process to be encompassed into the daily life work of a teacher but rather it was construed as an artefact of the practicum which is not seen to connect to 'real' teaching. As pre-service teachers enter the teaching discourse through public displays of knowledge (for example through conversations with peers in staffrooms), the question remains whether they engage in a critical analysis of their teaching within discussions about the broader issues of education and use this information to effect professional action and change. Can they in fact go beyond 'a recount of what happened' to consider the placement of talk at the level of improvement and of the profession in the global context?

If sustainable reflexivity is desired, then teacher educators must also reflect on their own teaching and assessment practices in an explicit, overt and transparent way to legitimatise reflection as valid, informative action that contributes to the reframing and re-making of their practices. (Our reflections in this chapter will assist us in redesigning the practice architectures of our course to overcome some of the confusions and negative reactions this study has revealed.) This will enable transference and positive action affording pre-service teachers opportunities to experience reflection at all of the levels outlined in Table 5.1. What is put on offer for pre-service teachers in the university and in schools requires some pragmatism and symmetry between the purposes, practices and parallels of reflection and its connections to life in schools. Further, accounts of *how* the practice of reflection assists in one's ongoing development as an educated professional needs to be drawn into the debate about what counts as valid professional activity. Utility and sustainability are often driven by whose interests are being served. If indeed reflection is only captured by the intentions of the university (as an exercise), rather than as a valid and desirable activity for the profession with inherent professional merit as teachers work towards *praxis*, then its place in the lifeworld of teachers will remain superficial at best or non-existent at worst.

CONCLUSION

Teacher education aims for the formation of knowledgeable communities of committed professionals who act in the educationally 'right way'; that is to act as *praxis*-oriented professionals. And since reflection is considered an integral feature of *praxis*, the capacity universities have to empower pre-service teachers to develop this *praxis* orientation should be closely scrutinised. Throughout this chapter the emphasis has been on understanding the connectivity between the experiences pre-service teachers have with reflection in their teacher education courses to their perceptions of its utility in the lifeworlds of teachers. The connection is important for establishing information about the particular orientation these people will have towards the goal of sustainable reflexivity, and towards *praxis*, as they begin to teach. Reflection can act as a catalyst for focused growth and improvement throughout the careers of teachers enabling them to actively evaluate, adjust and fine-tune their work with a high degree of control. By responding decisively and analytically to their own reflections, pre-service teachers ideally should, with guidance, be able to act in the full knowledge of what they are doing and why, and be able to engage in focused discussions with others about their discoveries, moving them towards a *praxis* orientation.

This chapter presents the case that reflection for the particular group of pre-service teachers in this study is predominantly experienced as assessment. Although the production of reflective artefacts may be necessary, they are simply not sufficient if they are taken to be an end in themselves. To sustain reflective practice post-university, pre-service teachers need deeply embedded knowledge about the rationale for utilising reflection. The treatment of 'reflections' primarily as assessment products seemed to generate antipathy to reflection and reflective activities in the teacher education program and presumably towards these teachers' professional learning in the longer term. This was evident in pre-service teachers' lack of authentic engagement with reflections which was sharply at odds with our intention that the pre-service teachers would be empowered to sustainably use a range of reflective technologies to conceptualise and reconceptualise teaching practice. In addition, the pre-service teachers' reflections often remained at the surface or 'recount' level rather than reaching a deeper more critically analytic connection. Furthermore, opportunities for focused and in-depth discussions about the substance of individual pre-service teacher reflections were visibly absent. In a significant way, this would not strengthen the predilection for the development of a *praxis* stance held by the university.

As education is a moral enterprise (see Chapters Two and Three, this volume), so too must be the practices that constitute it. Pre-service teachers need to be given a clear and explicit understanding that the intention of reflective practice is to develop educational practice in its moral as well as its technical dimensions. Furthermore, to teach pre-service teachers to develop as reflective practitioners, universities need to reconceptualise their own practices. University practices need to authentically and intellectually engage their students in conceptualising and contextualising teaching through reflection by relocating the practice of it within a moral framework in such a way that students explicitly understand that the way they 'do' education will express *their* moral ideologies. Therefore, to regain reflection as a valid, authentic and intellectually rigorous pursuit for teachers in the profession, it must not be considered only as a product for assessment in teacher education. It must be experienced as a practice which provides pre-service teachers with an authentic way to learn, and to continue to learn, about teaching.

An interrogation of the place of reflection within the assessment regime is required to validate the relevance and connectedness of reflection to the teaching profession. If the aim is to have reflection as an inherent part of the *praxis* ideology and situated practice of teachers, then its strategic development over time is required. To be taken to the level of critical valid action, explication is required to serve reflection for pre-service teachers (as learners of their profession) as a sustainable, useful endeavour; one that does not deny access to its inherent value by engaging in implicit and unsystematic courses of action.

To be constructive and perceived of value, reflective practices need to demonstrate a deeper analysis and higher order thinking about its utility and what it means for teachers in the wider context. Without sustained focus and responsive action, reflection is unlikely to be a 'motor' for continuing transformation and self-transformation; it is not likely to contribute to the development of a *praxis* stance to one's own teaching. Therefore, for sustainable reflexivity there is a responsibility on the part of the university sector to make reflective practice, as it is connected to a *praxis* orientation, overt at all levels and developmentally embedded into the practice architectures of the education courses which herald its use in the profession longer term.

Perhaps part of the issue is with the teaching profession itself. If pre-service teachers do not recognise reflection in action within the professional actions of the teachers they engage with as a part of their practicum, it may well be the case that education systems themselves offer little in terms of availing teachers (both novice and expert) the communicative space to engage in meaningful, critical reflection. Limiting the opportunities for teachers to become fully functioning professionals with a *praxis* orientation restricts the possibility of a flourishing *praxis*-oriented profession. If in the longer term, teachers in the field continue to report lack of time, opportunity and support for ongoing professional reflective opportunities then sustaining a *praxis* stance is compromised.

In conclusion, the case presented in this chapter asks for teacher education programs, and even beginning teacher programs, to take pre-service and early career teachers to a deeper level of thinking about their teaching. An explicit approach which injects challenge and promotes and guides them to engage in focused thought on very specific aspects of practice, ideology and student learning is needed. This is an educational enterprise which can be made available through reflective practice. Clarity and explicit connections need to be drawn between 'reflective practice' at the university level and the realities of the profession in a pragmatic way. Assisting pre-service teachers to think deeply and critically about details of their practice is a feature of effective teacher development and a responsibility of the university systems if reflective practice is to take its place as a useful, overt, relevant and sustainable activity in the daily lives of teachers as they continue on their professional journey.

NOTES

[1] All pre-service teacher statements are taken from the corpus of interview data gathered in the Gray study (2006).

REFERENCES

Cochran-Smith, M. and Lytle, S. (1999). The teacher research movement: A decade later. *Educational Researcher, 28*(7), 15-25.

Dewey, J. (1933). *How we think: A restatement of the relation of reflective thinking to the educative process.* D.C. Health and Company: New York.

Edwards-Groves, C. (2003). *On task: Focused literacy learning.* Primary English Teaching Association. Newtown: Australia

Edwards-Groves, C. (1998). *Reconceptualisation of classroom events as structured lessons: Documenting and changing the teaching of literacy in the primary school.* Unpublished doctoral thesis Griffith University, QLD: Aus

Gray, D. (2006). *Learning to listen: Pre-service teachers' views of reflective practice in the Bachelor of Education (Primary) course.* Unpublished Honours Thesis, Charles Sturt University: Wagga Wagga, NSW, Aus

Griffiths, M. & Tann, S. (1992). Using reflective practice to link personal and public theories, *Journal of Education for Teaching, 18*(1), 69-84.

Griffiths, V. (2000). The reflective dimension in teacher education. *International Journal of Educational Research, 33,* 539-555.

Groundwater-Smith, S., Ewing, R. & Le Cornu, R. (2003). *Teaching: Challenges and dilemmas,* 2nd Ed. Nelson: Australia Pty Ltd

Groundwater-Smith, S. & Mockler, N. (2003). *Learning to listen: Listening to learn.* Division of Professional Experiences. University of Sydney, Aus

Grushka, K., McLeod, J.H., & Reynolds, R. (2005). Reflecting upon reflection: Theory and practice in one Australian university teacher education program. *Reflective Practice, 6*(2), 239-246.

Hart, L.C. (1992). Essentials. *AMP Connection 2.* Spring 2.

Hatton, N. & Smith, D. (1994). *Reflection in teacher education: Towards definition and implementation.* School of Teaching and Curriculum Studies: University of Sydney.

Kemmis, S. and McTaggart, R. (2005) Participatory action research: Communicative action and the public sphere. Pp.559-603 in N. Denzin and Y. Lincoln (eds.) *The Sage handbook of qualitative research,* 3rd edition. Thousand Oaks, California: Sage.

Porter, A., & Brophy, J. (1988). Synthesis of good teaching: Insights from the work of the institute for research on teaching. *Educational Leadership, 45,*8.

Schön. (1983). *The reflective practitioner: How professionals think in action.* Basic Books: New York.

Schön, D.A. (1987). *Educating the reflective practitioner.* Jossey-Bass: San Francisco.

Smyth, J. (1987). *Educating teachers: Changing the nature of pedagogical knowledge.* The Falmer Press: London.

Valli, L. (1997). Listening to other voices: A description of teacher reflection in the United States. *Peabody Journal of Education, 72*(1), 67-88.

van Manen, M. (1995). On the epistemology of reflective practice. *Teachers and Teaching, 1*(1), 33-50.

Wenger, E. (1998). *Communities of practice.* Cambridge University Press, Cambridge.

Zeichner, K.M. & Liston, D.P. (1996). *Reflective teaching: An introduction.* Lawrence Erlbaum: New Jersey.

AFFILIATIONS

Christine Edwards Groves
School of Education,
Charles Sturt University, Wagga Wagga, NSW, Australia

Deana Gray
School of Education,
Charles Sturt University, Wagga Wagga, NSW, Australia

HELEN RUSSELL AND PETER GROOTENBOER

6. FINDING PRAXIS?

The impetus and motivation for this book began with a group of education academics sharing ideas about *praxis*. Writing the book involved many rich and enjoyable discussions about the nature of *praxis* and about how crucial it is to education. Each of us shared our passion for our own particular area of interest in education, and together we considered how the promotion and development of *praxis* would enhance educational experiences and outcomes for learners. It was a wonderful time, academically stimulating and engaging.

As we proceeded, however, we became aware of two anomalies in our discussions: (1) they were often theoretical, and; (2) they focused on the educational practices of others. Regarding the first: the theoretical tenor of the discussion was probably not surprising given that this was the work of a group of academics, whose work is often theoretical, and given that theory development is as crucial for advancing educational ideas as it is in any other field. The issue for us was that *praxis* is a form of action, not just thinking or theorising about action (see Chapter One). If it does not involve action then it is not *praxis* and our academic discussions risked diminishing the 'doing' quality of *praxis*. In this chapter we will not devote a great deal of space to theory, not because we do not value theory, but because we want to present a very practical account of our particular journey in trying to understand and develop our own *praxis*. The theoretical framework for this book is outlined in the first three chapters and we situate this report within that broader theoretical framework.

Regarding the second anomaly: as education academics, our work often centres on the activities of schools and the professional tasks of in-service and pre-service teachers. We became concerned in our discussions that while we were making a case for teachers to engage in *praxis*, we were not necessarily turning this same lens on ourselves. Given that *praxis* is "morally-committed action, oriented and informed by traditions in a field" (see Chapter One), it might be argued that we would be acting unethically if we did not, firstly or simultaneously, examine our own teaching as a form of *praxis* before presuming to offer advice about the *praxis* of others.

With these two overarching concerns in mind, we set out to explore *praxis* in our particular context – pre-service teacher education. As we began to consider our actions as tertiary teachers, we continued to read and reflect to help us articulate and understand the moral tenets that underpinned our teaching *praxis*.

This chapter presents a case story of our interaction with some of the literature, our exploration of our intentions and self-understandings, and some of the implications these ideas require of our action as educators. As our exploration

Kemmis, Stephen and Smith, Tracey J. (2008) Enabling praxis: Challenges for education.109-126

proceeded, we were faced with tensions and constraints that impelled us to consider how we would act and to question our prior actions. Our chapter is a shared account of tertiary teachers trying to engage in *praxis* within the constraints of a university degree program. In presenting this account of our journey, we have been particularly aware of some of our short-comings and at times have felt quite vulnerable, but we have come to see this exposure as an integral part of exploring our teaching *praxis*.

This chapter is the story of that process and the themes and issues that emerged. Peter alluded to these aspects in a contribution to a shared blog (weblog) called 'Finding *praxis*' that we created to record our reflections along the way. (The online blog will be described in the section 'The exploration'):

> *Although we have sketched some broad parameters for our journey ahead, there is a real sense of mystery and uncertainty about what experiences lie before us. It is possible that we may experience a 'break-through' or 'earth-shattering' moment, but we may not, and so I think we need to try and identify how we are becoming more conscious through the moment-by-moment experiences of the mundane and ordinary. I think the difficult process of trying to see the ordinary as extra-ordinary and the seeds of the spectacular amongst the routine is important – indeed critical. Those 'aha' moments are important and worthy of study, but they are indeed rare, and the ongoing realisation of praxis is deeply interesting.*

As we began to consider the routine activity of our teaching practice we had no script to follow and our course was not mapped. However, we were influenced by the principles of phenomenology and hermeneutics in the interpretation of our lifeworlds as tertiary teachers and in the interpretation of the lifeworld of the pre-service teachers with whom we work. We believed that a phenomenological perspective would contribute to our understanding of the taken-for-granted practices that shape our *praxis* and that the discovery-oriented and inductive nature of the phenomenological approach would enable us to find unforeseen and emergent insights into our practice and *praxis*. Likewise, the hermeneutical perspective would also help us to be responsive to emerging themes and relationships. This responsiveness was important to our exploration because of the tentative nature of our analysis and interpretation of our *praxis*.

Histories

As we present the case story of our search for *praxis*, we are aware that our journey did not begin at our first meeting. As relatively recently arrived teachers in our regional inland university, we were becoming Charles Sturt University teachers, shaped by the practice architectures our university has already constructed. Nevertheless, we are equally aware that we were forming our own particular roles as teachers out of our own acts and deeds. It is clear that our unfolding experiences were shaped and pre-figured by our histories and we continued to make connections between our past, present and future as university teachers. With this in mind, we briefly present a synopsis of our backgrounds to help readers understand a little of our context and backgrounds.

Helen

I work mainly with pre-service primary and secondary teachers as an information technology educator. I came to my current position after many years of teaching computer education in secondary schools. As a secondary school teacher, I had many fruitful discussions with colleagues about balancing the here-and-now (the pragmatic) with the responsibility to provide the best possible opportunity for learners to learn. However, as a teacher educator in a university, my concerns about *praxis* have shifted in compelling ways that have provided an imperative to explore my *praxis* in greater depth. My interest in the notion of *praxis* stemmed partly from reflecting on the evaluations my students submit at the end of each teaching session. These gave me insights into my own practices and the disjuncture between what I was espousing as 'good teaching practice' for students and my own practice as a university teacher. I became aware of my own teaching in the sense that I began to see my teaching from the perspective of my students and I began to wonder about a kind of hypocrisy in my actions. In an environment where it might be expected that teaching decisions are supported by theories, I appeared to be acting contrary to the theories I was espousing.

I had a further concern about inherent messages I may have been conveying to the pre-service teachers I was teaching. The following narrative is just one example. In an evaluation of one subject I teach, a student referred to my lack of feedback on an assignment. I agreed that this was true; I had provided little feedback. I knew this and had known it at the time, but had not considered that it was the kind of practice I should question. It was only after reflecting on the student's comments that I began to ask some questions I needed to have answered. First, my reason for not providing feedback was that I believed students just wanted to 'jump through the hoops' and that they regarded assessment simply as a necessary evil. This presupposed that I also believed that real learning only took place in other places in the subject and not in the assessment. If this were so, then my practice was not aligned with what I was espousing: that assessment is a learning opportunity. This led me to scrutinise the assessment tasks in all the subjects I taught and to explore my *praxis* to find a closer fit between my teaching practices and what I encouraged in pre-service teachers. Newman (2006, p. 153) cites Brookfield's (1995) notion of 'critical-incident analysis' in which a critical incident is held up to scrutiny so its significance can be exposed and examined, and so the analyst can reach a deeper understanding of why they deemed this particular incident to be critical and to 'identify the values that underpin actions' (Newman, 2006, p. 154). The issue of feedback on assignments had been made 'critical' for me by this student's evaluation comments, and it allowed me to discover how I could better realise my views and values through my teaching, in this case by giving richer feedback on students' assignments.

Peter

I am a university mathematics educator working primarily with pre-service primary and secondary teachers. My main area of interest is the affective dimension of learning. When I began working with pre-service primary teachers in their initial teacher education programs in mathematics education, I was surprised at the negative attitudes that many displayed towards mathematics. This led into my doctoral research that explored the affective responses of pre-service primary teachers to mathematics. One particular finding that stood out for me was the critical role that these students' previous mathematics teachers had played in forming their largely negative perceptions, beliefs and feelings about mathematics. It was confronting to realise that as a school mathematics teacher I had probably inadvertently caused some students to develop beliefs and attitudes about mathematics that were similarly not positive or enabling. This disconcerting revelation pierced at the heart of what I perceived my role to be. As I had moved into the role of mathematics educator, I had certainly experienced feelings of uncertainty and dissonance, and I came to recognise that I was not just a teacher of skills and knowledge, but that I also had a significant role in shaping students' beliefs, values, attitudes and feelings. This revelation brought to the fore the moral and ethical dimension of my practice that I have since reflected on and written about (Grootenboer, 2006). It continues to focus my attention in my teaching as a university teacher educator, and has shaped the inquiry into my *praxis* presented here.

ANALYSING TAKEN-FOR-GRANTED ASPECTS OF TEACHING PRACTICE

There is a certain inevitability about the practices of teaching in formal learning environments. When teachers and learners enter a shared space there is both an inevitability and an expectation about what will occur. There is a pattern and predictability to the behaviours in which both parties – teachers and students – are expected to 'stick to the script'. As these practices are repeated, they become routinised, anticipated and something like 'second nature'. Their continual practical success guarantees their reliability and they become habitualized as recipes – a 'guaranteed formula' for success. In teaching, the repetition of routines that reliably produce expected outcomes can diminish *praxis* to *poiēsis* – that is, it can diminish morally-committed action that is informed and oriented by tradition to instrumental action aiming only to produce reliable results (see Chapter Two). The disposition of *phronēsis* (to act wisely and prudently, guided by practical commonsense) is replaced by the disposition of *technē* (to produce an expected result). This transformation of *praxis* to *poiēsis* can occur for teachers simply by virtue of past success and established routines. The successful employment of a particular set of actions may mean that the practitioner no longer needs to consider a particular kind of situation as new or different, nor to require new ways of acting.

Under such conditions, which we might describe as a '*technē* experience', practitioners might behave as if they 'know all there is to know' in relation to a particular practice. The '*techne* experience' includes the repetitiveness, the sameness, the automation and the routine that subsequently flow from adopting this perspective. If technique is thought to have been perfected, there is no reason to seek new solutions or to examine the particular, different and unique conditions of practice in this or that particular case, in this or that particular time and place. If the practice 'works', the practitioner may believe, then they can repeat past successful acts and that each time things will be the same, with the same outcome. Under such conditions, there appears to be no need to examine the taken-for-granted. For teachers with these beliefs there may also be a certain expectation that nothing changes between teaching/learning events and that it is possible to repeat behaviours without unforeseen outcomes. The conditions of practice are also assumed to be unchanged.

This kind of experience of practice may also entail an assumption by teachers that others in the shared space – particularly students – will accept and comply with past and expected ways of behaving. There is an expectation that the meaning of the behaviour will be known and that this meaning will be accepted without question by all participants. It is only when something novel occurs that the individual is made aware of the deficiency in their personal 'stock of knowledge' that previously had been taken-for-granted (Schutz & Luckmann, 1974, p. 8). This stock of knowledge is an expression to explain prior experiences. The unexamined ground of practice remains taken-for-granted as routines and patterns of behaviour while ever the mechanical devices and techniques (*techne*) used continue to result in anticipated outcomes.

The perspective of *praxis*, however, requires a different way of looking at things. In *praxis*, the unexamined, taken-for-granted ground of practice is examined. Without the exploration, the ground remains taken-for-granted. In *praxis*, the everyday and perhaps unspectacular moments of our teaching practice are opened to scrutiny and exploration. In Chapter Four, Smith referred to three qualities that Dewey (1933) believed underpin a *praxis* stance or a disposition towards *praxis*. (A similar way of describing the *praxis* stance is that given by Edwards-Groves in Chapter 8 as a '*praxis*-oriented self'.) One of the qualities identified by Dewey that was particularly relevant for us was the quality of open-mindedness, that is, the ability to consider perspectives other than one's own. We believed that by approaching our journey of finding *praxis* from a hermeneutic phenomenological perspective we would demonstrate an open-mindedness that could not only expose our shortcoming but also allow us intersubjectively to encounter the lived experience of others – that is, to encounter their subjectivities as they engaged with ours in a shared encounter and a shared experience.

In attempting to understand the nature of the *praxis*-oriented self, Peter made an early contribution to our blog (see below for description of 'The exploration'), in which he questioned how we could investigate our *praxis* while also being immersed in our own *praxis*. Peter's insight suggested that this was going to be a difficult and yet eventful journey:

I wonder how we can imagine this idea of developing the self that teaches – the 'praxising' person. I think this is a big topic that warrants thoughtful consideration. All of the faith traditions seem to include a dimension that requires some sort of inner journey, and perhaps there is something to be learned here. Often this seems to include times of solitude and reflection – a time away from our practice. Praxis can only be realised in action, and so I am not suggesting the monastery-type lifestyle, but it seems very difficult to remove oneself from the humdrum of our practice in order to rejuvenate/refresh something so we can 'praxis'.

In other words, in looking for what counts as *praxis* for a teacher in an education faculty, we were reflecting and becoming reflexive about our own *praxis*. In this state of being critically conscious of our *praxis*, we attempted to identify, question and analyse the ethics of our teaching practices. This involved scrutinising our ideologies and values, and the taken-for-granted – those aspects and qualities that influenced and constrained our ways of thinking, feeling and acting as teachers. This involved taking a step back and attempting to distance ourselves from the personal nature of the landscape we were inhabiting along with our students and being dispassionate about our practices in that landscape. In doing this, we trusted that exposing our practices to others would allow us to gain insights that might be uncovered and revealed by the critical discussions that would follow.

IN LOOKING FOR *PRAXIS*, WHAT WERE WE LOOKING FOR?

In Chapter One, Kemmis and Smith defined *praxis* as "morally-committed action, oriented and informed by traditions in a field" (p.2). This, then, defined what we were looking for, but our immediate concern was about more tangible things. If we were looking for *praxis*, what would it look like? And if we saw it, would we recognise it? How would we know? We were saturated in the theoretical machinations of *praxis* as morally informed practice, but were more perplexed about how we might notice it within ourselves, let alone others. It became clear that *praxis* cannot necessarily be seen or heard because any given action or practice can be moved or enacted from a range of different motivations. Hence the same teaching behaviour could be a form of *technē* or *praxis*, or more likely, some complex amalgam of positions and strategies. This was a profound moment, for in this relatively simple quest we experienced at a very personal level the complex and difficult agenda we were promoting for others.

We understood in more than a theoretical way that a commitment to scrutinising our own practices would require a personal dedication to community and collegiality, reflection and self-disclosure if we were to explore the moral intent of our actions. Furthermore, we realised that this sort of journey could only begin with a sense of trust and mutual respect. For our small group this characterised our relationships and it emerged as much through shared meals and coffee as it did through our more formal interactions.

Peter further wrote in our 'Finding *praxis*' blog (see below for description of 'The exploration'):

I see us as "searching for praxis" or "journeying towards praxis development" or something like that, because, as has been highlighted by Stephen (Kemmis) and Helen, it is not arrival that is important but the "exploration towards". It is trying to be more conscious of and deliberate about pedagogy as praxis. To me this will be rooted in our experiences, and I'm hoping that our collegiality will help me see and think about those experiences in a deeper and more morally-conscious way. I also hope that we reflect upon our shared experience in some way – not just as a collection of individual experiences, but somehow capturing the complexity and richness of our togetherness. I'm not sure how we can do this but perhaps it will involve times of "looking back" and trying to specifically focus on certain features of our shared work, practice, praxis and humanity.

THE EXPLORATION

The journey we describe in this chapter centres on our attempts to begin a process of *praxis* development in our own tertiary teaching. The events took place over a ten month period that included two semesters of teaching in 2006 and 2007. Our exploration was built around three sorts of activities that were bound together and synthesized by continuous thought and conversation: reading, discussing and acting in our role as tertiary teachers. Formal and informal discussion was central, in face-to-face situations and through a shared online blog (weblog). The blog provided a communication space that enabled us to see and read the contributions of all participants and to respond to the text and graphics in our own time and place. Being part of a discussion that was not dependent on time and space gave us immense freedom to reflect and to keep up with the discussion.

In this account of our journey we draw on all of these three types of activity and give readers some insight into our thinking, struggles and the issues we faced. Our account is not a recipe for others to follow, but rather a very situated and personal story of how we tried to enter the potentially-treacherous space of collegial self-review searching for morally-informed *praxis*. Indeed, it seems to us that to regard what follows as a recipe or method for *praxis* would immediately be to risk changing it into a form of *technē* or instrumental action to produce an external product. As Kemmis and Grootenboer suggested in Chapter Two, *praxis* is a process of self-formation that changes the person who acts.

How did we go about it?

Our exploration involved a range of reflective collegial activities. This chapter has been written by two of the participants, but other colleagues were involved to varying degrees. In short, we listened and told teacher and student narratives in corridors, informal discussions and formal meetings. Our online blog provided a further venue for critically reflecting on these stories. We created communicative spaces for collaborative reflection. We started writing and exchanging scripts about our teaching and events where we were conscious of our *praxis* or occurrences that challenged our attempts to enact *praxis*. At the same time, we read the work of some key writers in the literature of *praxis* (for example, Dunne, 1993).

There were many instances when we attempted to make meaning of a situation using metaphors as a way of interpreting the experience. One metaphor from the blog that created some excitement was that of a bike spoke in helping us to grapple with the many tensions that characterized our professional landscape. Initially we spoke disparagingly about the unavoidable and seemingly oppositional forces that constrained our attempts towards *praxis*. Theoretically we were not unaware of these sorts of tensions, as has been discussed in Chapters Two and Three in this volume. We noted that the discussions about these external constraining influences appeared to lead to a sort of inactivity or paralysis because of events and decisions apparently beyond our control. However, we came to view the tensions differently through the metaphor of the bike spoke. A bike spoke is a relatively flimsy piece of metal but it functions well because it is held in tension with the other spokes around the wheel. The tension keeps the wheel centred and able to function but without the tension the wheel collapses. So we saw the parallel with our situation for two reasons.

First, such tensions keep us from extremism and perhaps from being captured by our own agendas without due consideration for our colleagues, community, students and the profession at large. Second, such tensions mean that *praxis* is required. If the professional landscape was free from tensions and competing agendas, there would be no need for morally-informed practice because the decisions required would be straight-forward and the action steps clear-cut. On a well-charted and issue-free journey, *technē* is sufficient – in fact probably desirable, because it takes away the opportunity for unnecessary moralistic vacillation. In our journey, however, the dilemmas, the uncomfortable feelings, the sense of unease, the critical incidents, and the occasional clashes of personal beliefs and ethics all created an essential tension. For our wheel to spin in a balanced way, the spokes could not be slack. Without tension, there would be no issues and no need to explore the taken-for-granted. These tensions will be discussed in greater detail in the next section.

The tension-filled nature of our teaching context was inevitable, but our responses were not and the choice to do nothing seemed morally indefensible. With this in mind, Peter encouraged us in our endeavours in one of the early blog postings:

Fellow journeyers, I'm expecting that we will be different (better?) in a few months time! In fact, I'm sure we will be different, but I'm hoping we will be more aware of the changes and that we might be better 'praxisers'.

THE TENSIONS OR ISSUES

In this chapter, we explore a number of issues that relate directly to our experiences (and not necessarily to the experience of others). We can make no definite claims here about others' experience, though we assume that some of our experiences may resonate with others. We noted that our journey towards *praxis* was charted in a terrain characterised by tensions. These included the tensions between:
- integrity and pragmatics;
- teacher and students, humans in a shared space;
- teacher and students in separate time and space;
- *technē* experience and sincerity;
- acting morally or acting moralistically, and
- enacting *praxis* and explaining our practices.

We have deliberately called these issues *tensions* rather than *problems* because we came to view each pair of terms not as opposed ideas each intending to overthrow or obliterate the other, but as poles held in relation with one another by stresses that kept us from extremism. As poles, they defined a space that demanded morally informed action – that demanded *praxis*! Below we discuss each tension in turn, although they did not arise and we did not necessarily identify them in the order in which we discuss them here. In each case, the tension is illustrated with a particular example from our shared experiences and often we cite the *praxis*-focused questions that piqued our thinking, and that still remain open and conscious-raising for us now, as we continue the exploration of our *praxis*.

Integrity and pragmatics

There exists an area that could best be described as the pragmatics of teaching: the expedient, the means to an end, the purely technical solutions to problems that arise during the event. These are the solutions that are perhaps *easiest* to explain, in terms of logical explanation, but *least easy* to explain in terms of a philosophical perspective or *praxis*. Perhaps it is a combination of practice (i.e. *technē*) and pragmatics that drive the immediacy of teaching that seems to work in opposition to *praxis*. Could *praxis* be *technē* and more, that is, good technical and pragmatic skills + the moral, ethical concern that underpins decisions? It seems to us that *praxis*, as action, enacts the ability to 'think on your feet', enacts the capacity to evaluate what is happening as it unfolds, and enacts the theory that underpins one's actions.

One of the first tensions we noticed in our teaching was an apparent mismatch between some of the material we presented to our pre-service teacher education students and our own modes of teaching and acting. A specific example of the contradiction was apparent when trying to explain the theory and principles of constructivism in a formal lecture setting. This teaching strategy created a disparity between what was being espoused and what was being enacted. So why did we find ourselves doing it? Why did we act in contradiction with the constructivist principles we were espousing? Why this perversity, this seeming contrariness, this disparity? When we examined these questions we came up with pragmatic answers, such as the session being scheduled in a lecture theatre, large numbers of students, it was easier this way, there was less need for organisation of students and resources, less preparation involved for the teacher. Our university timetables distinguish different types of session as 'lectures' and 'workshops'. The taken-for-granted text suggests that lectures will be teacher-centred and that workshops will involve student-centred activities. Locking ourselves into these assumptions allowed our teaching decisions to be rationalised by 'pragmatic' concerns.

On the blog, Helen described an instance of the tension between personal human values and institutional bureaucracy that has potentially far-reaching consequences.

After teaching in one of the computer rooms, I encountered students waiting for their next class. Their teacher had not yet arrived to take the class. University regulations require that students may not be left alone in a computer room without supervision, so I asked them to wait outside a locked door until their teacher arrived. My underlying sense of ill ease meant that I was in a relationship with these students and I was communicating a lack of trust in them, an expectation that they would not be honest or 'do the right thing'. How will this expectation be played out in other situations and contexts when I want them to know that I do trust them and when I espouse the values of teacher/student relationships based on trust and respect? What does it say to the students and how can I expect them to believe me, when I say I respect them, that there is mutual-ness in the teacher-learner relationship? What does it also say about how they will approach their students when they come to teach in the school environment? Will they say they trust them and then lock the door at lunch time so the students are not able to use the room without a teacher present?

A particular aspect of teaching in computer rooms that gives cause to stop and think is the topology of the room, the configuration, the layout and placement of the resources and students, and the expectations and constraints these impose on the teacher and the students. Schatzki (2002) refers to the 'spatial relations' and 'how artifacts enable and constrain one another's actions depends not just on their physical properties, but also on the organization that human activity imposes on them' (p. 98). In a computer learning environment, the topology is often such that it restricts collaborative learning or makes collaborative learning difficult. Unlike a 'normal' classroom with tables and chairs that can be re-arranged, the computer teacher is locked into an existing topology because she cannot re-arrange fixed computers and power outlets, data projector, scanner and printers. The topology is 'prefigured' and pre-arranged in a practice architecture (see Chapter Three) in which these resources are screwed down and fixed in place. Both the teacher and the students are bound by the placement of teaching and learning resources. In this situation, with these conditions of teaching and learning, the following questions are raised in relation to the 'spatial relations' of computer learning environments:

- How do the classroom configurations of furniture and resources influence the
  learning?
- How does the configuration position the teacher and students?
- Who is privileged and why?
- On what basis is the topology determined?
- Is there a rationale for the topology based on learning theory, or is it
  determined by other circumstances, such as comfort, shape of room, position
  of power outlets?
- Is the topology an architectural decision or a design decision?
- Who makes these decisions?

The computer teacher is faced with the tension of the fixed topology of the room
and the potential clash with their preferred way of teaching. The set configuration
of the room also potentially influences the nature of the teacher/learner
relationship. The dilemma for the teacher is how to maintain integrity amidst the
fixed configuration and architecture of the room that dominates and determines the
pragmatics of actions. How is the teacher able to teach over and around the fixed
placement of furniture and resources with no possible choice in re-arranging
furniture and providing alternative learning spaces for students? A final question in
this section relates to the next tension and provides a link to the tension of humans
in a shared space, that is, who occupies the dominant space and 'drives' the actions
within the space?

Teacher and students, humans in a shared space

Although learners are the chief actors in the drama of learning, each Being is also a
member of a human family (Kidd, 1973) so any individual experience is never
truly just one person's experience, it is inexplicably linked to the social. Humans
are in constant interaction with their surroundings and "these interactions constitute
the framework of all experience" (Dewey, 1933, p. 36).

In reflecting on relationships with learners, qualities such as understanding,
patience and generosity come to mind. Enacting these virtues is quite a challenge
when many students in a computer learning environment insist on personal
attention. It is very difficult, as a teacher, to be *understanding* when learners are
not understanding about the demands on the teacher's time, and when they expect
and demand instant teacher-focus. It is also difficult to be patient after explaining
something to a class in different ways and then to have students want it explained
again to them, individually, because during the earlier explanations their attention
had been elsewhere while they were listening to music via an earphone, or sending
a text message on a mobile phone, or checking their email on the computer. It is
difficult to be generous when students have their own agendas (they are people too)
and seek to strengthen their position by attempting to undermine other students or
the teacher. Like it or not, learning institutions are halls of power. Hence, the
tension and the need to remind ourselves that teachers are also people.

This shared situation is spatial, temporal and social. Teachers are learners too, so, from an existential perspective, the journey of learning is a shared journey. From a physical perspective, teachers and students are confined within rooms and buildings they share. All participants are influenced by the topology of the room, the placement of furniture and resources. Teachers and students are bound by the university regulations and each has expectations of what will take place within the shared space. Members look for behaviours that will remind them that everyone is following the same script. "I share (an everyday) reality with other men, with whom I have in common not only goals but means for the actualization of these goals. I influence other men and they influence me. The everyday lifeworld is that reality in which reciprocal understanding is possible" (Schutz & Luckmann, 1974, p. 35).

The work of Paolo Freire (for example, Freire, 1972) has been influential in the field of teaching and learning, and we were drawn to his notion that the teacher should be a student among students. However, as Stephen Kemmis remarked on our 'Finding *praxis*' blog, being accepted as a fellow student by our own students requires a difficult action of positioning, and may not even be possible:

What is it that makes me seem distant from their lives, their stories? How can I find a way around or under or through the barriers that separate us? Can I assure them that our relationship is really one of mutuality, of co-learning, of collaborating in the project of their education, or will the regulatory discourses of university teaching, learning and assessment mean that we remain on opposite sides of a fence – implacably opposed in the dualities of teacher and learner, assessor and assessed?

We come into the learning situation with a past and a future that is with us in the present. Our future is what we are mainly concerned about; it contains the anticipation, the expectation of something from learning, dreams, hopes, aspirations. We are limited by the shared space we occupy and the constraints of the university system. This limitation sets up a tension. Because we conform to the expectations conventional for these shared spaces, we are able to live up to the expectations of others sharing the space. If we do not, then we risk wasting our time and theirs.

The existentials of corporeal, temporal and spatial relationships clash when teachers and students are waiting outside a room for another class to vacate the room. Together, sharing that 'waiting' space, teachers become aware that they are not students, and students that they are not teachers, and that there is a corporeal, time, spatial and relationship distance and difference between them. Newman (2006, p. 173) says "We can disrupt another person's orderly universe simply by being there." Helen wrote in the blog about the experience of waiting outside the room for the class to begin:

It is painfully evident that I am a trespasser and then I become aware of myself, my behaviour and being able to overhear their conversations, as they too are aware of my presence and my being able to hear them. If I talk to them, what do I talk about? They become the owners of the territory, they have territorial rights and I take my cue from them; it is only in the classroom that I have authority. Outside I am a person, but I carry a tag, I am a teacher and in a few minutes I will transform into being the facilitator and assessor of their learning.

The tensions that emerged as we reflected on our teaching were not limited to teaching that occurred in a shared physical space. We also work with students through distance education (DE), and there are tensions in that setting, too.

Teachers and students in separate time and space

In the distance education (DE) mode, we have experienced a unique way of relating to students in assessing their assignments without having met or taught them. Outside of face-to-face teaching, there are many related activities (such as preparation, designing the subject outline, developing assessment tasks, gathering resources, referring to texts and to the literature, student interviews, setting up online activities and contributing to online forums for students). These activities influence the relationship between teacher and students and are an integral part of *praxis*. Hence, it seems restrictive to limit our discussion of *praxis* only to face-to-face teaching and to classrooms where time and space are shared. The culture of the classroom and the behaviours within them may be the main focus of this book, but the distance education component of our teaching is significant.

Peter wrote in our blog:

I was struck by the distinction between technē – which focuses on 'what you do', compared to praxis with its focus on 'who is the doer'. It seems to me that as we prepare for our teaching we need to spend at least as much time preparing ourselves – as a sort of embodied curriculum – as we do preparing our material. Perhaps praxis is about the complex connection and interplay between the self that is teaching and the material being taught (and the students of course). Even as I write this I see the folly of not including the students in the loop, but I guess we have more direct control over the first two.

We were also aware of the effects of the policies and regulations of our university as they are played out in the relationship with students; not just in the classroom and in interactions with students in the same space, but also in distance teaching. Can *praxis* also lie in action that crosses the separations of time and space in distance teaching or is it restricted to face-to-face teaching? This question highlights once again the *relational* nature of teaching and learning, and how a kind of retreat to *technē* might be perceived as a way to cope with the tensions that arise when teacher and student must meet and interact across these separations. *Praxis* is called for, we believe, in such a tension-rich environment.

Technē experience and sincerity

Contributing to our shared blog forced us to consider our teaching, the way we approached it and what we think we are doing when we are interacting with students. *Technē* suggests that teachers are machines with numerous well-tried and tested strategies – even if these strategies also lack heart. We would like to have experiences with students that truly reflect the potential we have to act as humans when we interact with others and to attempt to understand their personal journey of learning and our role in their journey. Are we actors with a script – the script – when we are devising a lesson plan, a set structure for our teaching sessions? There is a further tension here – the tension of providing a structure versus determining what is to happen in the session.

In our shared blog Helen wrote:

> *As I put into place strategies to 'get to know' students' names as quickly as possible, I wonder what I am doing. Am I really reaching out to another human, just as I would remember a name of a person I have met socially as an acknowledgment of their self, their individuality? In social situations (where there is no assessment and no imbalance of the relationship as there is with student and teacher) when someone I have met previously doesn't remember my name, I feel slighted, as if I am not important enough for that person to remember my name. Further I want to say to students: "you are not a collective and I want to know each of you by name and to recognise your face". But is this really why? Or do I want to know their names so that when the assignments come in, I am able to put a name to the work submitted and in some form be influenced by my personal experiences with that student? Why does it make it harder to assess the work if I don't know them, as happens with distance education students? Is my wanting to know their names truly an acknowledgment of their separateness and selfhood, or is it a strategy a teacher can use to assist with behaviour management and assessment? I assume that students want me to know who they are and so, on some level, it just seems the human thing to do, to want to remember a person's name, a person who will be sharing experiences with you for a period. But is this just a technique that seems to work for giving students a false sense of your interest in them? Does it become a part of our 'bag of tricks'?*

Allied to these concerns is the moral dilemma inherent in teacher education of trying to develop, but not demand, certain values and practices that are perceived as desirable (or even essential) in teaching and teachers.

Acting morally or acting moralistically

Central to the venture that has underpinned this chapter is the tension between acting morally and acting moralistically. This is a bind that is peculiar to teacher education where we are teaching new teachers how to teach. In this position, we promote certain kinds of educational knowledge, values and practices and aim to undermine or dismiss other perspectives on teaching. We want to promote *praxis* as the foundation of good teaching. But what right have we to impose a particular form of *praxis* (our interpretation of *praxis*) on our students in their role as teachers? Newman says (2006, p. 11) we may be "laying out unwanted futures". We believe it may be arrogant and presumptuous of us to prescribe a *praxis* of our own interpretation. We were concerned that we were imposing our form of *praxis* on our students and thereby "laying out unwanted futures" or futures that would take our students on a particular path. We were cognisant of the potential we held in our hands to influence their thinking in relation to teaching, but we were equally cognisant that there might be other possible alternatives. Newman suggests that we should teach our students defiance: to question, to scrutinise and to be in a position to be heard, noticed and taken seriously. We should teach them how to analyse problems and to empower them to take these problems to others. Beginning teachers are hardly in a position of having their voices heard – perhaps they are quite the opposite, on the bottom rung in the hierarchy of roles in the profession. We recognised that we also needed to attend to this tension: to be able to regard our students as our equals in their status as persons, as Others, even while we regard them as novices in teaching. Perhaps that is why it is incumbent upon us to teach them their Otherness and their equality, by teaching them that they can defy us and be themselves, doing their best in their way.

A further consideration in the tension of acting morally or acting moralistically relates to the question of freedom. Newman (2006, p. 109) cites Jean-Paul Sartre who argued that in exercising freedom we restrict the freedom of others. In the context of our freedom to impose a particular form of *praxis* on our students, perhaps, in Sartre's terms, we thereby impinge on the freedom of students to choose their preferred form of *praxis* for learning – their "morally-committed action, oriented and informed by tradition" in their own learning. Since, as university teacher educators, we also supervise some of our students' professional experience placements (practicums), we have a further opportunity to impose *praxis* on pre-service teachers, not just in their learning but also in their teaching. Our freedom to impose a form of *praxis* impinges on their freedom to practice another form of *praxis*.

Our constraints are not the only ones that impinge on the freedom of our students in their learning and their practice teaching. We must also consider the intractable nature of university rules and regulations, the intractable nature of professional experience placement (practicum) requirements, and the intractable nature of state accreditation processes and compliance procedures. Are we seeking to serve the interests of the educational system, the politicians and the expectations derived from the hierarchical structure of schools and institutions? Are we encouraging our students to be submissive and passively accept the objectives of the school organisation? Are we 'training' students to be 'good' teachers in our model of good teaching? Are we encouraging them to act in their own best interests?

Neither we nor our students turn out to be entirely free; like them, we are constrained (and enabled) in our practice by rules, regulations and the best interests of others. *Praxis* always occurs within constraints; indeed, as we have suggested, *praxis* is called for precisely because we encounter constraints that require us to respond in conscience or in the best interests of others insofar as they are compatible with the good for humankind. As Sartre was aware, freedom is not unconstrained and acting freely is always a matter of will and conscience. In the tension between our own freedom and that of our students, Newman's idea that we must teach our students defiance seems all the more appropriate – we must teach them to do what they believe is right, in their own interests, in the interests of the others they encounter, and in the interests of humankind. If we teach them that, and if they prove willing to learn it, we may have taught them (or they may have learned) *praxis*.

Enacting praxis and explaining our practices

In the last semester of the reflective process reported here, we became more conscious of making explicit to learners what teaching decisions are made and why. We recognise now, with much greater clarity, that our students are simultaneously learning to learn and learning to become teachers. They are both learning to Be and learning to Become. In these processes they are sometimes not very confident about what is happening to them. Modelling the sort of practice we want to encourage the students to do in their future practice as teachers is by itself a good enough reason to make our teaching decisions transparent. We believe we can enable this to happen by making teaching and learning more explicit for our students, including by drawing attention to our own teaching decisions. Schuck & Russell (2005) believe that we should make learning about teaching explicit by communicating our reasons for designing activities and tasks in particular ways, based on our specific intentions for learning, and in relation to our own educational philosophies.

On our blog, Peter wrote (on this dilemma refer also to Edwards-Groves & Gray, Chapter Five in this volume):

> *A vexing issue I noted was the dilemma of a pedagogy that desires praxis for our students. The notion of praxis imbues deep, thoughtful, ethical and moral qualities, but it seems problematic when we 'demand' these things from our students. It would seem to me that a student is no longer enacting a form of praxis if they are doing it to meet my agenda. Can we, in a sense, be inadvertently promoting an artificial praxis by overtly promoting praxis?*

CONCLUDING COMMENTS

At the beginning of this chapter we said that we wanted to avoid any suggestion that we were presenting a recipe or model for *praxis* development. We said that, if we did, we would be in danger of changing the very nature of *praxis* into something more like *technē* or a product. That said, we do think that there are some characteristics or principles of *praxis* development that seem to be very important if not essential.

First, we believe that the development of *praxis* is a collegial venture. We believe our understandings and interpretations of *praxis* developed through our conversations with each other, in our blog and in discussions with other contributors to this book. And these discussions, in turn, took place against backgrounds of our own experience and the experiences of others, some of whom have long preceded us in the educational traditions in which *praxis* has its origins and in which it evolves to meet the challenges of changing times and circumstances. Even as individual action, *praxis* turns out to be a collective enterprise – the enterprise of communities of practitioners jointly committed to the development of their own practice and the practice of their profession.

Second, *praxis* is by its very nature, a kind of action. It is what is done, beyond the dispositions, ideas or intentions which may guide or orient the action of *praxis*. In this chapter, we reflected on tensions and issues we encountered in our striving for *praxis* in two semesters of our teaching careers. Some of the examples we have given may hint at the moments when we became conscious, in the action or afterward, of our action as *praxis* – as something more than 'going through the motions' of teaching. As suggested in Chapter Two of this volume, whether we did well or badly by our *praxis* will be a matter for history to judge – when the consequences of our actions might be more clearly known.

Finally, we understand *praxis* to be or to involve a reflective process that necessarily involves symbiotic consideration of theory/literature and action. Of course, these characteristics are also central to other educational processes such as Carr and Kemmis's (1986) action research and Schön's (1987) reflective practice, but, as has sometimes happened with these developmental practices, reflection can be captured and routinized, and become a form of *technē* that can be used as a bureaucratic form of control in educational situations.

In researching our *praxis* development, we found that we were, to some extent, caught in a hermeneutical bind: we were searching for 'aspects of *praxis*', but in a sense all we had access to were our acts or products – things that are more aligned with *technē*. We were trying to better understand something internal (*praxis*), by looking at something external (*poiēsis*). By recording what we might regard as evidence of our *praxis* – in our blog, for example – we risked treating it as external to ourselves, with the attendant danger that we might miss the thing most intrinsic to what we were doing – our commitment to doing the best we could under the circumstances; our actions and their consequences, not just our words about them.

Similarly, this chapter has now become a product – an object crafted according to a set of rules. Is it no more than the product of *poiēsis*, of 'making action'? Or is it the product of an act of conscience, an act of doing the best we could under the circumstances, willing that the consequences of our writing will be to enable *praxis* and to constrain the instrumentalization and bureaucratization of education? Of course, we hope it is, and that readers will understand it to be, the latter.

We conclude by asking, once again, that readers not see the activities described in this chapter as any sort of formula or recipe for the development of *praxis*. Equally, we hope we have not overly theorised our story. Our goal has been to lay bare some of our attempts to develop our disposition to act wisely and justly in our educational practice in our university teacher education program. At the very best, our efforts have refreshed our sense of what is at stake whenever we teach.

REFERENCES

Brookfield, S. (1995). *Becoming a critically reflective teacher.* San Francisco: Jossey-Bass.

Carr, W., & Kemmis, S. (1986). *Becoming critical: Education, knowledge and action research.* Geelong: Deakin University.

Dewey J (1933). *How we think.* (1998 ed.) Boston: Houghton Mifflin.

Dunne, J. (1993). *Back to the rough ground: 'Phronesis' and 'technē' in modern philosophy and Aristotle.* Notre Dame, Indiana: University of Notre Dame Press

Freire, P. (1972). *Pedagogy of the oppressed* (M. B. Ramos, Trans). Harmondsworth: Penguin.

Grootenboer, P. J. (2006). Mathematics educators: Identity, beliefs roles and ethical dilemmas. In P. Grootenboer, R. Zevenbergen, & M. Chinnappan (Eds.) *Identities, cultures and learning spaces* (Proceedings of the 29th annual conference of Mathematics Education Research Group of Australasia, Vol. 1, pp. 270-277). Canberra, Australia: MERGA.

Kidd, R. (1973). *Relentless verity: Education for being-becoming-belonging.* Syracuse, NY: Syracuse University.

Newman, M. (2006). *Teaching defiance: Stories and strategies for activist educators.* San Francisco: Jossey-Bass.

Schatzki, T. (2002). *The site of the social: A philosophical account of the constitution of social life and change.* University Park, Pennsylvania: University of Pennsylvania Press.

Schön, D. (1987) *Educating the reflective practitioner: Toward a new design for teaching and learning in the professions.* San Francisco: Jossey-Bass.

Schuck, S., & Russell, T. (2005). Self-study, critical friendship, and the complexities of teacher education, *Studying Teacher Education,* 1(2), 107 - 121.

Schutz, A., & Luckmann, T. (1974). *The structure of the lifeworld* (R. M. Zaner & H. T. Engelhardt, Trans.). London: Heinemann Educational Books.

AFFILIATIONS

Helen Russell
School of Education
Charles Sturt University, Wagga Wagga, Australia

Peter Grootenboer
School of Education
Charles Sturt University, Wagga Wagga, Australia

7. THE PRAXIS-ORIENTED SELF

Continuing (self-) education

Professional development, teacher learning and effective classroom practice are issues that have, for many years, been on the educational and research agenda and are singled out as crucial factors for attention as the political media reports on the crisis of the teaching profession. This chapter brings these issues together in a discussion which centres on what teachers learn about their teaching if the object of professional learning focuses on classroom interactions. The chapter rests on the conviction that the centre point for transforming pedagogy and understanding *praxis* is on the interactions that occur in classrooms. The moment-by-moment interchanges between teachers and students and the details of learning and teaching events reveal valuable insights about what it means to be a *praxis*-oriented teacher. The research study, its findings and the follow-up discussion being presented here go part way in offering a new direction for understanding and interpreting *praxis* in relation to fostering ongoing teacher learning and improving classroom practice.

The perspective taken in this chapter considers a *praxis*-oriented teacher to be a committed professional who consciously and continuously acts and interacts with moral integrity in an educationally right and sound way. The practical question about what this means for teachers relies on assisting them to understand what educationally 'right' teaching looks like in their own classroom lessons and how interaction shapes a culture of authentic learning in classrooms and within the professional learning communities to which they belong. This chapter does this by casting a critical, but retrospective, eye over the findings of an ethnomethodological study that investigated teacher transformation by viewing the same data through a *praxis* lens. This exercise serves to inform a deeper understanding of *praxis* development; that extends beyond the notion of practice architectures, and teaching with good intention, to consider actions made visible in the transcripts of classroom interactions.

The chapter is informed by the results of a twelve-month action research study focused on the interactive practices of teachers working in primary school classrooms with the aim of fostering teacher change. It presents one way a particular group of teachers worked to understand themselves as teaching professionals, their teaching context and their *praxis* development. This study involved five experienced teachers (ranging from 5 to 25 years experience) who were located in a range of contexts (small rural schools to a large regional centre in inland Australia). Individual teachers were assisted to systematically study their classroom interaction practices, analyse information gathered from their context,

Kemmis, Stephen and Smith, Tracey J. (2008) Enabling praxis: Challenges for education. 127-148

and use findings to work toward improvement. Examining elements of their own classroom interactions offered teachers the opportunity for critical inquiry into the role of interaction in effective pedagogy and teacher learning. The research was based on the premise that learning events (for students and teachers alike) are socio-cultural constructs. For *praxis* to be demonstrated, teachers need to be actively involved in the change agenda and be able to account for changes in their theorising and discourse.

The chapter reports the efficacy of transforming teaching by assembling information about what is, and can be, accomplished by examining the talk of the classroom within professional communities of inquiry. By making teacher-student interactions the object of professional learning through the use of transcript and/or video technology, professional learning outcomes for teachers can be individualised, and the empowering nature of classroom talk can be demystified. In this way teachers are led to a deeper understanding of what it means to be a *praxis*-oriented self; a teacher who examines and reframes their own classroom practice as he or she seeks to think and act educationally in the right and proper way.

Too often professional development for teachers has involved attending in-service days driven by an external political, economic or administrative agenda. These 'one-size-fits-all' programs are not tailored to address teachers' individual learning needs, and often overlook the details of teaching at the micro level – the level of interaction. Therefore, the application of the research findings to subsequent programs of professional learning over a number of years has proved highly informative. By making interaction the object of focus within professional communities of teachers, it was found that all teachers had the capacity to view the moment-by-moment details of their current practice more critically. This chapter argues that the intervention presented here offers an alternative approach to teacher learning which is richer and more strategic, thus, enabling practice to evolve into *praxis*.

THE INTERACTIVE CONSTRUCTION OF CLASSROOM CULTURE AND PROFESSIONAL LEARNING: THE CASE FOR IN-DEPTH INQUIRY

Classrooms are unique social sites. They provide the interactive and physical context for learning in which students become 'enculturated' into school life through their interactive encounters with teachers. Students learn the ways of schooling by participating in it. Each classroom context affords a highly complex set of interpersonal interactions which serve to simultaneously assemble the educational and social relationships between teachers and students and organise student learning. These relationships are never neutral. Classroom participants (teachers and students) come charged with their own ways to view, interpret and act in the world (Gee, 1990). Therefore, learning how classrooms work interactively offers a powerful insight into how the organisation of classroom discourse impacts on learning and teaching. It situates the construction of classroom culture and learning within the interactions (or discourse) of students and their teacher. The reciprocity between interaction, classroom culture and learning can be understood through close observation and analysis.

Similarly, teachers enter their profession by engaging in the discourse and/or metalanguage of the profession with peers and mentors, students in classrooms and with other professionals (see also Chapter Six, this volume). Continuing development in the profession involves active participation and engagement in quality professional discourse. This discourse demands certain ways of using language, certain ways of acting and interacting and the display of certain values and attitudes (Gee, 1990). Particular ideologies and cultural expectations are enacted (made visible) through school (classroom and professional) interactions (see also Chapter One, this volume). Understanding the position these interactions have in enabling *praxis* is a critical responsibility for professional development and learning.

Interaction shapes learning and teaching events; these events unfold in interaction. The significance of interaction can be outlined in terms of what is accomplished by it in classrooms (Baker, 1991). Classroom talk assembles social relationships between teachers and students. At the same time it organises and displays particular teaching and learning practices. Talk shows the power and precision of verbal and non-verbal interactions in the production of classroom knowledge and is a vehicle through which teachers teach and learners learn as the curriculum meets the students. Embedded within classroom interactions is a particular moral order which illuminates the beliefs and ideologies of its participants. For the teachers in this study, analysing talk revealed what counts as important and the interpretation of these interactions proved crucial for their ongoing development, and indeed for their *praxis*.

The literacies of praxis

Teachers learn to 'read' their educational world as they participate in the discourse of teaching through a range of contexts and texts. In fact, teaching itself, and the contexts of school and education more globally, can be interpreted as texts to be understood and analysed (Groundwater-Smith, Ewing & Le Cornu, 2003). Classrooms, staffrooms and professional development arenas can be viewed as 'texts of context'. These texts are socially and culturally constructed. They are a visible display of organised patterns of meaning constructed and interpreted in, and by, the educational world. Like any socially literate practice they are able to be read: constructed and deconstructed, interpreted and analysed.

Participation in text (or discourse) construction and interpretation along with substantive dialogue focused on teaching (with colleagues, peers, coaches, mentors, outside professionals and school administration) takes on different dimensions in different situations (in classroom lessons or in professional interactions). The texts of teaching and the literacies of *praxis* are highly contextualised and dependent on individual situations; that is, for each text, its purpose (what are we doing this for, for what moral good), its field (what are we focusing on), its tenor (who is the audience or the interactive participants involved)

129

and its mode (how are we interacting or engaging with this text) is different in each instance. Therefore, in this sense, one 'reading' of any teaching text is not sufficient because the relationships between and across classrooms or professional groups differently shape the discourse (or the texts they construct in actions and interactions). Therefore, analysing teaching texts from multiple lenses enables a more complete understanding of how these texts shape and inform the professional discourse and knowledge about *praxis*.

Praxis demands that teachers are literate in their professional texts within the domain of ever-shifting educational discourse. Therefore, understanding how the literacies of *praxis* operate with moral integrity in the educational world is necessary. To better make sense of these literacies it is important to consider the interplay and reciprocity between the meanings and knowledge brought to the teaching situation (as a text of and for schooling) and those taken from, and demanded by, the situation. Therefore, continuing professional self-education requires teachers to explore in depth their understanding of these contexts and texts throughout their careers. How these literacies of *praxis* and pedagogic knowledge are understood and constructed both individually and collectively through a range of discourses and textual opportunities require attention. The discussion presented here offers teachers a way of interpreting and deconstructing their own interactive contexts and texts.

The utility of ethnomethodology for understanding interactive contexts

Classroom talk has long been recognised as an important pedagogical feature but its place in professional learning and in learning the profession has been undervalued. In fact, interaction at the micro or classroom level is generally a 'taken-for-granted' feature of teacher development. Attention directed towards the understanding and in-depth study of everyday, commonplace, taken-for-granted or even mundane aspects of classroom life is often neglected when considering what is taken to be effective and important in professional development. However, logic suggests that *praxis* demands the identification of these 'taken-for-granted' features of classroom life if a well-balanced, morally-reasoned, richly-informed teaching profession is desired.

With the evolution of ethnographic studies, 'taken for granted' features of the ways classrooms work have been made visible. By paying particular attention to the organisation of discourse, these studies offer a powerful way of illustrating the situated construction of classroom life, literacy and culture and have enabled the deconstruction of these as 'texts of context'. Ethnomethodology, in particular, is regarded as a useful tool for understanding the patterns of interaction in a range of social circumstances, ethnomethodology shows how classroom participants interpret (hear and understand) the social and cultural dimensions of their individual contexts.

Each individual situation, or classroom, generates its own distinctive culture and its own distinctive set of interactive routines. Therefore, the 'principle of local interpretation' (Brown & Yule, 1983) needs to be theorised both individually and collectively by teachers in practice. Understanding one's own context from a situated perspective is an essential ingredient to understanding and developing *praxis*. An important premise of applying an ethnomethodological perspective to the notion of *praxis* is summarised by Freiberg and Freebody (1995) in the following statement:

> ...rather than examining one site or types of site and then describing its features as if they define interaction in and for that site, the task is to compare talk in differing sites to determine the features that are distinctive to each.

Accordingly, ethnomethodology has the potential to provide teachers with important information that leads to *praxis* development as it illuminates what is distinctive about their context and how this relates to the effectiveness of their teaching practice and consequently on-going learning about their teaching. Whilst ethnography enables the documentation of observable courses of action within a situated perspective and how these actions are understandable by the interactive participants, ethnomethodology recognises that it is principally in the talk of the classroom that teachers draw the attention of students to what features and routines of pedagogy are prioritised. Ethnomethodological studies highlight the way the social organisation of classroom activities contributes to student understanding of what learning is and how learning is achieved. Further, such studies have the potential to show how teachers and students display understanding of the classroom experience through, and within, the moment-by-moment interactions encountered.

Ethnography and ethnomethodology as research methods are often used by non-participant observers to understand participants in interaction. However, the ethnomethodological perspective can also be taken by participant observers. The case for careful observation, by teachers, of the classroom interactions of which they are part can and should have a significant role in the pre-service and continuing education of teachers. In the study to be reported here, transcriptions of classroom talk were made the object of focused thinking, dialogue and analysis. Transcripts were presented to participating teachers to give them evidence of their everyday interactions so they could explore and develop their classroom interactions to reflect on and improve their own teaching.

THE INTITIAL COLLABORATIVE ANALYTIC ACTION RESEARCH

The first phase of the study was to record and transcribe a series of literacy lessons across one week in the classrooms of five teachers. The next step was to re-convene with the teachers individually to present them with their own transcribed lessons along with samples from across the entire corpus of data (used as explanatory material). This meeting primarily consisted of an introductory presentation, informal 'reading' of their work (via transcribed or videoed lessons), a collaborative analysis of their own practice (patterns of talk) and discussion and review of the main findings of the analysis of initial classroom observations. Teachers were assisted to establish a conceptual framework for transforming their teaching, selecting a change focus, collecting and organising data, analysing and interpreting data, and taking purposive action.

In the second collaborative analytic phase of the research, teachers were assisted informally but systematically to examine their own instructional and interaction practices and routines in literacy lessons. Here the categories for focused change (see below) were negotiated and developed as the teachers examined and worked through their own lessons and a sample of transcripts from other teachers. It was found that although self understanding by analysing transcripts from one's own lessons is necessary, it is not sufficient. Using transcripts from other teachers enabled teachers to come to know themselves in relation to others within the broader context of the field.

The aim of the third intervention or collaborative action research phase was to work in the field with the target group of five teachers on a daily basis over a four-to-six week period. Informal discussions and systematic documentation, related to the main themes or categories for change (which were taken up as a matter of focused reflection and review) provided opportunities for coaching, on-going monitoring and evaluation. The direct daily feedback or debrief sessions provided formative review and were an opportunity for teacher self-assessment. One teacher, a self-paced teacher, worked independently on the intervention categories over a ten-week period with weekly phone contact with the researcher and supported by four researcher visits to the school over that period. Concluding comparative lessons from each participant were recorded over the final two weeks of intervention.

Finally, the fourth and concluding phase consisted of semi-formal interviews. These were conducted to construct an account of how the participating teachers interpreted the findings and the process of the intervention phase of the study. This linked teacher action (evident in the transcripts) to the themes emerging through the interview data. The interview also enabled a detailed description and explanation of how the teachers viewed the intervention as an approach for understanding *praxis*, continuing professional education, improving and changing pedagogy and informing personal literacy learning theories. The results offered valuable instructive insights for *praxis* development.

Transcripts as instructive tools

As one of the 'players' in the classroom context — one of the interactive participants — a teacher cannot realistically stand back and be an effective analyst of her/his own practice during a learning event. A second phase is needed, one that enables the teacher to revisit (view, hear or think about) the lesson in a focused and analytic way. Transcripts offer a practical way to closely observe the classroom context and illuminate the existing architectures and relationships. Transcripts, like video and peer coaching, are ethnographic techniques which make available evidence of classroom activity and interactivity; they can show what *really* happens interactively in classrooms, and illustrate how learning events unfold.

They are instructive because teachers can learn about their practice architectures and interactions and subsequently use this information to shape future action.

Transcripts (along with videos of teaching) are situational texts which offer teachers a forum to read, interpret and analyse the context in which they work. What is important here is that one's reality is the instructive instrument. And, just as learning from oneself is a main centrepiece for development, so too must one learn from the realities of others. In this study, further work with peers or learning partners enabled teaching as a critical focus to become the object for observation and critique. Reading transcripts enabled teachers to 'work over' lessons (transcript or even video-taped lessons) and examine what was revealed on a moment-by-moment, turn-by-turn basis.

Transcript and lesson analysis reveals what the students hear and understand in any given lesson which is indicated by student responses and interactive engagement. Student responses need to be interpreted by teachers as feedback upon which to respond. Through transcript analysis, student responses became observable courses of action displaying what students really take to be going on. This process fostered responsive teaching - a key feature of effective pedagogy and an outcome for teachers who focus on the interactive dimension of classroom life. This study illustrated that transcripts: allowed teachers to interpret, critique and analyse the context in which they work; enabled focused reflection about whether similar or different approaches might be useful for student learning in future lessons; and positioned teachers in a way that enabled them to develop as *praxis*-oriented teachers.

Specifically, what is made visible by transcript analysis is the systematic ways in which the culture and moral order of the classroom learning context is created through mutually formed relationships between teachers and students. Furthermore, what counts as meaningful instruction is revealed if the details of moment-by-moment interactions through transcript technology are critically analysed. The benefits of this process are firmly established in the testimony of participating teachers as seen in the following teacher's commentary:

> *As a result of reading my own lesson transcripts and the intervention, I now know that a lesson really relies on more than the syllabus, or the books or the activities I planned or like to do. It is more about how I interact with my students— how I engage students in their learning through my talk. I didn't realise the importance of it until I looked at some of those transcripts. I now continually listen to myself and ask "What did the kids hear?" and "Is that what I want them to focus on?*

Teacher Mr M

Talk is not only an entry into written language, it is a main way in which students encounter and learn about the ways or the culture of the school (Baker & Freebody, 1989). Regardless of what texts or curriculum documents are used for example, it is through the talk and patterns of interaction that the learning is enacted and made visible. And, importantly, transcripts offer a record and a description of what 'learning' is made accessible to the students in classrooms; they have the potential to instruct teachers as they develop in their profession. Consider below this lesson introduction where the teacher aimed to teach students about procedural texts using TV guides (as identified by the teacher before the lesson):

Transcript 7.1

> Teacher: *What we're talking about is what we did on the weekend.*
>   *Now I've already told you I went skiing and stuff like that on*
>   *the weekend as well, but, also I watched some TV shows.*
>   *Hands up if you watched TV on the weekend? (Children put*
>   *hands up) Whatya watch James?*
>
> James: *Ah, Umm/*
>
> Teacher: */Whatcha watch, Lucy? Did you watch any television on the*
>   *weekend?*
>
> Lucy: *Cartoons*

Transcripts, such as this demonstrate how talk is at the core of the interpersonal, social and intellectual relationships between teachers and students within the context of the classroom. Further, how teachers control and organise classroom interactions by directing the topics for talk or learning. For example, *"what we are talking about is what we did on the weekend"* is inextricably linked with cultural social organisations and routines of the classroom and *"hands up if you watched TV on the weekend"* indicates where the teacher nominates who has the next turn at talk. Looking at transcripts demonstrates to teachers that classroom talk is a main tool for teaching, thinking and learning. What unfolded, in reality, was a lengthy discussion about favourite television shows (lasting approximately 40 minutes) which ultimately had no clear link to the previously identified lesson goal nor did it legitimately assist students to understand the text with which they were working. This introductory transcript segment (and others like it) offered the teacher the opportunity to 'read' how the lesson intention aligned with the 'reality'.

After examination of this transcript, the teacher considered the importance of explicit orientations to the lesson purpose and was able to explicate adjustments made to teaching in subsequent lessons. The following view typifies the positive impact of teachers reviewing transcripts of their own lessons:

> *Having cooperative classrooms and being partners in learning have always*
> *been important, yet explicit teaching as an effective teaching practice is a*
> *very basic area in which this ideal has been lacking. Until I looked at*
> *transcripts of my own lessons I thought I conducted focused and explicit*
> *teaching and learning. I realised I didn't really understand what it meant for*
> *the children. No one seems to have picked up on that and that's why it came*
> *as a surprise to me that I wasn't doing it. It hit me as a powerful way of*

creating an inclusive educational environment that puts kids at the centre of the learning. We expect that children are to be partners in developing self-discipline for example, we sit them down and fully discuss expectations and implications, we allow them in on that, but I believe we haven't taken it that step further towards fully allowing them in on their own learning. Learning about my own effectiveness as a teacher in relation to explicit teaching and classroom interaction is now a fairly big area of professional development for me.

Teacher Ms Mac

This teacher recognises that focused review of one's own teaching practice (via transcript technology) enables teachers to make clear statements about the effectiveness of their own work and about how to act in an educationally right way, a feature of *praxis*. Teachers in this study redefined their view of what a literacy lesson should look like and strongly suggested the importance of this insight for all teachers. Teachers recognised that, by changing their interactive practices, they could explicitly prioritise student learning.

Transcript materials (pre and post intervention) provide explanatory and instructive information. The findings of this study not only inform the debate surrounding the efficacy of practice and *praxis* development but the examination of transcripts of teaching reported here demonstrates how a group of teachers reconceptualised their understanding of a lesson, reconstructed teaching and learning events and transformed practice. As a professional learning tool, targeting the micro-analytic level is effective in instituting changes in pedagogical practice. Teachers not only come to 'know thyself in order to understand and interact with others' (Schmidt, 2003) but they are informed and transformed by committed action, continued growth, on-going learning and inquiry.

Towards praxis: A summary of changes after collaborative analytic intervention

The collaborative analytic intervention showed that establishing a communicative space for teachers to engage in substantive, focused professional talk about the classroom context provided them with an opportunity to make significant changes to how they perceive and demonstrate what counts as effective teaching. By focusing on the talk generated in their own lessons (via audio- or video-taped lessons and transcript technology), teachers were able to observe, establish and value those aspects of their practice that were working well. Equally, they were able to recognise arenas for professional learning, growth or improvement. The taped or transcribed documentation offered an analytic basis for self-monitoring and appraisal, resulting in a motivation for growth and transformation. The challenge for individual teachers everywhere is to develop efficient tools and approaches for analysing, reflecting and adjusting practice in a meaningful, yet simple, way as indicated here:

Looking at transcripts of my own lessons forced me to think about what I am doing and why in a very focused way, something I would not normally have the chance to do. If we are serious about improving our practice then I think all teachers should reflect critically on their practice in relation to the classroom talk, especially on how they set up their lessons and about what our kids are actually learning. They need to be clear and ask for clarity to ensure students really understand the messages we are giving in our lessons...

Teacher Ms Mac

Teachers acknowledged that it is through talk that the work of classroom lessons gets done. They recognised, demonstrated and articulated their reconceptualised understandings of the interactional factors affecting student learning. Furthermore, they oriented to the highly constructive nature of the changes - they approved of and acknowledged the importance of the changes; they transformed teaching and the thinking about teaching. Teachers demonstrated changes in practice that potentially enabled the skills and knowledge of literacy and the literacy curriculum to be more accessible to the diverse group of students in their classrooms. The explicit teaching resulted in the maintenance of the literacy topic whereby lessons became highly focused on learning, and could be recruited to explain the less frequent orientations to behaviour management issues which tended to cut across learning. The main aspects of teacher learning about their own teaching are presented below in Table 7.1:

Table 7.1

Collaborative Analytic Professional Learning Summary of changes to instruction		
Features of Teacher Learning	**Description**	**Explanatory Comment and Supporting Teacher Statement: Towards a *praxis* orientation**
Teaching and learning as interactive practice	Quality interactions produce quality classroom action and activity.	Focus on the classroom interactions revealed lessons are accomplished as mutual courses of action and interaction. After time teachers valued the role of classroom interactions for successful learning. They came to view lessons to be focused learning events which rely on interactive action and supported by genuine interactions (as opposed to lessons largely being about management or talking about culturally familiar topics and textual themes). *...[teaching] is more about how I interact with my students — how I engage students in their learning through my talk. I didn't realise the importance of it until I looked at some of those transcripts...*
Explicit and systematic teaching	Shared understandings of the lesson focus and topics for talk (procedures and process) foregrounded, maintained and reviewed.	What was offered to students as the learning focus was made explicitly, and heard by the students as relating to learning about specific aspects of literacy. Learning goals, processes and procedures were clearly explicated and

		maintained. Topics of talk were centred on the lesson focus. *...I thought I conducted focused and explicit teaching and learning. I realised I didn't really understand what it meant for the children...* Behaviour management became less of an issue. *..I could see that the management of behaviour can rally run in a take way a lot of valuable time from actual teaching and learning...it affected lesson continuity for the students... now my lessons appear to run more smoothly, I guess the kids know what is going on...*
Explicit teaching as an inclusive practice architecture	Explicating the learning focus equalises the opportunities students have for accessing the curriculum.	The upfront explication of the lesson focus throughout the lesson clearly prioritises learning. This was recognised as an 'enabling' practice. *...[Explicit teaching] hit me as a powerful way of creating an inclusive educational environment that puts kids at the centre of the learning... ...letting them in on the big secret...towards fully allowing them in on their own learning...*

Engaging in critique, posing questions and seeking answers related to the details of their own teaching and professional experience led these teachers towards *praxis*. It enabled them to refine and improve the learning experiences for the students in their classrooms as they considered how interactions shaped the moral order of their classroom. It was evident that teachers do not need extensive theoretical input to change practice at the micro-analytic level of instruction; but they do need support within a context of collegiality and professional inquiry. Other studies have also reported on the significance of classroom interaction (Edwards-Groves, 1998, Freebody et al, 1995). Teachers can, through exposure to their own teaching (via transcripts or videos), reconceptualise 'what counts as a lesson'. They are able to show it in their talk in the classroom setting and in their accounts of effective literacy instruction in professional dialogue. The findings show that instruction can be improved by direct feedback concerning the details of interaction, and is accounted for in the following teacher comment:

Being able to read my transcripts and listen to my lessons on tape and discuss them in a way that focused on the talk was a real challenge. But it was so practical because it was all about my teaching. Without the guide questions [provided by the researcher] though I probably would have not gone beyond what the children were doing, their behaviour in the lesson, and maybe how well they were working. I don't think I would have thought about me and aspects of the actual teaching and think about what I was saying. It was a real eye opener. Now I know how to improve my teaching that will make a difference to kids, I know what to change...

Teacher Mrs C

The program of teacher learning reported here successfully targeted practice at the micro-analytic level of instruction. The collaborative professional development intervention used in this study lies in the way in which it draws on the actual practice of classroom teachers. A summary of the distinctive features of this intervention are presented in Table 8.2

Table 8.2

Collaborative Analytic Professional Learning Summary of features of the intervention approach		
Features of the approach	*Description*	*Explanatory Comment and Supporting Teacher Statements: Towards a praxis orientation*
Substantive Professional Dialogue	Communicative space for substantive professional dialogue is provided. Teachers (as individuals and as a collective) focus and refocus their teaching practices; they frame and reframe questions about teaching.	Having time and opportunity to enter quality professional discourse facilitates change. It enables teachers to be supported and challenged about the details of their teaching and their thinking about teaching. The opportunity to engage with other professionals enables the development of metalanguage required to generate collegiality for the collective good. Feedback mechanisms offer opportunities for teachers to uncover covert actions. ..Normally you don't have time to reflect, at the end of a day you think about the housekeeping things.... But to make the time to reflect is vital, the (research) intervention (focusing on classroom interaction) has been good, because it has made me think about realistic and practical ways to improve my practice that really do make a difference [to student learning]....
Connecting Theory with Practice	Collaborative analytic methodology provides a way of working which explicitly links theory and practice.	The collaborative analytic research methodology enabled teachers to trial learning within their own context as a means of improving practice and developing knowledge about the curriculum, teaching and learning. It worked to strengthen the relationship between theory and practice (what we do and why) resulting in improvement in what happened in the classroom and schools, and further provided teachers opportunities for seeking clarity, articulating, justifying and developing a *praxis* orientation. ...learning as professionals is an essential aspect of what we do. Teachers need to become partners in our profession and in our learning. We need to trust each other to talk about issues.. and in that way create a system of informed professionals that can discuss and debate so we can learn more about our teaching and ourselves. It is through talking and learning about our difference of opinion and interpretation that we can debate and clarify and grow and change..
Professional Learning as Interaction	Interacting with other teachers (with individuals or in groups) about areas of interest and concern takes teachers beyond their own	In their own accounts of this process of change, teachers oriented to the highly constructive nature of collegial interaction as a foundation for teacher learning and the development of the profession. Teachers developed their own

	situation to consider the profession as a whole.	theorisations about explicating the benefits of teacher learning networks when focusing on the issues and concerns of their profession at both a local and wider level. ..what I have learnt is the importance of professional discussions. Talking about these things has helped me clarify a lot of things about my children and my teaching. We need the chance to talk about [professional] issues in a structured way…
Teaching as Ethical Practice	There is reciprocity between learning about self and learning about the professional world which consider acting with moral integrity and 'right' educational practice.	Commitment to learning about and improving teaching is demonstrated. The moral order of the classroom is maintained with primacy. Learning is not just fixed within the context but also enables teachers to move and think outside the local context to consider what this means for teaching and learning in other contexts. …If we are serious about improving our practice then I think all teachers should reflect critically on their practice in relation to the classroom talk, especially on how they set up their lessons and about what our kids are actually learning. They need to be clear and ask for clarity to ensure students really understand the messages we are giving in our lessons… .. Now I know how to improve my teaching that will make a difference to kids, I know what to change…
Localising Learning	Learning about teaching and the profession is situated within the context of teachers settings (classrooms, schools, local areas). Teaching is strengthened within its situated context.	School leadership recognises, values and supports the professional space required for learning and offers teachers a local (and regular) forum for debate, dialogue and discussion about issues of importance and relevance to them as a professional learning network. Professional learning forums require a teaching focus, centring on teaching activity and learning, students and their learning and the teaching profession. …Being able to read my transcripts and listen to my lessons on tape and discuss them in a way that focused on the talk was so practical because it was all about my teaching…
Technologies for focused reflection, response, critique and review are utilised	Transcript analysis, peer observations and viewing videos of teaching enable reconceptualised understandings of what teachers take a lesson to be and to be about.	Change and redirection in teaching and understandings are possible because the focus is directly on the teacher's own teaching practices. Their own teaching becomes the object of observation, critique and redirection. Teachers 'read' their lessons and cast their eye over covert practices and make these overt.
Change Over Time	Professional learning is viewed as an ongoing individual endeavour, not addressed with a 'one-size-fits-all' approach.	Opportunities are provided for practice, trialling and focused feedback in a regular and ongoing way within a supportive and collaborative professional learning network.

139

What is compelling about the findings of this study is that after examining their own practice, the teachers recognised the need to change and went about transforming practice; they demonstrated it in their lessons and were able to recognise and articulate changes. Through the intervention, teachers demonstrated *praxis* development that was grounded in classroom action. They showed that not only does interaction shape the pedagogy, but that it serves to shape the moral and social order in classrooms. Participants in this study did not view the intervention as a 'stop-gap strategy' or a 'top-down' intervention to improve literacy practices in classrooms, approaches that appear to form the basis of many professional development programs. From the corpus of intervention data, the reconceptualisation of classroom lessons as mutually accomplished interactive events has been shown and accounted for in the theorising of teachers. This research shows comprehensively, that for *praxis* development, the relationship between teaching and learning is strengthened by professional development that aims to collaboratively target the *primordial* level of instruction.

CONTINUING SELF EDUCATION: INDIVIDUAL PRAXIS AS AN ON-GOING, SELF-EXTENDING STANCE

In this discussion *praxis*-oriented teachers are viewed as those who do not simply do 'practice' (engage in the 'technē' or the technical aspects of teaching), they have a philosophy for teaching and learning about teaching that inspires, guides and even provokes ongoing improvement, re-direction and transformation of teaching. *Praxis*, therefore, is not static or an endpoint goal, but rather an on-going dynamic and transformative process that is ever-evolving and developing. Transformation involves much more than mere change at the level of action. Transforming existing ways of thinking and doing has been described as requiring people to be convinced that there is a need for transformation (Apps, 1994, cited in Gravett, 2004). The teachers participating in the study discussed throughout this chapter were able to identify the need for transformation by analysing, critiquing and sharing their own lesson transcripts. This process involved them not only in presenting a new or desired way of thinking and doing, it also involved them in examining, enhancing or adjusting their personal reality and changing the direction of their futures (Gravett, 2004). More importantly it generated teacher action that responded to their context and circumstances in a morally right way; in order to do what was right and good for the students in their classrooms. Educational *praxis* involves the visible display of educationally right action; it is recognisable and articulated by self and others.

Praxis-oriented teachers like the ones in described in this chapter learn from their own teaching and the teaching of others; and, as they do, they construct new knowledge and form an ever increasing foundation for improvement and growth. They develop a philosophy and an approach to their own development that engenders a greater depth of knowledge about teaching and learning, pose more questions and probe deeper to address problems and seek solutions. This belief shapes their professional activity as they regulate, monitor and evaluate their own learning and respond to what they have learned with positive action. Furthermore, they articulate the benefits of change in terms of instructional talk and its impact on the students in their classroom context. In fact, the self-extending characteristic of *praxis* emerges; one that is not a culminating ideal but a self-generative approach which challenges one to keep learning, as encapsulated in this teacher comment:

It is our job to be as effective as we possibly can be. We need to be continually mindful of what we want our children to learn and ensure our teaching methods allow children to be clear about their learning, and focus on their learning. After reading my transcripts and working collaboratively on improving teaching, I realised why and how I had to change, and using the framework for presenting a lesson has helped me to do this. It is something I always do now. It has become a natural part of the way I teach and think about teaching. And it has helped me understand what explicit teaching means for the children in my class. I can never go back, now; I will always be thinking about how the talk influences the thinking and learning for the children in my room.

Teacher Mr M

Praxis is positioned throughout this chapter as an enduring and self-extending stance. Its development hinges not only on teachers having opportunities to engage in professional learning opportunities and reflect on their teaching but purports an intrinsic desire to be prudent and responsible for their own learning: to take charge and become self-regulated. *Praxis*-oriented teachers are independent on-going learners who address issues relating to their own practice which consequently provides the self-extending, professional, substantive ownership over, and commitment to, improving teaching. *Praxis*-oriented teachers have controlling power over their own interactions, action, the consequences of their actions and practical change. Once a teacher develops such a self-extending philosophy the *praxis* pathway becomes a moral imperative, as indicated clearly in the above teacher commentary.

The self-extending professional develops reflexivity which is sustained over time and does not remain within a fixed context; that is they constantly think about, learn from and respond to current and new situations and experiences. It affords opportunities for teachers to engage in responsive problem solving and provokes a climate whereby teachers are constantly adjusting and learning from their own experience, as indicated by this teacher:

Normally you don't have time to reflect, at the end of a day you think about the housekeeping things -Have I got their artwork up on the wall? Have I corrected all the maths? And then you just want to go home and relax for a while. But to make the time to reflect in a focused way is vital, the intervention has been good, because it has made me think about realistic and practical ways to improve my practice that really do make a difference... I know what I am doing, and why... I know how it affects the learner...

Teacher Mrs J

Praxis-oriented practitioners are reflective. Reflection is a strategic *praxis* action when it is planned for, instructive and followed with focused improvement to practice. Merely reflecting on teaching action or on the artefacts of teaching is not enough for *praxis* development. Reflection needs to affect practice so teachers respond to their discoveries in a morally defensible way, as shown by the public accounts of teacher change presented in this chapter. Therefore, reflection is a dynamic feature of *praxis* when it is conducted at the critically analytic level (refer also to Chapter Five, this volume). It is a *praxis* action when it assists teachers to not only think about their teaching and the issues concerning the profession, it assists them to ask questions routinely and deliberately and use the answers to their questions to challenge and guide changes to instructional practice in a highly focused way. Critical reflection enables teachers to focus and refocus classroom talk so that it becomes a principled and informed endeavour.

COLLECTIVE PRAXIS AND COMMUNITIES OF PROFESSIONAL INQUIRY

Praxis involves teachers working towards self-knowledge, self-extension and growth but importantly also involves working towards the good of the profession collectively. A strategic focus on interaction and the utility of the technologies of ethnomethodology have been highlighted in this chapter as effective ways to foster collaborative professional learning networks. These networks incorporated in-class support, focused reflection and lesson evaluation and oriented individual teachers toward specifically improving their interactive practices in relation to their own understandings of the profession.

Substantive dialogue, coupled with an orientation to collective professional development, formed a principled program of improvement that assisted teachers to make well-informed choices about learning rather than 'a hope for the best' approach reflected by one-size-fits-all programs. Furthermore, the collaborative analysis of lessons and peer observations rather than individual analysis added an transformative and instructive aspect to professional learning that held intrinsic value. As teachers observed and collaboratively critiqued lessons or transcript examples from other sites, they could transpose experiences and knowledge from their own classroom learning events (Edwards-Groves, 2003). Teachers considered how *they* would have presented *that* learning criteria more effectively or differently and could rethink how the talk could progress differently to make the opportunities for learning more effective. This proved to be a powerful way of reflecting on teaching and learning on the one hand; and on the other, it advanced teachers' capacity as critical thinkers. Such theory-practice interconnectivity becomes grounded when teachers are given opportunities to practice and trial learning activities, explore connections, and act and interact within a community of professional inquiry.

Collaborative focused reflection

Reflection which generates productive professional dialogue and connects teachers so that they can learn about teaching in a deliberate and conscious way is *praxis*-oriented action. Opportunities for focused professional dialogue, sharing the resources and artefacts of teaching, observing teaching, researching and solving problems together in a focused way enables groups of teachers to develop a 'collective *praxis*'. Collective *praxis* is a term used by Mayo (2004) to describe a group of people operating within a 'self-organising system' for growth and development. This system enables individual teachers to come together to focus on a common interest or area of concern, where patterns are recognised and investigated, individual and group feedback are welcomed and valued and group directions emerge (rather than be predetermined). Teachers, as members of a mutually supportive community of professional inquiry, therefore share in knowledge construction: knowledge about their profession. Success and enlightenment as a community of teachers learning together - a collective - generates a desire to improve and transform individual practice. Collective *praxis* development leads to individual *praxis*.

Whilst Mayo's definition opens up fresh understandings of relationships between collaborative professional development and teacher learning, the need for understanding meaningful reflection and the negotiated level of guidance that supports and scaffolds the learner through collaborative focused reflection remains a rising issue. All teachers reflect on, or informally think about, their lessons from time-to-time; however reflection is not constructive on its own. For *praxis* development it needs to be an activity which must be focused on how to act on the knowledge about teaching in the right way and more importantly the right way to interact with students and engage them in their learning. It is followed with purposeful action that affects a shift in thinking and transforms practice. In fact, the proposition here is that for the development of *praxis*, reflection needs to be learned and practiced, ongoing and purposeful.

Collective *praxis* development within a climate of positive scaffolding or coaching, focused professional dialogue and inquiry enables accelerated individual learning. As teachers are supported within collaborative learning communities they learn to articulate what they know and are thinking in order to extend their learning and professional growth. The more teachers' own perspectives and priorities are used to segue into a change paradigm (or shift in theoretical positioning), the more sustained the learning (Lyons and Pinnell, 2001). As teachers connect teaching approaches, theories and observations with their own practical issues in the classroom they gain a deeper understanding of the interplay between teaching decisions, student learning, classroom approaches and theoretical perspectives. The process comes together as teachers coordinate their own accumulated and organised understandings into a theoretical framework and system of professional, self-generative learning.

Self-generative learning is promoted through active participation within a community of learning professionals. In such a community, teachers engage in collaborative focused reflection, classroom interaction analysis, critical thinking and professional dialogue clearly centred on the details of teaching. In order to develop an ongoing, productive, self-extending system teachers require planned and systematic opportunities to work individually and within communities of professional inquiry where they work with other teachers to learn from each other.

Building a 'collective *praxis*' demands teachers engage in focused professional dialogue with others about their reflections and their teaching that enable them to develop, through use, the language of teaching. This activity is then a principled and prudent activity that fosters *praxis* development as teachers engage in substantive dialogue. They develop the ability to describe their actions and interactions, or to write about their teaching in a focused and critically analytic way so they can interpret and learn from their own teaching and the teaching of others. However, as an important matter for educational administration, teachers need 'planned for' opportunities for purposeful, relevant dialoguing to generate options for changing and transforming practice, a point identified in the following teacher commentary:

> *Learning as professionals is an essential aspect of what we do. Teachers need to become partners in our profession and in our learning. We need to trust each other to talk about issues like classroom talk, explicit teaching and effective teaching and learning practices. And in that way we could create a system of informed professionals that can discuss and debate the issues so we can learn more about our teaching and ourselves. It is through talking and learning about our difference of opinion and interpretation that we can debate and clarify, and grow and change.*

Teacher Mr M

A key feature of the community of professional inquiry described in this chapter has been focused reflection that enables teachers to work as an interactive community who learn, through interaction, about teaching. Professional learning communities aim to seek out and unravel the intricacies of teaching practice and how conscious and unconscious knowledge and ideologies bring life to pedagogical approaches in every classroom context. Importantly the professional community captured in this case aimed to develop more collaborative, articulate, theoretically-informed teachers whose shared goal was to foster learning through ongoing action research, action learning, collective knowledge construction, supported practice, robust professional dialogue and collaborative focused reflection (Anstey, 2002; Edwards-Groves 2002; Mayo, 2004).

As an approach to professional learning, collaborative focused reflection goes beyond the scope of traditional collaborative methodologies by focusing specifically on patterns of interaction and social organisations in lessons in a critical and analytic way; and its benefits are accounted for in the following teacher excerpt:

What I have learnt is the importance of professional discussions. Talking about these things [classroom talk, explicit teaching] has helped me clarify a lot of things about my children and my teaching, and I think it has made me become a better teacher. I think that as teachers we need to have the security of knowing what is really going on in our classrooms, we then can become better learners and evaluators of our own learning and our teaching. We need to have to chance to talk about these issues in a structured way...

Teacher Ms Mac

Teaching well is about building strong theory and practice links. The teachers in this study did not just think about teaching in relation to theory and practice, they constructed a complex system of learning and teaching *over time* and appeared to develop an intrinsic motivation for self-improvement and ongoing learning. Further, in learning about teaching, the teachers became constructive learners. They learned more about how to teach, what to teach, why to teach in a particular way, as they became accustomed to their context (their group of students) and flexibly responded to the transcripts of their own practice.

Teachers must have opportunities to take a step back and review their teaching in a focused way. But they also need to know *what to think about* and what to focus on in order to improve. Therefore professional development programs should primarily help teachers to interpret classroom experiences aiming to extend and improve quality in the full consciousness of what they are doing and why, and in examining the effects it is having on the students they teach. Such actions foster a language to talk about and think about teaching in a self-extending system that obliges them to question, challenge and formulate new pathways for learning and teaching.

Quality professional talk: entering the discourse of praxis

Self-extending professionals engage in substantive talk about their profession. They come to understand that classroom talk is classroom action, and moreover professional talk is professional action. But it cannot remain fixed within the context; it must lead to action, to change in teaching. Quality enters the picture when the action is focused on deepening the knowledge and skills of the profession that improve the context and learning opportunities for students. Since pedagogical efficacy probes the social cultural aspect of classroom life, it cannot be neglected when establishing a *praxis*-oriented self. It accounts for, but more importantly goes beyond, the surface level of instruction. Reflecting on and attending to the visible features of classroom lessons (classroom texts, the physical environment, the syllabus, the organisation of seating and so on) can be deceptive. In fact, focusing on these issues alone can mask the realities of classroom life. Along with an understanding of the interactions of the classroom context, a *praxis*-oriented teacher is immersed in the profession and talk about the profession. *Praxis* emerges as professional talk shapes learning and future action.

Publicly and rationally accounting for teaching action and the ways meanings are shared, understood and mutually constructed within each social context are considered by the *praxis*-oriented teacher. In this way, knowledge of the classroom as an interactive context makes the 'reading' of this recognisable context a rich and powerful forum for professional dialogue. As the teachers in this study gathered self knowledge about classroom interactions from their situated perspective they moved to a way of understanding the efficacy of teaching and the ways in which classroom life is talked into being a socially culturally defined learning event.

CONCLUSION

Teaching and learning is a complex and unique social interplay of physical, political, cultural and interpersonal influences. It is as individual as the location and the interactive participants (the teachers and students) themselves. Just as the social nature of classrooms has a critical impact on student learning, teacher learning is influenced by social dimensions within the professional-development context. Quality professional talk about the classroom context is a key factor of successful on-going teacher learning and for *praxis* development.

Learning the profession is not static but a dynamic and an ongoing lifelong process. Effective teaching and learning depends not only on what one does, but also on the depth and quality of the understandings and theories by which it is guided. The findings of the study presented in this chapter address this notion by offering teachers an interactive space to engage in deep analysis and dialogue about their own teaching. It has been argued that *praxis* only develops as an on-going self-extending stance when an intrinsic value and understanding of the ideologies of schooling, the discourse of teaching and learning, self-regulation, focused reflection and inquiry are clearly understood, enacted and articulated. *Praxis*-oriented teachers are highly literate in their profession and continually ask more challenging questions about their teaching and act on the answers in a way that visibly demonstrates a strong ethical stance; they do what is right and prudent for the good of the students they teach.

The collaborative analytic action research model presented here emphasises the importance of involving teachers as active participants in professional learning within their own situated context. The orientation towards *praxis* requires teachers to become actively involved in intentional, committed and enduring professional transformation: one that is self-moderated and evaluated as they shape the directions of pedagogy at the fundamental level of practice. By looking practically at the level of talk, teachers in this study reconceptualised teaching in light of the interactive construction of classroom life, a characteristic which acted as a springboard for focused teacher growth and development. Individual teachers made changes to their practice with firm justification. They had power over their own learning; a pivotal feature of *praxis*.

Self-education is sustained when a strong sense of purpose and focus drives classroom observations, reflections and professional dialogue. The approach presented in this chapter advocates the move beyond a one-size-fits-all model of professional learning to one of continuing self-extending professional learning; one that not only responds to individual needs or realities but offers a dynamic blend of committed action, self regulation, self generative learning within communities of professional inquiry. Substantive dialogue within these communities of professionals generates knowledge of the profession and builds on the knowledge of schooling both individually and as a collective or collaborative endeavour.

Making clear space for communicative and professional discourse needs to be given priority by school communities if the effectiveness of teaching and learning is to be addressed in a sustainable way. To accomplish sustained professional growth in schools, administrators must assist teachers to carve out time for quality professional discourse that enables focused sharing and reflection about practice architectures and classroom interactions. If such programs of professional change are supported and integrated into daily classroom life, teachers can maintain a *praxis* stance. *Praxis*-oriented teachers will always consciously act and interact with moral integrity if they can be continually renewed and energised through meaningful and productive professional interactions. Enabling *praxis* requires a visible pathway for teachers who use professional learning opportunities as vehicles for understanding the work they do both for the individual and the collective professional good.

REFERENCES

Anstey, M. (2002). Analysing literacy practice. In G. Bull & M. Anstey (eds), *The literacy lexicon*. Sydney: Prentice Hall

Baker, C. & Freebody, P. (1989). *Children's first school books*, Oxford: Basil Blackwell Ltd

Baker, C. (1991). Classroom literacy events. *Australian Journal of Reading*, (14)2, pp. 103-108.

Britzman, D. (2003). *Practice makes practice*. State University of New York Press. Albany: US

Brown, G. & Yule, G. (1983). *Discourse analysis*, Cambridge University Press

Darling-Hammond, L. (1998). Teacher learning that supports student learning, *Educational Leadership*, 55(5), pp.6-11.

Darling-Hammond, L., & McLaughlin, M. (1995). Policies that support professional development in an era of reform. *Phi Delta Kappan*, 76(8), pp. 597-604.

Edwards-Groves, C. (2002). Building an inclusive classroom through explicit pedagogy: A focus on the language of teaching, *Literacy Lexicon*, Sydney: Prentice Hall, Australia Pty Ltd

Edwards-Groves, C. (2003). Connecting students to learning through explicit teaching, *MyRead: Strategies for teaching reading in the middle years*, DEST, ALEA, AATE Sydney: Australia

Edwards-Groves, C. (2003). On task: Focused literacy learning, *Primary English Teachers Association* (PETA), Sydney, NSW: Aus

Edwards-Groves, C. (1998). The reconceptualisation of classroom events as structured lessons: documenting changing the teaching of literacy in the primary school. Unpublished doctoral thesis, Griffith University, QLD Aus

Freiberg, J. & Freebody, P. (1995). Analysing literacy events in classrooms and homes: conversation-analytic approaches. In Freebody, P., Ludwig, C., and Gunn, S. (1995), *The literacy practices in and out of schools in low socio-economic urban communities*, Commonwealth DEET; pp. 185-369.

Gee, J. (1990). *Social linguistics and literacies*. London: Falmer Press

Gravett, S. (2004). Action research and transformative learning in teaching development, *Educational Action Research*, *12*(2), pp 259-272.

Groundwater-Smith, S., Ewing, R. & Le Cornu, R. (2003). *Teaching: Challenges and dilemmas*, 2nd Ed. Nelson: Australia Pty Ltd

Lyons, C.A. & Pinnell, G..S. (2001) *Systems for change in literacy education: A guide to professional development*. Heinemann: Westport

Mayo, H.E. (2004) Toward collective *praxis* in teacher education: Complexity, pragmatism and post-structuralism. A paper submitted to the *33rd Annual Philosophy of Education Society of Australasia Conference*, Nov 26-28

Schmidt, PR (2003) Know thyself and understand others, *Promising practices for urban reading instruction*, Mason P.A. & Schumm J.S. (eds), International Reading Association Inc., Newark, DE: USA

AFFILIATION

Christine Edwards-Groves
School of Education,
Charles Sturt University, Wagga Wagga, Australia

IAN HARDY

8. A CASE STUDY OF TEACHER LEARNING

Professional development policy, practice and praxis

This chapter explores *praxis* development amongst a group of teachers engaged in professional development (typically described as "PD") at a particular moment in the formation of Australian and Queensland state policies about professional development. The chapter focuses on the activities of the group as they collaborated across their respective schools to try to orchestrate sustained, coherent cross-school professional development for themselves and their colleagues, during a time of significant educational reform. The group of teachers orchestrating these processes was known as the "Curriculum Board", and the schools from which they were drawn were described collectively as the "Future Schools Cluster".

The chapter explores the work of the Curriculum Board as a locally mandated response to a broader policy context in which the reform of public schooling in Queensland was being advocated. It describes the work of the Curriculum Board and its effects as the product of a complex policy setting which simultaneously encouraged and discouraged the orchestration of active, sustained, teacher-led professional development practices. The chapter focuses on the interrelations between Board members, and the nature of the teacher learning which transpired within the Board in the context of pertinent teacher learning policies, and the histories which informed these policies. The chapter is divided into two sections to help the reader make sense of the way in which both the present and the past inform the mutually constitutive interplay between a particular group of teachers, and the context in which they undertook their work.

The first half of the chapter describes the learning which occurred, and the work of the Board more generally, as evidence of policy support for context-specific, teacher-led, ongoing and genuinely collaborative approaches to teacher learning, and also, perhaps contradictorily, support for more technicist, economistic and accountability-oriented approaches. The data presented provides insights into the tensions evident within and across these disparate positions and emphases. These tensions are not simply the product of one specific policy moment, however.

The second half of the chapter puts these tensions in an historical context. It describes the professional development practices which transpired within the Curriculum Board more broadly in terms of historical tensions which have influenced relevant policies related to teacher professional development over the previous thirty years, and describes the way in which these tensions have been

Kemmis, Stephen and Smith, Tracey J. (2008) Enabling praxis: Challenges for education.149-170

interpreted by teachers and school administrators as they struggled to make sense of them. That is, the chapter provides insights into how teacher learning has been influenced by the broader policy context, and how these policies have served as metapractices or practice architectures (see Kemmis & Grootenboer, Chapter Three, this volume) that operated to enable and constrain the professional development that ensued.

THE POLICY CONTEXT

Australian federal professional development policy initiatives

The principal federal professional development policy initiative influencing the nature of the teacher learning associated with the Curriculum Board and the Future Schools Cluster was the *Commonwealth Government Quality Teacher Programme* (since renamed the *Australian Government Quality Teacher Programme*; see Commonwealth of Australia, 2000). This policy served as a practice architecture which provided targeted funding to support professional development in schools on the proviso that agreement could be reached between the individual Australian states (of which Queensland is one) and the Commonwealth of Australia about how such monies should be expended[1]. The Quality Teacher Programme (hereafter "QTP"), encouraged ongoing, individual and collaborative teacher learning, but it also constructed teachers in ways geared towards making them more responsive to broader, more economically oriented and managerial policy pressures.

The QTP sought to promote teacher learning in specific curriculum areas, especially literacy, numeracy, science and information and communications technology (ICT), all of which were perceived as crucial to improving the performance of the Australian economy. Such targeting reflects the influence the impact of a broader Australian Government policy, *Backing Australia's Ability* (see Commonwealth of Australia, 2001), the construction of which served as a metapractice for the design of more specific policy initiatives (like the QTP), and which exerted influence on the way these more specialised policies would be enacted. *Backing Australia's Ability* emphasised learning focused on promoting innovation and broader economic improvement. Within the framework of *Backing Australia's Ability*, teacher PD policy was to be focused more intensively on literacy, numeracy, scientific and technological skills, on the view that these were especially important for students as future citizens. These emphases were continuous with earlier policies advocating increased expenditure on these areas, and, like some of those earlier policies, included mechanisms for increasingly close scrutiny over the use of resources in general. While *teacher learning* in the QTP was described as being aimed at improving *student learning outcomes* in general, the Programme was also undertaken within a broader, more economistic framework. During this particular policy moment (that is, a particular moment in the formation or transformation of policy), reference was made to the need for students to be able to participate in global marketplaces, and to develop skills of "innovation, creativity and flexibility so students can contribute to Australia's future entrepreneurial culture and progress" (Commonwealth of Australia, 2002, p. 8). It followed that the content of the *teacher learning* being advocated was that which was considered most likely to result in national economic benefit. This emphasis on economic goals was criticised by groups like the Australian Council of Deans of Education, which championed a broader focus on what should be considered as worthwhile learning – for example, education for democracy and democratic participation (ACDE, 2001; 2004). Restrictions were built into the QTP funding model to limit how funds could be used, including restrictions on the release of teachers during school time, and on payment to employees of education systems receiving funding. In these ways, the expenditure of QTP funds was tightly managed, albeit from a distance – a situation which gained traction during tighter fiscal times (see Kickert, 1991). This broader practice architecture, dominated by economic interests and concerns, exerted influence over the expression of alternative perspectives, and encouraged a narrower technical approach to the provision of opportunities for teachers' learning.

At the same time, however, the distribution of QTP funding was also informed by considerable understanding of how teachers learn best. There was an emphasis on collaborative workplace-based learning that involved teachers in addressing their own learning needs. Teachers were encouraged to engage in learning initiatives related to their daily work practices, and involving active inquiry into the nature of the circumstances of their work (Commonwealth of Australia, 2000).

This emphasis upon teachers as active agents responsible for their own learning was not new. It was apparent in many key policy initiatives that were precursors to the QTP. These previous policies had also been sites of contestation between competing pressures, however, and those older contests also played through into the QTP and its enactment.

Educational reform in Queensland

At the state level, *Queensland State Education 2010* (QSE2010) was the principal policy guiding educational reform and the PD associated with it. As with its federal counterparts, this policy, and associated policy effects, reflected multiple and complex approaches to teacher professional development – some supportive of *praxis*-related approaches and some antithetical to them. As with the QTP, QSE2010 also included broader economistic and accountability-oriented influences alongside more genuinely collaborative, teacher-led, context-specific approaches to teacher learning. QSE2010 (Education Queensland, 2001) explicitly advocated learning related to teachers' specific classroom practices, and for teachers to be active producers of knowledge in these contexts. At the same time, however, QSE2010 was also more prescriptive about what teacher learning would be supported, focusing on several specific curriculum and pedagogical reforms which were then being developed in response to both economic and social concerns in Queensland. In particular, QSE2010 aimed to orient teachers' learning towards more "productive" teaching practices, and towards the development of curricular activities likely to enable students to participate more effectively in complex, technologically advanced societies. Finally, QSE2010 also aimed to ensure that the expenditure of resources led to measurable outcomes, typically construed in terms of narrow quantitative measures of student academic learning.

These more prescriptive emphases reflected the technicist way in which the educational bureaucracy in Queensland engaged with the findings of a large-scale study into teaching practices in Queensland public schools. Known as the *Queensland School Reform Longitudinal Study* (QSRLS), this study was informed by a detailed literature review and empirical research in over 1,000 classrooms. The QSRLS identified a need for more engaging teaching practices in public school classrooms, and whole-school capacity-building through individual and collective teacher professional development. One of the outcomes of the study was the development of a series of resources, including information packages and videos exemplifying "productive" pedagogical practices which teachers could use to generate professional dialogue around their own and colleagues' classroom practices. These resources were drawn from what were described as "Productive Pedagogies", which were desirable teaching attributes generated from the QSRLS's extensive literature review of effective classroom practices and empirically validated through its observations of 1,000 primary and secondary classrooms throughout Queensland. In particular, the QSRLS identified Productive Pedagogies as those characterised by twenty elements in four broad groupings: the *intellectual quality* of the class work undertaken by students, the extent of *connectedness* of such work to the world beyond the classroom, the levels of *supportiveness* for students, and whether or how teaching practices took into account and valued *social difference* (for example, differences associated with class, race, gender) (QSRLS, 2001). In some quarters, the identification of these twenty elements of productive pedagogies had the effect of encouraging a "check-list" approach to critiquing teaching practices, rather than the deeper exploration of teachers' practices originally intended by the authors of the QSRLS. Increasingly, when the concept of "Productive Pedagogies" was invoked, teachers thought not so much about the rich research-based critique of classroom practices that QSRLS had advocated, but a list of twenty elements which they believed they should incorporate into their classroom lessons.

More prescriptive professional development policy emphases in Queensland also arose in response to calls for a more engaging, relevant curriculum in schools. In particular, there was considerable advocacy for learning associated with a more holistic approach to curriculum, described as the "New Basics". The New Basics approach was described as a reconceptualist curriculum model which aimed to provide accessible, socially supportive and intellectually demanding learning experiences for all students, including those most economically, socially and politically marginalised (Education Queensland, 2000). The New Basics conceptualisation of curriculum was in contrast to the more piece-meal, outcomes-based Key Learning Area curricula which dominated curriculum development in the Australian states (and which were supported by the federal QTP initiative). The New Basics curriculum was assessed via project-like "Rich Tasks" which approximated "real world" activities. Knowledge associated with the New Basics was organised under four "organisers" or broad themes: *life pathways and social futures, multi-literacies and communications media, active citizenship,* and *environments and technologies* (Education Queensland, 2000). However, like the Productive Pedagogies, the way in which the New Basics was framed in policy reflected a more reductionist approach to curriculum development than was originally intended. For example, a series of specific "rich tasks", originally designed only to be exemplars of the approach, were expected to be implemented in schools trialling the New Basics approach, and were reified to such an extent that the principles undergirding them were marginalised. In a number of trial schools, only those exemplars provided by the state were regarded as "real" rich tasks. During the data collection phase of the research presented in this chapter, the New Basics approach to curriculum was being formally trialled in 59 schools around Queensland, including the secondary school mentioned in this study.

To add to this broad policy mix, there was also considerable contemporary interest in the area of middle schooling in Queensland. This took on an increased urgency with the release of the QSRLS which found that the quality of teaching practices was particularly low for students in the middle years (QSRLS, 2001).

The Future Schools Cluster

These policies had a significant impact upon many teachers in Queensland, including a group of four schools known as the "Future Schools Cluster" located in the hinterland region of a coastal community in south-east Queensland. The cluster included four primary schools, "Cresswell[2] Primary", "Merton Primary", "Laramie Primary", "Qando Primary", one secondary school, "Cresswell High", and an environmental education centre, "Chandall Environmental Education Centre". A group of teachers was charged with promoting cross-school professional development within the Cluster, in relation to the reform agenda driven by the policies described above. Because so much of the reform agenda was curriculum-based, the group was described as the "Curriculum Board" (hereafter, "the Board").

The data presented here focuses on the nature of the learning which occurred within the Curriculum Board, and on how Board members endeavoured to foster what they considered to be beneficial teacher learning for other teachers in schools in the cluster. The data is drawn from tape-recording and transcriptions of meetings of the Curriculum Board, interviews with key administrators and Board members, and observation notes relating to professional development practices undertaken in the cluster.

TEACHER LEARNING AND THE CURRICULUM BOARD: POLICY IN
PRACTICE AND PRACTICE AS *PRAXIS*

Establishing the Curriculum Board

The Board was created in response to the decision by the administrators from each of the six schools to collaborate with one another as part of a coordinated response to the broad educational reform agenda in Queensland. The response included engaging with the New Basics which was being trialed in the secondary school in the cluster, alongside the ongoing implementation of more traditional discipline-based "Key Learning Area" (KLA) curricula. It also involved promoting more productive pedagogical practices within the schools, with particular emphasis on improving the learning experienced by students in the middle years.

Initially, the principals and deputy principals from the six schools decided that representative teachers from across the schools should be approached to form a body to coordinate professional development opportunities. It was envisaged that these PD opportunities would relate to the development of a cross-school curriculum, with an emphasis on the middle years, and addressing issues pertaining to both KLA and New Basics curricula, as well as calls for improvements in the quality of teachers' pedagogies. To assist them with this work, the administrators applied for and received $AUD 27,000 from the federal QTP policy initiative.

In keeping with federal policy emphases on those KLAs regarded as most relevant to increasing economic productivity, the initial stages of the Board's development focused on the development of a series of networks across the schools focusing on literacy, numeracy, science and information and communications technology (ICT):

> The main focus of the project is the development of the middle school through teacher networks in the areas of Technology, Literacy, Numeracy and Science. A curriculum board comprising teachers from each school coordinates teacher networks and provides leadership and direction for that section of the project (Proposal submitted for QTP funding, p.1).

The emphasis on middle schooling reflected state concerns about schooling flagged by the QSE2010 policy initiative, and reinforced by the findings of the QSRLS which revealed that pedagogies in the middle years were particularly impoverished.

These initial stages of the work of the Curriculum Board bore traces of the more accountability-oriented policy pressures outlined above. Ostensibly, the establishment of the Board was in keeping with those pressures to try to promote more engaged and engaging classroom pedagogies at a time when teachers' classroom practices were under increased scrutiny in light of the adverse findings of the QSRLS. At another level, however, the establishment of the Board was a product of administrative fiat – a way in which the administrators could keep track of what was occurring in their schools, and a means of responding to central pressures for improvements in pedagogical practices. In part, this was borne out by the teachers involved:

> But they see us as an adjunct, and perhaps a way of them keeping a finger on the pulse of what's happening in the school, what teachers are actually thinking (Kim, teacher, Cresswell Primary).

Under these circumstances, the administrators were concerned to ensure that their schools were involved in the reform agenda, and they approached teachers to be involved as members of what would become the Curriculum Board. Such a response could be construed as indicative of the disposition of *technē*, rather than *praxis* (see Kemmis & Smith, Chapter Two, this volume): the establishment of the Board was an instrumental response to a particular policy setting which demanded much from schools in a relatively short period. Teachers themselves seemed to play little role in its instigation. Instead, they were positioned as the recipients of directives made elsewhere, directives which were seen to have a significant impact upon their work practices and to which they had to respond:

> Well, I think from the point of view of New Basics, we had certain things we had to do. There were these Year Nine Rich Tasks that we had to implement so we, as a school, had to come up with a way of doing that within our school setting. So [Education Queensland] Departmental requirements led to change … in our theme structure and the way we had to operate (Lisa, teacher, Cresswell High and Chair of the Board).

In this way, members of the Board were aware of and responding to pressures from Education Queensland to ensure that teachers and schools were engaging and complying locally with the reform agenda. The Board appeared to regard itself as not having a choice about whether to comply; it appeared to accept the legitimacy of the centralised prescriptions for practice. Such an approach was in keeping with policy emphases since the 1980s to prescribe the work of teachers centrally: the notion of 'teacher as technician' resonated strongly in these circumstances, and the practice architectures which were apparent seemed to constrain rather than enable *praxis*-oriented approaches.

Over time, however, there was also evidence that some teachers responded much more proactively to their circumstances:

> I was basically told I had to go and that's because there's only two of us at the Centre. I mean as Gordon has got principal things to do, I was basically told that I needed to go to start with, to see whether it was worthwhile for us to be a part of it, simply because we don't do what everyone else does. So that is the start of it, and I was given the option to say if I didn't think it was worthwhile that I didn't have to belong to the group any longer but I thought it was important (Hilary, teacher, Chandall Environmental Education Centre).

While Hilary's involvement may not have been optional initially, her decision that it was "important" to be engaged in the work of the Board revealed a more agentive relationship with the reform agenda. That is, there was evidence within the Board of more active involvement by teachers as time progressed. Consequently, within a relatively short period of time, there was evidence of both passive and active engagement with the reform agenda – the latter being most evident as teachers came to construe the work of the Board as an opportunity for growth rather than an imposition. A more optimistic and enabling approach to teacher learning seemed possible as teachers engaged more actively with the broader socio-political circumstances in which they were operating. In this way, there was evidence of both more instrumental and more *praxis*-oriented approaches to teacher learning occurring simultaneously.

As time progressed, the more instrumental aspects of the Board's work, although still evident, were challenged by Board members' desires to continue their involvement in an initiative which was seen as addressing their own needs and desires, as well as those of the state:

> I know the Board – much less so now than at the start – it was always, the fact that I think we thought that the principals had more power or more say and that they would veto any decisions, some decisions we made, or maybe that we would look to them for guidance, or that it seemed to be that we were in opposition. But I think it's evolved now – the fact that we both have got the same agenda. They have a few more guidelines, a few more requirements, placed upon them by the district office than we do (Kim, Cresswell Primary).

While engagement in the Board may have initially been indicative of little more than how a group of administrators had succeeded in ensuring that teachers in their schools were engaging in the reform agenda during a period when there were both considerable resources and pressure for reform, and to be seen to be engaged in reform, the active decision by teachers to continue their involvement also gestures towards a much more agentic response on their part. That is, the decision by teachers to continue with the work of the Board exemplified more than simply rule following, but instead provided at least some evidence of *phronēsis*, a *praxis*-oriented disposition, and a challenge to those practice architectures at the policy level which encouraged narrower, more technicist approaches.

Accounting for QTP & QSE2010 requirements

Further evidence of *praxis* was evident in the way in which teachers became engrossed in their efforts to try to promote beneficial teacher learning as the Board continued to meet. This was apparent when the Chair described how the group had been involved in a variety of initiatives to promote teacher learning within the cluster:

> And this is the form [holding it up] we're meant to have filled out, which I've been doing as we've gone along, but I went through my diary and found a whole heap of things we'd done that I had never put onto this form. So this is my attempt to put in everything we've done since our initial meeting (Lisa, during Curriculum Board meeting, 28 August, 2002).

While the compilation of "the form" was also necessary to satisfy accountability requirements associated with the QTP, it was apparent that many of the activities undertaken by the Board had not been done solely for this purpose. During the Board meeting in which the QTP form was being discussed, the Chair of the Board also took the opportunity to encourage participants to reflect upon what they had achieved to date, as a precursor to trying to determine how to continue their work in the future. These teachers were committed to trying to engage with the reform agenda.

At the same time, however, such reflection was a fraught process, and always at risk of being appropriated for less educative purposes such as satisfying accountability concerns:

> Is there the capacity to meet one of our needs to, you know, in the vein of revisiting… Can we do it as a view of where we've progressed? So having – getting people to reflect on where they were and where they are, and then in doing that they're reflecting on the productive pedagogies but it's also providing some data which is a bit thin on the ground in relation to well … where have we moved? Where have you as individual teachers moved as a result of us spending 18 months, you know, a considerable amount of effort in productive pedagogies? (Tom, senior administrator, Cresswell High, during Curriculum Board meeting, 28 August, 2002).

This comment about "data which is a bit thin on the ground" could be understood in multiple ways. It could be construed as a call for teachers to reflect on whether the work they had undertaken as Board members actually had an impact upon student learning. However, it could also be understood as a plea for data to satisfy accountability regulations within the QTP funding scheme, and within public policy in general. Furthermore, the way in which the teachers were identified as "individual teachers", rather than as a collective endeavouring to foster reform, was also indicative of how a particular notion of the person as an individual – 'the neoliberal subject' (see also Adlong, Chapter Eleven, this volume) – has permeated PD policy and practice, thereby reducing the likelihood of potentially *praxis*-oriented approaches. Finally, the comment from Tom, an administrator who had been instrumental in writing the application to secure the QTP funds reveals how accountability-oriented practice architectures embedded within the QTP policy exerted influence on the discourse employed in Board meetings. In this way, PD policy-making associated with the QTP served as a metapractice which influenced the way teacher learning was construed within the Board.

At times, the tensions between accountability-oriented concerns and more intrinsic educative concerns were palpable:

> I have seen more involvement in kids and their learning in the last couple of years than I've seen for many a day in secondary. I think there should be more emphasis on the pedagogies…you know. Why are kids interested in learning whereas three years ago they weren't? This is what the Board has done or what…? [We need] more intense survey approaches rather than a

fairly bland survey approach that we have tended to do. Coupled with fairly intense observations about what is going on. I don't think we observe classes very well and we don't have that skill [at high levels]. Now, that's not really good quantitative data, I know. I need teachers… who will tell me that the kids are going much better. But what I would really like is someone to show me that that is the case, so that I can say to the Director-General, "These kids … their critical thinking skills have gone from there to there, as a result of the program." Now I don't have that information from people here at the moment. All they can tell me is that critical thinking has improved a hell of a lot because of the approach that is adopted. And I'm not sure that I really know what that means if I am trying to convey the success of the Board (Andy, senior administrator, Cresswell High).

While there was considerable emphasis on student learning for the sake of student learning, and of an intrinsic desire to see improvements in such learning, there was also much emphasis on the need to satisfy calls for accountability. In this instance, it was the desire to be able to satisfy the concerns of the Director-General of Education which served as perhaps the most significant motivator for one of the senior administrators in the secondary school in the Future Schools Cluster. Furthermore, it was "good quantitative data" which was valued, rather than what was construed as the more 'subjective' qualitative indicators of student learning then available from the teachers involved. Such concerns about accountability have a considerable heritage (outlined briefly in the second part of this chapter) and have steadily gained traction since the 1980s in policy and practice. They also have the potential to distract educators' attention from more *praxis*-oriented approaches to teacher and student learning.

The extent to which members of the Board were actually able to foster *praxis* – morally-committed action oriented and informed by educational traditions – was also made problematic by the restrictions on the use of QTP funds and the Board's responses to these restrictions. The result was advocacy for and the dominance of "one-off" teacher professional development days that were not part of a deliberate, designed, developmental program of professional learning for teachers. There were several instances when such disjointed learning initiatives were considered appropriate simply because they were seen to comply with the regulations about the use of QTP funds, which included limits on the funds used to release teachers during school time, and which prevented Board members from paying Education Queensland employees. When the suggestion was made by a Board member who wanted to provide funding for the release of a teacher in a local Education Queensland school who was recognised as an exemplary curriculum planner, the response reflected the influence of the QTP policy regulations, and how members complied with these restrictions:

Well, I was really looking for outside people. Now, that's not to say that classroom people aren't doing good things. But because I was, in my head thinking, QTP funding, this is a really good opportunity to invite a lecturer from wherever, who has good information and does a workshop on... (Lisa, during Board meeting on 7 Feb., 2002).

The result was the continuation of traditional one-off workshops and a lack of coherence across the PD experienced by teachers. In this way, more *praxis*-oriented approaches were limited and substantive teacher learning oriented towards student learning struggled to gain traction. The practice architectures of the QTP policy bore heavily upon the decisions made by Board members, as did the history of reliance on "one-off" PD days as the dominant mode of professional development in schools.

Similarly, during the concluding stages of a later Board meeting, the suggestion was made to purchase an on-line software package, "e-learner" – a program designed to assist teachers in developing lessons – simply because it would satisfy restrictions on the way in which QTP funds could be utilised:

> I mean, the reason I suggested it is that we were struggling with the legitimate expenditure of funds. I think we can all think of lots of ways to expend $4,000, but do they meet the criteria that we have to meet? (Lisa, during Board Meeting on 28 Aug. 2002).

Again, complying with the accountability requirements of the QTP diverted Board members from developing a more sustained approach to teacher learning. Under such circumstances, cultivating a disposition of *phronēsis* proved difficult, and under these circumstances, the development of *praxis* might remain elusive.

Finally, in spite of decades of policy advocacy for more sustained, rigorous inquiry-oriented approaches to teacher learning, including within the QTP and QSE2010, there was also evidence of how such learning could be sidelined by conflicting pressures and practice architectures embedded within policies. A suggestion was made by a visiting academic that Board members should systematically document what they were doing as part of the process of reflecting upon and critiquing their practice:

> Lauren: If someone's got a really good idea, or they're trialling something around assessment, that then gets documented and that's fed back to the big group. Then you've got a really good record for an action research project.
>
> Lisa: Any further information?
>
> Ted: Just, ummm, what do teachers need to bring on the day?...
>
> (Combined meeting of academic advisers, Curriculum Board and Cresswell High Curriculum Committee, 7 Dec. 2001)

The way in which the value of action research was marginalised by more administrative procedures and concerns reflects how the more active learning typical of a *praxis*-oriented approach is fragile in schooling contexts. Substantive PD could be construed as more of an "absence" rather than a "presence". Although policy initiatives like the QTP and QSE2010 expressly support more active engagement in collaborative, workplace-based learning by teachers, other parts of these same policy initiatives undermine that support – for example, some of the particular restrictions on the use of funds and requirements to produce certain kinds of reports on what schools have achieved in terms of improved student learning outcomes. Under such circumstances, teachers struggled to resist those cultural-discursive, socio-political and material pressures which emphasise more technical and technicist approaches and dispositions.

Exploring the nature of collaborative practices

Nevertheless, and at the same time, there was also evidence of more *praxis*-oriented approaches to teacher learning as a result of QTP and QSE2010 policy advocacy for inclusive interactions between teachers. The Board made efforts to ensure its membership was always properly representative of each of the six schools in the cluster, as prescribed in the QTP proposal, despite the work-related pressures that made full representation difficult to guarantee. Efforts to maintain a robust membership were evident – a propensity towards *praxis*. For example, when a deputy principal from one of the primary schools, who had originally been involved in helping to foster the idea of the Curriculum Board, left the school to take up another appointment at a neighbouring school, a Year 7 teacher from the school agreed to attend the meetings:

> He was transferred out and on his leaving I said, 'Okay, I would take over.'
> And that basically was my first little experience (Barb, early-stage Board member and teacher at Merton Primary).

This person's involvement in the Board also provided examples of how a more *praxis*-oriented disposition could exert influence in other ways as well. As a new member of the Board, she emphasised the need for teachers to continue to focus upon their own learning. She was an experienced teacher with a wide repertoire of skills in the classroom and a well-developed sense of constructive collegiality; she also believed that teachers should engage in sustained critique of and inquiry into their practice – something she saw as central to her own identity:

> For me, see I'm the sort of person that I believe I can never stop learning (Barb).

Other members of the Board saw the value of having such a member as part of the group. They were open in engaging with Barb during the initial stages of her involvement:

> Well, they've always been open in providing – and initially for example, I would say to Lisa, "What the hell are you talking about?" And she would fax me what was there. Then when they came on board with her sending emails and things, you know, if there was anything needed through that, I would be able to do that. If I wanted to go into anything further, well then I could ring

or just email the bird that was at Laramie and say ... "What have you got, Liz?" (Barb)

At the same time, however, there was also evidence of resistance to a more *praxis*-oriented disposition regarding pedagogical issues associated with the reform agenda. This was apparent when Barb sought to explain how she and her colleagues had approached the reform agenda in her school:

> Barb: Well, Dana [teaching partner] and I are attacking it from the viewpoint of ... we've got outcomes, we've got the outcomes. And we've been doing Rich Tasks per se for years. What we're doing now is having a look at how the Rich Tasks we do fit in with the New Basics concept, because our feeder school is New Basics...Dana's written the task and I think they're a bit – you're doing this [points to documentation], so I just worked on the matrix, just as a start.

> Lisa: The Year 7 to 9 meeting is at the reading recovery room of the Cresswell Primary school...

(Curriculum Board meeting, 24 April, 2002)

Instead of engaging with this teacher about the way the reform agenda was being approached in her school, Lisa responded by turning to administrative matters like organising upcoming meetings. In such ways, more active engagement with their own learning was sometimes resisted within the Curriculum Board. In this instance, administrative matters constrained rather than enabled *praxis*. In these ways, the material-economic, socio-political and culturally-discursive practice architectures enabling *technē* and constraining the disposition towards *phronēsis* shaped not only the actions but also the self-understandings of Board members as organisers responsible for orchestrating the professional development of others in their schools.

Teacher learning for student learning

In spite of this, there was at least some evidence of the influence of a focus on student learning, and how being a member of the Board was construed as having a positive impact upon student learning:

> I think it's ... I think overall it [membership of the Board] probably does improve the standard of work, that's what I've seen just this year so far with these ones, because I've changed what I do. They're actually working to a higher standard overall ......than what I would normally expect of Year Sevens at this stage in the year; [with] the ones this year, just because we've changed our approach, you're actually getting better work ... and we are getting tougher on our standards (Kim).

The point about teachers "getting better work" was important because it resulted from specific changes prompted by the Curriculum Board. Teachers were expecting more from their students, and the students were delivering on these expectations with improvements in standards. In part, such responses reflect how policy metapractices can contribute to the development of practice architectures in teacher learning which encourage teachers to be actively involved in assessing their needs within their own specific contexts, and to act to redress identified shortcomings.

This emphasis on student learning also enabled some teachers to become more discriminating about the success of some of their activities arising from involvement in the Board, and where they needed to continue to focus their efforts:

> My thinking is that when you're looking assessment-wise, you can only get out what you put in, and so for us here, these two years have been a time of learning, a time of growth, a time of experimentation. Our assessment practices lag behind our planning expertise but we can't get the assessment up until we get the planning up. So, if we're looking at outcomes from kids' work, I don't know that we yet have that data to say, "Yes, this worked for the kids." We can certainly see from the end product of units of work that the kids have been able to articulate – "What have you done? Why have you done that? What does that mean?" They've been able to articulate that, and thinking about the presentation of the Year Seven students using skills like PowerPoint presentation – they've got a number of skills there, and are motivated pretty well (Cilla, Board member and teacher, Qando Primary).

There was considerable evidence of members of the Board grappling with the nature of the learning their students were experiencing, and being reflective about whether the work they were engaging in as Board members was influencing student learning. The critical comments about assessment practices lagging behind planning skills reflected evidence of a *praxis*-oriented disposition, as did the ability to point to some evidence of improvements in student learning in the knowledge that the evidence for such learning was incomplete. In these ways, there was at least some proof of members of the Board being the serious learners that teachers were encouraged to be in the relevant policies, but there was also evidence of the need to go further.

CONTEXTUALISING PROFESSIONAL DEVELOPMENT POLICY:
PRACTICE AND *PRAXIS*

In many ways, the tensions experienced by these teachers were a reflection not only of the interplay between specific policies, policy contexts, individuals and groups in which they were undertaking their work. The tensions were also a reflection of the specific historical conditions which influenced these policies and contexts, and of the ways in which teachers and administrators in schools have responded to this policy heritage. That is, the specific practice architectures within which members of the Curriculum Board and the Future Schools Cluster more generally were operating were not simply those associated with the material-economic, socio-political or discursive structures or practice architectures apparent in the QSE2010 and QTP policy initiatives alone. Instead, these practice architectures were influenced by previous policy 'pushes' for particular types of professional development during earlier and sometimes very different policy moments. In each of these moments, more *praxis*-oriented approaches to teacher PD have existed alongside systemic pressures antithetical to such approaches. In some periods, these *praxis*-oriented approaches have been marginalised by broader systemic pressures; in others, *praxis*-oriented approaches have been in alignment with and informed the way in which the state has construed teacher learning.

This section provides a brief account of some of the earlier moments in Commonwealth and state professional development policy formation which influenced the current policy setting, previous and current practice architectures, and, in consequence, the work of teachers in schools. Such a genealogical approach helps to make sense of the work of the Curriculum Board and the Future Schools Cluster whose members engaged with a particular set of historically-informed practice architectures which simultaneously enabled and constrained more *praxis*-oriented approaches to teaching and teacher professional development.

The *Schools in Australia Report* (ICASC, 1973) was perhaps the first federal policy which emphasised the need for teachers to engage in meaningful professional development in Australia. The *Report* served as a significant metapractice of educational design for future professional development practice. Known as the "*Karmel Report*", after its principal architect, Peter Karmel, an economist and university Vice Chancellor, it has had a long-standing influence upon the way teacher learning provision, and educational reform in general, have been framed in subsequent policies and practices. The *Report* gave special emphasis to the professional development of teachers – teacher learning. Such learning was considered of most value when it was instigated by individual teachers themselves and systemically supported by the state (ICASC, 1973). The *Report* advocated both long-term individual and collaborative learning. These emphases have persisted in subsequent policies, including the QTP policy which in turn influenced the local work of the Curriculum Board.

The *Karmel Report* recognised that it was insufficient to conceptualise teachers' learning needs only in terms of knowledge they did not possess, or only in terms of knowledge that would be immediately applicable to their specific teaching contexts. While traditional short courses and conferences were used to transmit knowledge teachers may not have possessed, and which may have been perceived as of immediate practical benefit by those involved, it was also recognised that on their own, such initiatives were inadequate. These approaches were described as:

> ... someone else's diagnosis of what [the teacher] requires. Consequently, there is a need for other approaches which move outwards from the teacher's own experience and are based on his [sic] own developing conception of what it might mean to be a competent practitioner. Such alternatives recognise that while some teachers are obviously more skilled than others,

there is no single pattern to which good teachers conform. The objective of this approach to growth is to help the teacher become progressively more sensitive to what is happening in his classroom and to support his efforts to improve, assisted by theoretical studies arising from his need as he perceives it (ICASC, 1973).

This perspective emphasised teachers' engagement in fostering their own learning, the content of which would be determined by the specific needs of teachers, as they construed them. The advocacy of such principles reflects a more *praxis*-oriented disposition towards teacher learning than is often the case in practice. Such tensions were apparent on those occasions when members of the Curriculum Board engaged in teacher learning oriented towards their own needs as they perceived them.

The approach to teacher learning presented in the *Karmel Report* reflected a much more social democratic, *praxis*-oriented, and potentially emancipatory, ethos which pervaded public policy-making in its time. Such emphases have left their traces in subsequent policies, including the QTP, but are even more apparent in the QSE2010 and policy effects such as advocacy for more engaged, contextually-responsive approaches to curriculum and pedagogy. The conception of professionalism advocated in the *Karmel Report* was one which framed teachers as able and willing to take and make decisions about what was in their best interests and the best interests of their students. Arguably, however, these more social democratic emphases in the *Karmel Report* have since been challenged by more neoliberal emphases which currently resonate through both federal and state policies pertaining to teacher PD. Such contested positions within policies reflect the changing balance of influence of more and less dominant practice architectures at particular moments in time.

Changing times, changing approaches to teacher PD

The QTP and QSE2010 policies, and the ways they played out in practice in the Future Schools Cluster, also reflected the influence of earlier policies and contexts antithetical to *praxis*-oriented traditions. The practice architectures of the post-Karmel era often did not foster open engagement and active modes of learning amongst teachers. The gradual disassembling of the Bretton Woods agreement (that in 1944 established an international monetary system with exchange rates fixed in relation to gold and the US dollar), accelerated by the OPEC oil crisis of 1973, meant the mid to late 1970s was a period of increasing fiscal restraint. Against such constraints, government support for teacher learning decreased. Further substantial changes to the public sector occurred through the 1980s, as public administration was increasingly influenced by private enterprise management models, with their emphasis upon improved efficiencies (Pusey, 1991; Yeatman, 1990). These practices are often described as the "new managerialism" (Yeatman, 1990) and they became increasingly dominant to the practice architectures of public policy, despite the influence of hybrid versions of corporate managerialism – such as that espoused by Wilenski (1986), a key Labor bureaucrat at the federal level – which sought to maintain more supportive social democratic practices, while at the same time addressing concerns about efficiency and effectiveness. The increased influence of corporate managerialism resulted in a vacuum in support for the provision of teacher learning as expenditure on teachers' learning was not seen to be a priority in the harsher, post oil-crisis era. The result was considerable discontinuity around PD issues, which has also played through subsequent policies and the practice architectures to which they have contributed (and which have reflexively influenced them).

Early economism

By the late 1980s this lack of emphasis upon PD practices was partially challenged when the federal government again made funds available for reform-oriented teacher learning. More restricted than the measures outlined in the *Karmel Report*, this later support was premised, in part, upon specific concerns to ensure that teacher learning fostered student learning which was perceived as providing students with the knowledge and skills to enable them to contribute to improved economic performance when they entered the workforce. This was but one indicator of the narrower, economistic paradigm on the ascendant amongst policy-makers. An example of how such economistic emphases have played through later reforms is the way, in the case presented here, the Curriculum Board was originally construed as a body to promote teacher learning in curriculum areas deemed most likely to contribute to economic improvement.

Perhaps the most prominent policy associated with teacher PD in the late 1980s was the Commonwealth Schools Commission's *In-Service Teacher Education Project* (ITEPC). While there was an emphasis upon *praxis*-oriented and more emancipatory approaches to teacher learning, the content of this policy also revealed concerns about narrower, more economistic matters. In particular, the policy was influenced by contemporary concerns about workforce flexibility. It contained arguments in favour of educating a more diverse student population to utilise new technologies and media, and to be able to respond to the constant changes in the world of work, in order to improve economic productivity (ITEPC, 1988). In some ways, the *In-Service Teacher Education Project* was a harbinger of later, more intensive scrutiny of resource utilisation, greater competition among educational systems, states and countries, growing demand for higher quality of service, and increasing demands from the community to be accountable for expenditure in all areas of educational spending and for ensuring that education delivers what are perceived as desired results (Smyth, 2001). Again, the effects of the practice architectures informed by such positions were evident in the way members of the Board struggled to sustain a more *praxis*-oriented disposition in the face of calls to be accountable for resources.

Teachers as researchers

The PD associated with the Curriculum Board also bore traces of earlier policy support during the early 1990s for teachers to be engaged as researchers of their own practice. The *National Schools Project* was a particularly notable initiative which sought to address the educational needs of teachers in a much more systematic manner than many previous policies. The *Project* was designed to align teachers' learning with a research program concerned with how best to promote beneficial organisational restructuring and change (Ladwig & White, 1996). It was premised upon creating working relationships between teachers and academics, aimed at enabling teachers to take a more active, research-oriented stance to their own learning to take the circumstances and needs of their local contexts into account in their teaching. In short, *the National Schools Project* supported the disposition of *phronēsis* and the development of educational *praxis*.

The design of the *National Schools Project* had a significant impact upon the practice architectures within which teacher PD was practised. The project resulted in the development of the *National Schools Network* (NSN) and the *Innovative Links between Universities and Schools for Teacher Professional Development Program (Innovative Links)*. These initiatives were designed to contribute towards systematic and systemic education reform (Angus, 1996). Both the NSN and *Innovative Links* emphasised collaboration amongst educational partners. The NSN was designed to better understand the link between the organisation of teachers' work and student learning, as a precursor to assisting teachers to improve their teaching (Sachs, 2003). The emphasis was on teachers being involved in action research projects to determine factors inhibiting schools from engaging in renewal. The *Innovative Links Program* forged connections between schools and teacher education faculties in universities as a means of fostering teacher learning for renewing teacher professionalism (Sachs & Groundwater-Smith, 1999). Part of the purpose of the *Program* was to promote whole-school reform by advocating the development of learning communities, which embraced students, teachers and academics as learners (Yeatman & Sachs, 1995). Traces of this earlier policy heritage have filtered through into current policy and practice, as is revealed in the case presented in this chapter by those instances of more active engagement by Curriculum Board members in their own learning, and advocacy for more substantive learning and for action research within the cluster.

Neoliberalism, individualism and PD

The Curriculum Board struggled to embrace the substantive elements of this earlier and more overt policy advocacy for more substantive teacher learning practices, however. Their struggle reflects the shifting pressures which shape practice architectures which frame teachers' work. While the QTP and QSE2010 policies explicitly advocated teachers' engagement in more substantive learning for educational reform, these messages were often drowned out by the more neoliberal and managerialist approaches to PD which gained traction during the 1990s and continue to exert influence today.

The emphasis upon more neoliberal and managerialist ideals threatened the co-operation sought in earlier initiatives like the *National Schools Project* and the *Karmel Report* despite the subsequent influence of those earlier policy initiatives. The dominance of these economistic and neoliberal tendencies was evident in the complex and patchy ways teachers engaged with substantive learning initiatives in the Curriculum Board and the Future Schools Cluster. The work of the Board was an example of part of a broader devolutionary process in which governments have devolved responsibility to teachers, but within narrowly defined parameters. Such an approach constitutes a particular set of practice architectures aimed at ensuring state control, albeit from a distance (Kickert, 1991). This is the hallmark of a managerial regime which seeks to place tight strictures upon resources, whilst simultaneously increasing pressure for reform.

At the same time, and in apparent contradiction to increased control on the part of the state, an increasingly neoliberal agenda, usually termed "economic rationalism" in the Australian context, has resulted in the retreat of government support, and an emphasis on individual responsibility (Pusey, 2003). Neoliberalism has subverted the principles of the welfare state not by encouraging a laissez faire ethos or the unfettered individualism of the nineteenth century, which was relatively unencumbered by the state apparatus, but rather by actively advocating a particular type of government which constructs the individual as responsive to the changing needs of the fast-capital state (Rose, 1999; see also Adlong, Chapter Eleven, this volume). Neoliberalism is premised upon the assumption that all participants in processes of government are "opportunistic egoists" (Painter, 1997, p.153) who strive to satisfy their own individual needs rather than those of the society as a whole. Policy initiatives designed to control the behaviour of these "opportunistic egoists" thus include practice architectures aimed at restricting the activities of those upon whom they have an impact, - as evidenced in the more managerialist regime encountered by the Curriculum Board as it implemented the QTP and QSE2010.

These neoliberal and managerial emphases have been further complicated over the last decade in Australia by increased 'ministerialisation' (greater control by Government ministers of the departments for which they are responsible), expressed in the increased politicisation of policy production. This more muscular and direct control has been exerted as pressure has increased to ensure public funding is utilised expeditiously, usually in narrowly-targeted and outcomes-oriented ways, in more uncertain times (Knight & Lingard, 1997). In relation to the provision of teacher learning, this has meant a narrowing of the kinds of learning initiatives considered worthwhile by policy-makers and a tendency to downplay the value and validity of teacher learning that was regarded, in the era of the *Karmel Report*, as valuable for its own sake and for the sake of the professionalism of teachers in general. In many instances, teacher professional development for its own sake became an "absent presence" in both policy and practice. This was also evident in the case discussed here, in the somewhat sporadic way in which teachers engaged in substantive learning in the professional development opportunities and activities created by the Future Schools Cluster.

In this section, we have seen how several conflicting principles co-exist in changing and contested balances in the heritage of current policies. Each set of principles, in its own way, influenced the practice architectures that shaped teacher professional learning and professional development. Traces of each are found in current policies, having more or less influence in the ways teacher learning is currently designed and practised. These principles form part of the contested tradition of professional development policy in Australia, and are played out in a similarly contested and complex manner in teacher development practice. The result is approaches to teacher learning in which *praxis* is both enabled and constrained.

CONCLUSION

While the case study of the Curriculum Board has provided evidence of *praxis*-oriented approaches to the way in which PD policy is enacted in practice, it has also indicated that this can be difficult work. In large measure, the difficulty of the work lies in its being an intimate local manifestation of a wider context in which teachers made efforts to enact *praxis*. *Praxis*-oriented approaches and the learning opportunities and activities fostered by the Curriculum Board reflected not just the reactions of an aggregate of atomistic individuals who were responding to state-endorsed policies supportive of educational reform. Rather, they were indicative of a particular set of practice architectures which influenced and were influenced by the particular policy settings in which they evolved, and by the way in which individuals and groups responded to them. Importantly, these particular practice architectures bore the traces of the influence of previous policies and practices. The local and contemporary struggle for *praxis* observed in the Future Schools Cluster was described in terms of an historically informed, mutually constitutive relationship between the broader socio-political, material-economic, and cultural-discursive practice architectures within which practice was undertaken, on the one hand, and, on the other, the individuals and groups who influenced and were influenced by these structures. The policy heritage of contemporary teacher professional development policies is expressed in the understandings and self-understandings of the teachers involved in the professional development practices of the Future Schools Cluster, as in thousands of other settings around Australia. It is carried in the discursive arrangements that allow people to understand themselves as people of a particular kind, doing work of a particular kind, in the activity-structures that enable and constrain particular kinds of work and professional development activities, in the rules and arrangements governing the use of resources, and in the social arrangements that bind teachers in schools to wider social, administrative and political arrangements.

In part, the result of these mutually constitutive relationships, within a complex and contradictory moment in the history of professional development policy and work, was the initial establishment of the Board as little more than a reactive response to a plethora of state-endorsed reforms. Furthermore, there was also evidence of instances of superficial engagement in teacher learning by members, rather than the active, interrogative identity position encouraged by a truly reflexive stance, or a disposition towards *phronēsis*. However, and at the same time, the Board also served as an opportunity for some teachers to come together and collectively consider the nature of the learning experienced by their students, and within their respective schools more broadly, thereby in fact altering the nature of the learning some teachers and students experienced. There was also some evidence of members striving to understand the nature of the reforms in which they were participating, and to promote an inclusive and critical inquiry community. The Curriculum Board was a policy response which did foster worthwhile learning for some members, some of the time, as it served as a mechanism for informing teachers about the complexity of the educational reform process in which they were engaged.

Given the evidence of the need to "recover" *praxis* outlined in Chapter One of this volume, it is important to flag instances of active and engaged teacher learning, and the conditions under which such approaches might be enabled or constrained. There is clearly a need to explore further those occasions when such *praxis*-oriented learning is evident, albeit cautiously and in the knowledge that while specific instances of teacher learning may be promising, they are rarely unproblematic. Rather, they are always and everywhere influenced by local and broader policy settings in which they are developed, and by the peculiar policy (and practice) heritages which have informed these policies, and the practice architectures of which they are a part, and to which they have contributed. Being cognizant of this complexity will assist in promoting resilience to combat the disappointments and conflicts which invariably arise when engaging in this important work, and for forging opportunities for the promotion of *praxis*-oriented teacher learning now and into the future.

NOTES

[1] Such agreements are possible because, in Australia, the states expend the majority of their educational budgets on teachers' salaries and physical infrastructure, resulting in relatively little funding being available for teacher professional development. In this way, QTP funding represents a significant point of leverage of the Commonwealth over the states.
[2] Pseudonyms are used for the names of all schools, teachers and other participants in this study.

REFERENCES

ACDE. (2001). *New learning: A charter for education in Australia*. Canberra: Australian Council of Deans of Education.
ACDE. (2004). *New teaching, new learning: A vision for Australian education*. Canberra: Australian Council of Deans of Education.
Angus, M. (1996). Award restructuring in schools: Educational idealism versus political pragmatism. In T. Seddon (Ed.). *Pay, professionalism and politics*. (pp.117-152). Hawthorn: Australian Council for Educational Research.

Commonwealth of Australia (2000). *Commonwealth quality teacher programme.* Canberra: Department of Education, Training and Youth Affairs.

Commonwealth of Australia. (2001). *Backing Australia's ability: An innovation action plan for the future.* Canberra: Department of Education, Science and Training.

Commonwealth of Australia. (2002). *Teachers for the 21st Century: Making the difference.* Canberra: Department of Education, Science & Training.

Education Queensland (2000). *New basics project technical paper.* (pp. 1-125) Brisbane: Education Queensland.

Education Queensland (2001). *Queensland State Education 2010* (QSE2010). State of Queensland: Department of Education.

Fullan, M. (2003). *Change forces with a vengeance.* London: Routledge Falmer.

ICASC - Interim Committee for the Australian Schools Commission (1973) *Schools in Australia.* Canberra: Commonwealth of Australia.

ITEPC - Inservice Teacher Education Project Committee (1988). *Teachers learning: Improving Australian schools through in-service teacher training & development.* Canberra: Commonwealth Department of Employment, Education & Training.

Kickert, W. (1991). Steering at a distance: A new paradigm of public governance in Dutch higher education. Paper presented at *European Consortium for Political Research.* University of Essex.

Knight, J. & Lingard, B. (1997). Ministerialisation and politicisation: Changing structures and practices of australian policy production. In Lingard, B. & Porter, P. (Eds.) *A national approach to schooling in Australia.* (pp. 26-45) Australian College of Education, Canberra.

Ladwig, J. G., & White, V. (1996). Integrating research and development in the national schools network. *Australian Journal of Education, 40*(3), 302-310.

Painter, M. (1997). Reshaping the public sector. In B. Galligan, I. McAllister & Ravenhill, J. (Eds), *New developments in Australian politics.* (pp. 148-166). South Melbourne: Macmillan.

Pusey, M. (1991). *Economic rationalism in Canberra: A nation-building state changes its mind.* Melbourne: Cambridge University Press.

Pusey, M. (2003). *The experience of middle Australia: The dark side of economic reform.* Cambridge: Cambridge University Press.

QSRLS. (2001). *The Queensland school reform longitudinal study* (QSRLS). State of Queensland: Department of Education.

Rose, N. (1999). *Powers of freedom: Reframing political thought.* Cambridge: Cambridge University Press.

Sachs, J. (2003). *The activist teaching profession.* Buckingham: Open University Press.

Sachs, J. & Groundwater-Smith, S. (1999). The changing landscape of teacher education in Australia. *Teaching & Teacher Education, 15,* 215-227.

Smyth, J. (2001). *Critical politics of teachers' work: An Australian perspective.* New York: Peter Lang.

Wilenski, P. (1986). *Public power and public administration.* Sydney: Hale and Iremonger.

Yeatman, A. (1990). *Bureaucrats, technocrats, femocrats: Essays on the contemporary Australian state.* Sydney: Allen & Unwin.

Yeatman, A. & Sachs, J. (1995). *Making the links: A formative evaluation of the first year of the innovative links project between universities and schools for teacher professional development.* Perth: Murdoch University

AFFILIATION

Ian Hardy
School of Education,
Charles Sturt University, Wagga Wagga, Australia

JANE WILKINSON

9. LEADERSHIP PRAXIS IN THE ACADEMIC FIELD

A contradiction in terms?

The focus in the book thus far has been upon teaching *praxis*. How applicable is the concept of *praxis* to other, related fields within education, such as leadership and what explanatory force might it have in such cases? This chapter signals a shift to an exploration of educational leadership as *praxis*. If human conduct or action in general can take the forms of *praxis* or *technē*, for example, then the distinction must be equally applicable as we consider different kinds of conduct in educational leadership.

This chapter poses three key questions: Firstly, what might it mean to lead with *praxis* within educational organisations? Secondly, is it possible within the transformed climate of new managerialism that characterises the contemporary Australian educational field, to lead in agentic ways that are underpinned by a notion of *praxis*, that is, "moral action that is theoretically grounded" (Shields & Oberg, 2006, p. 19)? Finally, what are the attendant risks and rewards for those who attempt to do so?

The location in which these questions are examined is that of contemporary Australian academe. Why choose the university sector? As part of broader global trends within education, Australian universities have undergone one of the most significant forms of industry restructuring, reflecting the "major role that they are seen to play in the nation's attempts to move from a Fordist to post-Fordist or knowledge economy" (Marginson & Considine, 2000, p.11; Ozga & Deem, 2000). Underpinning this transformation is a shift to neoliberal modes of rationalist governmentality and in particular, new managerialism, as a means by which to achieve the goals of increased economic productivity. One consequence of the transplantation of private sector principles into university management and leadership has been a focus upon efficiency and productivity gains at the "expense of older forms of academic leadership such as collegiality; and more recent trends towards democratic leadership that included greater representation of women, Indigenous peoples and other equity groups in university decision-making bodies" (Marginson & Considine, 2000, p.11).

What are the implications for leadership *praxis*? The prevailing climate thus engendered in Australian universities as a result of these reforms has led to the production of forms of management that might best be described as *technē* (Kemmis & Smith, Chapter Two, this volume) and as a hegemonic norm from

Kemmis, Stephen and Smith, Tracey J. (2008) Enabling praxis: Challenges for education.171-195

which leadership dispositions within universities are constructed and understood. Such *technē* nurtures a leadership and overall academic identity which "privileges the individualistic entrepreneur, able and willing to sell their expertise to the 'highest bidder', as opposed to previous discourses of academic professionalism as an 'advocacy role for public good'" (Blackmore & Sachs, 2003, p. 144). Though not wishing to perpetuate the dualism between managers as " *'people who do things right'*" versus leaders as those who "*do the right thing*" (Bennis & Nanus, 1985, p.21, cited in Gronn, 2003, p.282), the new managerialism preserves an unrelenting instrumentalist focus upon economic gains that subsumes questions about the "purpose and values, which underpin academic leadership" (Furman, 2002, p.205).

To explore the questions posed at the start of this chapter, I will discuss data based upon interviews conducted with ethnically and socioecomically diverse senior Australian female academics located in a variety of universities and leadership roles. The interviews were conducted as part of a larger study which analysed dominant discourses of ethnically and socioeconomically diverse women's leadership in the Australian media. The larger study interrogated how diverse Australian female academic leaders, challenged/resisted and/or took up these discourses in their leadership work (Wilkinson, 2005). Six women of European, Anglo, Asian and Aboriginal origin, who were from working and middle-class backgrounds, were selected for interview. They held various positions ranging from senior lectureship to senior management and were diversely located in research-only; research and teaching; and management/administration roles. The women were based in a variety of universities, including the oldest and most elite, as well as the new universities formed as a result of Australian Federal Government reforms in the late 1980s. They came from a wide variety of traditionally 'feminised' as well as 'non-traditional' disciplines. The decision to select women leaders from a range of ethnic and socio-economic origins was based upon the need to begin to challenge the hegemonic norm that still underpins much contemporary feminist leadership research in terms of an assumed (white, middle-class) construction of female leadership. In this chapter (as in the larger study), Pierre Bourdieu's thinking tools of capital, habitus and field, along with Bob Lingard and Pam Christie's (2003, p. 328) notion of "productive leadership habitus" are utilised as helpful "thinking tools" (Wacquant, 1989, p. 50) to use in this exploration of the possibilities, tensions and dilemmas for leadership *praxis* amongst this group of senior women academics.

Why choose this particular group of senior women academics for analysis? Women leaders from backgrounds other than those of the hegemonic norm are positioned in particularly contradictory ways in the current academic environment. On the one hand, their diversity is viewed as "positive capital – a source of fresh ideas and change for 'greedy institutions' such as universities" (Coser, 1981, cited in Thomas & Davies, 2002, p.384; see also Yeatman, 1995) and a valuable selling point to potential clients in a sector eager to promote its adherence to equity principles. On the other hand, their gender, ethnicity and class continues to position them as "second-class citizens" (Thomas & Davies, 2002, p. 381) in a management hierarchy characterised by a construction of leadership based upon male, middle-class and Anglophone norms (Wilkinson, 2005). The relatively low numbers of women in the more senior ranks of academia and the slow rate of their progress – particularly for those from non-Anglophone and lower socio-economic origins – signals their precarious status as an overall group[1].

Moreover, much leadership research in universities ignores how masculinist, Anglophone and middle-class discourses dominate the logic of the field, with the (diverse) "feminine excluded, downplayed and subordinated" (Thomas & Davies, 2002, p.376). For example, the advocacy of "individualistic academic subjectivities which new managerialism promotes" (Thomas & Davies, 2002, pp. 383-384) connotes a gendered subtext of competitive masculinities, as opposed to more feminised discourses of collaboration and collegiality. The material effects of this devaluation of such qualities are a silencing and marginalisation of many women and of diverse and alternative forms of leadership (Halford, Savage & Witz, 1997, pp.264-5, cited in Thomas & Davies, 1997, p.383).

This chapter examines gendered assumptions about leadership and hence, *praxis*, for at the very core of dominant constructions of leadership and management in Western society lie a series of fundamentally gendered beliefs about authority as naturally being the possession of generally white, middle-class males. Hence, diverse women leaders are situated as "double deviants" (Bagilhole 1994, p. 15) in the academic leadership game, for they are outsiders both in terms of their gender and their ethnicity and/or class. As such, they provide a useful touchstone for analysing the gendered, raced and classed consequences of the shift to academic managerialism upon the formation of leadership identities and the potential impact upon the possibilities for their leadership *praxis* in this field.

The chapter is divided into three key sections. The first problematises how reification of the practical nature of leadership work feeds into new managerialist tropes of business efficiency, means-end and instrumentalist rationalities. In so doing, the new managerialism functions as a metapractice of administration, that is, a practice which structures other practices (Kemmis & Grootenboer, Chapter Three, this volume), discouraging considerations of the broader moral purpose of leadership and entrenching competitive masculinity as the *raison d'etre* of academic leadership (Halford, Savage & Witz, 1997, pp.264-5, cited in Thomas & Davies, 2002, p.383). Arguably, the new managerialism enables abstract, rationalistic approaches to (and procedures of) management and leadership, and, by so doing, it constrains the highly situated practical and moral deliberation and decision making characteristic of *praxis* as a mode of human conduct. The second section of the chapter defines how the terms 'leadership' and 'management' are used within the chapter. It examines how new managerialism has reshaped the logics of practice within educational leadership in academia and explores the material effects of this transformation in regard to the opening up/closing down of productive spaces for leadership *praxis*. The third section draws upon semi-structured interviews with diverse academic female leaders, located in a variety of contexts and leadership roles. It teases out the possibilities and conditions for agency and leadership *praxis* which the women's practices enable, and contrasts those practices with ones which favour a form of rule-following that treats individuals (including leaders and managers themselves) as operatives of academic management systems (on agents versus operatives, see Kemmis and Smith, Chapter One, this volume).

EDUCATIONAL LEADERSHIP: JUST DO IT?

As a field of study, educational leadership and management has been characterised as largely atheoretical, often priding itself upon its applied and practical nature (Bush, 2007). The trend towards a technical or instrumental emphasis, shorn from a broader, non-instrumentalist concept of leadership and management imbued with moral purpose, has been one of the unintended consequences of the wholesale adoption of private sector management techniques and principles into education and the Anglophone public sector more broadly over the past two decades. Such an adoption is part of a broader political strategy to reform education and make universities and other public institutions more accountable to their constituents (Bush, 2007). The fetishisation of instrumentalist-driven management practices means that theories of leadership and management are then discursively positioned as distant from the more immediate realities of universities, particularly in a globalising economy in which reification of economistic practices and principles has led to a major questioning of the role and identity of universities in the post-modern era.

Arguably, the diminution of both leadership and management to a narrowly defined set of competencies/skills/outcomes ignores the moral and social purposes with which both leadership and management practices are imbued (let alone the moral and social purposes of education and public service). The fostering of a disposition towards leadership *techne*, that is, a focus upon narrow, and in the past few years, economically-driven 'means-end or instrumental reasoning' to achieve economic gains, invites us to think in instrumentalist ways that exclude *phronēsis* – the "moral disposition to act wisely, truly and justly" (Kemmis & Smith, Chapter Two, this volume). The disposition of *phronēsis* includes the capacity to be critically reflective about one's actions, to learn from one's mistakes, take judicious risks and sustain a broader view of leadership, for example, the "narrowing of social and educational disparities between groups of students" as a *telos* or goal of education or the *telos* of a liberal democratic society (Shields & Oberg, 2006). An exclusive focus upon *techne* ignores the fact that the dialectical interchange between theorisation and critical reflection upon practice and action, is a crucial trope of leadership *praxis*. Discursively, the technically-focussed conception of leadership as purely a set of management skills positions as "old-fashioned or out of touch" (Blackmore, 1997, pp. 90-91) those who may wish to ask more challenging questions such as what is or should be the purpose of leadership in education? What difference does and should leadership make both in relation to one's individual context and society as a whole? In addition to occluding these general questions, the technically-focussed conception of leadership also occludes practical, day-to-day questions that arise when people act and interact in workplaces. On a technical view of leadership and management, it is the job of leaders or managers to employ established procedures and rules that are regarded as more or less universal. If they rely too heavily on established procedures and rules to guide them, they may ignore or overlook the situated moral deliberation necessary for wise, prudent and proper conduct in the 'messy' situations in which people find themselves, even in the best-run organisations. An orientation to *praxis* is necessarily an orientation to the people and situations in which leaders and managers, and those they lead and manage, find themselves, not just to the goals, roles, functions and imperatives that constitute the organisation and its work.

An exclusive emphasis upon *technē*, ignores the reality that the practices of leadership and management do not take place in a vacuum. Such practices are part of a broader system of architectures that differentially enable, constrain, marginalise and/or regulate individual leaders and leadership and management as a collective set of practices (Kemmis & Grootenboer, Chapter Three, this volume). What such practice architectures enable and constrain in specific settings, depends upon the various kinds of social, economic and symbolic capital which individuals bring to their leadership work; and the valuation placed upon these capitals in terms of the logics of practice (Bourdieu, 1990) within the specific field in which the individual may be located (Wilkinson, 2005, 2006). Moreover, practices, like discourses, are constitutive; that is, they have material effects upon real human beings. The boast that leadership and management are (instrumentally-oriented) "practical activities" (Bush, 2007, p. 5) both conceals and sustains the asymmetrical power relations that underlie them. They naturalise "objects of knowledge" such as the leadership practices within universities, thus rendering invisible the concrete processes by which such practices "are *constructed* and not passively recorded" (Wacquant, 1989, p. 43). Moreover, the veneration of "idealized forms" of technocratic leadership "operate[s] to produce effects of power, such as knowledge about what count as leaders and communities" (Lingard, Hayes, Mills, & Christie, 2003, p.128).

Before turning to an examination of individual case studies in order to examine these points further, it is necessary to explore some of the key terms used in the chapter. Specifically, how are concepts such as 'leadership', 'management' and 'managerialism' discursively constructed by the contemporary working conditions and key practices in the Australian tertiary education sector?

LEADERSHIP AND MANAGEMENT: WHAT'S IN A NAME?

The term 'leadership' is hotly contested in the educational literature. Since the 1970s in particular, the emphasis upon leadership as a set of narrowly defined technical management practices (that is, seen from the perspective of the disposition of *technē* and enacted as *poiēsis*, see Chapter Two, this volume), allied to a neoliberal agenda which fuses educational goals within the economic, has led to a marginalisation of questions about the broader aims of educational leadership. Recently however, there has been a "resurgence of interest in engaging at a deeper level with questions of leadership, including its moral purpose and the underlying values by which it is sustained" (Bush, 2007, p. 7). This critical re-evaluation marks an important shift away from preoccupations with how leadership is done and by whom, to an engagement with "the critical-humanist, moral and artistic dimensions of leadership" (Furman, 2002, p. 205). In accordance with these views, and rather than attempting an iron-clad definition of the term, the term 'leadership' will be used in the chapter to denote a "deliberate intervention that requires the moral use of power" (Bogotoch, 2000, cited in Shields & Oberg, 2006, p.4). It is worth noting that such an intervention is not necessarily tied to hierarchical roles within an organisation. Regarding the positions of the academic women interviewed in the wider study upon which this chapter draws, nearly all held positions of recognised authority as managers and/or researchers; what was crucial about their work practices was that they exemplified how it is possible to exert influence and lead with *praxis* by acting with integrity, humanity and morality within their management roles. One might even say that they aimed to lead *praxis* by *praxis* – that is, to lead others' *praxis* by demonstrating *praxis* in their conduct.

A distinction needs to be drawn between leadership and management. For the purposes of this chapter, the term 'management' will be used to refer to the formal, administrative roles designated within an organisation, and the carrying out of the functions associated with those roles, especially in relation to overseeing and coordinating the work and functions of others. In contrast, leadership extends beyond the positional (roles), referring both to informal and formal positions of influence, and beyond the purely functional, referring also to practices that concern the conduct of lives within and beyond any particular organisation. In the cases under examination in this chapter, one may posit that the object of management is primarily people, whereas the object of leadership is that of education. As Lingard et al in their analysis of productive leadership in schools (Lingard et al., 2003, p.52) note:

> (w)ithin organizations, leadership can be exercised at most levels and in most activities ... Management, in contrast ... relates to structures and processes by which organizations meet their goals and central purposes, and arguably, is more likely to be tied to formal positions than to persons ... leadership is not necessarily tied to position power and its influence is not mandated.

Given that this chapter is examining leadership *praxis*, why utilise the term 'management'? Increasingly since the 1970s in Anglophone nations such as Australia and England, the word 'management', borrowed from the private sector, has come to signify the leadership work of those in formal positions of authority within education (for a more detailed explanation of new public management and the neoliberal ideologies which underpin this force in the context of teacher professional development, refer to Hardy, Chapter Eight, this volume). The discursive turn towards management within the educational leadership field connotes a reductionist focus upon techniques of private enterprise, which in turn has had major material effects upon academic leadership practices and identities. As a discourse, new managerialism has "set the terms" to which all other discourses of leadership "have to respond" and hence, operates as a form of hegemony within the field of educational leadership (Hall, 1988, p.62 & p.71).

This is not to suggest that management as a formal organisational function must of necessity lack a moral or social purpose. Nor is it to imply that because the women under examination in this chapter were employed as managers at varying levels within the system, that they were doomed to act as operatives of the new managerialist orientation impacting upon universities. However, what it does suggest is that the current overemphasis upon accountability tied to economically rationalist ideologies leaves management as particularly vulnerable to a form of "bureaucratic rationality ... attuned to capitalist, materialist endeavours rather than the formation of a moral reasoning" (Adlong, Chapter Eleven, this volume). It was striking that the majority of the women leaders interviewed in this study refused to accept this new managerialist disposition, continued to engage with the broader moral purposes of leadership, and maintained their commitment to a wider social collective that was fundamental to their views of their leadership and management practices. This collective disposition towards a leadership *phronēsis* reminds us that discourses of change such as new managerialism are "not uniform in ... (their) ... effects" and that their "impact on alternative or oppositional positions is as important as ... (their) ... success in producing the subjects of change" (Clarke & Newman, 1997, p. 54). In this sense, an unintended material effect of discourses of power may be that they are not only coercive and regulatory, but also productive of new and alternative bodies of knowledge about leadership (Foucault, 1990).

Numerous tensions may be generated as a result of the dialectical interplay between a leadership disposition (*phronēsis*) oriented towards *praxis* and a management disposition (*technē*) oriented towards positional and functional management *poiēsis* (illustrated in the neoliberal fetishisation of the techniques of new managerialism). Tensions may be productive of leadership *praxis* (P. Ponte, personal communication, February, 2007) but the *situated nature* of the contexts in which leadership practices were played out (Kemmis & Grootenboer, Chapter Three, this volume), including the different working conditions within the women's various universities, also played a key role in enabling, constraining and/regulating participants' attempts to lead in ways that modelled a leadership *praxis* different from the instrumentalist-focussed management orientation currently privileged in Australian universities. Let us turn to three examples of participants' practices in order to explore this point more deeply. The case studies include 'Ruth', who is a middle manager/lecturer/researcher in a leading Australian university; 'Lauren', who is a senior manager located in one of the new universities formed as a result of the major reforms of the Australian tertiary sector in the late 1980s; and 'Amelia', who is based at one of Australia's oldest universities and holds a figurehead role which nonetheless garners a great deal of symbolic capital.

TELLING TALES FROM THE FIELD: LOCATING LEADERSHIP *PRAXIS*

'Ruth'[2] occupies a dual management and teaching/research position in a leading Australian university. She is also active in the field of Aboriginal civil rights and sits on a number of key Indigenous/governmental committees. As an Aboriginal feminist located in a range of different fields[3] she is subject to competing tensions in her leadership work. This is how Ruth compared the contrasting ways in which she was able to exercise leadership within the different fields in which she principally operated. She noted:

> (Y)ou're so stifled by educational institutions and they're a bureaucracy. And I've always hated working in a bureaucracy and increasingly more I find it very frustrating working in an educational institution because I'm starting to feel straitjacketed ... particularly as now I'm Acting ...(Manager) for three months that ... there are all these administrative things that you have to do and answer to ...(Boss A) or take it up to ... (Boss B) who'll take it up to ... (Boss C) and I find those issues of negotiation very difficult to deal with. Whereas I'm a lot freer person in terms of being an Indigenous woman and leader in politics because in a very real way I can say what I want to say. I'm not a public servant. I'm not hamstrung to Governments. I can say what I really feel ... there's a lot more freedom out there to be an Indigenous woman leader in politics.

Ruth's criticism of the bureaucracy of her university and the way in which it stifles innovation and stifles the disposition towards phronesis, is damning. Her critique of the hierarchical and bureaucratic nature of her university, suggests the intensification of workload and the increased surveillance and regulation of academic freedom that has accompanied changes to governance within "enterprise universities" (Marginson & Considine, 2000). Moreover, she draws a strong contrast between the relative autonomy and freedom she experiences as a political operator in her committee work which allows her to exercise leadership *praxis*, in terms of furthering Indigenous rights; and her university work, in which she feels very much dictated to and regulated by administrative and bureaucratic structures which appear to stifle opportunities for moral activism. In so doing, Ruth draws attention to how administrative structures may function as metapractices, that is, in terms of their '"regulating" and "constraining" capacities which in turn shape the possibilities for leadership work within academe' (Kemmis & Grootenboer, Chapter Three, this volume). In contrast, the relative freedom to influence government which her Indigenous committee work affords, reveals the '"enabling" and "informing" opportunities that the metapractice of administration may open up' (Kemmis & Grootenboer, Chapter Three, this volume) when it is situated outside traditional bureaucratic boundaries, be they within the public service or private organisations.

Ruth observes:

> I really believe within my own self that working within the institution doesn't hold much weight ... I've had experience of doing both of that in the last year, working within an institution and working without. ... You're like this small cog in a huge machine and it just keeps revolving ... and you can get caught up with all that machinery ... I think it's far more important for me to

be working outside institutions and bureaucracies rather than working within them because … I could get really swallowed up.

As a middle manager in her university, Ruth may be a "small cog in a huge machine" and, as such, is structurally and discursively positioned as a "management operative within the practice architectures that shape and structure administration" within her university (Kemmis & Grootenboer, Chapter Three, this volume). Nonetheless, her gender, Indigeneity and high levels of education carry considerable symbolic capital in the current academic field. As the "only Aboriginal woman at a senior level" in her university, she has led changes, such as working in conjunction with university senior management to produce Indigenous "protocols and policies". She notes that senior management "had been very encouraging in terms of getting (Indigenous issues) throughout the institution … being taught in core subjects …"

According to Ruth, the small changes she has been able to lead at her university pale in comparison to the freedom and power to make a real difference, afforded through her political activist work. For example, she notes in regard to the leadership work involved in the Indigenous relations committee of which she is a member:

It was about engaging people, meeting people, speaking with … the key political leaders, talking to Governments, stuff that I don't do in my job at the Uni of course because what I do at Uni is mostly … teach … administration and I look after the place …

What Ruth is pointing to is the productive spaces that have opened up at this point in time for some Australian Aboriginal women in universities and the public sphere more generally, in contrast to their relative invisibility prior to the 1990s[4]. Moreover, despite Ruth's limited success in leading change in a field in which academic middle managers are increasingly expected to act as "boundary riders" between senior and junior staff, the fact that she is taken seriously by the university's senior management and can affect changes, suggests that there may remain a submerged but ongoing commitment to egalitarianism within the academic field – one of the values upon which Western academia is based and upon which equity strategies in universities are partially drawn (Yeatman, 1995, p.196). In addition, given the fierce competition for funding in Australian universities, Ruth's institution may well see that there is both symbolic and economic capital and a positional advantage to be gained by being seen to be sympathetic to equity initiatives. Furthermore, in and of themselves, Indigenous students are a small but key group of consumers in the Australian academic field.

That Ruth is even given the flexibility in her academic role to move between the fields of academia and governmental politics, suggests some productive spaces may have opened up for women academic leaders. For example, despite the "less collegial, less fratriarchal" culture of academe, Jeff Hearn suggests that in contemporary Anglophone universities, managerialism has both "affirm(ed) … existing patriarchal relationships … yet also create(d) the spaces for some women

179

to do more management … in different ways" (Hearn, 2001, pp.83-84) to enact a form of leadership *praxis*, albeit in limited ways. However, this tendency also has an exploitative edge to it, for in viewing female leaders as the potential "agents of change", there is a risk that such women may also face exploitation and "burn-out" in these new academic "hard times" (Yeatman, 1995, p.203).

What are the practices which Ruth draws upon in order to lead purposively, guided by a "form of doing that constitutes right conduct"? (Kemmis and Smith, Chapter Two, this volume). Moreover, where do these practices originate from and what are the working conditions that allow them to flourish or wither? One key source of her leadership practices is the moral disposition towards egalitarianism ingrained in Ruth's cultural background. She states:

> I know that I have positions of power but when people have said, "You are a leader" then I'm quite complimented by that which is coupled by … the cultural expectations of Aboriginal people never having true leaders in the sense that we are today. We were once a fairly egalitarian society where men and women had separate roles, separate responsibilities, separate spheres of knowledge of sacred sites and custodianship to land and I think that philosophy is ingrained in me. That's why I feel almost embarrassed. One very important part of Aboriginal culture is that you don't bignote yourself.

Furthermore, she draws on strong feminist elders within Aboriginal communities who enact this egalitarian tradition in their leadership. For example, Ruth notes that the older feminist chair of a major committee upon which she sits, has initiated some important changes in practices that have led to a transformation of the dynamics and culture of the group. These include: giving "women the absolute opportunity to have a say; mak(ing) … half the … (executive of the committee) … women; "hav(ing) … a very deep and keen interest in women's issues"; and "absolutely shar(ing) … that responsibility". The chair of her committee provides Ruth with a clear role model for wise and committed action which in turn has led to the "blossoming" of her "womanism" and a feeling of "being more powerful … strong and … determined in the work that we do not only in … (this committee) … but in all aspects of my life".

Ruth's growth in leadership is "not purely an individual exercise but is experienced intersubjectively" (Kemmis & Grootenboer, Chapter Three, this volume). It is clearly based upon interactions with significant individuals within her life; in her place within the broader Aboriginal community; in her position as a senior Aboriginal female academic in an elite university; and in her location within the fields of Aboriginal civil rights and feminism. Finally, the 'metapractices' of academic leadership which are increasingly borrowed from private enterprise, shape, and, according to Ruth, increasingly constrain and regulate her leadership practices' (Kemmis and Grootenboer, Chapter Three, this volume). In a Foucauldian sense, they act as disciplinary and disciplining technologies of management so that she experiences her university work as acting largely as an operative within the metapractice of administration that is university management (Kemmis and Smith, Chapter One, this volume). These experiences stand in vivid contrast to the relative freedom Ruth experiences in the field of government/Indigenous Affairs. How then, does she lead in ways, which suggest resistance to the status quo of academic managerialism, and yet retain legitimacy within the academic field? It is here that Pierrre Bourdieu's theorisation of practice, through his use of the concepts of habitus, field and capital; and the notion of leadership habitus (Lingard & Christie, 2003) is productive in analysing further the development of a disposition towards leadership *praxis* for women such as Ruth.

THEORISING LEADERSHIP *PRAXIS* IN THE ACADEMIC FIELD

I have used the terms 'field' and 'capital' in the preceding discussion when referring respectively to the site of academia in which Ruth carries out her leadership work; and the varying degrees of varying degrees of economic, cultural, social and symbolic power which she brings to her leadership role. In utilising this term, I draw upon Bourdieu's (Bourdieu, 1998, p. 4) definition of a field as

a structured social space, a field of forces, a force field. It contains people who dominate and others who are dominated. Constant, permanent relationships of inequality operate inside this space, which at the same time becomes a space in which the various actors struggle for the transformation or preservation of the field.

What of individual leaders such as Ruth who compete and struggle within specific social sites such as academe? She develops a sense of herself as a player in this field, in the 'game' that characterises the field. Bourdieu uses the notion of habitus to "surmount the sociological dichotomy between subjectivism", in which social practices, such as those which make up leadership, "can be understood solely in terms of individual decision-making"; and objectivism, in which the practice of individuals is solely "determined by supra-individual 'structures', such as class" (Jenkins, 1992, p. 74). Bourdieu has defined the habitus as

the product of a *practical sense* ... of a socially constituted 'sense of the game' ... (which) ... posits that objects of knowledge are constructed and not passively recorded ... practical – as opposed to cognitive – functions ... (Wacquant, 1989, p. 43).

Each field produces its own specific habitus, its own action "guided by a feel for the game" (Bourdieu, 1990, p. 68). Bourdieu also points to the dialectical relationship between a field and the habitus, for the

field structures the habitus, which is the product of the embodiment of the immanent necessity of a field ... On the other side ... habitus contributes to constituting the field as a meaningful world ...endowed with sense and value, in which it is worth investing one's energy (Wacquant, 1989, p. 44).

What of academic leadership? Where might *praxis* be located in a theory of leadership practices based upon Bourdieuian concepts? A contemporary characteristic of the Anglophone academic field is a major rupture in the internal logic of the field, characterised by a shift from "the freedom to 'play seriously'", with intellectual ideas and theories (Bourdieu, 1998, p. 128) – a freedom which was largely the possession of white, middle to upper-class males – to a marked interdependence between the fields of business/economics, politics, and the tertiary education sector. This, in turn, has led to a "transformation in the values underpinning social fields" such as academia (Lingard & Rawolle, 2004, p. 369) including the production of the new habitus of the academic manager, characterised by an adherence to individualistic rather than collegiate decision-making based upon economic, rather than educational outcomes (Marginson & Considine, 2000; Blackmore & Sachs, 2003, p.144).

Where is Ruth positioned in such a field? As an academic manager, lecturer, researcher, player within the field of Aboriginal/government relations, feminist and mother, Ruth is subject to the competing tensions of the varying and often contradictory logics of practice within these fields. As a manager, she is located in the academic field at the nexus of new managerialism. Thus, she is vulnerable to the latter's regulatory forces. On the one hand, she expresses her frustration at the lack of collegiality in decision-making and her lack of freedom to make major decisions without referring them to upper management. Yet, on the other hand, she draws upon the symbolic capital that her Indigeneity and gender affords her within the academic field, in order to affect broader changes to Indigenous policy, protocols and curriculum within her university. In Bourdieuian terms, she appears to have achieved at least some measure of legitimacy within the academic field. Moreover, the individual habitus Ruth brings to the field, based as it is upon a family and communal history of activism, produces a logic of practice and commitment to social action, which shapes her leadership *praxis*, in defiance of the broader managerialist logic underpinning the academic field.

Let us take Ruth's story one step further. A normative concept of leadership implicitly underpins any discussion of leadership *praxis*, given that *praxis* may be defined as "a form of doing that constitutes right conduct" (Kemmis & Smith, Chapter Two, this volume). What might a normative model of leadership look like? Bob Lingard and Pam Christie's conceptualisation of productive leadership habitus within schools (Lingard & Christie, 2003) provides a glimpse of what is possible. The authors argue that schools, like universities, have been subject to an economic rationalist agenda which has led in the principalship/headship to a higher valuing of performativity and new managerialism, rather than attention to pedagogy and students' educational and social outcomes. As such, the authors argue for a "normative concept of leadership habitus" (Lingard & Christie, 2003, p. 328) which places emphasis upon a broader valuation of what matters in educational leadership terms. They outline three elements to this concept, that is:

> Reflexivity ... a "critical or reflective disposition", which includes the work of "awakening of consciousness and socioanalysis" by which the habitus may be changed (Bourdieu, 1990, pp. 16, 116) cited in (Lingard & Christie, 2003, p. 328);

A preparedness to "do the most good and cause the right change" (Lingard & Christie, 2003, p. 329); and

A capacity and disposition to deal with the "wholeness of the school and educational system as fields" (Lingard & Christie, 2003, p. 329).

A major strength of these elements is that they maintain the dialectical tensions between habitus and field, that is, the interplay between agents and the social, political and economic structures or practice architectures which, on the one hand, enable and constrain individual and collective actions, and, on the other, are in turn influenced and shaped by these same actions. This brings a new theoretical richness to our understanding of the practice and concepts of leadership. The notion of a dialectic interplay between agents and practice architectures is particularly important when attempting to understand how the habitus of individual female academic leaders such as Ruth operates in relation to the gendered, raced and classed power relations which are played out in the games for legitimacy within the academic field (Wilkinson, 2005).

If Ruth's leadership is examined utilising these elements, it would appear that her work as a feminist Indigenous leader within a range of fields has led to the production of a habitus which is predisposed to reflexivity, as well as a preparedness to "do the most good and cause the right change". She clearly possesses a sufficient practical sense – a socially constituted sense of the game as it is played in the higher education field – as witnessed by her success in gaining positions of leadership within this site of practice and within the challenging field of Indigenous/government relations. Her leadership work within the latter field and in particular, the opportunity to learn from the feminist elder who chaired the committee upon which she sat, appears to have afforded her key insights into the wholeness of the field of Indigenous/government relations and the wider field of power in which it operates (Jenkins, 1992, p. 86). These are crucial insights, which simultaneously broaden her capacity to deal with the wholeness of the fields in which she is operating but which also exacerbate her dissatisfaction with the obstacles to *praxis*, which the academic field constructs.

Ruth's example also reveals that an ability to engage with the wholeness of the fields in which one operates is both linked to individual capacity and disposition but also to the possibilities for leadership that are made available to individuals within a field. The latter is a situation that is often denied to female academics, with "women traditionally corralled into the lower status areas of teaching and course administration rather than research" (Thomas & Davies, 2002). In this sense, Ruth's Indigeneity operates as a form of positive capital in the Australian tertiary field in opening up leadership possibilities, for she notes that in terms of her positions within both the academic and the political fields:

I'm not constrained ... by my Indigeneity. In fact, it is a real bonus in both ... Certainly, as a woman, in both of them; at times I have felt very subjugated.

However, Ruth's university is one of a small number of elite institutions whose comparative weight within the Australian academic field has given it the capacity to attract major researchers who possess the symbolic capital to 'resist managerialism' to a greater extent than newer institutions (Marginson & Considine 2000, pp.193-194). What of women leaders located in the newer, less elite universities? What enabling and/or constraining factors are at work and how might Lingard's and Christies' framework of 'productive habitus' assist in an examination of their leadership *praxis*? Let us turn to two other case studies, that of Amelia and Lauren, in order to examine these questions.

LAUREN AND AMELIA: TOWARDS REFLEXIVITY?

Lauren is a senior manager of Anglophone origin, located in one of Australia's new universities. Amelia is an Indigeous feminist, who holds an honorary role of much prestige in one of Australia's oldest universities. Lauren displays a great pride in the working-class roots of her extended family, noting, "I am who I am and ... whatever comes with that, and people can either take it or leave it". Both women entered academe from other fields in which they had established themselves as leading national players. Amelia strongly identifies herself as a feminist, while Lauren identifies more strongly with the field of her professional subject specialisation in which she had carved a niche for herself in her previous employment. In terms of Lingard and Christie's framework of leadership habitus, how might the two women's commitment to *praxis* be characterised?

Amelia's lifework appears to have cultivated within her, an acute, critical awareness of the damages wrought by racism and sexism and a fierce commitment in her leadership role to challenging the asymmetrical power relations that have inflicted these wrongs. She observes:

> (I)f you think about ... the ... power structures in society which are law, government and the fourth estate ... they are very powerful male constructs ... I ... challenge the paradigm ... the ideology ... the practice ... that's a ...massive threat.

Growing up in a society in which she "learnt that Aboriginals were lazy, shiftless, untrustworthy," infused Amelia with the knowledge that in the legal and academic fields, "as an Indigenous person" she had "an added responsibility" to challenge such stereotypes. For example, in the field of law where she also practices, Amelia comments:

> I really do believe that people are entitled to justice ... The overwhelming majority of people we get in the local courts are people who are under-educated, unemployed or ... casually employed ... very often they lack life skills and ... their families ... come from communities where there's been generations of that experience ... You find that you're actually having to take those kinds of issues into account ... in dealing with people as individuals.

Amelia's primary habitus[5] as an Indigenous child experiencing poverty, racism and sexism are powerful, developmental influences in terms of her leadership development. She clearly displays a capacity for critical reflection and self-awareness in regard to these early experiences, particularly in terms of how they have moulded and shaped her leadership ethos. Her location as a feminist as well as a prime mover in the struggle for Indigenous rights provides her with powerful reflexive tools from which to fashion a stinging critique of how Indigenous women and women as a group, continue to be unequally positioned within society. She then translates this awareness into her leadership practices. For example, she notes:

> I do try to treat everybody around me – and I don't care what position they hold ... as a human being. I know ... of men who walk past and don't even acknowledge the presence of people like typists or ... their PAs ... they treat them like dogs ... I have the view that everybody ... has a view on how the institution can run ... So that's important to try to include everybody in the team rather than being ... the head honcho ...

Amelia's clear capacity for resistance and agency reveals a rejection of the "corporate culture discourse" of senior academic management (Blackmore, 1997, p.8) in favour of a boundary-crossing feminist equity discourse which privileges democratic and inclusive forms of decision-making. Amelia's freedom to draw upon such a discourse suggests that the drive towards an increasingly centralised, "peak masculinist discourse" within Australian academic management may not be monolithic (Currie, Thiele, & Harris, 2002, p.9) and that one needs to examine the particularity of the context in which discourses of leadership are played out. It also suggests that Amelia has the power within her university to enact alternative kinds of knowledge about leadership and to be taken seriously within the leadership stakes of her university. Crucially, Amelia also holds a central position of authority in a university which is struggling to reinvent itself as the Australian university sector undergoes major transformations. She had been appointed to her role in the university because she was viewed as an "Indigenous female role model", thus signalling in a similar way to Ruth, the other Indigenous female leader, that at certain times and in certain fields, her Indigeneity can function as positive capital.

Amelia was appointed at a time when the university was "in such a condition that it was necessary" for her to take a lead role in terms of major reforms. This included the overhaul of upper management and the appointment of a senior feminist leader who shared her commitment to social justice. Thus, she had a unique "opportunity to have a major impact on the higher education sector in this country". Amelia's university has lower stakes in the academic field and less symbolic capital within the broader field of power compared to Ruth's. In this sense, it is "precariously free to reinvent ... (it)self" by appointing an Aboriginal feminist figure at its head – a person who comes from outside the academic field and complements the student profile (Marginson & Considine, 2000, p. 202). Hence, Amelia's self-reflexivity combined with a position of power in which she is able to exercise an ability to do the "most good and cause the right change" (Lingard & Christie, 2003, p. 329) is a powerful brew in terms of leadership *praxis*.

Where does Lauren fit in terms of a leadership habitus that combines self-reflexivity and doing the most good in often difficult circumstances? Lauren is less senior than Amelia but nonetheless holds a position of considerable authority as a senior manager in her university. Her leadership disposition reveals an acute awareness of and commitment to collegiate and collaborative leadership models. She notes that her experience coming from an extended working-class origin family has been a valuable quality "in this university" in particular, as many of its students are the first people in their family to go on to tertiary studies. Her previous leadership experiences in a very different setting have provided her with a sense of legitimacy that her traditionally imputed 'feminine' style of leadership is valid and positive. She observes:

> I suspect there's a stereotype ... that any leader has to be hard-nosed, authoritarian, aggressive ... extremely decisive ... my ... natural approach is different ... I think I still do my own thing very much, regardless, because I have the confidence of having been the leader of a group ... that worked extremely well and I have no intention of changing my style ... It's more to do with bringing people along than kicking them into submission ... a softer style ...

In this quotation, Lauren identifies the emergence of two distinct styes of leadership within new managerialism, each underwritten by a distinct, gendered sub-text. The "first is a hard management discourse modelled on a form of corporate 'macho' management that privileges hierarchy and line-management structures and concentrates decisions within fewer hands. It thus runs the risk of further marginalising equity groups such as women at all levels" (Marginson & Considine, 2000, p.11). Lauren's observations suggest that the various practice architectures in which she and other managers within her university make decisions encourage this discourse as the primary or default position. The "second is that of 'soft management' in which women come to be viewed as 'change agents', providing a fresh 'source of leadership for the greedy organisation'" (Blackmore, 1997, p.4). Such discourses open up certain limited leadership possibilities for women such as Lauren as they privilege traditionally feminised qualities such as "team-building, collaboration, consultation and communication" (Karpin, 1995, p.xxxix; see also Mackinnon & Brooks, 2001). However, the danger is that the second kind of discourse may "reproduce existing gender stereotypes by placing expectations upon women leaders that they will do the emotional 'housework ... (and) the nurturing' of staff required in these tougher times" (Currie & Thiele, 2001, p.98). Of course, such styles of management are not necessarily new to institutions such as academia, but what is different in universities is the advocacy for such styles over "older traditions of patriarchal governance such as collegiate decision-making, and over more recent moves towards inclusivity of equity groups which now are frowned upon 'as an obstacle to managerial rationalities'" (Marginson & Considine, 2000, p.11).

Like an invisible cloak, Lauren's Anglophone whiteness confers upon her a privileged position within the largely white leadership stakes which Amelia can never assume. Hence, it is Lauren's experiences of sexism and class snobbery, which are most acute in her accounts of academic leadership. In her previous field, Lauren's professional habitus became that of the expert, 'honorary male' researcher and was so pervasive that she observes:

> (eventually) I didn't really think much about being a woman although I was so alone in the beginning. I ... worked my way into being able to speak up ... without anybody thinking, "Oh, she's a woman".

Crucially, however, Lauren was able to gain much of her research and eventual leadership experience in a small, supportive team environment which exhibited the more traditionally feminine qualities of co-operation, nurturing and communication – qualities which soft management discourses capture and exploit. Her researcher habitus became, "the product of a *practical sense* ... of a socially constituted 'sense of the game'", thus allowing Lauren to become a "'fish in water' and take... the ... (scientific) ... world about (her)self for granted" (Wacquant, 1989, p. 43). It is this taken-for-grantedness, which was disrupted when she moved to academia and experienced a subtle, but very pervasive sexism. She notes in regard to her experiences within senior management:

> I've been surprised ... I feel that I'm a fairly seasoned warrior, that I'm capable of making myself heard in an assertive manner... But I can't just seem to break through ... it's like a sound barrier ... in where it counts ...

Although Lauren's critical awareness and self-reflexivity have grown greatly as a result of the sexism she experiences within academic management, it has been at great personal and professional cost. She notes:

> (H)ow much better could it have been for me and how much aggravation has it been? How have individuals suffered in achieving those ends? Many have prospered but I think many have suffered too.

Lauren carried into her previous role as senior manager, the positive capital of specialist expertise within her field of research which she had built up over many years. She was well known and widely respected in her area, thus allowing her to become a legitimate player within its senior management game. She was far less well known in academe and was forced to adopt a new leadership disposition as academic manager, rather than specialist researcher and manager. It is a role in which she appears to have received very little mentoring support and has instead encountered a great deal of hostility from some other senior male members because her leadership style is frequently at odds with the material circumstances in which she works. Her comments invoke the particularity of circumstances within the academic milieu in which she is forced to operate, and suggest how her efforts at agency are stymied by the pre-existing arrangements/practice architectures, with which she must contend. Her observations signal the difficulty women leaders as a group may have in gaining the third element of Lingard and Christie's (2003) leadership habitus, namely, a "capacity and disposition to deal with the wholeness of the" ... (university) ... and "educational system as fields" (pp.328-329) when they are denied the crucial support that would provide them with this capacity. It is to this final quality of leadership habitus that we will now turn.

DEALING WITH THE WHOLE: CHANGING THE SYSTEM FROM WITHIN

How might one lead with *praxis*, illustrating how to "deal with the wholeness of" universities and the "educational system as fields" as well as utilising a critical reflexivity and a "preparedness to do the most good and cause the right change" (Lingard & Christie, 2003, p.329)? Amelia provides a telling response when she is asked whether it is possible to bring about major changes within the fields of law and academia whose practice architectures are so constraining of individual and collective agency:

> You need to be absolutely clear about why you are there, what is your agenda, what is it you think you're going to achieve and how do you think you're going to achieve it ... You've got to keep your eyes on the prize – you don't waver.

> The big challenge is to find your way through the morass of rules and regulations and conventional practices ... but ... if you've got a very clear idea of what it is you want to do and how you want to do it, you soon find your way through those things ... I think it's because people are impatient or that they haven't done their own work on themselves ... So they become acted upon instead of acting upon themselves.

Amelia's habitus as an ex-head of a public service department and member of the judiciary, provides her with a very strong *"practical sense ... of a socially constituted 'sense of the game'"* (Wacquant, 1989, p.42) of the fields of power in law and the public service which she brings to her senior leadership role. As fields of power, the dominant fields of politics, law and academia produce "certain commonalities of habitus and practice as they are translated within the differing logics of ... (the) ... separate fields" (Jenkins, 1992, p.86). Thus, Amelia is not confused by the inner logic of academia's habitus of "subtle barriers" and "clubbiness", for it has parallels within the cultures of the legal and public service fields – locations whose games she has "master(ed)" and in which she is situated as part of a metafield of power (Walker, 1997, p.336).

Amelia's seniority within the fields of power of the law and higher education and her regular presence in the dominant field of the media, locates Amelia within a "metafield ... which acts on other fields and influences their practices" (Webb, Schirato, & Danaher, 2002, p.85). It provides her with the necessary analytical tools and experience of the games of power as they are played out in academic leadership. Allied to her self-reflexivity and moral disposition as a leader to "do the most good and cause the right change" (Lingard & Christie, 2003, p.329), Amelia becomes a rule-maker as well as a rule-breaker within the academic field (Henderson, 1999, p.144). Her leadership habitus is powerfully shaped by her location within the fields of feminism, law and academe and she calls upon feminist discourses to enact change at the most senior level of her university. Moreover, she possesses the formal authority to bring about change within her university to a far greater degree than Lauren and Ruth, while simultaneously being subjected to the power that arises from her location within the metafield. In sum, she is more watchful and conscious of how to influence the course of events, compared to Lauren and Ruth. Moreover, she has more of the cultural-discursive and social-political resources at her disposal and, crucially, chooses to deploy these differently from the way they are typically framed in the current context of the enterprise university.

Lauren's struggle within academic management reflects both the gendered nature of the practice architectures which frame current educational leadership practices (Kemmis & Grootenboer, Chapter Three, this volume) and the intersubjective nature of the formation of her academic leadership identity in relation to other individuals and groups within her university (Kemmis Grootenboer, Chapter Three). There is a fundamental switch in leadership identity, disposition and practices entailed as part of her shift from being a key senior researcher and senior manager to a management role in the different, though related field of academe. A major problem with this switch is the lack of support and overt sexism she encounters within her individual university when entering academic leadership as the sole senior woman, in particular in terms of the lack of mentoring in regard to the unwritten rules of this new game. In short, how does Lauren gain a sense of the wholeness of the field when those gatekeepers who can provide her with access to the leadership experiences that will provide her with this disposition block opportunities at each turn? Lauren's experiences of isolation and not being heard are common features of the "outsider status" (Acker & Feuerverger, 1997, p.137) and considerable pain that sole senior women often experience in both academic leadership and senior roles in other fields more generally where they are located as double deviants in a "male-dominated world" in which they expect to "receive equitable rewards and recognition" (Bagilhole, 1994, p.15).

Despite all of this, Lauren learns tactics of resistance and maintains a clear sense of agency. For example, she recounts strategies that she utilized to deal with the sexist behaviour of senior management, by insisting that other women's suggestions in key committees be formally dealt with rather than passed over. However, she speculates that such acts of resistance may have led to her exclusion from the inner sanctum of the "boys' club" of senior management (Montgomery, 1997, p.70).

Hence, Lauren's ability to effect leadership *praxis* and in particular, to gain an overall sense of the system and the educational field is severely restrained by the 'mobilisation of bias' which occurs for women who assume management positions within academia (Connell, 1987). Her experiences illustrate the dangers of a lack of problematization of concepts such as leadership and *praxis* when they are uncritically transposed to an analysis of practices, devoid of consideration of 'how asymmetrical power relations must be constantly remade in the micropolitics of everyday leadership actions and practices' (Morley, 1999, pp.4-5). Nonetheless,

Amelia, Lauren and Ruth's experiences hold out hope for strategies of resistance and agency, for they point to the reality that the establishment of new managerialist practices of leadership within academe is not a taken-for-granted process but an active process characterised by "a *field of struggles* aimed at preserving or transforming the configurations of these forces" (Wacquant, 1989, p.40).

CONCLUSION

Leadership praxis is currently being enacted in Australian universities despite the climate of new managerialism that prevails. It is particularly telling that tales of leadership praxis come from Amelia and Ruth, the two women leaders whose Indigeneity appears to bring with it a form of capital that bestows a sense of legitimacy in their specific location within the academic field. It suggests how this may be a political position which can be exploited for positive effect under circumstances in which the cultural-discursive, social-political and material-economic conditions make space for such recognition. Amelia, Ruth and Lauren's experiences imply that praxis may be cultivated in challenging times, but that an individual "capacity and disposition" towards critical reflexivity, a commitment to "do the most good" and engender "the right change"; and see the system as a whole (Lingard & Christie, 2003, pp.328-329) are nurtured in material circumstances that are not always of our own making. Nonetheless, the strength and wisdom of collective leadership practices, which Amelia and Ruth in particular draw upon from the fields of feminism and Aboriginal civil rights, gesture towards productive spaces from which models of leadership praxis may be enacted.

One of the crucial messages from the three women's narratives is that there is no simple formula of recipe-driven success from which individual leaders enact their *praxis*. Hence, any discussion of leadership *praxis* needs to take into account the broader socio-political contexts which inform the institutional discourses and practices of leadership; the specific local contexts, which may optimise or subvert *praxis*; and the particularity of experiences, which each person brings to their work as leaders. It is in these fruitful and "multiplaced" locations, which evoke both oppression and liberation, that leadership *praxis* may become a site of "power and resistance" (Pallotta-Chiarolli, 1996, p.98).

NOTES

[1] For example, at level A, the most junior of all academic levels, Australian women remained clustered as the majority of the lowest paid academics (1996 – 52 percent; 2003 – 53 percent). Despite male academics being a minority at 47 percent, in 2003 men still comprised the overwhelming majority of all professorships – 85 percent – only a slight decrease from 90 percent in 1996. In 2003 at senior lecturer level (Level C) – the key lecturing level from which positions of leadership commence and at which the springboard into the professoriate occurs – women's representation declines from 46 percent at Level B to 34 percent, or just over a third of all academics (www.avcc.edu.au/documents/universities/key_survey_summaries/Uni_staff_profiles_19-2003.xls Accessed 17/01/05).

[2] All names of interviewees are pseudonyms.

[3] Given the small numbers of women from diverse ethnic origins in leadership positions in Australian universities, there is a possibility of identification of participants within the larger study from which these examples are drawn. Hence, descriptions of the women have been kept as general as possible.

[4] Aboriginal women have always exercised considerable leadership within their communities and women such as Faith Bandler have been at the forefront of social activism. However, it is only in the past two decades that they have emerged within the white media and public sphere more generally in terms of their location as "(an)other public identity ... the ... (female) ... Aboriginal political actor'" (Mickler, 1998, p.129).

[5] Primary habitus is the term used to describe the ' "practices and dispositions acquired in very early stages of childhood maturation" , which subconsciously mould one's life trajectory' (Zipin and Brennan, 2003, p.358).

REFERENCES

Acker, S., & Feuerverger, G. (1997). Enough is never enough: Women's work in academe. In C. Marshall (Ed.), *Feminist critical policy analysis II: A perspective from post-secondary education* (pp. 122-140). London: The Falmer Press.

Bagilhole, B. (1994). Being different is a very difficult row to hoe: Survival strategies of women academics. In S. Davis, C. Lubelska & J. Quinn (Eds.), *Changing the subject: Women in higher education* (pp. 15-28). London: Taylor & Francis.

Bennis, W., & Nanus, B. (1985). *Leaders: The strategies for taking charge.* New York: Harper.

Blackmore, J. (1997). Disciplining feminism: A look at gender-equity struggles in Australian higher education. In L. G. Roman & L. Eyre (Eds.), *Dangerous territories: Struggles for difference and equality in education* (pp. 75-96). New York and London: Routledge.

Blackmore, J. (1997). Gender, restructuring and the emotional economy of higher education. Paper presented at the Annual Conference, *Australian Association of Research in Education*, Brisbane, Australia.

Blackmore, J., & Sachs, J. (2003). Managing equity work in the performative university. *Australian Feminist Studies, 18*(41), 141-162.

Bogotoch, I. E. (2000). Educational leadership and social justice: Theory into practice, *Annual Conference of the University Council for Educational Administration.* Albuquerque, NM.

Bourdieu, P. (1990). *In other words: Essays towards a reflexive sociology* (M. Adamson, Trans.). Cambridge: Polity Press.

Bourdieu, P. (1990). *The logic of practice* (R. Nice, Trans.). Cambridge: Polity Press.

Bourdieu, P. (1998). *Practical reason: On the theory of action.* Cambridge: Polity Press.

Bush, T. (2007). Editorial: Theory and research in educational leadership and management. *Educational Management Administration & Leadership, 35*(1), 1-8.

Clarke, J., & Newman, J. (1997). *The managerial state: Power, politics and ideology in the remaking of social welfare.* London: Sage Publications Ltd.

Connell, R. W. (1987). Gender and power. Cambridge, MA: Polity Press.

Coser, R. L. (1981). Where have all the women gone? Like the sediment of good wine, they have sunk to the bottom. In C. F. Epstein & R. L. Coser (Eds.), *Access to power: Cross-national studies of women and elites.* Boston: George Allen and Unwin.

Currie, J., & Thiele, B. (2001). Globalization and gendered work cultures in universities. In A. Brooks & A. Mackinnon (Eds.), *Gender and the restructured university: Changing management and culture in higher education* (pp. 90-116). Buckingham: The Society for Research into Higher Education & Open University Press.

Currie, J., Thiele, B., & Harris, P. (2002). *Gendered universities in globalized economies: Power, careers, and sacrifices.* Lanham, Maryland: Lexington Books.

Foucault, M. (1990). *The will to knowledge: The history of sexuality Volume One* (R. Hurley, Trans.). London: Penguin Books.

Furman, G. (2002). Introduction. In K. Leithwood & P. Hallinger (Eds.), *Second international handbook of leadership and administration, Part One* (2nd ed., pp. 205-207). Dordrecht: Kluwer Academic Publishers.

Gronn, P. (2003). Leadership: Who needs it? *School Leadership & Management, 23*(3), 267-291.

Halford, S., Savage, M., & Witz, A. (1997). *Gender, careers and organisations.* London: Macmillan.

Hall, S. (1988). The toad in the garden: Thatcherism among the theorists. In C. Nelson & L. Grossberg (Eds.), *Marxism and the interpretation of culture* (pp. 35-57). Houndmills: Macmillan Education Ltd.

Hearn, J. (2001). Academia, management and men: Making the connections, exploring the implications. In A. Brooks & A. Mackinnon (Eds.), *Gender and the restructured university: Changing management and culture in higher education* (pp. 69-89). Buckingham: The Society for Research into Higher Education & Open University Press.

Henderson, A. (1999). *Getting even: Women MPs on life, power and politics.* Sydney: Harper Collins.

Jenkins, R. (1992). *Pierre Bourdieu.* London: Routledge.

Karpin, D. (1995). *Enterprising nation - Renewing Australia's managers to meet the challenges of the asia-pacific century: Report of the industry task force on leadership and management skills.* Canberra: Australian Commonwealth Government - Department of Employment, Education and Training.

Lingard, B., & Christie, P. (2003). Leading theory: Bourdieu and the field of educational leadership. An introduction and overview to this special issue. *International Journal of Leadership in Education, 6*(4), 317-333.

Lingard, B., Hayes, D., Mills, M., & Christie, P. (2003). *Leading learning: Making hope practical in schools.* Maidenhead: Open University Press.

Lingard, B., & Rawolle, S. (2004). Mediatizing educational policy: The journalistic field, science policy, and cross-field effects. *Journal of Education Policy, 19*(3), 361-380.

Mackinnon, A., & Brooks, A. (2001). Introduction: Globalization, academia and change. In A. Brooks & A. Mackinnon (Eds.), *Gender and the restructured university* (pp. 1-11). Buckingham: The Society for Research into Higher Education & Open University Press.

Marginson, S., & Considine, M. (2000). *The enterprise university.* Cambridge: Cambridge University Press.

Mickler, S. (1998). *The myth of privilege: Aboriginal status*, Media Visions, Public Ideas. Fremantle Arts Centre Press, Perth.

Montgomery, A. (1997). In law and outlaw? The tale of a journey. In L. Stanley (Ed.), *Knowing feminisms: On academic borders, territories and tribes* (pp. 58-71). London: SAGE Publications.

Morley, L. (1999). *Organising feminisms: The micropolitics of the Academy.* New York: St. Martin's Press.

Ozga, J., & Deem, R. (2000). Carrying the burden of transformation: The experiences of women managers in UK higher and further education. *Discourse: Studies in the Cultural Politics of Education, 21*(2), 141-153.

Pallotta-Chiarolli, M. (1996, 20-21 September). Educating Voula'/la mestiza educating: Interweaving cultural multiplicity, gender and sexuality in education. Paper presented at the *School days: Past, present and future. Education of Girls in 20th Century Australia*, University of South Australia, Magill Campus.

Shields, C., M., & Oberg, S. L. (2006). *A praxis-oriented framework for educational leadership*, Commonwealth Council of Educational Adminstration and Management.Cyprus.

Thomas, R., & Davies, A. (2002). Gender and new public management: Reconstituting academic subjectivities. *Gender, Work and Organisation, 9*(4), 371-397.

Wacquant, L. J. D. (1989). Towards a reflexive sociology: A workshop with Pierre Bourdieu. *Sociological Theory, 7*(1), 26-63.

Walker, M. (1997). Women in the academy: Ambiguity and complexity in a South African university. *Gender and Education*.

Webb, J., Schirato, T., & Danaher, G. (2002). *Understanding Bourdieu*. Sydney: Allen & Unwin.

Wilkinson, J. (2005). Examining representations of women's leadership in the media and Australian universities. Unpublished PhD, Deakin, Geelong.

Wilkinson, J. (2006). Policy as practice: Senior women academics and the "risky business" of diversity policies in enterprise universities: Charles Sturt University.

Yeatman, A. (1995). The gendered management of equity-oriented change in higher education. In J. Smyth (Ed.), *Academic work: The changing labour process in higher education* (pp. 194-205). Buckingham: Society for Research into Higher Education & Open University Press.

Zipin, L. & Brennan, M. (2003). The suppression of ethical dispositions through managerial governmentability: A habitus crisis in Australian higher education'. *International Journal of Leadership in Education*, 6(4), pp.351-370.

AFFILIATION

Jane Wilkinson
School of Education
Charles Sturt University, Wagga Wagga, Australia

ROSLIN BRENNAN KEMMIS

10. FREEDOM FOR PRAXIS

An unburied and unforgotten tradition

Vocational Education and Training (VET) in Australia has a long history. White colonial settlement brought the VET traditions and practices from Britain. These, in turn, had been strongly influenced by Western European practices that stretch back to the 16th century. Apprenticeships, as an approach to trade training, were based on the tradition of the craft guilds (Misko et al, 2005, p7) and were attached to wage structures that equated with the level of progress through the apprenticeship (Smith and Keating, 2003, p11). The European tradition was based on a craft relationship between a 'master practitioner' and a 'novice'. These individual relationships gradually amalgamated into 'guilds' or groups of masters involved in the same craft. The guilds were the sites at which the *technē* or disposition to make a product and the *poiesis* or making of the product were contextualised by *phronesis* or the commitment to act wisely in your trade and *praxis* or behaving professionally and morally as an integral part of life and work. In the apprenticeship and the guild, we see one form of the nexus of tradition, practices, institutions and the "narrative unity of a human life" described by Macintyre (1984, p.36). Vocational Education and Training had its own virtues, its own characteristics and its own particular relation to the *technē* (disposition) and *poiēsis* (making action) characteristic of the various crafts. It held its own sense of place in the society, and had a set of practice architectures embedded in these traditions.

The virtues of contemporary teachers in Vocational Education and Training in Australia may thus be understood against a long-standing history and set of traditions that accompanied white settlement from 1788. Within the traditions and history of the apprenticeship system their particular responsibility was not only the teaching of the technical craft but also the socialisation of novices to the craft and its history, as well as the development of the whole human being who would enact values that aligned with relevant traditions. They had a duty to the craft, and their technical expertise in teaching was imbued with a sense of responsibility both to their students and to the craft. Teachers in formal training organizations whose

Kemmis, Stephen and Smith, Tracey J. (2008) Enabling praxis: Challenges for education.195-215

brief it was to teach vocational skills were committed and permitted to teach both the skills and the culture of the trade. Pride in workmanship was not a meaningless aphorism. Alexander McCall Smith's fictional creation Mr J.L.B.Matekoni articulates the dimensions of these traditions beautifully (2006, pp.14-15):

> Mr J.L.B. Matekoni sighed. He had been tempted to abandon the task of teaching these apprentices anything about life, but persisted nonetheless. He took the view that an apprentice-master should do more than show his apprentice how to change an oil-filter and repair brakes. He should show them, preferably by example, how to behave as an honourable mechanic. Anybody can fix a car – did the Japanese not have machines which could build cars without anybody being there to operate them? – but not everybody could meet the standards of an honourable mechanic. Such a person could give advice to the owner of a car; such a person would tell the truth about what was wrong with a car; such a person would think about the best interests of the owner and act accordingly. That was something which had to be passed on from generation to generation of mechanics, and it was not always easy to do that.

> He looked at the apprentices. They were due to go off for another spell of training at the Automotive Trades College, but he wondered if it did them any good. He received reports from the college as to how they performed in the academic parts of their training. These reports did not make good reading; although they passed their examinations – just – their lack of seriousness, and their sloppiness was always commented upon.

Vocational Education and Training was, and continues to be, about developing the skills and knowledge appropriate for a specific trade or industry, and about the 'virtues' associated with the trade – virtues like perseverance, reliability, precision, honesty and ethical behaviour. In the current Australian context of high levels of government regulation of the VET sector, where national organisational imperatives are shaping practice in VET, teachers and trainers are confronted by structures and compliance regimes that threaten their concepts of *praxis*. The scale of this colonization, the tensions and problems it creates, and – despite the colonisation – the persistence of ideas relating to the moral and social purposes of education and training is the subject of this chapter.

VOCATIONAL EDUCATION AND TRAINING TRADITIONS IN AUSTRALIA

By 1788 the European craft guilds and their apprenticeship arrangements were beginning to respond to the new industrial, economic and social circumstances of the Industrial Revolution.

> It was the industrial revolution, which forged the regulated trades in industrialised countries, including Australia, a central element of which has been the apprenticeship system. Features of the system have been the

government endorsed regulations governing the practice of the trade; industrial awards for the tradespeople, based on skill levels; and regulations for the conduct of the apprenticeships, including the contract of training and the wages to be paid to apprentices (Smith and Keating, 2003, p10-11).

In Australia, these effects on the traditional apprenticeship system were slower to emerge. Australia was settled as a penal colony and it was not until the country was regarded as a source of produce and trade for Britain specifically, and Europe generally, and free settlement had begun, that the possibilities for any kind of 'industrialisation' were realised. The colonial needs were 'basic' and the free settlers and emancipated convicts divided clearly into two groups: those with the privilege and capital to take up large tracts of land for agrarian purposes and those who would service their needs. It was not until the gold rushes of the second half of the nineteenth century that the advent of large-scale immigration to the Australian colonies created the preconditions for a reinvigoration of the apprenticeship system. As the economies of the Australian colonies boomed, the demand for the traditional trades increased. By this time, however, the impact of changes in Britain and Europe had percolated through the older arrangements and a nexus had been made between the state-administered industrial relations systems and apprenticeships. English law prescribed the relationships between master and apprentice and in 1901 the Australian state of NSW was the first to introduce legislation, modelled on its British forerunner, that enshrined a range of practices for the industrial protection of the parties in the apprenticeship relationship (Ray, 2001).

The traditions of the guilds were partially preserved in organizations such as the Mechanics Institutes in Australia. The roles of these organizations were educative, protective and broad based. They had an egalitarian commitment to the education of their members and they often brought together industry, government and labour into loose knit and not altogether effective alliances.

Government intervention in the VET sector, beyond regulation of the apprenticeship system, began to take shape following World War I as governments recognised the need for more a more highly skilled labour force to promote international competitiveness and economic growth. These initiatives were state and territory based and took a back seat to other education policy reforms associated with school-based education and the higher education sector. The combined pressures of reduced immigration numbers, economic growth and the prospect of skills shortages led the Commonwealth Government in 1973 to make large injections of funds to support apprenticeships in Australia via the National Apprenticeship Assistance Scheme. The Kangan Review in 1974 confirmed the assertive involvement of the Commonwealth Government in the VET sector.

The Kangan Report was a watershed for technical education in Australia. It effectively established the TAFE sector, and it argued for a more liberal concept of technical and further education that Murray-Smith (1967) believes was abandoned in Australia in the early part of the 19th century. It placed TAFE as a broadly based vocational and education training sector, rather than a more narrow focussed vocational skilling sector (Smith and Keating, 2003, p.9).

The weaknesses in the economy that culminated in the 1980s in Australia as they did in many countries, led to a major reassessment of the structure of the Australian economy and the levels of skills needed to service the economy and contribute to its growth. Governments became more interested in the relationships between training and economic health, and became committed to reforming the training system. One of the central planks of the new policies was award restructuring, the structuring of the award system by which minimum wages for particular occupations and skill levels were set. In this new context, wages would be tied to demonstrable productivity increases and training was seen to be the vehicle for attaining these. Agreements between the unions, governments and business gave rise to a raft of new policies on training, and the growing trend towards a federal rather than an individual state or territory response, created the National Training Reform Agenda. One of the major planks in this Agenda was the Commonwealth creation and subsidisation of traineeships. Traineeships were a "major response to youth unemployment" and "were promoted mainly as quality training options for jobs in service industries" (Ray, 2001, p.25). Apprenticeships were "virtually left alone for many years" (Ray, 2001, p.25).

The National Training Reform Agenda has grown and changed since 1985. Some significant landmarks have been the opening up of the training 'market' to a much wider range of providers, the introduction of competency based training with agreed national industry competency standards, contracts for apprentices and trainees that are nationally consistent, a national framework for the recognition of credentials, the negotiation of national strategies for VET, the Australian Qualifications Framework, the Australian Quality Training Framework and the introduction of Training Packages. This prodigious growth in government regulation has created a highly elaborated new practice architecture in VET designed to constrain practitioners in the name of consistency and accountability. It is a practice architecture where skills and knowledge are disjoined from considerations of the morality of teaching. However, while teachers acknowledge these constraints they continue to assert their freedom to teach.

In many ways, then, the Australian VET sector is a reflection of the nineteenth and twentieth century growth of rationalist ways of thinking about society, the economy and the world. The increasing focus on individualism and competition and the concomitant loss of social and community responsibilities and the absolute assertion of the rights of the 'market' have both demanded and encouraged high levels of regulation. According to Huberman (1999), Gertrude Stein commented that we are entering an age that has just about given up on answers (p.307). In this uncertain political climate, the response has been an ever more elegant system of interlocking mechanisms for the control of the uncontrollable. VET 'practitioners', many of whom were participants in the more traditional forms of apprenticeship of long ago, are now the teachers and trainers within this context of compliance and legislative determinism. They are thus at the threshold of a new era, imbued with understandings of the virtues of practice in their trades but also agents or operatives of a training system that does not countenance the idea of virtue, at least in its regulatory framework. It is therefore fascinating to consider whether and how they reconcile their work as accredited trainers with the idea of *praxis*. How do their understandings of the traditions of their 'trades' and the lessons that they learnt intersect with these new regimes of control? To what extent are they the passive recipients of regulation versus morally informed and socially responsible members of a trade, a society and a nation? Is there still room for negotiation? Are there ambiguities, randomness and under determined influences (Huberman, 1999, p306) that allow *praxis* to survive despite the apparent collision between these two opposed ways of understanding a trade and the training for it? Do the elements of *praxis* expressed in the traditional concepts of apprenticeship survive in contemporary VET pedagogical practices?

As we address these questions we might recall and consider the following statement by Basil Bernstein (1996, p.5) about how forms of education have cultural and social as well as economic effects and consequences:

> Education is central to the knowledge base of society, groups and individuals, yet education, like health, is a public institution, central to the production and reproduction of distributive injustices. Biases in the form of content, access and opportunities of education have consequences not only for the economy; these biases can reach down to drain the very springs of affirmation, motivation and imagination. In this way such biases can becomes, and often are, an economic and cultural threat to democracy. Education can have a crucial role in creating tomorrow's optimism in the context of today's pessimism. But if it is to do this then we must have an analysis of the social biases in education. These biases lie deep within the very structure of the educational system's processes of transmission and acquisition and their social assumptions.

Government regulation in the VET sector

The Australian VET sector is now highly regulated, and compliance is enforced through legislation. Training Packages that specify the skills to be accredited in industry provide assurance that Nationally Accredited Training is consistent between states and territories and offer students guarantees of mutual recognition of qualifications irrespective of location.

The diagram on the next page shows how the various component parts of the system interlock through legislation and agreement.

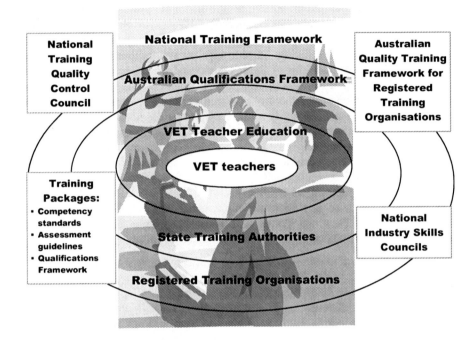

The National Training Reform Agenda is a complex web of legislative interrelationships. Within this Agenda, *Training Packages* provide accreditation to students on the satisfactory completion of specified Units of Competency that are bundled in particular ways at particular levels within the *Australian Qualifications Framework* These different levels of accreditation are frequently linked to wage levels. Training Packages claim to cover all the skills needed for practice at each specified level within the Australian Qualifications Framework.

Training Packages are developed by *National Industry Skills Councils* or enterprises "to meet the identified training needs of specific industries or industry sectors" (Australian National Training Authority, 2004, p.1). They are a vital component of the *National Training Framework* that has been agreed to by all Australian states and territories. Training Packages form part of the *Australian Quality Training Framework* and have been endorsed by the *National Training Quality Council.* Training Packages can be delivered and assessed only by *Registered Training Organizations* who have registered the units of competency in their scope of registration, or who work in partnership with another Registered Training Organization, which has the units of competency on their scope.

Each Training Package includes *Endorsed Components* that "must be used" (Australian National Training Authority, 2004 p.2). The Endorsed Components establish and require specified *Competency Standards, Assessment Guidelines* and the Qualifications Framework.

– The Competency Standards are organised in units and levels within the AQF. "Each unit of competency identifies a discrete workplace requirement and includes the knowledge and skills that underpin competency...the units of competency must be adhered to in training and assessment to ensure consistency of outcomes" (Australian National Training Authority, 2004, p.2).

– The Assessment Guidelines "provide an industry framework to ensure all assessments meet industry needs and nationally agreed standards as expressed in the Training Package and the *Standards for Registered Training Organizations*. The Assessment Guidelines must be followed to ensure the integrity of the assessment leading to nationally recognised qualifications" (Australian National Training Authority, 2004, p.2).

– The Qualifications Framework sets out the information relating to the various levels of awards that can be given to students who have successfully completed Units of Competency. "The packaging rules must be followed to ensure the integrity of nationally recognised qualifications issued" (Australian National Training Authority, 2004, p.2).

Training Package qualifications are nationally recognised through the process of mutual recognition under the powers of the Commonwealth established by the Australian Constitution, that is, recognition by all Australian states of certain matters regulated in any other state. The levels of competency specified by the Training Packages have created a new industry classification system that has taken over many spaces previously occupied by Industrial Awards (the system of minimum wages for particular kinds and levels of employment in particular occupations). Currently Training Packages cover a gamut of industries including Hospitality, Tourism, Building and Construction, Information Technology, Fishing and Education. The control mechanism used to enforce these standards for training in every industry is the Australian Quality Training Framework (AQTF). This legislative mechanism regulates the operation of the Registered Training Organizations that deliver training and assess student competence. It is composed of Standards endorsed by the National Ministerial Council on Employment, Education, Training and Youth Affairs that must be complied with if a training organization is to be registered. Each State and Territory has a rigorous auditing and compliance system with the power to register or deregister Training Organizations on the basis of their compliance with these Standards. "Together with Training Packages, the standards under the AQTF provide a common foundation for the national recognition and integrity of vocational education and training (VET) providers and the qualifications and statements of attainment they issue" (Australian National Training Authority, 2005, p.2). The AQTF specifies 12 Standards with 48 sub-regulations. These Standards cover the operation of the Registered Training Organizations delivering Nationally Accredited Training and the Standards regulate:

1) Systems for quality training and assessment;
2) Compliance with Commonwealth, state/territory legislation and regulatory requirements;
3) Effective financial management procedures;

4) Effective administrative and records management procedures;
5) Recognition of qualifications issues by other Registered Training Organizations;
6) Access and equity and client service;
7) The competence of Registered Training Organization staff;
8) Registered Training Organization assessments;
9) Learning and assessment strategies;
10) Issuing Australian Qualifications and Statements of Attainment;
11) Use of national and state/territory logos; and
12) Ethical marketing and advertising.

Implications of government regulation

Within this crystalline structure of regulation and legislation Statements of Competency have replaced the kinds of standards employed by masters imbued in the traditions of the guilds. The intricately elaborated framework of Statements of Competency requires no acknowledgement of the sense of solidarity amongst the members of an industry; it leaves no space for creative reinterpretation of the new or the innovative, and there is no place for preserving the ethos or culture of the 'brotherhood'. The new systems acknowledge skills and competencies but the practitioner, whether apprentice or master, trainee or trainer, is absent and excluded by the disinfected language and the architecture of the Training Packages. Discussions of curriculum, pedagogy, the centrality of student learning and the responsibilities of all those involved in facilitating student learning have likewise been excluded at worst and devalued at best by the discursive environment that has come to dominate the VET environment. The official language of the VET sector is mechanistic, rhetorically political and hard edged. For instance, 'knowledge' has been replaced by 'competencies', 'teachers' by 'practitioners' and 'students' rarely appear in anything but purely transactional relationships. Legislation ensures compliance and Training Packages provide the details of the mandated reality. The complexity of the interlocking systems controlling the VET sector is not necessarily badly intentioned but the functional effects are that practitioners are swamped by the bureaucratic and the mechanistic. The matrix of values embedded in education and training that makes explicit the link between education and social and political health explicit is nowhere to be found. "In other words, it is silence which carries the message of power; it is the full stop between one category of discourse and another; it is the dislocation in the potential flow of discourse which is crucial to the specialization of any category" (Bernstein, 1996, 20). This 'silence' creates a bubble of 'insulation' that surrounds the official definitions of the VET sector. The VET sector is Australia is a clear example of Bernstein's 'strong classification system' (p.21):

In the case of strong classification, we have strong insulation between categories. In the case of strong classification, each category has its unique identity, its unique voice, and its own specialised rules of internal relations.

The model of standardisation in Australian VET described above and the consequent strong levels of 'classification' in the curriculum might have the effect of creating teachers and trainers whose practices are 'domesticated' by prescriptions of competencies and outcomes, even if the teachers and trainers themselves are not (or are they?). This might create a conflict with the traditions of the trades, and perhaps put praxis itself at risk of replacement by regimes of compliance. These regimes are in the form of practice architectures that exclude rather than include the traditions within VET. Better and more historically and morally located architectures need to be developed and these should begin with the aspirations and realities of those teachers and trainers in VET who articulate and aspire to retain the traditions of their work.

REGIMES OF COMPLIANCE AND PRACTICE

The focus on only those skills specified by the Training Package agenda threatens to confine students to the acquisition of *technē* and *poiēsis* by excluding the context and culture of their actions (*phronesis*) and the wider social and moral consequences of their actions (*praxis*). However the narrowing of the definition of vocational education and training and its reduction to a neat articulation of skills and competencies denies the traditions of VET practice (Macintyre, 1984, p.87):

> To enter into a practice is to enter into a relationship not only with its contemporary practitioners, but also with those who have preceded us in practice, particularly those whose achievements extended the reach of the practice, to its present point. It is thus the achievement, and a *fortiori* the authority, of a tradition which I then confront and from which I have to learn. And for this learning and the relationship to the past which it embodies the virtues of justice, courage and truthfulness are prerequisite in precisely the same way and for precisely the same reasons as they are in sustaining present relationships within practices.

The question is: Do trainees and trainers in the Australian VET system give up their induction into these traditions and the authority of tradition when they follow the intricate scripts of the Training Packages, or do these traditions and this authority somehow survive in the interstices – the spaces between the lines – of the specifications of competency? The development of Training Packages is heavily influenced by 'industry' – although who constitutes the voices of industry is a complex political question in itself. The content of the Training Packages is said to reflect the most current appreciation of the skills that are needed in any particular industry area arranged in levels of complexity from Certificate I to Advanced Diploma level. The content as specified by the Units of Competency is a definition of the work required within any industry area. Despite the inherent arguability of any particular determination of what skills are most essential in any industry there seems to be no room for contestation of the definition given in a Unit of Competency. It is presumed that all this debate has happened within the confines of the Industry Skills Councils that have the unequivocal power to make final decisions (after consultation) about levels of achievement and the nature of work. The only concession to a broader discussion of 'work' has been the development of a list of generic employability skills that are taught and developed in conjunction with Training Package implementation.

The results of a study reported at the Australian Vocational Education and Training Research Association 2006 (Peddle, 2006), however, indicates that 'industry' is not of one heart and mind about the skills that are needed. Peddle showed that an industry-acceptable tradesperson is one who is as ethical as they are skilled. Loyalty, commitment, honesty, enthusiasm, motivation, adaptability, commonsense, reliability, sense of humour, a balanced attitude to work, positive self esteem and ability to deal with pressure were attributes ranked as highly as the specified technical competencies in the Training Packages. Industry itself is reasserting the importance of *praxis*.

VET TEACHERS AND PRAXIS

VET teachers also assert the importance of *praxis*. The objective realities of compliance and regulation, however constraining, have not destroyed the historically-constituted commitment to ideas and ways of being that are both human and contributory. The comment below from a VET teacher education student captures this 'inheritance of *praxis*' and the strength of the living tradition that influenced his career choice (Deilman, 2006, p.1):

> I always wanted to be an Electrician. My father was one and my brother was an Apprentice Electrician. I grew up waiting for that phone call late in the night when the Tip Top Bakery had a breakdown that needed urgent repair. I would jump into Dad's panel van as he zoomed off to fix the mixer or oven or whatever else had stopped. When we arrived there would always be the big welcome and 'thanks for coming so quick'. It made Dad feel special and it made me feel proud of Dad, and the respect shown to him by the factory staff when he got their production line on the move again. This is a feeling I wanted to get when I grew up, and this was my inspiration to be an electrician and now a teacher. Dad died when I was 14 and I vowed to be like him.

Praxis as it developed in the traditional apprenticeship model clearly survives in the work and conduct of many contemporary VET teachers and trainers. These teachers and trainers continue to reassert the moral and ethical dimensions and responsibilities of the work itself and the contributions that their students can make as morally informed participants in the communities into which their students will go as qualified and credentialed members. They model in their teaching and training those conditions under which the development of moral reasoning accompanies the acquisition of skills. Hamilton and Lempert (1996, pp.453-454) report the results of two longitudinal studies into the situations under which apprentices develop moral reasoning – conditions that seem identical to those which VET teachers and trainers in many situations would aspire to create for their students:

1. Involvement in manifest (instead of repressed or transferred) social problems and conflicts of interest.

2. Free (instead of standardized, one-way, or manipulative) communication.

3. Participation in cooperative decision making (instead of subordination, rivalry or mere talk).

4. Abiding empathy, love, care and recognition (instead of indifference, hatred, rejection, depreciation or contempt).

5. Information about the social impact of individual and collective behaviour and action (instead of unfounded rules prescribing or proscribing certain actions).

6. Substantial involvement in contradictions between individual expectations, interpersonal rules, social norms, and cultural values that preclude one-sided solutions (instead of either enforced harmony or lack of common maxims)

7. Ascription of responsibility for one's own life and (subsequently) for others according to one's growing capabilities) instead of either distrustful strict control or uncontrolled laissez-faire).

Who are VET teachers?

The Training Reform Agenda generally and the de-regulation of the training market particularly has meant that VET teachers are now difficult creatures to apprehend and describe. They may be teaching and assessing 'on the job', in a workshop, business or enterprise; or 'off the job' in a small Registered Training Organization; or working in an institutional VET provider such as a Technical and Further Education (TAFE) Institute.

They are working in full time and part time positions, with the latter group often having a cocktail of employment in a range of different sites. These teachers, by definition and constraint, must hold qualifications in the content area in which they are teaching and assessing. For example, if they are teaching Building and Construction Certificate Level 3, they must have this qualification. Increasingly, they are also asked to be marketers who will generate business for their Registered Training Organization since their Registered Training Organizations rely on the profits of training for their continued existence.

The growth of traineeships and new apprenticeships in industry has also impacted on the profile of the VET practitioner. Increasingly more experienced employees are being asked to supervise and assess apprentices and trainees, particularly in large enterprises and this task is subsidiary to their substantive position in the organization. Often this training and assessment role is part of a larger human resource function. To do so they must gain the relevant qualifications – often while doing their usual work. Teaching in the context of a workplace is very different to the teaching that takes place in an organization like a TAFE Institute whose primary function is the delivery of VET.

VET teachers come from a very varied set of backgrounds – education, business, industry, human resource management, traditional trades, social welfare and the armed services, to mention only a few. Similarly, their students cross all age barriers and statuses and any one class may have students from 16 to 65 with a wide range of ethnic, social and educational backgrounds. There is thus a multiplicity of relationships between teachers and students in the VET sector. The specificity of the skills prescribed by the Certificate IV in Training and Assessment (the minimum qualification needed by any person delivering Nationally Accredited Training) represents an attempt to capture all the basic competencies needed by teachers who are working in these diverse circumstances. Similarly, the prescriptions of competencies, performance criteria and specific evidence requirements within every Training Package across all industries, are meant to make the delivery of the qualifications practitioner proof in the face of this diversity.

In the highly rationalised world of Training Packages, where the skills are so highly regulated and specified, there is no explicit and official role for the VET teacher. To people not familiar with the Australian VET sector, this persistent and obvious absence may seem surprising – amazing even. Teachers have no documented role in any other responsibility area other than to facilitate or perhaps to guide the acquisition of the required skills in their students. These other responsibilities still exist but they have been deliberately occluded through omission. Training Packages are free of pedagogy and free of curriculum, and VET teachers are ostensibly free to take whatever unofficial actions they choose. The fact that teachers and trainers rise above the exigencies of Competency Based Training and supply the missing links about work, a working life and the morality and ethics of work means that the void is often – perhaps crudely – filled. The success of the National Training Agenda may not in fact be the result of the Agenda itself but may rather be due to the efforts of those charged with its practical implementation in the classroom or the workplace: the teachers and trainers who have been written out of the scripts they perform.

TEACHER PREPARATION FOR THE VET SECTOR – TENSIONS AND ASPIRATIONS

VET teachers may once have learned their teaching skills on the job in Technical and Further Education (TAFE) Colleges; increasingly they learn their craft as teachers in University courses. University Teacher educators in the VET sector are a relatively new phenomenon. Generally they see their role as being respectful of the differences that exist between the VET sector, school, University and adult education. They wish to preserve the specific solidarity of values of the VET sector. They have a sense that they are preparing teachers for a sector that is characteristically different from any other. Teacher educators also have a commitment to encouraging the development of *praxis* in their students. In this way, the dilemmas that confront teachers in the VET sector also confront VET teacher educators.

Teacher educators in Australia are confronted by two sets of standards; one set emanating from the Australian Quality Training Framework and one which comes from the history and traditions of universities.

The first of these sets of standards places teaching in the VET sector as equivalent to working in any other industry area for which there is a Training Package. The Certificate IV in Training and Assessment prescribes "the skills and knowledge needed to perform effectively in the workplace without prescribing how people should be trained" (Australian National Training Authority, 2004, p.1). The Certificate IV is the minimum teaching qualification for any person delivering nationally accredited training.

The Training Package for VET teachers (TAA04) is a large volume of 776 pages. The Certificate IV in Training and Assessment (TAA40104) was developed after a major review of the previous Training Package in Assessment and Workplace Training (BSZ98). "It was developed in conjunction with contracted consultants, critical friends and thousands of individuals and hundreds of organizations who contributed their time and input into the development process. The project was undertaken under the guidance of a Project Steering Committee comprising representatives of key stakeholders and a Reference Group comprising representatives of State and Territory Authorities and the Commonwealth government" (Australian National Training Authority, 2004, p.7). The TAA40104 has 12 core Units of Competency and 2 elective Units. These Units of Competency are organised into 4 major fields:

– Learning Environment;
– Learning Design;
– Delivery and Facilitation; and
– Assessment.

Within the 12 core Units of Competency for teachers in the VET sector there are *56 elements of competency* and *264 performance criteria*. Each Unit of Competency comes with an accompanying *Range Statement* that "establishes the range of indicative meanings or applications of these requirements in different operating contexts and conditions. The specific aspects that require elaboration are identified by the use of italics in the *Performance Criteria*" (Australian National Training Authority, 2004, p.429). The *Evidence Guide* in the Training Package sets out the Evidence Requirements in detail. The Evidence Requirements specify the knowledge that needs to be demonstrated, the required skills and attributes, the Key Competencies relevant to the Units, the products that could be used as evidence, the processes that could be used as evidence, the resource implications, the collection of evidence and the specific evidence requirements. A section then follows this on the possibilities for integrated assessment. There is little room to misunderstand.

The developers and reviewers of this Training Package would argue that they provide "a clear set of benchmarks to support both initial competency achievement and ongoing staff and professional development" (Australian National Training Authority, 2004, p.8). However a number of questions emerge from this statement of apparent curriculum neutrality:

207

– What is the extent and nature of the influence that Training Packages exert over teachers?
– What definitions of work and learning are being endorsed by the Training Packages?
– What is missing from the Training Packages and who is responsible for the advocacy of these missing components?

It comes as no surprise that many VET teachers feel that they have been written out of the teaching profession in the Training Packages. The cold edges of the competencies leave little room for asserting the values, influence and responsibilities most of these teachers associate with teaching. Similarly there are no references to students beyond their capacities to demonstrate competence is missing. The spokespeople for the national agenda strongly assert that it was never the intention of the Training Packages to do anything beyond specifying the competencies – as if this were a neutral activity, without implications for standards, and traditions that will develop and unfold beyond their intervention. The Standards within the AQTF are intended to provide the necessary guidance about issues such as learning and assessment strategies, access and equity and the competence of RTO staff to respond to student needs, but there is no mention of human responsiveness to the needs and circumstances of students or people their work will affect.

The reactions of teachers and students suggest that *the specification of action* is being mistaken for *the action itself* – real action that has real consequences for the VET students and their teachers, for VET teacher educators, and all those whose lives are affected by the qualified tradespeople the VET students will become. A prodigious bureaucracy intent on documentation has attempted to tame the chaos of the real world of VET, though, as always, the messiness of reality may have been obscured rather than obliterated. The strange mixture of apparent flexibility within the VET sector that provides students with real and valuing opportunities – flexible time, portability of credentials and mixed mode delivery and assessment are juxtaposed beside, rather than captured within, the highly structured and mechanistic procedures that surround the delivery of VET. Delivery and assessment must stay within the bounds of the Training Package and while experienced teachers are far less intimidated by the pressures of compliance than newer teachers, it is undeniable that they are being asked to deliver and assess within very narrow limits. There appears to be very little space for interpretative teaching beyond a creative combination and integration of the Units of Competency

The environment in which the VET teacher is working is highly competitive and firmly regulated. The "National Curriculum" in VET is nationally endorsed and enforced. Its level of prescription is designed to make it 'practitioner-proof' and whilst there is some room for "customisation" and "reasonable adjustment" within the legislative systems, the exigencies of audit and compliance often press more powerfully on practice than do VET teachers' intentions and opportunities to adapt and become responsive to the local needs and contexts of the students.

Teacher educators are confronted with the task of exposing student teachers to this interlocking system of legislation and agreement in ways that acknowledge and facilitate compliance with these requirements but nevertheless encourage critical thought. VET teachers need to be able to questions the assumptions on which these systems have been built and need to have the capacity to interrogate the effects and consequences of their teaching on their students' learning and the industries and societies in which they will work. This can only be done by developing an understanding of history, politics, sociology, learning theory and pedagogy as these relate to VET, and by using the tools of knowledge and experience to find the paths in teaching that generate inclusivity, equity, social justice and excitement for their students. Generally speaking, teacher educators for the sector are committed to the development of a local, national and international set of perspectives in their students so that the 'here and now of regulation' might be regarded as always open to revision rather than a final determination on questions that are, by their very nature, contested and open to change in the light of changing circumstances.

A scan of the VET teacher preparation programs around Australia indicates that Universities focus on the following themes:
– the practical development of teaching and assessing skills;
– the multiplicity of workplaces for VET practitioners;
– an understanding of the social, economic and political context of VET;
– teacher reflection and research as powerful tools for improving practice;
– the assertion of teacher agency and the development of resilience;
– flexibility, change and leadership;
– the social and moral dimensions of teaching and learning; and
– a commitment to the development of the forms and domains practice that are not colonised by legislation.

University VET teacher educators are not frequently invited to participate in debates about teacher competency in the VET sector. We have to make our own invitations and forums for expressing our views. The Australian Vocational Teacher Education Colloquium (AVTEC) is one of these. In these forums, university VET teacher educators have a responsibility to reinvigorate the debates about what constitutes legitimate work, equitable working conditions, a healthy civic life and a well informed and critically thinking public.

The Certificate IV in Training and Assessment aims to make competent assessors and trainers. It excludes consideration of people either as teachers or students. The Training Package makes minimal reference to students and focuses on what they can make, and not what they are, or what they could be. It describes actions without actors, skills without the skilled, competencies without the competent, assessment standards without the bearers or providers of those standards. The Training Package is based on skills with no reference to *praxis* or to the traditions of teaching. It is based on a narrowly performative view of education and training. Its reserve in leaving persons and personnel out of its specifications is at once modest and monstrous – a pretended neutrality that threatens to suffocate the teachers and students who must pick their way through its regimes of performances and demonstrations.

University teacher education programs aim to go beyond *techne* and work towards respecting the craft distinctive traditions of the VET teacher by codifying these traditions. Most importantly University teacher education programs recognise that education and training are capable of being contributory to the building of the 'good society' and that the nature and consequences of good teaching are significant.

The practicum: opportunities to develop praxis

Within teacher education programs for VET practitioners, the Practicum (practical experience on the job) provides the opportunity to discharge the system responsibilities for teacher accreditation and to explicitly incorporate those things that have been left out of the Certificate IV. It gives the chance to include Macintyre's practices, institutions, traditions and the narrative of human life in ways that bind the cold skills of the Certificate IV into a new fabric of education and training. The Practicum provides context, demonstrates the relevance of learning and acknowledges the experiences of the students.

Many students participating in VET teacher preparation programs in Australian universities are already experienced practitioners, both in the trades and occupations that they want to teach, and in teaching itself. They are working in a huge variety of teaching and training contexts and blending teaching activities across a variety of contexts. These students have practitioner knowledge of very particular kinds, knowledge that far exceeds the experiences of their university teachers. University VET staff accept these backgrounds with a mixture of admiration, excitement and some trepidation. Many see their academic role as one of building on this expertise and extending practitioner knowledge by locating practice in a more critical framework (Carr, 2003, p.1):

> As well as teaching practitioners to think about their practice historically, practical philosophy also teaches them that the understanding...of their practice is neither immutable nor fixed and that, in the course of the history of their practice, previously established modes of practical knowledge and understanding have been continuously reinterpreted and reconceived by previous generations of practitioners.

Tensions remain, however, in terms of the balance between the provision of skills for compliance, registration and accreditation, and the need to critically examine the formation of the context of practitioner work. This is seen most clearly in the Practicum components of the university courses.

Some Australian universities involved in VET sector teacher preparation have chosen to deal with these tensions by excluding a practicum component from their programs. Others like Charles Sturt University (CSU) have tackled these tensions by offering two qualifications, both a VET sector qualification (via the award of transfer credit through a Registered Training Organization) and a University sector qualification, where the Practicum offers a contribution to both. In many ways, the Practicum is the bridge between the prescription of the VET sector teacher qualifications framework, on the one hand, and, on the other, the university aspirations for the development of critically evaluative and reflective practitioners and for the development of *praxis*.

The Practicum in CSU VET teacher education programs is designed to fulfil a number of functions. It provides the opportunity in the workplace for students to apply the knowledge they have gained through their formal University studies. It also provides the opportunity for students to display the competencies specified in the Certificate IV in Training and Assessment. The Practicum is structured so that the competencies are displayed in the first two Practicum subjects. The students then move into a third Practicum subject where the more complex dimensions of teaching are explicitly studied and assessed. These tasks are the more complex and difficult for CSU teachers and students because CSU VET teacher education programs are offered by distance education.

The Practicum pathway is based on three important assumptions made by academic staff in the design of the program. The first is that students will iteratively develop new questions about their work informed by literature and tertiary study. The second is that while students come with occupational trade based competence and some teaching experience their educational and teaching knowledge is in a state of development – they need to develop the craft and *praxis* of education. The third is that students will become committed to developing their professional roles and engage with the excitement of learning through the application of new knowledge to their work.

These assumptions, while laudable, deny a number of important realities. Firstly, the assumptions are unilateral in their conception of the 'student'. While every effort is made to ensure that the diversity of sites is acknowledged and accommodated, the gap between the university and the location of the student can never be adequately transcended and hence requires interpretation, discretion, judgement and a tolerance of uncertainty. This raises questions about the relevance of the constructed Practicum experiences for the student in a distance education mode. Secondly, the assumptions demand that the materials provided for the support of the students are equivalently regarded as useful and extending. While it would be extremely comforting to take this point of view, experience and feedback indicates otherwise. Thirdly, the assumptions deny the 'dip and dive' nature of any learning. Learners at some stages can be observers of their own and others' behaviours or participants. They can be in control of the content of their learning or lost in the flow of it. They can contribute to their own practice through interrogation, evaluation and reflection or simply float with the current. They can decide on what to attend to and what to ignore at any time.

Perhaps the best that can be done is to create conditions for learning and encourage the enquiring, curious disposition in the students that moves them to a point of greater control and influence over the conditions of their work by providing them with both the literacy of *praxis* and the opportunity for *praxis* (as distinct from *technē*).They must have a counter discourse available to them that allows them to critically analyse the language and practice architectures of the regulatory regimes in which they work. A place to begin is with a view of practice that emphasises the value of communication, transaction and development, a view that is more relative than settled, and a view that acknowledges that the same situation can be seen from a multiplicity of perspectives. Given this view, the political, moral and ethical dimensions of teaching and training are repatriated and with this repatriation comes the healthy contest between opposing or simply differing views.

CONCLUSION: TWO VIEWS OF TEACHER PREPARATION – *TECHNĒ* AND *PRAXIS*

In this chapter, two approaches to teacher education for the Australian VET sector have been presented. The first of these is the legacy of the Australian Training Reform Agenda that has culminated in the Certificate IV in Training and Assessment. It is a rationalistic and non-confrontational view of teaching and training. It is permissive in the sense that it simply stipulates outcomes. However the impact of this qualification is felt more in the omission than the inclusion. The official silence on matters of pedagogy, curriculum and values is corrosive, and the apparent tolerance about these issues masks the reality that only institutional VET providers and individual teachers with high degrees of resilience can afford the luxury to interpret the Training Packages in ways that include the older values.

History, tradition and practice are excluded in the specification of competencies. The voices of the unions and the teachers are muffled. There has been a silent *coup d'etat* of *technē* over *praxis* in official documentation relating to teaching.

The Training Package certainly has the capacity to produce competent assessors and trainers but this production alone is not sufficient. It is the capacity to use what we produce wisely and to act rightly that is critical.

Praxis, when applied to VET teachers and trainers, ideally refers to their ways of being, their practical and social histories and the set of embedded traditions that accompany such a sector. The 'society' of VET teachers has been a strong one although this older society is breaking down in the face of national regulation and changes in work practices such as casualisation. The battle for parity of esteem with other tertiary organizations such as universities created a tradition of trades-based practitioners confident in their abilities and somewhat dismissive of the type of learning that has been stereotypically ascribed to universities. It is not that university learning is illegitimate, just questionable in its immediate relevance to the working lives of many VET sector participants. The tradition of the guilds is very strong in the more traditional trade areas. The newer industries are less like this, but they pride themselves on their practicality and the immediate applicability of the learning they are providing. In this, they sustain a valuing of craft knowledge. In this, too, they demonstrate that their practice has been shaped by traditions.

In VET in Australia in recent years, both pedagogical practice and the practitioner have occupied a very lonely position. Those with political power and influence have had their eyes firmly focussed on the structures and procedures that maintain a highly regulated system. This focus has meant that many aspects of the work of VET practitioners have become obscured. In many instances, teachers and trainers report feelings of disempowerment and disengagement from the processes of formal curriculum formation. They also report that their practices seem to be devalued and ranked poorly in discussions of the VET sector.

Learning in VET has always been situated and aligned with strong employment outcomes. Preparation for industry has been a clearly articulated goal of VET teaching and training. This has provided fertile ground for the implementation of more strongly rationalistic views of this relationship. Currently, the links between industrial relations, wage rates, awards and VET qualifications are strong. The advent of much less structured and freer market practices that exclude the influence of the unions is relatively new. The Australian Qualifications Framework (AQF) with its levels of competency and the development of Training Packages that specify in small discrete parts the essential components of the qualification have replaced in many ways the power of the unions in establishing wage rates and career progression. This process has coincided with an increase in the discourses of rationality and standardisation and it is difficult to argue with such an internally consistent set of rules. To attack a part is to attack the whole.

The overlay of a new class of national regulatory agencies gives the impression that tradition has been discounted and a new way of being a professional in contact with others has been discovered. On the other hand, as has been suggested here, one of the roles of VET teacher preparation involves the reclaiming of past traditions, an acknowledgement of, and comfort with, these traditions as the basis for developing a new kind of practical resilience based on a broad appreciation of the location of the professional in the society, the economy and the political definition of the current world and an ability to think about the kind of world the professional has a responsibility to shape.

The development of the VET system in recent years has also been characterised by a particular kind of communication – selective or representative but not participatory or genuinely open. In the end, the coercive force required to shore up this system will fail, as this is way of being is not genuine consultation among people mutually worthy of recognition and respect. Coercion is a key part of the reconstruction of relations within the sector that began with the reforms of Laurie Carmichael and the assertion of new levels of control in the VET sector.

The voices of teachers and teacher educators have been replaced by the influence of the professional representatives of 'industry' with practitioners having a role in the sometimes-uncertain process of consultation. This 'after the event' role can be explained by reference to the policy documents and political debates of the last ten years. The commitment to economic growth, the passion for competition, the deregulation of the employment markets and the privatisation of public infrastructure have all contributed to a view of education and training as an instrument of national policy. In the VET sector, this has meant that those with direct links to the operationalisation of this agenda exert powerful influences.

The practitioner is buried deeply inside the new regulatory framework and apparently the system no longer relies on the practitioner for its livelihood. The blandness of the Training Packages that choose to refer to 'students' only as 'clients' or 'customers' and occasionally as 'learners' ostensibly guarantees fairness and objectivity to all. However the absence of explicitness about values does not mean that the curriculum is value-free. The assumption is that if everything is carried out in the order prescribed, using the assessment tools presented, and giving due attention to the specific evidence requirements and by consulting the glossary of terms that accompanies each of these Training Packages, then learning and practice is unambiguous, transparent, valid, reliable and fair. Equivocation and contestation are removed by specificity and accountability measures – or so it is asserted.

Contrary to this bleak picture, however, the observable reality is that teachers in both in the VET sector and the tertiary sector are keeping alive the traditions of *praxis* in spite of a VET system that has denied reference to the external world of teacher, students and pedagogy. The strong workplace focus and apprenticeship experiences of many VET teachers and trainers are based in living traditions in these workplaces. This dual focus means that pedagogical practice is brought by the practitioners to their teaching and training, with the support of many university programs. The personal craft model stands in stark contrast to the industrial model of regulation and compliance. The traditions of VET teaching are neither buried nor forgotten but they do need continual revitalisation in the face of the cold and consistent silence of the Training Packages and the National Training Agenda. As one of our VET teacher education students remarked recently (Murphy, 2007, p.29):

> Twenty six months ago I was happy and content plodding along on the building site, esky and kelpie in the back of my ute [an Australian term for what in the US might be called a 'pickup']. Shorts, boots and a blue singlet were my uniform, and my language was not quite as cultured or socially acceptable as it is now. I had never been in front of a class until February 2005 when I started as a causal teacher at Campbelltown TAFE. I consider myself fortunate. I love my trade and I love helping people to learn. My personal philosophy of teaching in VET is to attempt to provide the best possible opportunity for my students to learn the skills and ethics of carpentry. Carpentry is a very traditional trade and many of the basic construction principles have been around for centuries. As a custodian of the trade I feel morally bound to maintain high trade standards of both workmanship and attitudes, and instil these in my learners through effective training. We should strive to make the experience an enjoyable and enriching one for our learners.

REFERENCES

Australian National Training Authority (2004). *TAA04 Training and assessment training package.* IBSA.

Australian National Training Authority (2005). *Australian quality training framework- Standards for registered training organizations.* Canberra, Australia.

Bernstein, B. (1996). *Pedagogy symbolic control and identity.* London, Taylor and Francis.

Brennan Kemmis, R. Kemmis, S., Pickersgill, Rushbrook P. & Thurling, M. (2006). *Indigenous staff in VET: Policies, strategies and performance.* Adelaide: National Centre for Vocational Education Research.

Carr, W. (2003). Educational research and its histories (unpublished paper). In D. Hamilton, *Participant knowledge and knowing practice. Proposal to the Swedish Research Council.* October, 2003.

Deilman, M. (2006). *Reflective practice in VET.* Subject assignment. Charles Sturt University.

Hamilton, S.F. & Lempert, W. (1996). The impact of apprenticeship on youth: A prospective analysis. *Journal of Research on Adolescence, 6*(4), 427-455.

Huberman, M. (1999). The mind is its own place: The influence of sustained interactivity with practitioners on educational researchers. *Harvard Educational Review, 69*(3), 289-319.

Knight, K. (1988). *The Macintyre reader.* Notre Dame, Indiana: University of Notre Dame Press.

Lempert, W. (1994). Moral development in the biographies of skilled industrial workers. *Journal of Moral Education, 23*, 451-468.

Macintyre, A. (1984). *After virtue.* (2nd ed.), London: Duckworth.

McCall Smith, A. (2006). *Blue shoes and happiness.* Edinburgh: Polygon.

Misko, J. (2005). *Linking vocational education and training with industry in China and Australia.* Adelaide: National Centre for Vocational Education Research.

Murphy, A. (2007). *Reflective practice in VET.* Subject Assignment. Charles Sturt University.

Peddle, B. (2006). TAFE at the local level: how research informs contemporary practice. Paper presented to the *Australian Vocational Education and Training Research Association,* 9th Annual Conference, Wollongong.

Ray, J. (2001). *Apprenticeship in Australia: An historical snapshot.* Adelaide: National Centre for Vocational Education Research.

Smith, E. and Keating, J. (2003). *Training reform to training packages.* Tuggerah: Social Sciences Press.

AFFILIATION

Roslin Brennan Kemmis
School of Education,
Charles Sturt University, Wagga Wagga, Australia

WILLIAM ADLONG

11. EDUCATION AND SUSTAINABILITY[1]

Praxis in the context of social movements

Our societal responses to the issues of environmental sustainability and social justice have been inadequate. A way of building adequate responses to sustainability issues may be to cultivate communicative spaces that can engender commitment, educate participants and co-extend their social action with social movements. Participation in such communicative spaces contributes to the formation of a collective identity, a 'public', that can then enable *praxis*, an informed and moral orientation in action[2] that is closely associated with the development of character and prudence (Kemmis & Smith, Chapter Two, this volume). The 'formation of a public' thus entails a process of self-formation for each practitioner or citizen who participates in it. Such a communicative process can engender a consciousness of the modern 'prejudices' (Gadamer, 2004) toward objectivism (or value-neutrality) and individualism. This chapter describes some aspects of a research project oriented towards communicative action in response to climate change, discusses some relevant theoretical resources, and considers some implications for educators and other *praxis*-oriented citizens.

The main theoretical points to be made in the chapter are founded on insights into the origin and pervasiveness of the modern orientation to objectivism and individualism (with reference particularly to MacIntyre and to Habermas). Recognising that the bureaucratic rationality associated with a late modern worldview excludes subjective factors and consideration of the moral, this chapter advocates a reinstatement of aspects of the Aristotelian tradition, with groups of committed citizens together exercising communicative rationality. The communicative spaces that citizens can open for themselves can connect with and be part of wider communicative networks that make up public spheres and social movements. Deliberating on and working toward shared visions in such social formations is regarded here as an avenue for the development of *praxis*. Such participation is a practical and transformative form of education – and democracy – that admits to the political nature of all education and provides new opportunities for the constitution of identities (Calhoun, 1994). The solidarity experienced in social movements provides support for the development of identities and norms that are more rational in view of the risks faced by society.

Kemmis, Stephen and Smith, Tracey J. (2008) Enabling praxis: Challenges for education.217-240
© *2008 Sense Publishers. All rights reserved.*

This chapter asserts that we are in the midst of social movements. These social movements are built on educative processes and are important in setting new directions for society. Through social movements and other processes of democratic deliberation (for example in informal settings in different practices), educators can cultivate responses to sustainability issues and find an important fulfilment of their commitment to the good of humankind. In this chapter, the focus is less on education as it is conducted in formal educational institutions and more on processes of informal education and collective self-education that occur when people deliberate together toward shared understandings in relation to issues of common concern, recognising norms and discourses that work against rational response to their situation – in this case, the shared predicament of global warming and climate change.

FACILITATING CLIMATE CHANGE MITIGATION

When I started my PhD, I had an interest in 'sustainability' and I wanted my PhD to make a difference outside the academic world. I had grown up with experiences of and a reverence for 'nature'. A close friend, an environmentalist in town, had been explaining to me why climate change is the critical environmental, or sustainability, issue of this epoch. His logic was convincing to me. Other environmental areas of concern such as biodiversity, water and the health of particular species and ecosystems would be engulfed by the damage anticipated in credible climate change projections. Also, the welfare of many, particularly among the poor, would likely be harmed or at risk. The facilitation of greenhouse gas abatement became the focus of my PhD project in the Faculty of Education.

My initial surveys of the literature made me aware that nearly every nation in the world had signed a United Nations convention to prevent 'dangerous climate change'. Very credible reports called for a 50-60% reduction of greenhouse emissions from 1990 levels by 2050 in order to prevent dangerous climate change (e.g. UK Government, 2003; RCEP, 2000; EEA 2005). Yet the reports published by the Federal Government's Australian Greenhouse Office (AGO, 2005) projected Australia's emissions to rise by 22% over 1990 levels by 2020, even with planned mitigation measures. Clearly the responses to climate change were not proportionate to the magnitude of the problem.

Part of the problem might have been environmental programs in schools and elsewhere that focused mainly on the individual dimension of practice and neglected the extra-individual and intersubjective dimensions (Kemmis & Grootenboer, Chapter Three this volume). Such programs risked constructing the individual as a consumer, as suggested in Collins' (2004) study. Many environmental education and behavioural change programs did not allow for the ability of people to plan, imagine, creatively resolve problems and organise with one another; that is, the programs did not orient people towards addressing some of the social and cultural prefigurings of their practices that Kemmis and Grootenboer describe in Chapter Three (this volume). Regarding material-economic prefigurings of practice, figures from the Australian Greenhouse Office (AGO,

2002, p.v) showed that the emissions that people were responsible for through their *personal* use of electricity, gas and private vehicles was less than 20% of national emissions. This meant that being very environmentally conscientious in one's personal and family use of transport and energy would not by itself produce the dramatic reductions in emissions regarded as necessary to avoid dangerous climate change. Citing Finger (1989, p.27), Clover (2002, p.317) notes how the "'awareness-raising/individual behaviour change' educational agenda" ignores powerful structures and policies that lead to environmental destruction and instead "chastises" the individual.

I considered these questions: How could responses to climate change become more effective and significant? Was there a way of thinking about education which could better enable change in relation to sustainability? In its review of the contributions of education for sustainability, UNESCO (2002, p.9) writes "society must be deeply concerned that much of current education falls far short of what is required." Many assessments have pointed out that only modest progress has been made with the thousands of sustainability projects since the 1980s (Tilbury & Cooke, 2005, p.2).

Whelan, Flowers and Guevara (2004) point out that there is a tendency to think of environmental education as something that occurs in schools and universities. They state that there is a lack of in-depth examination of the educational aspects of environmental activism and people's movements. They call for more research on a blending of activism and education, a middle ground between the two that they refer to as 'popular education' (see also Whelan, 2005). Whelan (2005, p.120) recognises social action as an inherently rich opportunity for learning.

There has come to be an emphasis in environmental education, or education for sustainability[3], on engaging learners in critical reflection and participatory action research (Tilbury, 2004; Sterling, 2004). Tilbury asserts that education for sustainability must "engage learners in critical reflection" (2004, p.99, citing Huckle, 1996, Sterling, 1996 and Fien, 1993). Drawing from Habermas, she describes critical reflection as including a recognition that instrumental rationality and positivism have distorted people's relations and views (p.99, citing Huckle, 1997 and Fien, 1995). To achieve sustainability, we need to "Change the mental models which have driven communities to unsustainable development" (Tilbury & Cooke, 2005, p.2). UNESCO (2002, p.7) makes a similar assertion in its review of education for sustainability: "Social learning also involves reflection ... on the appropriateness of the mental models and assumptions that have traditionally guided thinking and behaviour."

Literature in natural resource management also advocates group action, action research, mutual learning, collective action, and communicative rationality (Bawden, 2005; Kilpatrick, 2002; Jiggins & Roling, 2000; Roling & Wagenmaker, 1998). Other sources advocate the use of collective inquiry in order to address irrationality in practices (Kemmis & McTaggart, 2005; Carr & Kemmis, 1986; Beck, 1997; Montuori & Purser, 1996). These moves in natural resource management and education for sustainability (Tilbury & Cooke, 2005) bring into these fields an element resembling 'practical philosophy', which cultivates dialogue in order to submit theories embedded in practice to critical examination (Carr, 2006). Carr actually describes action research as "nothing other than a modern 20th century manifestation of the pre-modern tradition of practical philosophy" (p.421).

Recognising these trends in education for sustainability, natural resource management and elsewhere, I formed my research questions largely around creating conditions to support the quality or 'symmetry'[4] of dialogue. The proposal was formed around convening "collaborative inquiry groups" and conducting interviews and participant observation, all with the action orientation of facilitating greenhouse gas abatement. The broad site for the case studies would be the city of Wagga Wagga in rural New South Wales, Australia, where I have lived for nearly 20 years. This proposed project was more than an intellectual exercise. It was also a moral response to a looming historical dilemma (as well as a protective response aimed to help assure my children's future). In Habermas' (1976) terms, I saw the lack of legitimacy in current practices; scores of millions of people likely to be adversely (and severely) affected by the unintended consequences of modern industrial practices were having no say in those practices or how they should be changed. One could say that my own *praxis* was driving the project.

Organising/researching locally for response to climate change

The fact that I chose to focus the case study in my home town of Wagga Wagga meant that I already had many established connections and hence more chance of achieving the aims of the research. Since I lived in the area, I could also participate in many more activities. Wagga is a rural city of 57,000 residents located a few hours drive from major metropolitan centres. The likely consequences of climate change for the region include: increased risk of bushfires; increased frequency, intensity and duration of drought; and increased incidence of severe storms. While I was aware of the work of some non-government organisation (NGO) and governmental programs in the metropolitan areas, I found no programs in Wagga designed to enable people to act collectively with a focus on climate change mitigation.

I recruited participants for the collaborative inquiry groups based on their existing concern about climate change. I used this approach partly because surveys by the Australian Bureau of Statistics (ABS, 2004) had shown that, of the adult population who were concerned about climate change, approximately 7% were not acting because they did not know what to do. Two collaborative inquiry groups formed and met for at least 8 sessions over approximately 9 months.

The Coffeehouse Group

One small collaborative inquiry group of four core members, including myself, met once a month from January 2006. The members had each been involved with some environmental organisations and programs before. Two members were a couple who lived together. We met in a restaurant where we could have coffee or wine. Conversations were wide ranging.

Conversations touched on different responses to climate change at the personal, national and international level, low emission and renewable technologies, risks to people and other species from climate change, the knowledge and attitudes of the general public, and criticisms of social norms of consumption. There were critiques of governmental decisions and the interests that were being given priority over rational interests for the common good. Comments touched on the power of media in shaping opinion and un-agentic orientations, but also on 'the power of the people' (the example of the fall of the Berlin Wall was given), particularly when networked together. Some commented on the importance of imagining an ideal future. The couple in the group voiced their intent to model good energy use personally and to model leadership. They saw this as necessary in the absence of governmental leadership. They spoke of the importance of taking personal responsibility for action on the issue. We discussed actions we were each taking in our lives.

The couple spoke of the effect that our meetings and conversations were having on them. The meetings had brought into the foreground of their minds the climate change issue that had long been important to them. Once in the foreground, the issue tended to get discussed and acted on. They sometimes now discussed the issue outside of the meetings. They accessed information on sustainable houses as they were planning a renovation. They exchanged their car for a more energy efficient one. They had solar photo-voltaic panels installed on the roof of their home – in spite of the fact that the price paid to residents for solar generated electricity was not high. The costs of the panels might not be recouped for twenty years.

The meeting conversations were informal, casual, and proceeded with very little direction from me or others. Discussions could also be animated as members expressed their views and sometimes expressed frustration or indignation at society-wide practices and at governmental decision-making. They perceived many governmental policies and decisions relating to climate change to be irrational and unjust.

At one meeting, I shared stories about climate change information sessions I had planned or given for local groups, and another member spoke of a radio interview he had given. One member suggested that we develop a PowerPoint presentation together to present to different groups in town. This was inspired by the work that Al Gore had been doing for years giving presentations to groups. At the next meeting, after working together on the presentation for a period, there was a suggestion and agreement that we would organise a public launch of a local climate action group. We drew a few others of like mind together with us in organising the launch. In those meetings we chose the name CROW (Climate Rescue of Wagga) for the group to be launched (described later). The meaning of the Aboriginal word Wagga has been interpreted as meaning crow (the bird), and so the crow has been the emblem for the city for many years.

The Campus Climate Care Group

Another group formed at Charles Sturt University (CSU), on the Wagga Wagga campus. The group grew to nine members who were all members of staff of the University. Most of the members had little experience with environmental campaigns. In introductions at the initial meeting nearly all expressed their concern about climate change and asked some version of the question, "But what can I do?"

The group met once every month or two for nine months, sharing information and discussing many topics. In response to the group's interest, another member and I got information about how fuel-efficiency was being considered in purchases for the University vehicle fleet. We were surprised to learn that it was very much a consideration, and that some of the University's vehicles were more efficient than hybrids (vehicles that are powered by a combination of batteries and internal combustion engine).

At one meeting, the group had a University officer talk to them about the energy plan for the University and a proposal that the University was considering to become greenhouse neutral. At another meeting, the members did calculations on their carbon footprint and buying greenpower (electricity that is generated from renewable sources). This led to an invitation to an officer from the local energy retailer, who spoke to the group about greenpower and related issues. I was the chair in this group and had to organise items for the meetings and did much of the talking, even though I had expressed a preference for others to take the lead role.

After a few meetings one member mentioned to me that "it's good to get together with people of like mind". A member of the Coffeehouse group had also made the same comment. One member of the University group started riding her bike to work; she said she had not ridden for many years previously. Another member had solar photovoltaic panels installed on his residence. Approximately half of the members (many times the state percentage) were buying greenpower and others were considering it. One member joined in a small local march to highlight the climate change issue. Several members of the group signed a letter to the Federal Government pointing out the need for more action to mitigate climate change.

In one meeting I asked members about the cultural influences that might be behind the lack of action on climate change. One member answered that at age 11 he had entered a path of schooling in the UK that would not lead to university. The sense he had of his parents and peers' views, and their place in the society, was summed up in the question, "Who am I to have an opinion on this?" Two or three members stated that, in considering what to do about climate change or other issues, they were careful not to be 'an activist', or to be seen as such.

The group chose to focus their ideas for action or intervention on the University. They decided to call themselves "Campus Climate Care." A senior executive in the University expressed support for the group. The group wanted a project to focus their efforts and chose the idea of working to reduce energy use with the staff in two buildings if the University could be persuaded to install electricity meters on the buildings. The University agreed. The staff of two buildings were contacted about participating in the project and enthusiastically agreed to be involved. Five months later, however, when the University had not been able to organise the installation of the meters, meetings of the Campus Climate Care group were suspended. There is some evidence, however, that the actions of the group have helped keep the University working with the energy retailer to organise having the meters installed.

A climate of response about climate change
From my interviews with a range of individuals and participant observation in the wider community, it was apparent that many practitioners, from farmers to local government officials to professionals, very often felt too busy to take action in relation to climate change. Other more immediate matters generally took precedence, especially for the farmers and local government officials. This corresponds to survey information from the Australian Bureau of Statistics (ABS, 2004); 49% of those concerned about the environment said that they did not act because of lack of time. A message in the research (and also widely understood) was that many farmers were 'on a knife-edge' – in crisis due to the drought. A sad representation of this is the high (Bryant, 2007) and rising (Hussey, 2007) rate of suicides among farmers.

Through document analyses, it appeared that significant organisations for which mitigation of climate change might have been a large concern, were not equipped by their strategic plans or institutional orientations to advocate for mitigation. Take the example of the state Catchment Management Authorities (CMAs), which have been set up to coordinate natural resource management in each catchment. While the CMAs were concerned with issues that were very much influenced or vulnerable to climate change, advocating about greenhouse gas mitigation or modelling efficient energy use was outside the range of activities encompassed in the local CMA's web documents. The Country Women's Association (CWA), a very large volunteer group with a long tradition of helping rural families, had recently put much effort into providing relief for farmers suffering from the 'longest drought on record'. Yet, the CWA had no position on climate change mitigation on their website. A speech about the future of farming from a manager of a locally influential state/University agricultural organisation made no mention of changes to farming in relation to reducing emissions. (Some people like the person making this speech, however, were changing quickly; this manager was quite responsive to and expressed an interest in information I sent to them afterward.) Naturally, the lack of orientation to preventative action and mitigation by such organisations is partly because the atmosphere cannot be managed through local actions only, but requires globally coordinated efforts.

The launch of CROW (Climate Rescue of Wagga)
In October 2006, approximately 35 Wagga Wagga region residents gathered in the city's Civic Centre for the launch of CROW. The launch grew out of the discussions of the Coffeehouse group described earlier. Participants discussed their interest in climate change and considered strategies to bring about mitigation. Using some democratic group processes to generate and select themes, participants

chose to focus particularly on possibilities for political action, education and awareness raising, promotion of renewable energy and other local practical actions. By December 2006, the number of people who had expressed an interest in being informed about the activities of the group had grown to approximately 65. Within a week of the launch, some members of the group had met again to plan or report on letters to different levels of government, industry groups and business. Weeks later, a group of CROW members met with the chief of staff of an elected federal parliamentary representative and others met with a local government councillor. The meeting with the federal representative's office led to a letter from the representative to the Prime Minister and other ministers asking for information and greater action. Some CROW members designed and produced a logo and postcards for local awareness raising and advocacy.

Several members of CROW met once per week over a number of weeks to plan a dinner called "The Food Less Travelled". The idea, which had emerged at the launch of CROW, was to highlight the issue of 'foodmiles' in a pleasurable way. 'Foodmiles' refers to the distance that food travels from production to customer. Generally, the greater the food miles, the more fossil fuels that have been burned to transport the food, meaning increased greenhouse emissions. Nearly all the food and drink consumed at the dinner was produced within 200 kilometres of the venue. 'The Food Less Travelled' dinner showed the climate implications of simple decisions we make day to day, and provided an opportunity to publicly present and discuss other information about climate change. Approximately 90 people attended and paid the $60-$75 charge, which will help fund future CROW activities. A number of attendees chose to join CROW as part of the dinner charge. A national senator – Christine Milne of the Green Party[5] – attended and was the main speaker for the evening. In its way, the dinner was an educational event.

The planning, organisation and meetings for the dinner were quite an intense effort for the organisers. I saw four of them about ten days prior to the event. There was a real sense of exhilaration amongst them. They were excited, an excitement that also involved some worry, enough to keep a couple of them awake some hours on previous nights. The solidarity that had grown among members of the group was almost palpable. They mentioned something about how close they were now to one another. They joked and chatted in a very comfortable and familiar way. They mentioned that the discussions at their meetings had been very animated and covered many issues related to the aim of the project, and not just the actual planning for the dinner. In terms of the learning and sense of support that the organisers experienced together, one said, "It's been *very* good for us". They joked that it would be like coming off an addiction when they no longer had the intensely social and meaningful weekly sessions together. No one seemed to be identified as the leader among the organisers. One said "We got along so well. Really fired off each other – lots of brainstorming."

Part of wider trends
Participants in the CROW launch commented on how there had been growing coverage of climate change in the media. Some felt that the launch of a climate

action group was especially timely since the Al Gore movie *An Inconvenient Truth*, which presents the scientific evidence for climate change, had launched in Wagga a few days earlier[6]. The increased media coverage was in part because of the regional failure of winter rain, the ensuing loss of crops and the continuation of drought, said to be in its fifth year in many areas. People in Wagga, who look out on the brown fields when the weather is dry, feel the effects of drought and are aware of the particular hardship that it causes to their fellow citizens on farms.

Before the whole CROW group met for the second time, media coverage of climate change had increased even more. The United Kingdom's 'Stern Review', an analysis of the expected economic losses from the effects of climate change – unless dramatic reductions in emissions are organised soon – undercut the Australian Federal government's argument that taking the necessary actions to reduce emissions would be too damaging to the economy. The fact that the Stern Review was chaired by the former chief economist of the World Bank gave the Review much credibility with the public and with business. Opinion polls showed that most voters wanted government to focus much more on generating energy from renewable rather than fossil fuel sources (*The Australian*, 2006). The Federal government, in what was seen to be a major change of direction, established a task force to investigate how a carbon trading scheme might be set up (*Sydney Morning Herald*, 2006).

The intensification of media coverage of climate change can be seen in the mentions of "climate change" in two major newspapers in Australia; Figure 1 shows the growth in the mentions of "climate change" in *The Australian* and the *Sydney Morning Herald* from 1999 to 2006[7]. In 2005, there was an average of 44 mentions of climate change per month in the two newspapers combined. In the four months following the Australian opening (in September 2006) of the movie *An Inconvenient Truth*, the monthly average of mentions of "climate change" in the two newspapers combined had climbed from 44 to 208! (This four month period included the release of the Stern Review.) Our location in the electoral cycle was another factor in the media focus on the issue. Being just a few months before the election of the state government and less than one year before the election of the federal government, politicians wanted to be seen to be responding actively to this issue of growing public concern. Climate change has come to be one of the top two or three issues for the forthcoming national elections (at the time of writing, likely to be held in October, 2007).

The growing intensity of public interest, reflected in the media coverage mentioned, was a worldwide phenomenon. There was a similar increase in coverage of the topic in major newspapers in other nations. As awareness of the reality of the situation (our climate prognosis, and the sustainability situation that it is emblematic for) has begun to permeate cultures, there has been a rising response. Paul Hawken (2006), environmentalist and co-author of the book *Natural Capitalism: The next industrial revolution,* claims that there are now 100 million people who work daily in a "bottom up movement" for "the preservation and restoration of life on earth" (¶2).

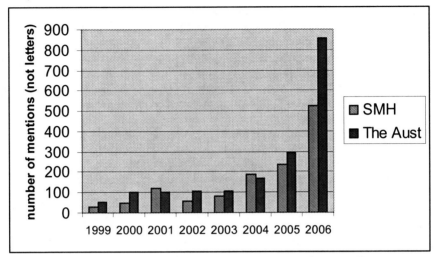

Figure 1. The number of mentions of "climate change" in two major Australian newspapers

Hawken (2006) expects to see a transformation of many institutions and the practices through which we build our future as a result of the recognition of the climate change and other sustainability crises: "We are experiencing something greater than 'greening'" (¶ 2). He states: "It will be a *hold-onto-your-hat* decade and beyond" (Hawken, 2006, ¶ 1). This portrays a phenomenon in relation to which educators need to position themselves. It represents a fundamental context for education and *praxis* in this epoch.

In the light of the local and global context so far presented, I will now discuss some theoretical resources and frameworks that can be used to conceptualise education and frame the development of *praxis* in relation to collective action needed to address the epochal issues of climate change and sustainability.

SOME COMMENTS ABOUT THE HISTORY OF REASON, THE INDIVIDUALIST AND SOCIAL FORMS ASSOCIATED WITH *PRAXIS*

In Chapter Three of this volume, Kemmis and Grootenboer call for an understanding of the context in which an action or practice is occurring. Similarly, Carr (2006, citing Gadamer) emphasises that we not only want to look at the context of individual practices but consider prejudices of the epoch that have conditioned those practices. Some historical perspective on the development of the modern concept of rationality can give insights into *praxis* development especially in relation to the dilemmas we face with action for sustainability.

MacIntyre (1981) writes of how the 17th and 18th century philosophical exclusion of moral attitudes, beliefs, intents, values –"all those aspects of the classic view of the world which were Aristotelian" (p.78) – from the concept of rationality meant that science, and then 'the scientific approach' to humans and human affairs, lost its traditional connection with moral reasoning. With the

Enlightenment, the 'moderns' prided themselves on stripping away interpretation and theory from 'fact'. After stripping away the moral, philosophy then had the task of establishing a rational basis for morals. Attempted particularly in the period 1630-1850, the quest to provide a rational justification for morality failed. A central thesis of MacIntyre's (1981) book *After Virtue* is that "the breakdown of this project provided the historical background against which the predicaments of our own culture can become intelligible" (p.38). He writes that "Twentieth-century social life turns out in key part to be the concrete and dramatic re-enactment of eighteenth-century philosophy" (p.83). One of the groups in the research study reported here sensed MacIntyre's insight, arguing that bureaucratic rationality is attuned to capitalist, materialist endeavours rather than the formation of moral reasoning or the collective definition of a desired future.

On the view that motives and beliefs could not be treated as 'facts' in the same way as facts in the natural sciences, much science, from the 18th through the 20th centuries considered such 'subjective' factors to be outside the ken of rationality. Bureaucracy has come to embody managerial expertise which has taken from the Enlightenment an "aspiration to value neutrality" (MacIntyre, 1981, p.83) and has the central task of "adjusting means to ends in the most economical and efficient way..." (MacIntyre, 1981, p.82). Hence, the definition of the 'science' of behaviour excluded values and morality, and this science became institutionalised, shaping the roles and practices that are anchored in bureaucratic institutions (perhaps through 'practice architectures'; see Kemmis & Grootenboer, Chapter Three, this volume). The self in modern society is (generally) significantly identified in a relationship with bureaucracy (MacIntyre, 1981, p.29). In this setting, the liberal individualist conception of the self, a modern concept, has become ascendant. Modern society abstracts the 'individual' and hence loses sight of the contextual connections which are a vital aspect of humanness (MacIntyre, 1998/1994)[8]. This mistaken concept of the individual is "embodied in institutionalized social life" (MacIntyre, 1998/1994, p.229), and distorts people's understanding of themselves, depleting their conceptual resources for understanding their intersubjective nature. As a consequence, we tend to be caught in a self-concept, a kind of self-understanding, that does not include the social and the political as intrinsic to our humanness. Also, many of our contemporary institutions tend to favour the rights for individual enrichment rather than collective identity, as was perceived by one of the groups in the research reported here, in its critique of governments favouring commercial interests over collective, truly public, interests.

MacIntyre (1981) asserts the possibility of a reinstatement of the Aristotelian tradition and discusses what would be involved. Aristotle's concept of *praxis* was something that was done toward 'the goods' of 'the blessed life' toward which each human was teleologically working. That is, there once were shared aims that were considered a part of a rational life. But these goods include relationships and shared commitments to the good of the social whole, so *praxis* is closely related to and dependent on intersubjectivity and being in a collective (not just in the sense of the collective nature of a professional practice, but in the sense of being part of a people, a *polis*, jointly concerned with the well-being of that polis). Dryzek (1990, pp.9-10) foregrounds the collective in the Aristotelian tradition: "...Aristotle clearly grounded practical reason in collective life. An individual isolated outside the polis could not be rational, for rationality was a product of collective interaction." In the research reported here, the Coffeehouse group, and then the Food Less Travelled group, developed shared aims through their discussions. The rationality of the aims arose from a shared commitment to the good and was dependent on intersubjective interaction.

The sense of closeness experienced by the Food Less Travelled group resembles the bond of friendship that Aristotle associates with "a shared recognition and pursuit of the good" (MacIntyre, 1981, p.146). MacIntyre writes: "We are to think then of friendship as being the sharing of all in the common project of creating and sustaining the life of the city, a sharing incorporated in the immediacy of an individual's particular friendships" (p.146). This is a kind of bond between citizens that Aristotle saw as essential to the polis. MacIntyre (p.146) believes that even contemporary societies of large populations can be informed by a shared vision of the good, through networks of small groups of friends sharing a moral orientation. Such social forms provide a context for the 'virtues' (p.153) and are "local forms of community within which civility and the intellectual and the moral life can be sustained..." (p.245). Perhaps groups like the Coffeehouse and Food Less Travelled groups can be regarded as reinstating the Aristotelian tradition, in which collective deliberation is a source of rationality.

Habermas also helps us to understand the cultural and conceptual conditions within which the groups in this study seek to understand their situation. At least in relation to the historical disruption of practical reason, Habermas' perspective is similar to MacIntyre's. He writes of "the many symptoms of a destruction of practical reason to be found in the history of ideas ..." (Habermas, 1976, p.124). He points out that prior to positivism, knowledge "referred to a scientific orientation in action" that "had its role to play with *praxis*..." (Habermas, 1974, p.263). Knowledge and commitment were inherently connected. "Science" included a commitment to, and interest in, the realisation of an aim of a society in which all human beings could actualise 'adult autonomy'[9] (p.262). As science was reduced to a productive force in industrial society, however, the concept of reason changed so that

> interest and inclination are banished from the court of knowledge as subjective factors. The spontaneity of hope, the act of taking a position, the experience of relevance or indifference and above all, the response to suffering and oppression, the desire for adult autonomy, the will to emancipation, and the happiness of discovering one's identity – all these are dismissed ... from the obligating interest of reason. A disinfected reason is purged of all moments of enlightened volition... (pp.262-263).

The move to collective action is an attempt to reincorporate these banished factors; to revive and enable *praxis*. We can see that a practitioner who chooses, in the terms of Chapter One, to be an 'agent' rather than an 'operative' will likely be correspondingly rewarded in meaning and individuation.

The wider cultural setting in which the groups in the study reported here were operating had been defined to a large degree by a system in which subjective factors have been 'banished' and in which there is an interlocking of science, technology, industry, and administration (Habermas, 1974). "The social potential of science is reduced to the powers of technical control..." (Habermas, 1974, pp.255-256). We are faced with the coalescence of science, administration, society, research, technology and production into a system which is the basis of our life but which we have difficulty overviewing, so the whole formation tends to be shut off from our knowledge and reflection. Attempts to overview the system are seen as dogmatic. The ascendancy has been so marked that even to suggest that there may be other sorts of rationality is to be accused of a prejudiced view (Habermas, 1974). Taylor's (1991, pp.17-18) words have a similar message: "...the liberalism of neutrality. One of its basic tenets is that a liberal society must be neutral on questions of what constitutes a good life." Carr (2006, p.430) writes:

> the assumption of a wholly ahistorical concept of reason that is independent of tradition is nothing other than a definitive 'prejudice' of the tradition of modernity...one of the illusions of modernity...

In empirical rationality, there is such an emphasis on efficiency that the end object and decisions about it are considered outside of rational review (Habermas, 1974). Habermas looks to critique, and critical theory, to show how dogmatic ideology is congealed in society, its institutions and the symbolic structures of speech and action. Building consciousness of, and overcoming, such constraints built into society requires a theory of reason that includes the interests of the good of humankind. Habermas seeks to rehabilitate the concept of reason in the notion of communicative reason (1996a, p.341), established through communicative action. Part of what Habermas would rehabilitate is that condition when knowledge is connected to *praxis*; when humans in society form themselves through communication "into a collective subject of the whole, that is capable of [practical] action" to guide the society's fortune, to choose where the society should go (Habermas, 1974, p.255). I believe that these ideas help to explain the exhilaration that the organisers of the CROW 'Food Less Travelled' dinner experienced. Their deliberation and action was an embodiment of critique. The solidarity they experienced provided them with a sort of liberation from the individualistic outlook and the way of experiencing the world embedded in many current norms.

PUBLIC SPHERES AND COMMUNICATIVE ACTION

The communicative rationality experienced by the 'Food Less Travelled' group was not just an isolated phenomenon. It was part of the 'public spheres', the communicative networks through which the public considers issues. Habermas explains the informal dimension of the public sphere: "A portion of the public sphere is constituted in every conversation in which private persons come together to form a public" (1997, p.105). Public spheres are constituted from the intersubjective space created in communicative action, when two or more people meet in uncoerced communication in which they have equal status, and suspend their judgements and agendas in order to reach understanding together. Benhabib (1996, p.78) refers to this 'ideal speech situation' (Habermas, 1987) as one of "egalitarian reciprocity".

Through discursive rationality people not only become more informed; there is also a tendency for commitment ('binding force') to form toward that which has good reasons (Habermas, 1974). That is, in their search for agreement, people not only come to *agreement*, they come to *commitment*. So *phronēsis*, understanding of and commitment to the good, actually develops in the ideal speech situation. Participation in communicative action leads to the "deepened self-awareness or self-presence" cited by Kemmis & Smith in Chapter Two (quoting Dunne, 1993). While the ideal speech situation in a pure form may well only happen rarely, if at all, communicative action can nonetheless be an experience of democracy, self-formation, the constitution of meaningful relationships, and solidarity among participants. Public spheres engender opinion-formation and will-formation.

Habermas (1996a) describes public spheres as sensitising the bureaucratic system. People in their lifeworlds experience imbalances caused by the system. They communicate with one another spontaneously and informally and these communications and developing learnings flow on through the public spheres. An intersubjective development of understanding about issues is generated that can be further amplified in other conversations, networks of public deliberation and the mass media. Through this process, discursively formed views can come to affect, or 'sensitise', parliamentary decision-making. The legitimacy of governmental decisions and policies is dependent on such flows from public spheres. The discussion of issues and solutions in the public sphere can be verbal or in writing (or in other forms), local and face to face, or global and indirect. The informal and spontaneous communications on the 'periphery' of the public sphere, however, retains a special place in the public sphere, for the meaning and authenticity that this generates is a foundation of legitimacy.

The connection with developments in distant or global public spheres was evident in a number of ways in the study reported here. For example, one of the members of the Coffeehouse and CROW groups dedicated time regularly to reviewing information and updates online about climate change. About once a fortnight he sent out an email to his own listserv of scores of people with key information or 'good news' stories about responses to climate change.

Beck (1999) argues that the integration of ecological principles in industrial societies requires the development of public spheres. These public spheres can work to challenge the authority of the coalition of bureaucracy, business and science and the associated paradigm of economic growth (Beck 1999)[10]. Though precipitated by awareness of the risks caused by industrial society, Beck regards this process of challenging as inherent in the Enlightenment and the underlying principles of modernity. Modernization subjects things – especially claims to authority – to disembedding and re-embedding and must do the same to itself

230

(Beck, 1997, p.13; Beck, 1994). An important dimension of deliberating on the risks caused by society, of questioning norms and asserting a global environmental agenda is found in international 'discourse coalitions' (Beck, 1999, p. 24, citing Hajer, 1996). The CROW group has made contact with similar groups in other cities and towns in the region in order to discuss their understanding of climate change and possible responses, and to share information that the groups have compiled. While having little direct contact with others internationally, there is a sense of solidarity with those sharing similar aims, and international written work (particularly via the internet) informs our local advocacies. It is worth noting that Beck (1999, p.25) also cautions that discourse coalitions oriented to causes such as the environment must assert themselves against powerful counter-coalitions.

What were the forces that had brought the change in media coverage and political commitment on climate change described earlier? Some of it was the result of scientific research, which has shown with increasing clarity the effects that emissions from human activities will have, such as the Intergovernmental Panel on Climate Change (IPCC) *Third Assessment Report* in 2001. Some of it was from the progress of international negotiations, such as the G-8 meeting at Gleneagles organised under Tony Blair's presidency in 2005 (G-8, 2005). But a substantial part of it was the result of the education that had been achieved by the agents in the activities and discussions of public spheres or social movements, not only in the immediate local situations of their own community but also reaching out to regional, national and international groups and movements. This has created a more informed debate enabling and pressuring local and national politicians and businesspeople to recognise the irrationality of certain courses of action and structures of our society and government and to recognise the kinds of initiatives needed to respond to our shared situation. The polls that were leading to changes in government direction (*Sydney Morning Herald*, 2006) were the result of opinion formation, a form of public, informal, collective and self education, that was occurring in the public sphere.

Habermas' views on the relation of developments in the public spheres with the legislative and policy making process were corroborated by the words of one senior New South Wales bureaucrat who stated at a 2006 conference of the Business Council for Sustainable Energy; "Don't assume that they [politicians and policy makers] know…[the key facts about an issue]." The agenda development and clarification of problems and potential solutions by civic associations (and alternative or unconventional industries) "can have a very big impact on the policy process." The bureaucrat encouraged everyone at the meeting to help to define the problem and could not "underscore enough" the importance of the breadth of experience and knowledge that advocates for alternative structures have in developing the understanding of the policy makers. "Community debate does make a difference in the policy process. It absolutely helps." Already having the context and dialogue around a needed policy can accelerate the development of policy from years to months. The policy formation process involves debate among perspectives that can be swayed by the knowledge accretion and thematization, and the proposal of solutions, in the public sphere.

231

SOCIAL MOVEMENTS

One of the conceptual frameworks that educators and CROW members can use to understand their role in sustaining the public sphere is that of social movements. Social movements set up and emerge from communicative action between people that results in cognitive, social and personal development of the participants (Habermas, 1987). Such development is a form of education; an education that shapes the social structures that learners – citizens – will live and work in. Understanding the collective extension of individual agency that occurs through communicative action and builds through social movements can help individuals to participate in shaping the circumstances of society so that there is less injustice and greater legitimacy. Participation in social movements provides individuals with an avenue for the development of *praxis* as they morally enact the potential to influence *collective* action. They might do so through initiating, democratically participating in, reflecting on, or providing material, theoretical, informational, or inspirational resources for such collective action. This development of *praxis* is also a development of meaningfulness for the individual. For example, one CROW member volunteered a comment about how their involvement had given them a greater sense of meaning and purpose in their life. Members of social movements have a chance to respond to that which they feel is most important historically, and to address that which is most irrational in their circumstances.

Participants in social movements are not necessarily linked through an organisation; they may instead be linked through a commitment to collective identities that reflect particular values (Haenfler, 2004). Cohen and Arato (1992, p.124) describe the possibility of "'norm-oriented movement' that is capable of positively influencing social change". Social movements or 'new social movements' are associated with 'post-materialist' values (Benhabib, 1996). They have succeeded in bringing about major changes in large scale political agendas (Beck, 1994; Benhabib, 1996). Beck (1999, p.18) describes how:

> Voluntary organizations play a crucial role in building a global civil society. They help to generate the public-mindedness and civic trust to open up the national agendas for transnational, cosmopolitan concerns. And they constitute a human flourishing in their own right.

Touraine (1987, p.9) even declares that social movements are the "principal agents of history." Giddens (1991, p.173, citing Lasch) contends that movements stimulated by the risks humanity now faces "represent our best hope for the future..."

Like the public spheres which they co-constitute, social movements are sites of will- and opinion-formation. Social movements build on communicative action, including the informal and spontaneous interactions at the periphery of public spheres (Habermas, 1996a). Part of the strength of the activities that comprised the Coffeehouse group and CROW was the enjoyment people had in the interaction. The commitment to broader moral engagement flowed from interaction that was inherently rewarding.

Being founded on communicative action, there is a transformative element in social movements. They provide the sort of social forms which, MacIntyre (1981, p.153) writes, are the context for the exercise and development of "the virtues." They provide a different context, a new setting, for the extra-individual dimensions of a practice (Kemmis & Grootenboer, Chapter Three, this volume) and hence opportunities for *praxis* development.

Giddens (1991) explains that social movements are collective attempts to reappropriate areas of institutional repression (p.207) and that they challenge "some of the basic presuppositions and organising principles" of modernity (p.208). Habermas (1981) similarly writes of social movements as protests against the roles institutionalized by the economic and administrative systems. He refers to them as 'counter-institutions' and 'alternative *praxis*' (1981). Habermas (1981, p.37) asserts "these institutions are supposed to counter the party system with new forms of an expressive 'politics of the first person' which, at the same time, is supposed to have a democratic base". Beck (1994) refers to the politics of the first person as 'subpolitics', a new dimension of the political with the possibility of shaping society from below (p.23). In Habermas' view, the counter-institutions of social movements reappropriate areas in which collective identities can be formed and in which participants can try out "new forms of cooperation and community" (Habermas, 1981, p.35).

Ray (1993) asserts that social movements come into being in response to problems or crises in the existing order. Habermas (1981, p.35) gives examples of social movements: the youth, environmental and peace movements. These groups share a critique of growth and perceive problem situations with great sensitivity (Habermas, 1981, p.35).

Participants in social movements will be the proponents for much of the change needed in institutions, society and individuals to achieve sustainability. The communicative action upon which social movements are built is a transformational educational paradigm. Education for the young is important, but time is too short for this alone (Kemmis, 2006). There needs to be an education through the civic sphere, through a revival of the '*praxis* of civic self-determination' (Habermas, 1996b) if the necessary changes are to be brought about in time.

Social movements and identity

One of the key ideas in the literature about social movements is that they are sites of identity formation (Habermas, 1981; Ray, 1993; Calhoun, 1994; Della Porta 2006). Participants individuate through the same acts that build solidarity. "Language 'unites through individuation…'" (Habermas, 2003, p.81, citing Humboldt, 1963). Cohen and Arato (1992, p.359) describe the 'emergent collective identity' associated with dialogue. Habermas (1981, p. 37) even suggests that, "The significance [of social movements] is hidden in the self-image of the participants…". McLaren & Giarelli (1995, p.8) propose that in 'new social spaces' we can forge our identities anew in ways guided in part by our 'sociological imagination'. The forging of these new identities is related to the formation of collective visions of the public good (McLaren & Giarelli, 1995, p.11). Beck (1997) suggests that such 'tinkering with' one's subjectivity can open spaces, ways of conceiving of the self, that can then be taken on by others. The members of the Coffeehouse group spoke of their personal responsibility for a better, or less dangerous, future, and then developed their identity through discussion and action. Their action in forming CROW then provided opportunities for others to take action and in turn develop their knowledge and identity. That is, as the Coffeehouse group members developed their own *praxis*, they enabled that of others. It seems that we depend, for our growth and our *praxis*, on the formation of public visions in communicative spaces.

Social movements and deliberative democracy

It is informative to consider briefly the settings for *praxis* development and groups such as CROW in terms of deliberative democracy. Della Porta (2006, p.239) claims that one of the key aims of most social movements is "the development of a new conception of democracy." The social forms that we saw associated by Aristotle with *praxis* (via MacIntyre) are deliberative and political. They are similar to the social forms implied in Dryzek's favoured definition of politics in his book on deliberative democracy (1990, p.10, quoting Fay, 1975, p.54): "'politics' refers to men's [sic] deliberative efforts to order, direct, and control their collective affairs and activities, to establish ends for their society, and to implement and evaluate these ends". Dryzek sees this as classical politics. He writes that "As one moves toward the participatory pole of the spectrum ... politics becomes increasingly discursive, educational, oriented to truly public interests, and needful of active citizenship" (1990, p.13). Participating in democracy is political. And it is educative.

Giarelli recognises the deliberative ideal of democracy in his comments on "the project of public formation" (1986, p.323). He regards the project of public formation as the point of politics and education:

> In this view, education and politics become merged. If democracy is not something that happens for us, but rather to us, then the political is the pedagogical and the point of both educational and political practice is to create ... self-cultivating publics and self-governing persons ... (Giarelli 1986, pp.322-323).

Giarelli's 'public formation' seems to be synonymous with the possibility of forming through communication "into a collective subject of the whole" (noted above, Habermas, 1974, p.255). This image of communication giving form to the public is supported by the notion of Cohen and Arato (1992, p.370) that processes of public communication form the we of collective action. Giarelli (1984) and Sullivan (1982) also write about this orientation in terms of "public philosophy" – "a system of beliefs and communicative practices through which a society can develop and maintain a widely shared sense of political meaning and direction" (Giarelli, 1984 p.10).

A tradition of working with social movements

One of the traditions closely associated with the development of educational practice – action research – is conceived in relation to social movements by Kemmis (1993; 2006) and Kemmis and McTaggart (2005). Kemmis (1993) explains that a connection with social movements has very much been a part of the history of action research from early on (predating Lewin). He writes that the "essential' nature of action research involved a connection with social movements…" (p.2 of 7). The versions of action research that he favours (p.3 of 7, citing Carr & Kemmis, 1986) "aim to make strong and explicit connections between action research and social movement". Kemmis (1993), like Carr (2006), points out that action research can be seen as a modern manifestation of Aristotelian practical reasoning. Quality (critical participatory) action research and practitioner research, "will explore themes of pressing contemporary interest, frequently in relation to contemporary social movements …" (Kemmis, 2006, p.471). The *praxis*-oriented educator seeking to open communicative space with others to address irrationality – for example, issues of sustainability as they are being defined in social movements – will likely find that they are enacting something akin to participatory action research (Kemmis, 2006; Kemmis & McTaggart, 2005).

THE CONSEQUENCES OF OR FOR OUR PRACTICES

Much of the problem of sustainability has emerged as a result of the institutionalisation of the liberal individualist viewpoint and a form of objective knowing that is prejudiced against the subjectivity of moral commitment. This has resulted in a depoliticized population (Habermas, 1974, p.4). The formation of solidarity, understanding, opinion and will in social movements and public spheres, which can be supported by educators, can counter the continued influence of the limited form of rationality in managerial or bureaucratic rationality. Perhaps Hoffman-Kipp, Artiles, and Lopez-Torres (2003, p.252) are correct in stating about teacher learning that "the telos of praxis is to become an organic intellectual and contribute to a social transformation project." Such an aim may include an aspiration to "create and nurture the kind of dialogical communities within which phronesis can be embedded and which the development of *praxis* presupposes and requires" (Carr, 2006, p.433).

Praxis, it turns out, is political. It expresses and realises a commitment to some ends, whether tacit or explicit. It reviews and reconstructs the social setting from which it arises (Carr & Kemmis, 1986, p.33). All "educational activities … take place against a social-historical background and project a view of the kind of future we hope to build" (Carr & Kemmis, p.39). Educators may want to ask what future is implicit in their educational activities.

In the process of thinking of themselves in relation to their practice, practitioners may internalise the concepts and boundaries of their role as it is defined by the institutions that employ them. These institutions are formed within the liberal analytic tradition that views self-interest as more basic than a "shared moral order" (Sullivan, 1982, p.214). Morally-oriented individuals may want to problematize and re-evaluate their concepts of their practice roles, especially in view of the kinds of theoretical and historical challenges discussed in this chapter.

CONCLUSION

The concepts of communicative spaces, public spheres and social movements help one to understand how to form an 'alternative *praxis*' to that instilled by the modern ascendancy of bureaucratic and economic rationality. Collective deliberation upon a shared vision of the good is a powerfully educative activity. When combined with the commitment that can arise out of such communicative action, the effects of deliberation can develop identity and solidarity among participants. It can also contribute, via public spheres, to setting agendas for governments and other institutions. Even spontaneous and informal communications can provide opportunities for collectively understanding solutions for the common interest; understandings that then flow on through communicative networks to influence others. It seems that these collective relations, deliberations and orientations, into which the Aristotelian tradition provides insights, offer an important basis for *praxis* development. Likewise, they provide an important basis for making the changes that sustainability calls for.

To say '*praxis* in the context of social movements' is to shift the concept of *praxis* beyond a relationship to an institutionally defined practice and role. It is to shift the concept of *praxis* to a historical context and to a relation with the historical agency of the individual. *Praxis* may be demonstrated in and have a focus in a practice, but it is by nature transformative and transgressive. Practical rationality, with its commitment to the betterment of humanity, accepts the enactment of a tradition to the degree that this enactment is a fulfilment of *the moral commitment of rationality*. *Praxis*-oriented practitioners work both within the traditions of their practices and within the wider tradition of disembedding and re-embedding – of questioning of the reasons for norms – that defined the Enlightenment and modernity (Beck, 1997; 1994).

We live in a time of social movements and it is through social movements that many of the most important issues of our epoch are being addressed. An educator's opening of communicative spaces with others about big issues, in an institution or in the civic sphere, particularly in a sustained way, is of significance. In such spaces not only understanding but also commitment and *praxis* can be formed. The role of initiator and facilitator of public discourse, in which the educator recovers and revitalises the collective *praxis*-orientation that once was a part of rationality, can be a powerful fulfilment of their identity.

NOTES

[1] Sustainability, like the 'triple bottom line' that it is frequently associated with, is traditionally thought of as having three dimensions; social, economic and environmental. It is a combination of

practicality and ethics. It aims for justice across groupings of people and across generations. 'Justice across generations' means that the environment should provide at least equivalent opportunities for future generations as for the present one. The practical importance of the economy for achieving the other dimensions of sustainability is acknowledged here.

[2] As described elsewhere in this book (especially Kemmis & Smith, Chapter 2 and Kemmis & Grootenboer, Chapter 3), Aristotle elaborated the concept of praxis (in the Nicomachean Ethics). Praxis is guided by the disposition 'phronesis', a practical understanding aimed at enacting 'the good' in different situations.

[3] 'Education for sustainability' incorporates and extends environmental education. It combines 'education about' the environment with the development of "the skills and capacity to plan, motivate and manage change towards sustainability within an organisation or industry" (Tilbury, Crawley & Berry, 2005, p.2). Recently, Tilbury and colleagues have been using the phrase 'learning for sustainability' (e.g. Tilbury & Cooke, 2005).

[4] That is, dialogue in which there are "relations of mutual recognition, of reciprocal perspective-taking, a shared willingness to look at one's own traditions through the eyes of a stranger, to learn from one another..." (Habermas, 2003, p.291).

[5] There was some concern with having a 'Greens' speaker for CROW, which wanted to remain non party-political. In the end, however, it was decided that her profile on the climate change issue, her willingness to keep party politics out of the speech and her willingness to come to the event outweighed the party-political association.

[6] The Wagga opening of 'An Inconvenient Truth' was more than a month after the national opening.

[7] The number of mentions was determined by using the database 'Factiva'.

[8] Carr (2006) notes that even the social sciences have adopted "a methodologically alienated form of self-understanding..." (pp.428-429, quoting Gadamer, 1975b, p.312).

[9] I.e. "the autonomy of action" and "the liberation from dogmatism" (Habermas 1974, p.256). Habermas (p.17) refers to 'mature autonomy' as the historical goal of enlightenment for Kant.

[10] Beck asserts that society becomes conscious of the environmental risks created by industrial modernity in a reflex-like way; hence he writes of "reflexive modernity." These conditions of risk also necessitate a reflexive self-determination within society which questions the assumptions of modernity: "The old ... grand coalition of economic growth between the administration, the state, business, technology and science is no longer viable" (1999, p. 101).

REFERENCES

ABS (2004). Environmental concerns and related activities (4102.0). Australian Social Trends. Australian Bureau of Statistics. Retrieved June 23, 2005, from http://www.abs.gov.au/ausstats/abs@.nsf/2f762f95845417aeca25706c00834efa/31bd15113714d0fcc a256e9e00295194!OpenDocument

AGO (2002). Australia's National Greenhouse Gas Inventory - 1990, 1995 and 1999; End use allocation of emissions – Summary. Australian Greenhouse Office, Commonwealth of Australia. Retrieved December 22, 2005, from http://www.greenhouse.gov.au/inventory/enduse/pubs/vol1-summary.pdf

AGO (2005). *Tracking to the Kyoto Protocol 2005: Australia's greenhouse gas emission trends 1990-2008-2012 and 2020*. Australian Greenhouse Office, Commonwealth of Australia. Retrieved December 8, 2005, from http://www.greenhouse.gov.au/projections

Bawden, R. (2005). Systemic development at Hawkesbury: some personal lessons from experience. *Systems Research and Behavioral Science, 22*(2), 151.

Beck, U. (1994). The reinvention of politics: Towards a theory of reflexive modernization. In U Beck, A. Giddens, S. Lash, *Reflexive modernization: Politics, tradition and aesthetics in the modern social order*. Cambridge, UK: Polity.

Beck, U. (1997). *The reinvention of politics: Rethinking modernity in the global social order*. Oxford: Polity.

Beck, U. (1999). *World risk society*. Malden, MA: Polity.

Benhabib, S. (1996). Toward a deliberative model of democratic legitimacy. In S. Benhabib (Ed.) *Democracy and difference: Contesting the boundaries of the political* (pp. 67-94). Princeton, NJ: Princeton University Press.

Bryant, N. (2007) Big dry takes toll on Australia's farmers. BBC News. Retrieved May 28, 2007, from http://news.bbc.co.uk/2/hi/asia-pacific/6679845.stm

Calhoun, C. (1994). Social theory and the politics of identity. In C. Calhoun (ed.) *Social theory and the politics of identity* (pp. 9-36). Cambridge, MA: Blackwell.

Carr, W. (2006). Philosophy, methodology and action research. *Journal of Philosophy of Education, 40*(4), 421-435.

Carr, W. & Kemmis, S. (1986). *Becoming critical; Education, knowledge and action research* (Rev. edn). Waurn Ponds, Vic.: Deakin University.

Clover, D. (2002). Traversing the gap: Concientizacion, educative-activism in environmental adult education. *Environmental Education Research, 8*, 315-323.

Cohen, J. & Arato, A. (1992). *Civil society and political theory*. Cambridge, MA: Massachusetts Institute of Technology.

Collins, A.J. (2004). Can we learn to live differently? Lessons from Going for Green: A case study of Merthyr Tydfil (South Wales), *International Journal of Consumer Studies, 28*(2).

Della Porta, D. & Diani, M. (2006). *Social movements: An introduction* (2nd edn). Carlton, Vic., Australia: Blackwell.

Dryzek, J. (1990). *Discursive democracy: Politics, policy and political science*. Oakleigh, Victoria, Australia: Cambridge University Press.

EEA (2005). Climate change and a European low-carbon energy system. Copenhagen: European Environmental Agency. Retrieved May 28, 2007, from reports.eea.europa.eu/eea_report_2005_1/en/Climate_change-FINAL-web.pdf

Gadamer, H. (2004). *Truth and method* (2nd revised edn). New York: Continuum.

Giarelli, J.M. (1984). A public philosophical perspective on teacher education reform. *Journal of Thought, 19*(Winter), 3-13.

Giarelli, J. (1986). Education under siege: The conservative, liberal & radical debate over schooling, by Stanley Aronowitz and Henry A Giroux. *Harvard Educational Review, 56*, 318-323.

Giddens, A. (1991). *Modernity and self-identity: Self and society in the late modern age*. Stanford, CA: Stanford University Press.

G-8 (2005). Gleneagles plan of action: Climate change, clean energy and sustainable development. UK: Foreign Affair and Commonwealth Office. Retrieved August 15, 2005, from http://www.fco.gov.uk/Files/kfile/PostG8_Gleneagles_CCChapeau.pdf

Habermas, J. (1974). *Theory and practice* (trans. J. Viertel). London: Heinemann

Habermas, J. (1976). *Legitimation crisis* (trans. T. McCarthy). London: Heinemann

Habermas, J. (1981). New social movements. *Telos, 49*, 33-37.

Habermas, J. (1987). *The theory of communicative action, Vol. 2, Lifeworld and system: A critique of functionalist reason*, trans. T McCarthy. Oxford, UK: Polity.

Habermas, J. (1996a) Civil society and the public sphere. In *Between facts and norms: Contributions to a discourse theory of law and democracy* (pp. 329-387). Cambridge: Polity.

Habermas, J. (1996b). Three normative models of democracy. In S. Benhabib (ed.), *Democracy and difference: Contesting the boundaries of the political* (pp. 21-30). Princeton, NJ: Princeton University Press.

Habermas, J. (1997). The public sphere. In R.E. Goodin & P. Pettit (eds), *Contemporary political philosophy: An anthology* (pp. 105-108). Oxford, UK: Blackwell.

Habermas, J. (2003). *Truth and justification*. MIT Press.

Hawkin, P. (2006). What's next? *World Changing*. Retrieved February 5, 2007, from http://www.worldchanging.com/archives/005670.html

Haenfler, R. (2004). Collective identity in the straight edge movement: How diffuse movements foster commitment, encourage individualized participation, and promote cultural change. *The Sociological Quarterly, 45*, 785-805.

Hoffman-Kipp, P., Artiles, A.J. & Lopez-Torres, L. (2003). Beyond Reflection: Teacher Learning as *Praxis, Theory Into Practice, 42*(3).

Hussey, J. (2007). Outback depression situation near crisis point, health conference told. Australian Broadcasting Corporation, Retrieved June 3, 2007, from http://www.abc.net.au/7.30/content/2007/s1925070.htm

IPCC (2001). Climate change 2001: Impacts, adaptation and vulnerability – Summary for policy makers. Intergovernmental Panel on Climate Change. Retrieved July 17, 2005, from http://www.ipcc.ch/

Jiggins, J. & Roling, N. (2000). Towards capacity building for complex systems management: Imagining three dimensions. In M. Cerf, D. Gibbon, B. Hubert, R. Ison, J. Jiggins, M. Paine, J. Proost & N. Roling (eds), *Cow up a tree: Knowing and learning for change in agriculture* (pp. 429-440). Paris: INRA.

Kemmis, S. (1993). Action research and social movements: A challenge for policy research. *Education Policy Analysis Archives, 1*(1), Retrieved July 11, 2005, from http://epaa.asu.edu/epaa/v1n1.html

Kemmis, S. (2006). Participatory action research and the public sphere. *Educational Action Research, 14*(4), 459-476.

Kemmis, S. & McTaggart, R. (2005). Participatory action research: Communicative action and the public sphere. In N. Denzin & Y. Lincoln (eds), *The Sage handbook of qualitative research* (3rd edn) (pp. 559-603). Thousand Oaks, CA: Sage

Kilpatrick, S. (2002). *Facilitating sustainable natural resource management: Review of the literature*, Centre for Research and Learning in Rural Australia (Paper D3/2003), University of Tasmania, Retrieved 2 September 2005, http://www.crlra.utas.edu.au/files/discussion/2003/D3-2003.pdf

MacIntyre, A. (1981). *After virtue*. Notre Dame, Indiana: University of Notre Dame Press

MacIntyre, A. (1998/1994). The thesis on Feuerbach: The road not taken. In K. Knight (Ed.), *The MacIntyre reader*, (pp. 223- 235). Notre Dame, IN: Polity

McLaren, P. & Giarelli, J. (1995). Introduction. In P. McLaren & J. Giarelli (eds), *Critical theory and educational research*. Albany: State University of New York Press.

Montuori, A. & Purser, R. (1996). Ecological futures: Systems theory, postmodernism, and participative learning in an age of uncertainty. In D. Boje, D. Gephart, & T. Joseph, (eds), *Postmodernism and Organization Theory* (pp. 181-201). Newbury Park: Sage.

Ray, L.J. (1993). *Rethinking critical theory: Emancipation in the age of global social movements*. London: SAGE.

RCEP (2000). Energy – The changing climate: Summary. London: Royal Commission on Environmental Pollution. Retrieved May 29, 2007, http://www.rcep.org.uk/pdf/summary.pdf

Roling, N. & Wagenmaker, M. (1998). *Facilitating sustainable agriculture: Participatory learning and adaptive management in times of environmental uncertainty*. UK: Cambridge University Press.

Sterling, S. (2004). Higher education, sustainability, and the role of systemic learning. In P.B. Corcoran & A.E. Wals (eds), *Higher education and the challenge of sustainability: Problematics, promise, and practice* (pp. 49-70). Dordrecht: Kluwer.

Sullivan, W.M. (1982). *Reconstructing public philosophy*. Berkeley, CA: University of California Press.

Sydney Morning Herald (2006, December 10). PM launches emissions trading taskforce,. Retrieved December 18, 2006, http://www.smh.com.au/news/NATIONAL/PM-launches-emissions-trading-taskforce/2006/12/10/1165685538179.html

Taylor, C. (1991). *The ethics of authenticity*. Cambridge, MA: Harvard University Press.

The Australian (2006, November 2). Howard dismisses climate change poll. Retrieved November 9, 2006, http://www.theaustralian.news.com.au/story/0,20867,20687562-29277,00.html

Tilbury, D. (2004). Environmental education for sustainability: A force for change in higher education. In P.B. Corcoran & A.E. Wals (eds), *Higher education and the challenge of sustainability: Problematics, promise, and practice* (pp. 97- 112). Dordrecht: Kluwer.

Tilbury, D. & Cooke, K. (2005). *A national review of environmental education and its contribution to sustainability in Australia: Frameworks for sustainability - Key findings.* Canberra: Australian Government Department of the Environment and Heritage and Australian Research Institute in Education for Sustainability (ARIES). (Publication available at http://www.aries.mq.edu.au/)

Tilbury, D., Crowley, C. & Berry, F. (2005). Education *about* and *for* sustainability in Australian business schools. Report prepared by the Australian Research Institute in Education for Sustainability (ARIES) and Arup Sustainability for the Australian Government Department of the Environment and Heritage. (Publication available at http://www.aries.mq.edu.au/).

UK Government (2003). The scientific case for setting a long-term emission reduction target, companion document of White Paper on Energy DTI. Retrieved May 30, 2007, www.defra.gov.uk/environment/climatechange/pubs/pdf/ewp_targetscience.pdf

UNESCO (2002). *Education for sustainability: From Rio to Johannesburg; Lessons learnt from a decade of commitment.* Retrieved February 10, 2007, unesdoc.unesco.org/images/0012/001271/127100e.pdf

Whelan, J. (2005). Popular education for the environment: Building interest in the educational dimension of social action. *Australian Journal of Environmental Education, 21*, 117-128.

Whelan, J., Flowers, R. and Guevara, J. (2004). Popular and informal education: The need for more research in an 'emerging' field of practice. In *Proceedings of the Effective Sustainability Education Conference*, NSW Council on Environmental Education, Retrieved 12 June 2005, http://www.epa.nsw.gov.au/resources/whelanflowersguevara.pdf

AFFILIATION

William Adlong
School of Education,
Charles Sturt University, Wagga Wagga, Australia

PART 3 CONCLUSIONS AND REFLECTIONS

JAN AX & PETRA PONTE, MATTS MATTSSON AND
KARIN RÖNNERMAN

12. REFLECTIONS ON 'ENABLING PRAXIS'

JAN AX & PETRA PONTE:
PRAXIS, RATIONALITY AND PROFESSIONAL SCOPE

Introduction

The editors of the series *Pedagogy, Education and Praxis* agreed to reflect on the text of this publication in the light of (1) points of interests, (2) conceptual issues and (3) empirical issues. They agreed to write their reflections within the framework of their own cultural and intellectual traditions. It was no easy task to do justice to the richness of the book and the broad theoretical and practical explorations of *praxis* as 'doing good for the individual and humankind' in a mere five pages. We cannot therefore discuss each chapter in detail. Instead we have tried to focus on what we think that the authors of the book have in common and the message they wanted to communicate. We read their message as a plea for a rationality that is more in tune with educational *praxis* than with the managerial way of thinking that is currently in the ascendancy. Two important themes emerge in our view. The first theme is the rationality that determines the educational practice of teachers and teacher educators; the second theme concerns how much professional say these professionals have over their own practice. These themes are the connecting thread running through our reflections.

Points of interest

The book led us to reflect critically on the concepts of 'substantial rationality' and 'functional rationality' defined by the sociologist Weber (1946). We have observed a tendency in education to accentuate the distinction between those who lay down policy and set rules and those who implement the policy and have to be managed. The distinction is central to Weber's conceptualisation of bureaucracy, which he saw as a system that prevented citizens from being treated unfairly and arbitrarily by officials.

Weber argued that functional rationality concerns the arguments about the way in which specific goals can be reached. This rationality determines the choice of means to be used to realise the desired goals. If such choices are based on a scientific-technological view of reality, rationality ideally comes into being

Kemmis, Stephen and Smith, Tracey J. (2008) Enabling praxis: Challenges for education.243-262

through logical deduction and knowledge of causality. 'Ideally' means here that in the ideal case there is 100% guarantee of success. The full research agendas of researchers in the educational field illustrate, however, that the discipline is not able to provide such guarantees. It cannot prescribe how to act in everyday practice, because it does not take account of choices that have to be made in local circumstances. The chapters in the book reflect this fact. They support the assumption that the discipline of education does not meet the logical and empirical requirements that would allow it to develop ideal functional rationality. The chapters by Tracey Smith and Christine Edwards-Groves & Deana Gray, for example, describe the obstinacy of substantial inquiry-based reflection in pre-service teacher education. Christine Edwards-Groves, in her chapter, advocates a substantive dialogue within communities of professionals, generating knowledge of the profession and building on the knowledge of schooling both individually and as a collective or collaborative endeavour.

By contrast with functional rationality, substantial rationality concerns the arguments that provide legitimacy for an action or purpose of the action. Substantive rationality is concerned with questions such as: What values am I realising through my action? What does this mean for others and myself? Why are these values in my actual actions important? According to Weber, the goals of public services, bureaucracies in other words, ideally are determined through a democratically organised, political, decision-making process. 'Ideally' means here that in the ideal case the greatest possible measure of agreement between, and justice for, the parties involved is respected. We believe there is a trend today to see education as an example of public service understood in this way.

Determining objectives for schools and for teacher education courses turns out to be far more complicated, however, than Weber's notion of substantial rationality suggests. Establishing educational objectives cannot therefore be only a matter of political and public decision-making via a majority of votes, but it also involves decision-making by people and agencies who design and develop the concrete aspects of educational practice. Pupils, teachers, teacher educators, academics and others also have expectations about what they want to achieve through education and how they want to achieve these things. These stakeholders include those who have a legitimate right to have their expectations met. Making decisions about objectives in education is therefore far more complex than Weber's theory of bureaucracy suggests. Decisions about proper objectives are surrounded by uncertainties, opposing tendencies and dilemmas. In their chapter, for example, Helen Russell and Peter Grootenboer show how they were faced in their practice as teacher educators with dilemmas inherent in the *praxis* of teacher educators.

The problem is that, in Weber's view on the way the public domain is organised, there is strict separation between the authorities who take substantial decisions and the bureaucrats who have to implement the policy by following set protocols. This hierarchical dichotomy can also be seen in the managerialism of today, in which politicians, school governors and school heads are apparently meant to be the ones who establish the policy in schools, while teachers are seen as the people who implement the policy these others have laid down. The same trend can also be seen in teacher education courses. This managerialism fails to recognise the fact that education is characterised by a complex configuration of diverse stakeholders, by moral import and by the impossibility, in practice, of acting solely on the basis of logical deduction and causality. This leads us to conclude that the divide between political policy-making and administrative decision-making on one side, and, on the other, the day-to-day practice of school teachers and teacher educators, cannot be drawn strictly along the lines suggested by Weber's theory.

That brings us to our second theme, namely the scope of the professionals' say. The studies in this book certainly show that teachers and educators must have the necessary degree of say; it is they who ultimately have to reconcile the diverse values of the different stakeholders, all of which may be legitimate in themselves, in a professional manner (Bull, 1988; Ponte, 2007). We could call this essential power to take decisions the *substantial rational scope* of the teacher and the teacher educator. However, substantial scope is not enough. The teacher also needs *instrumental scope* to be able to realise those interests in a practical sense, since the scientific-technological world view does not provide a valid representation of the practical realities of education.

The book includes contributions that criticise Australian education from this perspective. In the view of the authors, Australian schools are dominated by too many externally imposed regulations intended to increase chances of success. However, these regulations seem in fact to reduce the students' chance of success, because they curtail the teacher's scope for *praxis*. Expectations of the validity of functional rationality are inflated, and too many policy-makers believe that this rationality can be imposed from outside. Instrumentalism and centralisation are serious threats to educational *praxis* today. The various contributions to the book present a picture both of those threats and of the opportunities and counterbalancing forces that allow educators to claim that professional scope (see, for instance, the chapters by Tracey Smith, Christine Edwards-Groves, Roslin Brennan-Kemmis, Ian Hardy and William Adlong). Before returning to the empirical issues, we would first like to examine a number of conceptual issues.

Conceptual issues

Chapters Two and Three establish the conceptual basis for the combined analytic and interpretative framework employed in the later chapters: '*Praxis* Development' (Stephen Kemmis & Tracey Smith) and 'Situating *Praxis* in Practice: Practice architectures and the cultural, social and material conditions for practice' (Stephen Kemmis & Peter Grootenboer). The substance given to these concepts produced the necessary material for discussion at our meetings as part of the international 'Pedagogy, Education and *Praxis*' project (see the Editors' introduction). The differences that emerged from our discussions should, we believe, help to explain the difference between Anglo-American understanding of pedagogy as method and the continental European understanding of pedagogy as human science (see also Ponte, in press; Ponte & Ax, in press).

In the Netherlands and other continental European countries, pedagogy (pedagogiek) is a human science and a discrete academic discipline (Miedema, 1997). As a discipline, pedagogy encompasses the world of the theory, or the whole body of knowledge and opinions about help, guidance and support for cognitive growth from infancy to adulthood. It is the science of child-rearing, dealing with views on the nature of humankind, at all stages from baby to adult, and with practical knowledge that can be put to use in deliberately influencing the environment surrounding the child to be brought up. At its heart, the discipline of pedagogy – as a distinctive *human science* – makes a scientific contribution to optimising the process of becoming an adult. The human science of pedagogy makes the key assumption that human beings have a natural inclination to learn. We speak of pedagogic (*pedagogische*) *praxis* as the real existing practice of child-rearing. The practice of bringing up children is a practical reality which is the natural condition of the human being. In that sense, therefore, child-rearing has always existed, regardless of its quality or implications. Indoctrination, for instance, is a highly undesirable form of child-rearing but it is still child-rearing. Every form and act of upbringing, every *praxis* therefore, implies a social environment. We become people in and through the social environment and morality is the essence of this. After all, every social relationship has mores and every social relationship is culturally, socially and materially determined.

The concept of *education* is a differentiation of pedagogic *praxis*. Education concerns that part of child-rearing that takes place in institutionalised, professionalised settings (usually a school, a college or university). In our modern society, there is little disagreement as a rule about what we can call education, or the education sector[1]. The curious phenomenon that we see now is that, in Europe, education is a differentiated part of pedagogy (as human science) while in the Anglo-American literature it is precisely the other way round. In the English-speaking countries, pedagogy (as method) refers to the technical level of action within the broad domain of education. In the European literature, we usually use the terms 'teaching methods' and 'didactics' for that (though we will not go into the differences between these two concepts here).

The concept of *praxis* as we use it, was explained by Riedel (1977; see also Blankertz, 1969). *Praxis* is social and purposeful action, in which Aristotle's three key concepts (*phronēsis*, *theoria* and *technē*) come together in a concrete practical context (see also Ponte, 2002). Each social and purposeful action is based on morality. We saw earlier that the corollary of this is that it also applies to pedagogic *praxis*, because in *praxis* the educator is intervening in the life of the child or young person. That intervention is justified on the basis of an idea about what kind of person the child or young person should become. In *praxis* as action, therefore, *morality* (*phronēsis*, as giving meaning to experience), *knowledge* (theory, as knowing how things behave and are connected), and *skill* (*technē*, as knowing how to act) merge. *Technē* is not conceived by Riedel just as an instrumental algorithm, but as action based on scientific and ideological insights that is planned, evaluated and adapted in the reality of the school or the teacher education course. None of Aristotle's three main concepts can be separated from *praxis.* Each *praxis* brings about something that has moral meaning, each *praxis* makes use of knowledge and insights and each *praxis* involves an act. The concepts are only used in an analytical sense. Let us give an example for the purpose of illustration: an object can be described in terms of substance, form, content and colour, but it is not possible to say that an object is purely and only form. In the same way any social action in school or in the local environment of the school can be termed *praxis* (as the combined action of *phronēsis, technē* and theory), but not solely as *technē.*

What stands out from the pages of this book is that the interpretation of the concept of *praxis* is based, in our view, on what the individual person intends by his or her action. Stephen Kemmis and Tracey Smith state in Chapter Two that "An educator can be a *eudaimōn* if she or he lives and acts well, in the interests of individuals and the good of humankind, and is successful in living the sort of life that will allow people to say, when their life or career has ended, that she or he demonstrated a continuing commitment to those goods." This individual interpretation of *praxis* allows questions to be asked such as: 'To what extent do initial and continuing professional education courses develop *praxis* of the kind described here?' (Stephen Kemmis and Tracey Smith) and 'In looking for *praxis,* what were we looking for?' (Helen Russell and Peter Grootenboer). What also stands out is that *praxis* as individual action takes place in a separate culturally, socially and materially defined *practice.* A separate chapter by Stephen Kemmis and Peter Grootenboer is devoted to *practice,* which aims 'to show that practice and *praxis* are not dependent solely on the experience, intentions and actions of individuals, but rather to show that they are also shaped and conditioned by arrangements, circumstances and conditions *beyond* each person as an individual agent or actor'.

It will be clear from what we have said so far that this understanding of *praxis*/practice is not the same as the Dutch or continental European concept of pedagogic *praxis.* In the Dutch or continental European tradition, *praxis* is by definition a social situation that always has moral implications and can always be interpreted in a moral sense, so we make no conceptual distinction between *praxis* and *practice.* Practice for us is an inherent given of *praxis.* In other words, *praxis* is not a separate act of an individual to be identified, but a social circumstance in which the combined action of *phronēsis, technē* and theory determine the moral implications and effects. We also assume that every social action can be studied as *praxis,* even if it is bad or immoral, thoughtless or ignorant, or if it is carried out unknowingly or incompetently. This means that questions like 'Am I doing *praxis* or not?' cannot be asked, but questions like 'What are the effects of this *praxis* for specific groups of pupils?' can. The emancipatory perspective offers us something to hold on to when we try to put a particular interpretation on the relationship between theory, *technē* and *phronēsis* in those situations. The English concept of 'practice' (Dutch *praktijk*) mainly has neutral connotations for us. (For example, 'I intend to eat fresh vegetables every day but in *practice* I don't get round to it'.) The question now is whether and how these conceptual differences lead to different interpretations of present-day education as *praxis.* This question is interesting enough in itself to warrant a separate study; all we can do in the next section is to explore it very briefly.

Empirical issues

It is clear from the various contributions to this volume that there is great pressure on schools from outside bodies, and that there is great pressure on teachers from the management in schools to resign themselves to a managerial architecture. Teacher educators also recognise this trend. The situations in Australia and the Netherlands are very similar in this respect. The articles in the book give examples of managerial architectures in the Australian context. Roslin Brennan Kemmis, among others, refers to acting in accordance with this architecture as '*technē*', because it strips her of her own moral and situational choices. The absence of choice is described very clearly, and yet we can question whether this is '*technē*' in the sense in which we used it in the last section, following Riedel (1977).

Proceeding from the idea that every situation in education is *praxis*, we could also interpret the form of managerial architecture described by contributors to this volume as a specific form of professionalised action. All instances of professional *praxis* in a professionalised context are subject to quality standards and they are determined by the social environment. In many cases, they are established in formal rules, regulations and laws. Professional practice conforms to such institutionalised requirements, sometimes voluntarily, sometimes because it is compulsory, and often a mixture of both. The sociological concept of *institutionalisation* (Meyer & Scott, 1992) can be used to describe how this process takes place given the empiricism of modern societies. Educational *praxis* is highly institutionalised and cut according to the cloth of prevailing values such as economic effectiveness and efficiency, uniformity and manageability. We know that institutionalisation as such is unavoidable, but also that the intensity of the pressure to conform and the substance of the institutionalisation varies in time and place. There was a time when education was there to perpetuate the status quo and obedience and discipline determined the pedagogic sphere. There were 'rules' that had to be followed in those days, too, aimed at achieving compliance. The dominant thinking nowadays is what we, for the sake of brevity, call 'managerialism'. Many of the rules ensuing from managerialism, however, have little to do with pedagogic-educational *technē*. Were this to be '*technē*' according to Riedel's interpretation, then the whole body of rules would have to be built on action based on scientific and ideological insights that is planned, evaluated and adjusted in reality; that is, the concrete reality of learning and teaching in schools and in teacher education courses.

In the real world now, however, rules are based on a body of values that are imposed on public services in general, rather than on the empirical knowledge of the educational profession, as Riedel called it. In the terminology of organisational studies, what we are dealing with here is known as 'goal displacement' (Lammers, Mijs & Noort, 1997), because means are being elevated to goals: control through rules has ceased to be a means to an end and has become an end in itself. We prefer to speak of managerialism in this context rather than *technē*. Managerialism is the expression of a general modernist morality incorporated in architecture formats, and regulators across the board would like us to believe that it is *technē*. If we interpret it in this way, then Roslin Brennan Kemmis and the authors of the other contributions will certainly not rank themselves among the believers. Jane Wilkinson, for instance, showed how managerialism arouses tensions in the professional ethics of individual university leaders, especially when it comes to those from minority cultures. Ian Hardy showed that teachers' scope for *praxis* is pushed into a straitjacket by government policy and that both *technē* and the moral aspects of *praxis* are in difficulty because of this. Finally, William Adlong examines substantial rationality, that is the moral aims of education, in depth. Education does not exist for its own sake but is there to improve our future wellbeing. This can only be achieved if we live in harmony with our natural habitat. In a certain sense, therefore, Adlong is talking about *praxis* at a higher system level that can only be successful if it is supported by the community of individual education professionals.

Conclusion

We seem to be justified in coming to the conclusion that policy-makers and managers in education are making a sham of the definition of the good cause (the desired educational outcomes) and of the right way to achieve them. The concepts of substantial and functional rationality are confused and coloured by the mores of the times. In this sense, we can speak of a crisis of legitimacy in education and only critical reflection on our work, conceived as scholarly *praxis*, can offer us a way out of this crisis. We know that this solution will be bound by time and place, but we also know that Australia and the Netherlands have a great deal in common. We know that we live in a global village and that *praxis* geared to emancipation involves the combined action of *morality* (*phronēsis*, as giving meaning to experience), *knowledge* (theory, as knowing how things behave and are connected), and *skill* (*technē*, as knowing how to act).

MATTS MATTSSON:
A DIFFERENT MEANING OF PRAXIS

Phronēsis – as a challenge

This book is really a challenge. The authors deal with Aristotle in a most interesting way. *Praxis* development is the key concept. *Technē*, *phronēsis* and practice architecture are other concepts of importance. In each chapter, contributors approach different aspects of education. Some are mainly philosophical, clarifying ideas and concepts that are helpful in understanding what education is all about. The central message is that education is part of a process through which educators, by doing a good job, can make a contribution to improving this world. Other chapters are mainly empirical. They give detailed insights into the reality of classroom work and educational projects. Some deal with professional development, others with school leadership, vocational education and local collaborative inquiry groups for sustainability. *Praxis* development is explored from different angles.

Some authors focus on reflection and self-formation as important aspects of *praxis*. Others discuss *praxis* as a kind of action including "doings", "sayings" and "relatings". *Praxis* is analysed in relation to the individual, to social interaction, the educational system and institutional settings. *Praxis* development can be achieved in many ways and on many levels. It is a coherent discussion on education inspired not only by Aristotle, but also by Bourdieu, Dewey, Foucault, Gadamer, Habermas and others. They all approach essentials in education. Education is a practice that could and should be developed into *praxis*. *Praxis* is referred to as morally informed actions for the good of humankind. *Praxis* development is a commitment "to live a certain kind of life". The point of departure is that *praxis*, in this sense, is endangered. I agree.

The major threat to *praxis* development is said to be that teachers and school leaders are being deprived of their "moral agency" and their inclination and ability to "do the right thing" (*phronēsis*). The threat is formed by "the system world" (Habermas, 1992). Educators risk getting caught in a system compelling them to follow rules and to behave instrumentally (*technē*): "The disposition that guides the teacher who is only teaching to achieve certain pre-given learning outcomes is *technē*" (Kemmis & Smith, Chapter Two). The challenging thesis is, that teachers should act "educationally" which means that they should demonstrate practical wisdom. They should act wisely and prudently and with practical commonsense in response to particular situations, persons and circumstances, for the wellbeing of humankind. That is the meaning of *phronēsis*.

Strategies for praxis development

The message is important and challenging. But is it really possible to discuss education in such a normative way, giving credit to some attitudes, actions and experiences and not to others? On what basis could some approaches be referred to as good for humankind and others as "*technē*", "instrumental" and less morally informed? How can a researcher distinguish between actions that are good and actions that are bad?

Looking at the examples of *praxis* development offered in this book I understand that "doing the right thing" is to recognize, respect and live the traditions, the culture and the discourses of a professional practice. To become a full participant of a community of practice a person must get to know this practice from within, and be able to see the practice with the eyes of an experienced educator. And the person must live a certain kind of life – that is, do and say and relate according to the tradition and culture of this specific professional practice. At the same time, the person must learn how to analyse and how to change the practice architecture that threatens to deprive them and their colleagues of their "moral agency" and their inclination to act wisely and prudently.

This is a dilemma to be found not only in the Australian educational system, or in the tradition of action research. It is an old and general dilemma for humankind. It is difficult to change the structures that one is part of. How could this dilemma be handled by researchers and educators?

The general answer this volume gives is that people have to be moral agents. What strategies could be used by researchers and educators who would like to contribute to the wellbeing of humankind? Looking into different chapters, I can identify the following strategies for praxis development. They should not be understood as excluding each other.

(1) The agent can be a role model doing, saying and relating in a wise and prudent way. The commitment is to live and to demonstrate what is good for persons and for humankind. This agent knows his or her philosophy; it is a learned person who knows how to act in a specific context in relation to specific situations and in relation to the other people concerned. He or she personifies *phronēsis*. "He or she is acting on experience that has been thoughtfully reflected upon" (Kemmis & Smith, Chapter Two).

(2) Another strategy, or an aspect of the strategy just outlined, is to be a *reflective practitioner*. This agent knows how to stimulate and encourage pre-service teachers or other students to reflect upon their own experiences in relation to prevailing theories. This may lead to development of a *praxis-oriented self*. The *praxis*-oriented self will know how to find his or her way in classroom work and in life. *Praxis* is defined as "morally-committed educational action, oriented and informed by (educational) theories and traditions" (Edwards-Groves & Gray, Chapter Five).

(3) A similar strategy has a more *collective approach*. The idea is to involve teachers in active and *collaborative learning communities* within the situated context of their schools (Edwards-Groves, Chapter Seven). Members of such communities turn to their colleagues and friends in order to develop reflexivity. *Praxis* is a process of self-formation that changes the person who acts, but it is essential to note that the development of *praxis* is a collegial venture (Russell & Grootenboer, Chapter Six).

(4) Another type of agent has a more indirect approach. He or she takes the role of an *architect* forming the landscape in which student teachers make their experience. Teacher educators should form programs "that provide a balance between support and challenges and between theory and practice" (Smith, Chapter Four). Here, the focus is on *practice architectures* that enable and constrain teachers' professional development. In this landscape, pre-service teachers will hopefully find support for their reflections. They might "notice, name and reframe their experiences to nurture a praxis stance that will allow them to write themselves into *praxis*" (Smith, Chapter Four).

(5) A similar indirect approach may be called the *project leader*. This agent knows how to initiate and support projects for professional development. He or she is well informed about history, educational reforms, policies and

economy. The project leader knows how to involve teachers in *praxis*-oriented projects for improving the work of teachers and schools; he or she knows his profession (Hardy, Chapter Eight). A similar strategy is applied by the agent who knows how to identify, recognize and support good traditions among well experienced teachers, taking into account, for example, the history of vocational education and training and the practice architecture in that field (Brennan Kemmis, Chapter Ten). In leadership *praxis*, leaders need to take into account the broader socio-political contexts which inform institutional discourses and practices (Wilkinson, Chapter Nine).

(6) Another option is the *activist approach*. By participatory action research in social movements, people may, as a result of the process, have an impact on many levels. Together with other agents involved, participants may develop themselves and at the same time have an impact on the practice architecture that enables and constrains development of active and concerned citizenship. "We live in a time of social movements and it is through social movements that many of the most important issues of our epoch are being addressed" (Adlong, Chapter Eleven).

These strategies, suggested in this volume, seem to be most helpful for researchers and educators striving to "do the right thing for the good of humankind". Many authors make references to Habermas and to the importance of communicative action and a space for communication, a public sphere. I agree.

Conflicts and confrontations

From history, we know, however, that there are usually conflicts and confrontations involved when people try to move from one social identity to another and from one practice architecture to another. The tensions between agents and structures have often required a conflict-oriented approach, sometimes bold and militant. This observation prompts a critical remark. In this volume, it seems as if the agents and the strategies for "doing the right thing" seldom meet opposing groups and strategies. It seems as if they seldom meet resistance. Most (not all) case studies presented here, and the strategies outlined for *praxis* development, seem to exclude situations where conflicting ideas, groups, actions and strategies appear. It seems as if the *praxis*-oriented educator seldom confronts opponents. In my own research about community development, there is lots of evidence that conflicts and confrontations are part of the process when people struggle to change structures (Mattsson, 1986, 1996). For better or for worse, many situations in life call for a conflict approach. The literature on action research and organizational development has a lot to tell us about conflict strategies and the dialectical processes involved (see for example Alinsky, 1971; Crozier & Friedberg, 1980; Fals Borda & Rahman, 1991; Freire 1973)

From history we know that, in some situations, agents find no other solution than applying a conflict strategy. The oppressed, poor and victims of injustice may have to challenge the dominant power structure. Empowerment and emancipation are often main features in a strategy for fundamental change. Taking this into account, *praxis* development might be understood as a process and a result of asymmetrical power relations and the dialectical interplay between different groups (Wilkinson, Chapter Nine). *Praxis* development might be the result of conflicting ideas, agents, groups and strategies. Many important developments in history are the results of conflicts between oppressed groups and people in power.

A different meaning of praxis

So how is it that conflict strategies are more or less absent in this volume? There might be many reasons. One of them might be that I have misinterpreted the authors; that my reading does not do justice to their work. Another reason, however, might be the way they use the Aristotle inspired frame of reference and some of the key concepts. It might have to do with "*praxis* development" used as a concept for giving credit to some attitudes, actions and experiences and not to others. In such a normative perspective, it is difficult to analyse a complex situation characterized by competing agents, groups and strategies. From this perspective, it is difficult to analyse the dilemma which many educators face today. A dilemma suggests that the gap between what is actually done and what should be done is not just a matter of good and bad intentions, actions, agents and strategies.

In my understanding, the difference between practice and *praxis*, instrumentality and practical wisdom should rather be understood as part of a complex process which has not reached its final stage. That is why it may be hard for anyone to tell if and when someone has developed the disposition to "do the right thing" (*phronēsis*). Such a matter must be thoroughly examined, especially for researchers. There are often opposing agents and structures claiming to represent the "right thing". Finding ways to assess or evaluate *praxis*-related research, including action research, is a task that remains to be developed (Mattsson & Kemmis, 2007).

When people do and say and relate according to the tradition and culture of a specific professional practice, their approach may be understood as '*praxis*' in quite a different sense than the sense presented in this volume. In Sweden, '*praxis*' is generally understood as "general habits and customs", "traditions", "the way things are", "the taken for granted practices", "a settled practice that cannot easily be given up". Bourdieu's concept of "habitus" is related to "habits" in a way which comes very close to the way *praxis* is generally understood in Sweden.

Praxis, in Sweden, is generally not used as a normative concept. It is descriptive in relation to how people actually live their lives and how they do their jobs. *Praxis* in this sense could be good, it could be bad. *Praxis* has been formed during a long period of time. People have internalised the norms and the habits that are now taken for granted practices. Bourdieu (1993, 1999) talked about this phenomenon in terms of "sedimented intentions". He refers to habitus or sedimented intentions as frames of reference that are concealed in social fields as well as in peoples' cultures and actions (Broady, 1991). Such frameworks may be activated in particular circumstances. Bourdieu's habitus (acquired patterns of dispositions to act in particular ways in particular situations) includes actions informed by reflection as well as actions which merely express deep-rooted habits. Bourdieu introduced the concept of habitus as a tool for further investigation. Kemmis & Grootenboer (Chapter Three) use the concept "extra-individual formations" for a similar purpose. For better or for worse, *praxis*, habits and extra-individual formations represent continuity. *Praxis* interpreted this way makes it difficult to tell if a certain educational practice should be understood as good or as something that should be given up. *Praxis*, in this sense, is not a matter just for rational choice. It is embodied; it is integrated with culture and with peoples' emotions. It is part of a certain kind of life. As the concept of habitus suggests, our freedom to act in this world is limited. It is restricted by context, history and social capital. And it is restricted by other people's way of living and the strategies applied by other agents claiming support for other ideas.

To underline these aspects of settings in which *praxis* occurs, many cases of *praxis* development presented in this volume might turn out to be more complicated to analyse than now appears. *Praxis*, interpreted as I have interpreted it here, might make it difficult to conceptualise anyone moving from 'practice' to '*praxis*' and from 'instrumentality' to 'wisdom'. As I understand them, such transitions often requires empowerment, emancipation and agents that have a broad repertoire of strategies. *Praxis* development requires agents that are well experienced in many fields. They sometimes have to apply conflict strategies, which, of course, is no guarantee for success. In any case, even if a person were to manage making a transition from practice to *praxis*, it will be hard for an observer – a researcher, for instance – to tell if the person has really succeeded. Quoting the ancient Greeks, Kemmis and Smith, say "call no man good until he dies". They argue that "we cannot know, even in the case of a person who seems good, that all of their actions will be the ones they would want to stand by as contributing to their long term happiness and the wider and long-term good for humankind" (Chapter Two).

This edited volume is a challenge. The frame of reference and the concepts introduced are most fruitful. The authors deal with Aristotle in an interesting way. The case studies presented call for reflection. Some important and difficult questions have been raised, and some (as they always do) await better answers. How does a person move from one identity to another and from one structure to another? How does a person move from one context of meaning to another? What strategies can be applied by researchers and educators to encourage *praxis* development?

KARIN RÖNNERMAN:
A DIFFERENT MEANING OF PRAXIS

During 2007, Sweden has been celebrating the 300th anniversary of Carl von Linné's birth (Carl Linnaeus, 1707-1778). On the website http://www.linne2007.se/, we can discover that Carl von Linné was one of the most influential scientists in history, and that his work is crucial to our present-day understanding of how the species on this planet relate to one another. Linné, who was trained, and practised, as a physician, was the first person to define the human being as one animal among others, naming it *Homo sapiens*. In order to be awarded his doctorate in medicine, Linné was obliged to travel abroad. As was customary among Swedish doctoral students at the time, he went to the Netherlands for his disputation. With him he took the first manuscript of his pioneering magnum opus, *Systema Naturae* - a classification system for plants, animals, stones and minerals, that was based on his studies of flora in the University gardens at Uppsala, in the surrounding countryside, and on his travels in Lapland and elsewhere. This classification was based, in the case of plants, on their sexual characteristics. The animals were classified according to a variety of criteria, while rocks and minerals were ordered according to their external characteristics. All species in von Linné's system were divided into strict hierarchies, starting with the largest and ending with the smallest. Linné naturally placed man at the top of the hierarchy. The Linnaean system of classification has proved enduringly useful as a scientific tool for mapping and understanding the natural world.

Interesting points

Carl von Linné was not an educationist, but a scientist with a special interest in mapping and devising systematic ways of understanding the natural world. Educational ideas based on science and its systematic approaches to study have, throughout history, been in the foreground for "good education", where results should be predictable and measurable. Different methods have been developed to help students reach high scores on tests and, today, competition between countries in children's test performances is a matter of much debate. But does this result in good education for humankind? In *Enabling Praxis,* we meet a much older man, Aristotle, who was a philosopher with an interest in democracy and the conditions that enabled men to act in political and societal fields. *Enabling Praxis* details Aristotle's systematic way of separating and defining knowledge into three different forms. Whilst *epistēmē* is precise (theoretical – scientific) knowledge, practical knowledge takes two forms: *technē* (practical-productive knowledge) and *phronēsis* (political – ethical knowledge). These three categories of knowledge provide a theoretical background for arguments about how "good" education could be based more on *phronēsis*, which would then be realised in *praxis*.

The volume is interesting in the way it is packaged together. Chapter Two investigates the three different forms of knowledge and the concepts belonging to these forms, based on the ideas advanced by Aristotle. The most important contribution in this chapter is the attempt by the authors to connect these forms of knowledge to modern education by connecting them to teacher education. Another important contribution is how Aristotle's categorisation of knowledge is connected to Habermas's critical-emancipatory paradigm. The scheme is analytical and maintains a clear delineation between the different perspectives, even though it is important to be aware of how they are intertwined in practical work. This kind of scheme might serve well for discussions about and reflections upon how different courses are planned and carried out. A risk, though, is that a scheme like this could be used as a method of steering or in a technical/instrumental way, rather than as an analytical or reflective tool, as indeed is revealed in some of the cases presented in the volume. Most of the examples are taken from teacher educators' experiences from teacher education. The examples are presented as narratives in which *praxis* is conceptualised and discussed from various different angles.

The frame presented in Chapter Two is used in a fruitful way, for example in Smith's retrospective case, but also in the cases presented by Edwards-Groves & Gray (Chapter Five) and Edwards-Groves (Chapter Seven). In these chapters an interesting point discussed by the authors is how to develop a *praxis stance*. These three chapters deal both with pre- and in-service training. The latter is important since learning and development never end with education and are, on the contrary, an ongoing aspect of life as a teacher in continually reflecting over actions taken towards developing *praxis*. The obvious risk otherwise is that reflection is restricted to education and not used as a tool for developing *praxis* in schools and elsewhere. The examples of students resisting strategies for self-reflection presented by Edwards-Groves & Gray are recognized even in Sweden. Students, on the one hand, relate tools for reflection to their education and how they will be assessed, and have difficulties bringing self-reflection into practice and to the development of their roles and practices as teachers. On the other hand, teacher educators have difficulties in using and following up on these tools in education; that is to say how they can be used in practice and, in particular, how they can be used to develop *praxis* as Edwards-Groves & Gray show in their chapter. Indeed, this finding is confirmed by Swedish studies conducted in teacher education.

In Chapter Three, another frame is presented in which the focus is on *practice architectures*. The arguments for such architectures are that, in order to develop *praxis* in practice, you need to be aware of the circumstances that surround such practice. These are here defined as cultural-discursive, social-political and material-economic orders and arrangements, and labelled as 'extra-individual'. In the cases they present, Hardy (Chapter Eight), Wilkinson (Chapter Nine) and Brennan Kemmis (Chapter Ten) show how these features affect practice. No one would object to these arguments, but what possibilities do they offer to a teacher who, in these types of circumstances, strives to bring about change? On the other hand, these schemes are useful for understanding different circumstances that can occur in practice and might well provide a good tool to use in rewarding in-service teaching for teachers. Of course, teachers have their own experiences and will recognise such features as surrounding their practice and, further, even how they are steered by economic forms of knowledge rather than by *phronēsis*. One contribution to the volume in particular offers insights into, and an understanding of, the need to work politically and at a societal level with a focus on citizenship. The final case in the volume, Adlong's Chapter Eleven, explores challenges about how to handle the sustainability of the earth by being educational both in formal and informal educational situations. This is perhaps the most challenging issue today.

It would be a pity if the framework for understanding *praxis*/practice presented in the volume simply stays within the academy and is not used as a base to develop *praxis* among practitioners. A challenge would thus be to develop these frameworks further and to use them in practice (both in schools and in teacher education) as a means of developing *praxis*.

Conceptual issues

Knowledge is usually something associated with learning and education. But knowledge is also something that we come into contact with in reality: at work and in our everyday activities. In this sense, knowledge is usually divided into theoretical and practical, where theoretical knowledge is connected to scientific knowledge, and practical knowledge to everyday activities. A problem arises with such a distinction concerning the legitimacy and power of different forms of knowledge. A prevalent view, for instance, is that science is superior to practice and that it has greater power, so scientific knowledge takes precedence over practical knowledge. The Aristotelian division of knowledge, where practical knowledge is equally valued, appears to be fruitful in redressing this imbalance in favour of scientific knowledge. In Sweden as in Australia, there are discussions about how to understand teachers' work in forms of developing knowledge using an Aristotelian perspective in which the key issue is how to understand and use the interconnections between theory and practice in education. The concept of *praxis* is frequently used in this context, books are written about it, and research projects applying such a perspective are given financial support.

It should be noted, however, that concepts have particular meanings and significances within particular geographical and historical contexts. Using concepts created in another time, in another society, and for other purposes, is frequently problematic. However the problems encountered might not only be contextual: semantic problems also arise when concepts are used in different languages. For example, the concept '*praxis*' has two meanings in Swedish. In one meaning, it is the concept devised by Aristotle, to act in a way that is morally right based on *phronēsis,* whilst in another meaning it could be understood as custom or practice (*sedvana*), a way of doing things as they have always been done. Thus, when discussing the concept of '*praxis*' with teachers, it is important to know which meaning is intended when the concept is being used. Another angle could be that the concept *praxis* turns out to be an 'academic' way of talking about how to understand and develop knowledge through acting in schools. Somekh (1994) shows that language has significance for the ways in which practitioners will understand cooperation and research. A key challenge might be to find ways of cooperation between schools and the academy that encourage both teachers and researchers to strive to develop a *praxis stance*. If such an understanding simply remains within the academy, how then can education be for the good of humankind?

The other concept connected to practical knowledge is *technē*, and is connected to pragmatism, as is discussed by Russell and Grootenboer in Chapter Six.

Gustavsson (2000) writes that, in neo-pragmatism, the notion of the 'instrumental' has been transformed so that knowledge is seen as a part of the human work of making the world a better place. On this view, the instrumental is opened up towards *phronēsis*. This transformation also opens opportunities for the use of other concepts, like tacit knowledge.

A criticism of the volume might be that, overall, it provides an overdose of discussion on the development of *praxis* to the detriment of a discussion of *epistēmē*, which remains somewhat neglected. Is it not imperative to deal with both, or indeed all three forms of knowledge, if a better world is to be achieved? Gustavsen (2001) suggests another way to understand the mediation of knowledge. In his model, there is *theoretical knowledge*, on the one hand, whilst on the other there *is practical knowledge. The means of bridging between the two is via mediating knowledge* that covers parts of both theory and practice, meaning knowledge that does not occur exclusively in either science or practice, but which is derived when interaction between these two parts is achieved. Citing Ricœur, Gustavsson (2000) also argues for the use of knowledge that has a base in both the sciences and the humanities. He argues that, as science in modern times uses methods for interpretation and understanding, and that the humanities have developed methods for explanation, it could be useful to transfer the differences between these two dominant cultures.

Empirical issues

In this volume, the cases presented deal with well-known and recognised empirical issues. The individual or personal stance is consistently positioned in the foreground. Knowledge is a human concern that, as a result of hard work, is incorporated as something personal. It is acquired in an ongoing process, in which we gain overviews, understandings and deeper insights. Knowledge becomes something in ourselves that changes our perceptions and broadens our understandings of the surrounding world. Knowledge is thus both a personal and a societal occurrence embedded in a social and cultural context (Gustavsson, 2000). This is also shown in the analytical triangle presented by Smith in Chapter Four. Another such triangle could be added from the Norwegian researchers Handal & Lauvås (2001). They talk about the *praxis* triangle (based on Løvlie, 1974) as being divided into three levels. At the bottom there is acting, in the middle level there is action based on experiences and theory, whilst in the uppermost section of the triangle are values and ethics. All three levels are needed, they argue, in order to develop *praxis* (Lauvås & Handal, 2001). In the cases presented in this volume, many authors point out that, in order to reach a *praxis* stance, it is important to start initially with yourself. The question is, though, whether it is possible to include this in formal education and, if so, how should it be included? If, yes then new ways of teaching and of handling teaching situations in which students and teacher educators reflect over such things as "good" education need to be developed. But this then raises additional new questions, such as, who decides what good education is and for whom is it good?

As shown in the cases presented in the book, there are attempts to develop new ways of understanding, but there are always still more insights to be gained. This requires an approach characterised by open-mindedness in order to achieve new interpretive opportunities. Another way is to adopt the word '*bildung*' (in Swedish, *bildning*) as is grounded in the Swedish tradition of education. '*Bildung*' concerns knowing yourself and knowing how you are connected to the world. From the perspective of *bildung*, interpreting the world and interpreting or understanding oneself are inherently interconnected and form a central part in widening horizons and creating opportunities to find new meaning in new contexts. It is the path between the known in relation to the unknown, and then back to the known again. From this expanding relationship, new insights can contribute to change (Gustavsson, 1996).

In the cases, many aspects of *praxis*/practice are discussed. One aspect that perhaps does not receive as much attention as others, however, is the collaboration between schools and universities, or between university-based researchers and practitioners. There is a tension between theory and practice that has been widely discussed in recent decades. To open up and find new ways of enabling reflection and for in-service training, action research might prove to be a useful way of developing and connecting the forms of knowledge discussed in this volume. It is hard to believe that an education based solely on *phronēsis* can lead to the development of *praxis*, and thus other forms of knowledge must be presented too. Connecting *technē* to pragmatism and *epistēmē* to modern science might offer a way to transcend this dichotomy.

Collaboration between university-based researchers and practitioners through critical action research offers an opportunity to move forward, provided, that is, that there is an awareness of its danger of being overly technical, as Carr & Kemmis (2005) warned. These forms of collaboration are fairly new in education in Sweden, but are, at the moment, not left solely to teachers. Here, the university-based researcher is a facilitator who emphasises the linking together of different forms of knowledge. There is indeed a desire to link together explanation and understanding and, in this way, an opportunity to go beyond the division shaped by the taken-for-granted separation between the sciences and the humanities. A teacher with whom we have worked here in Gothenburg, who recently moved from a university city to a small town with no university connections, explained the importance of collaboration with the university. She mentioned that she was more up-to-date, more challenged to reflect on her own practice, and more motivated to initiate her own projects than some other teachers in the town. It seems that it is important both to have an up-to-date knowledge about theories concerning children's upbringing, as well as an awareness of the traditions of these theories.

When presenting empirical cases there is a tendency to cherry-pick the "good" examples. But what do we learn from such examples? In the cases, very few tensions or conflicts are presented. One can ask whether the world really is as harmonious as it is presented in these cases, or whether in fact we fail to identify and deal with tensions and conflicts when we present case studies from schools.

When developing *praxis*, and, in doing so, getting closer to a "good" education for humankind, another reflection of crucial importance for the current century is raised. Today, when talking about humankind and democracy it is not sufficient just to know what the world is like. Using the three forms of knowledge given to us by Aristotle, it is obvious that *epistēmē* and *technē* steer the world and that *phronēsis* is far beyond. Knowing this, it might be important not to talk simply about humankind, but to be more precise in identifying sex, gender, ethnicity, culture and religion as important factors to be aware of in education. Simply using the term humankind might blind us to the circumstances under which people live today. Although in Sweden there is legislation that requires that gender equality must be a goal for all schools, this goal is a long way from being achieved. Education has in history and by tradition been for men and, in many cultures, still is (Martin, 1985, 1994), as it was indeed for both Carl von Linné and Aristotle. One might finally ask how it is possible – and the extent to which it is helpful – to use theories in modern times that were created in bygone eras.

NOTES

[1] Some further explanation is needed to understand the situation in the Netherlands regarding the naming of academic disciplines at university. We also have a discipline of educational theory (onderwijskunde), as the science of education and teaching, which can be defined by analogy with pedagogy as explained above.

REFERENCES

Alinsky, S.D. (1971) *Rules for radicals. A pragmatic primer for realistic radicals.* Vintage Books Edition.
Blankertz, H. (1969) *Theorien und Modelle der Didaktik.* München: Juventa Verlag.
Bourdieu, P. (1993) *Kultursociologiska texter.* Stockholm: Brutus Östlings Bokförlag.
Bourdieu, P. (1999) *Praktiskt förnuft. Bidrag till en handlingsteori.*Uddevalla: Daidalos. [Bourdieu, P. (1998). *Practical reason: On the theory of action.* Oxford: Polity].
Broady, D. (1991) *Sociologi och Epistemologi. Om Pierre Bourdieus författarskap och den historiska epistemologin.* Stockholm: HLS Förlag.
Bull, B.L. (1988). The limits of teacher professionalization . AERA paper, 1988, New Orleans.
Carr, W., & Kemmis, S. (2005). Staying citical. *Educational Action Research, 13*(3), 347-358.
Crozier, M., Friedberg, E. (1980). *Actors and systems: The politics of collective action.* Chicago, Ill.: Univ. of Chicago P. Transl. by Arthur Goldhammer.
Fals Borda, O., Anisur Rahman, M. (Eds.). (1991). *Action and knowledge. Breaking the monopoly with participatory action-research.* New York: The Apex Press.
Freire, P. (1973). *Pedagogik för förtryckta.* Falköping: Gummessons. [Freire, P. (1970). Pedagogia do Oprimado].
Gustavsen, B. (2001). Theory and practice: The mediating discourse. In P. Reason & H. Bradbury (Eds.), *Handbook of action research. Participative inquiry & practice.* London: Sage Publication.
Gustavsson, B. (1996). *Bildningn i vår tid. Om bildningens möjligheter och villkor i det moderna samhället.* Stockholm: Wahlström & Widstrand.
Gustavsson, B. (2000). Kunskapsfilosofi: Tre kunskapsformer i historisk belysning. Stockholm: Wahlström & Widstrand.
Habermas, J. (1992/1973). *Legitimation crisis.* Polity press, Blackwell Publishers, Oxford.
http://www.linne2007.se/. (20070813).

Lammers, C.J., Mijs, A.A. & Noort, W.J. *Organisaties vergelijkenderwijs*. (7th edition). Utrecht: Het Spectrum.

Lauvås, P. & Handal, G. (2001). *Handledning och praktisk yrkesteori* (2 ed.). Lund: Studentlitteratur.

Martin, J. R. (1985). *Reclaiming a conversation. The ideal of the educated woman*. New Haven and London: Yale University Press.

Martin, J. R. (1994). *Changing the educational landscape. Philosophy, women and curriculum*. New York, London: Routledge.

Mattsson, M. (1986). *Det goda samhället. Fritidens idéhistoria 1900-1985 i ett dramatiskt perspektiv* Ordfront: RSFH:s förlag, Fritidsforum [Mattsson, M. (1986). *The Good Community, a story of settlements and community work in Sweden*].

Mattsson, M. (1996). *Vinter i folkhemmet. En studie av den svenska modellen på lokalplanet*. Doctoral dissertation, Göteborg University, Department of Social Work [Mattsson, M. (1996). *Hard times - A study of the Swedish Model on a local level*].

Mattsson, M.& Kemmis, S. (2007). Praxis-related research: Serving two masters? In *Pedagogy, Culture & Society*, 15(2), (s.185-214).

Meyer, J. & Scott, W.R. Scott (1992). *Organisational environments. Ritual and rationality*. London: Sage.

Miedema, S. (1997). *Pedagogiek in meervoud*. (5th edition). Houten/Diegem: Bohn Stafleu Van Loghum.

Ponte, P. & Ax, J. (in press). Action research and pedagogy as the science of the child's upbringing. In: Noffke, S & Somekh, B. (Eds.) *Handbook of Educational Action Research*. London: Sage

Ponte, P. (2002). How teachers become action researchers and how teacher educators become their facilitators. *Journal for Educational Action Research, 10* (3), 399-423.

Ponte, P. (2007). Postgraduate education as platform: a conceptualisation. In Van Swet, J.; Ponte, P & Smit. B. *Postgraduate programs as platform: A research-led approach*. (pp 19-39). Rotterdam: Sense Publishers

Ponte, P. (in press) Behind the vision – action research, pedagogy and human development. In Cambell, A. & Groundwater-Smith, S. (Eds.) *Ethical approach to practitioner research: Dealing with issues and dilemmas in action research*. London: Routledge.

Riedel, H. (1977). *Algemeine Didaktik und unterrichtliche Praxis. Eine Einführung*. München: Kösel-Verlag.

Somekh, B. (1994). Inhabiting each other's castles. Towards knowledge and mutual growth through collaboration. *Educational Action Research, 2*(3).

Weber, M. (1946 translation). *From Max Weber: Essays in sociology*, ed Hans H. Gerth and C. Wright Mills. New York: Oxford University Press (first published in 1906-24).

AFFILIATIONS

Jan Ax
Institute of Education
University of Amsterdam, the Netherlands

Matts Mattsson
Stockholm Institute of Education
University of Stockholm, Sweden

Petra Ponte
Graduate School of Education
University of Leiden, the Netherlands

Karin Rönnerman
Department of Education and Humanities
University of Gothenburg, Sweden

STEPHEN KEMMIS AND TRACEY J. SMITH

13. CONCLUSIONS AND CHALLENGES

Enabling Praxis

INTRODUCTION

In the light of discussion in the preceding chapters, we are now in a position to answer the five questions this book set out to address: (1) What is the nature of *praxis*? (2) In what ways can a deeper understanding of *praxis* inform and guide the actions of educators? (3) To what extent do the conditions of educational practice today, especially in institutionalised settings, enable, constrain or disable *praxis*? (4) How best can *praxis* be developed in initial and continuing education? (5) To what extent can *praxis* be safeguarded and preserved?

We will address each of these questions in turn.

1. WHAT IS THE NATURE OF PRAXIS?

In Chapter One, we defined *praxis* as *morally-committed action, oriented and informed by traditions in a field*. Throughout the book, we have tried to maintain a distinction between *praxis* and practice which aligns more or less with the distinction between the *participant perspective* in which a social practice has a powerful and indispensable moral dimension for the person acting, and an *observer perspective* in which the meanings, motives and intentions of actors may not be evident. In this view, *praxis* is social action understood from the *participant perspective*, while *practice* is social action seen from the *observer perspective*. This form of the *praxis*/practice distinction may be rather new to the fields of social and educational theory, but we believe it is also helpful, allowing us to interconnect traditions in practice theory that are usually understood as rather distinct, but all of which understand social practice as historically-, socially- and discursively-constructed (see Chapters Two and Three).

This distinction of *praxis*/practice as social action from the participant (moral) perspective and social action from the observer perspective differs from other accounts. For example, Giddens (1976, p. 75) sees practices as "regularized types of acts" (with which we concur) understood from a third-person, observer perspective, but he also describes *praxis* from an observer perspective ("the involvement of actors with the practical realization of interests including the transformation of nature through human activity", p.53, and as "an ongoing series of 'practical activities'", p.75), rather than (as we have done) from the participant perspective of the person whose action has been thoughtfully considered and warranted. Giddens also links *praxis* to the concept of agency (p.75), however, which suggests that he connects praxis with a participant perspective as well as the observer perspective[1].

By employing the *praxis*/practice, participant/observer distinction in the way we have tried to do in this volume, we have also attempted to connect and interrelate the two perspectives to show (as in the relationship between Chapters Two and Three) that the personal *praxis* of a person committed to acting rightly is not entirely due to the moral intentions, agency and capabilities of that person alone. Rather, their *praxis* is also shaped, formed, enabled, constrained and prefigured (Schatzki, 2002) as practices (what Giddens, for example, calls "regularized types of acts") which we also understand as situated in *and enacted in* collectively-established[2] conventionalised arrangements of *sayings, doings* and *relatings. These arrangements* pre-form and prefigure practices discursively, materially and socially (as we saw in Chapter Three).

We shall proceed by drawing together an account of the nature of *praxis* and practice using the six themes announced in Chapter One, now presented in a different order to make our account of *praxis* more coherent. These themes informed the case studies of *praxis*/practice presented in the second part of this volume, and now permit us to elaborate upon the qualities that embody *praxis* and practice a little further.

1.1 Praxis is doing

Praxis is right conduct – doing the right thing, or the best a person could do under the circumstances. It is the action itself, not the intention or the deliberation about what should be done (*phronēsis*) which may impel action. However, as was highlighted in Chapters Four (Smith) and Seven (Edwards-Groves), the nurturing of a *praxis* stance is crucial for enabling *praxis*. In much of this volume, the *praxis* concerned has been acting *educationally* including the education of pre-service teachers, the continuing professional development of teachers, or the educational work of teacher educators. We have also considered educational administration as a site for administrative *praxis* (Wilkinson, Chapter Nine) and a wider *praxis* of citizenship in collective action against global warming (Adlong, Chapter Eleven). These, we saw, were (and sometimes were not) sites and occasions for morally-committed forms of action, oriented and informed by traditions in the fields of education, professional development, public administration and citizenship.

Praxis is guided by the intention to do what is best in terms of the good for humankind, but there is no guarantee that this intention will be achieved. As Rönnerman reminded us in Chapter Twelve, humankind has multiple faces and identities such as gender, ethnicity, culture and religion. In its broadest sense, 'the good for humankind' can be all-encompassing but we should also be mindful that it can also refer more specifically to establishing a particular relationship between a teacher and a student or an educational administrator and a staff member. Thus, the good for humankind can be general or particular, but we evaluate *praxis* by its consequences, and we learn from experience how to act rightly under the variable and uncertain circumstances under which we find ourselves.

Enabling *praxis* in education, then, requires developing a teacher's or a pre-service teacher's capacities to *act educationally*. That is, it requires developing a practitioner's capacities to act in the interests of the development and self-development of each student, and in the interests of the development and self-development of the society and communities they serve, including the community of the classroom and school, the local community, and the community of practice of their profession. This, in turn, requires being informed about the nature and purpose of education, so that the practitioner of education is able to make wise and prudent decisions 'in the heat of the moment', as the action is unfolding, so that the action is always and in fact oriented towards serving the double purpose of education – the development of each individual and the development of the society and community. To do this requires a larger vision of the nature and purposes of education than the particular instrumental aims of developing students' knowledge and skills; it requires having a sense of the role education plays in the upbringing and formation of students as persons committed to the good, and the role education plays in the formation of a good society. Enabling *praxis* requires *enacting* these purposes, not just espousing them.

1.2 Praxis is action that is consciously moral and just

As we have seen, *praxis* is action that is morally-committed, always oriented towards the good for humankind. While there may be debate about what constitutes 'the good', it is frequently clearer to consider what might cause harm in a situation, and to avoid doing harm. The person wanting to conduct themselves rightly will consider how they might avoid doing harm in this or that particular situation.

Justice is part of what is good for humankind, so *praxis* is concerned with justice. Here, too, it is frequently easier to identify what might be unjust than what is just. The person wanting to conduct themselves rightly will want to avoid acting in ways that are unjust – what Iris Marion Young (1990) regards as the two faces of injustice: "oppression, the institutional constraint on self-development [and self-expression], and domination, the institutional constraint on self-determination" (p.37). For example, as Brennan Kemmis (Chapter Ten) concludes, Vocational Education and Training (VET) teachers are keeping alive the traditions of *praxis* as a moral commitment by maintaining high standards in their trades and in their relationships with those they teach. Similarly, Adlong (Chapter Eleven) demonstrates the commitment to intergenerational justice through education for sustainability initiatives.

Enabling *praxis*, then, requires developing an enduring commitment to acting in ways that avoid doing harm, and that avoid injustice.

1.3 Praxis embodies agency, subjectivity, being, identity and reflexivity

Personal *praxis*, as the action of an individual, presupposes an agent who acts deliberately, in a considered way, and, who could act otherwise. *Praxis* is action by an actor who aims and who acts in ways that avoid doing harm, including injustice, the harms of domination and oppression. It presupposes an actor, a person who acts, a person who inevitably sees the world and others from their own particular perspective, based on their own experience (or inexperience), and who deliberates (for example, taking into account others' perspectives) in order to act wisely and prudently, and to avoid doing harm.

Praxis, from the perspective of the individual who acts, is not just right action according to a set of rules. It is right and considered action by an actor who has made a decision to act in a particular way under the circumstances, even if it challenges the taken for granted traditions in a given field. It requires judgement about the likely consequences of one's action, and whether these are likely to cause harm. It is informed by experience – by learning from the consequences of one's actions (for oneself and for others) in a variety of circumstances. As we saw in Chapter Six, Russell and Grootenboer grappled with many tensions that continually caused them to question their own motives and identities and the taken for granted practices that constitute the practice architecture of their university setting.

Praxis is thus promoted by learning from experience – by reflection on one's experience and its short-term and long-term consequences. As several chapters in this volume have suggested, this self-reflection is learned, and it is not infallible. Self-reflection admits the possibility of self-deception about the character, conduct and consequences of one's actions. Thus, it is vital to notice the message from other chapters that reveal how collective or collaborative reflection by self with others offers additional resources to individual actors – the benefit of other eyes and minds that can help one to see beyond the limits of one's own private experience. Indeed, it has been argued that *praxis* itself is always collective (see for example, Edwards Groves, Chapter Seven and Adlong, Chapter Eleven), presupposing shared frameworks of understanding and interpreting the world, frequently accumulated in traditions that orient and inform what one does, and encapsulating ideas about the meaning and significance of particular practices.

We have argued, therefore, that developing one's capacity for *praxis* – whether the capacities of pre-service teachers or practising teachers or teacher educators or educational administrators – requires the development of a *praxis-stance* (Smith, Chapter Four) or *praxis-orientation* (Edwards-Groves, Chapter Seven). This stance or orientation includes a willingness to understand oneself as acting morally and in relation to traditions of practice, and an awareness that acting in particular ways may have good or ill consequences for others involved in or affected by what one does. At times, we have therefore suggested that our view of *praxis* sees it as an 'elevated' form of action – that is, action taken by an agent who is alert to the character, conduct and consequences of the action and willing to act accordingly. A number of the chapters illustrate how we have hoped to prepare our pre-service teachers to act in this way – to see their actions in terms of moral values and the avoidance of harm, and as concerned with social justice and the avoidance of injustice.

We have also emphasised that a *praxis*-stance – and *praxis* itself – require *moral agency* on the part of the actor. Contrariwise, we have also suggested that the actor cannot reliably act for the good of humankind simply by following rules or by being the '*operative*' of an institution or administrative system. Following rules is *technical* action or *poiēsis*; by itself, it is not *praxis*, though *praxis* may include or even require technical action – as when particular teaching techniques or strategies are adopted and orchestrated within a teacher's *praxis* of educating students. The key distinction that embodies *praxis* is that such techniques or strategies are thoughtfully selected by practitioners who can also give reason or warrant for their choice (see, for example, Russell & Grootenboer, Chapter Six). While we understand that technical action plays a role in *praxis* development, our concern is that the expansion of administrative systems and institutional imperatives, and the proliferation of rules and policies, may constrain action to a point at which the actor's sense of *praxis* is dulled or deadened. If this happens, we believe, the actor may no longer feel obliged to deliberate for themselves (*phronēsis*) on what may or may not cause harm or injustice, but simply act as the rules or the institution require. This is the kind of spectre of the end of *praxis* feared by the early critical theorists of the Frankfurt School, Max Horkheimer and Theodore Adorno (see, for example, Horkheimer, 1972) – a state in which morality itself would be overthrown by technical reason and technical action. It is the spectre feared by Hans-Georg Gadamer (1967, 1980) if human and social sciences follow the technical model of the objectivising physical sciences interested in controlling the world, not informing people's judgment and capacities for interpretation. If part of one's practitioner identity is becoming a *praxis*-oriented self, then practitioners need to have a well-developed and refined sense of moral agency and reflexivity.

Enabling *praxis*, then, requires developing a *praxis*-stance and a capacity to reflect on the character, conduct and consequences of one's actions – and a capacity to transform oneself, one's understandings and interpretations of one's practice, one's actions, and one's situation in the light of experience.

1.4 Praxis embodies connectedness, relatedness, order and arrangements
We have been concerned to show, by the *praxis*/practice distinction and juxtaposition, that *praxis* consists in the conduct of persons, but that persons do not act in circumstances and situations entirely of their own making or choosing, without presuppositions or assumptions that orient them towards action, or without discursive, social and material arrangements that constrain how they will interpret a situation and how they will (be able to) act in it. As Karl Marx (1851-2/1999) famously put it in his *Eighteenth Brumaire of Louis Napoleon*:

> Men make their own history, but they do not make it as they please; they do not make it under self-selected circumstances, but under circumstances existing already, given and transmitted from the past. The tradition of all dead generations weighs like a nightmare on the brains of the living (p.1).

By juxtaposing *praxis* and practice in the formulation *praxis*/practice, we have attempted to remind readers that personal *praxis* – one's own moral conduct – occurs under conditions which always-already contain pre-given circumstances and presuppositions from the 'dead generations' that enable and constrain, and sometimes disable, one's action. One may still conduct oneself as well as possible *under the circumstances*, but sometimes the circumstances may be very constraining, and one may have little freedom to act as one would prefer, to avoid harm and injustice. The formulation *praxis*/practice is intended to convey the idea that *praxis* is situated, it lives in 'the brains of the living', and that more or less established social practices like education or public administration or citizenship have both *individual* and *extra-individual* features.

In Chapter Three, Kemmis and Grootenboer showed how social and educational practices are constituted in related discourses (discursive arrangements, *sayings*), material and economic conditions (material-economic arrangements, *doings*) and social relations between the people involved and affected (social-political arrangements, *relatings*). These, it was argued, are bundled in ways that are or become characteristic of particular kinds and settings of practice, to the point where practices are to a greater or lesser degree *prefigured* – enabled or constrained so that they follow particular 'pathways' of action, so they can unfold in more or less regular, anticipated and conventional ways (which we understand in the sense that we "know how to go on" in them[3]), though also varying (often via *praxis*) to be adapted to local or particular circumstances and situations.

Being discursively-arranged, collectively-established practices like professional practices can be interpreted as meaningful, as doing certain things in the light of certain intentions – shaping what people think and say and mean (*sayings*). Being materially- and economically-arranged, collectively-established practices typically involve acting on particular kinds of objects in particular kinds of ways, using particular kinds of resources (*doings*). Being socially- and politically-arranged, collectively-established practices typically involve particular kinds of people in particular kinds of relationships with one another, with particular kinds of expectations about how they will contribute to the good of the people involved and the good for humankind. In this latter dimension of relating, practices may also involve particular kinds and characteristic constellations of emotions (like care or a sense of achievement), and particular kinds of social solidarities among groups of people involved (for example, among teachers, a shared sense of belonging to the education profession, or between students and teachers, relationships of respect and care).

Taking a cue from the notion of 'learning architectures' introduced by Lave and Wenger (1991), Kemmis and Grootenboer (Chapter Three) described practices in terms of *practice architectures* composed of these bundled arrangements of sayings, doings and relatings characteristic of particular practices in particular settings and situations. The notion of 'learning architectures' draws attention to the ways the learning of newcomers is shaped by the structure of a setting, so they learn how to participate in the setting like old-timers. 'Learning architectures' are structures in the setting seen from the perspective of the newcomer or learner. By contrast, we use the notion of a 'practice architecture' to describe the ways the discursive, social and activity-structures of a setting shape the way all people involved in a practice can participate in it, and we intend the notion to mean that these structures are enduring, more or less reliably shaping how people think and talk, what they do, and how they relate, in ways that are more or less stable over time, though they may be flexibly enacted and they can and do evolve over time. Practice settings like a school classroom or a doctor's surgery, are always-already pre-structured, shaping what people think and say, what they do, and how they relate to one another. In this sense, the settings, as sites for practice, are collectively 'designed' through traditions and expectations, in ways that shape how people will act when they enter and engage in the practice.

We used the notion of practice architectures in the later case chapters in this volume to explore how people's actions were enabled and constrained by these arrangements. Sometimes, we saw, *praxis* was enabled by these architectures, and sometimes, despite other intentions, *praxis* or the development of a *praxis* stance was disabled by the way a practice architecture worked 'in practice'. One example of this disabling was the way an initial teacher education course tried to develop the capacities of student teachers for self-reflection by a variety of self-reflective activities but unintentionally discouraged some students from self-reflection because they became confused or cynical about how they were meant to do it (Edwards-Groves and Gray, Chapter Five). A finding was that practice architectures may, and frequently do, enable action in line with what is intended, but that the discursive, social-political and material-economic conditions created by a particular kind of practice 'design' may produce unanticipated and unwanted consequences. Collective self-reflection may help to identify these kinds of consequences and allow those involved to amend or modify the arrangements in a setting to overcome irrational, unjust or unproductive consequences. By contrast, however, we also saw that apparently unpromising practice architectures like the highly-constrained circumstances under which Australian vocational education and training (VET) teachers must work, with highly detailed and highly regulated curricula and conditions of assessment, nevertheless give VET teachers unexpected freedom for *praxis* – freedom to act in line with the apprenticeship tradition, for example, and in the interests of VET students and the trades and the society they serve (Brennan Kemmis, Chapter Ten).

Enabling *praxis* thus requires understanding that one's actions as the practitioner of a professional practice are framed by practice architectures – like discourses, social relations and working conditions – that enable and constrain the ways one will understand and interpret things, the ways one will relate to others, and the ways one will do things. These discursive, social and material arrangements thus enable and constrain the possibilities for *praxis* in different settings and circumstances. Arguably, these arrangements may even be so tightly-constraining of the practitioner's action that they exclude the possibility of *praxis* – that is, the practitioner can be no more than the operative of the administrative or social system of which they are part – no more than 'a cog in a machine', as the saying goes. As Edwards-Groves showed in the case of the teachers studying their own practice in Chapter Seven, a critical understanding of the way particular discursive, social and material arrangements enable and constrain action will sometimes make it possible for a practitioner to act in ways that challenge or change what is currently possible – and thus create or restore the possibility of *praxis*.

1.5 Praxis is particular, concrete and material
As we have seen, *praxis* is real human conduct aiming to realise the good for those involved and for humankind. It occurs in real situations, especially in uncertain circumstances when one is called upon to deliberate as wisely as one can in order to act appropriately. Because it is real human conduct, *praxis* always occurs under real and existing conditions that are as they are, even if one might wish that they were otherwise.

Praxis is thus always particular. General rules or guidelines may or may not apply at *this* particular moment or in *this* particular place. One may bring familiar ways of understanding things to the situation but, by doing so, *misinterpret* or *misunderstand* what is happening or the people involved. *Praxis* and a *praxis*-stance require both an alertness and a capacity to see things otherwise, as well as to learn from others in the setting.

We have also seen that *praxis*, once done, cannot be undone. The concrete and material consequences of our actions may be other than we hoped or intended. We may be able learn to do things differently to avoid some unwanted consequences – and this constitutes the learning from experience that gives us wisdom and warrant for choosing further action.

Enabling *praxis* requires an understanding that one always acts, for better or for worse, in the here-and-now, in response to particular situations and circumstances, and not always in a uniform manner governed by abstract or universal rules. It requires understanding that one must learn from experience, from the consequences of one's actions, and, by reflecting on the consequences, envisage alternative possibilities for action if one encounters similar circumstances in the future. It also requires, as Joseph Dunne, quoting Hannah Arendt, suggested (see Chapter Two), understanding the need for forgiveness and for promising to do things differently if the need arises. As the next section shows, enabling *praxis* therefore requires understanding that one's actions are always acts of self-formation and transformation – making us who we are – as well as means to immediate external ends.

1.6 Praxis embodies our history, our biography and is always a process of becoming
Praxis is morally-committed action, that draws on theoretical, technical and practical forms of knowledge that constitute the traditions in a field. These traditions represent the collective learning of participants in a practice, especially in collectively-established practices like education, and established professions like the educational profession. For example, there are different traditions of *pedagogy* on which teachers can draw to orient themselves in what they do – like the tradition of progressive education championed by John Dewey at the end of the nineteenth and in the twentieth centuries (see, for example, Dewey, 1897, 1916) or the sociocognitive theory and social learning strategies introduced by Vygotsky (1978).

But human action – human conduct – also makes history. It makes what comes to be. Individual *praxis* and social practice shape what *can* be. In the process, as we argued in Chapter Two, our actions also shape what *we* become and what *we* can be. Our actions shape our biographies. The ancient Greeks said "Call no man good until he dies". In the *Ethics* (2003), Aristotle wrote that "One swallow does not make a summer", meaning that one good act does not make a good person. Learning to adopt a *praxis*-stance, contributors to this volume have argued (Smith, Chapter Four; Edwards-Groves, Chapter Seven), is necessary for teachers if they are to have the capacity to learn from experience and to improve their capacity to make decisions and act on them for the good for humankind. Adopting a *praxis*-stance is to adopt a moral stance and a moral commitment to acting with character, conduct and consequences that avoid harm and injustice. Even though, as we witnessed through the experiences of Russell and Grootenboer in Chapter Six, things may not work out as one hopes in every case, a praxis stance equips one to learn from experience and to do better next time. In Chapter Two, we quoted the ancient Greek poet Agathon, quoted by Aristotle in the *Ethics*, who said

For one thing is denied even to God:
To make what has been done undone again.

Learning to act rightly thus involves learning from experience, and learning to see how one's *praxis* and practice are constructed in sayings, doings and relatings that are drawn from a variety of forms of knowledge and have consequences both *for oneself* and *beyond oneself*, for others and for how things come to be.

Enabling *praxis* thus requires a commitment to one's own self-development, and one's development in connection with others. It involves a commitment not only to good acts but to living a certain kind of life: a life lived in pursuit of the good for humankind.

2. IN WHAT WAYS CAN A DEEPER UNDERSTANDING OF PRAXIS INFORM AND GUIDE THE ACTIONS OF EDUCATORS?

Morally-committed action, oriented and informed by traditions, is nothing very new to most people. Human beings engage in this kind of action as 'right conduct' whether or not they are aware that it can be called *'praxis'* or that it can be connected to a tradition with roots in ancient Greece. As when Aristotle first discussed *praxis*, the significance of the concept of *praxis* lies not so much in what it is but what it is not: its difference from other kinds of action, in particular technical action or *poiēsis*, guided by the disposition of *technē*, and contemplative or theoretical action or *theoria*, guided by the disposition of *epistēmē* (discussed in Chapters Two and Three). In particular, Aristotle threw light on the distinction between actions oriented towards success (*poiēsis*) – achieving a known end using known means – and actions oriented towards 'doing the right thing' (*praxis*) – actions that *are* 'doing the right thing' in a particular situation.

We believe that by clearly understanding what is implied by this distinction, educators and practitioners of other professions can distinguish between actions that are principally concerned with following rules or conventional ways of doing things (*poiēsis*) and actions they take explicitly in order to do what is good or, rather, to avoid doing harm including doing what is unjust because it dominates or oppresses others. At a time in which organisations and institutions are now more rule-bound, and more obliged to operate following specific and detailed policies and procedures, there may be conflicts between following organisational rules, policies and procedures (*poiēsis*) and 'doing the right thing' (*praxis*).

For example, a standardised examination or assessment or requirement may be unjust if it cannot be adapted to meet the needs of a student with special needs or difficulties. If a school system requires that all students take a particular written test for entry to high school, but does not take into account the special needs of a student with learning difficulties, for example, then this might constitute an unreasonable institutional constraint on the student's development and thus count as an injustice. *Praxis* or 'doing the right thing' in such a case might require that a teacher be an advocate for the cause of this student, and ensure that a fair and equitable alternative to the written test is made available for this student.

There are more complex examples, however. A school system might require standardised literacy and numeracy testing of all students at Grades Three, Five, Seven and Nine, with the declared purpose of identifying students who may be experiencing learning difficulties so teachers can give these students additional support. At the same time, however, the results on the tests might also be used by the school system for a very different purpose – to identify teachers and schools performing above and below expectations, and on this basis to allocate proportionally greater funding to schools and teachers performing above expectations. Such a funding procedure has the consequence of denying some support to students in schools or with teachers assessed as performing below expectations – that is, the procedure penalises the students as well as the schools and teachers. This constitutes an injustice if it is an unreasonable institutional constraint on the development of the students in the penalised school, and thus it is a potential harm to students at the school and at any school similarly penalised by the procedure. Doing the right thing in this case, for the teachers in the school, might require challenging and overturning the procedure for allocating funding on the basis of the results of the standardised test.

Doing the right thing in either of these cases requires challenging and overturning, or at least compensating for harm or injustice. It requires not accepting established procedures at face value, even if they are regarded as legitimate by an organisation or institution. Doing the right thing requires confronting irrationality, injustice, or unsustainable institutional practices or arrangements, and arrangements that cause harm or suffering. It might thus bring a professional practitioner into conflict with 'the powers that be', which may be the institution by whom they are employed or a professional body which accredits or reviews their conduct.

A professional practitioner who understands that praxis means 'doing the right thing' also understands that established institutional policies, rules and procedures do not always enable or constrain one to do the right thing. Indeed, some policies, rules and procedures do harm and cause suffering, particularly for some groups of people – employees or students with special needs, for example. Similarly, some policies, rules and procedures are discriminatory on the basis of attributes like gender or ethnicity or age. Professional practitioners who understand that policies, rules or procedures may in fact 'disable' them when it comes to doing the right thing may thus find that they are compromised, and that they must act to overcome what disables right conduct in a situation.

This means that professional practitioners must be more than employees or technicians whose conduct can be entirely governed and directed by institutional rules. Practitioners who understand *praxis* also understand that they must take responsibility for their actions and the consequences of their actions. Such persons must remain alive – and not allow themselves to become deadened or dulled – to questions of their own moral agency and responsibility. Sometimes, therefore, they must act around or against established policies, rules and procedures – even if their action is not to disobey the rules but to work towards changing them.

The professional practitioner who understands *praxis* also understands that their conduct must not be evaluated only in terms of efficacy or efficiency – whether it efficiently achieves given objectives – but also in moral and social terms. The relationship of the practitioner with the client (for example, the relationship of the educator with the student) must also be conducted rightly – as right action. That is, it must not cause harm, including injustice. The practitioner who understands *praxis* also understands that their overarching aim and responsibility is to do what is good for the people involved and good for humankind. Such a person is not solely a technician, good at the art or science or craft of education, but a person who is, in and through their educational action, actually doing good or, more precisely, *not* doing harm.

Most of us know that this is no easy task. As Mattsson rightly points out in Chapter Twelve, sometimes, history tells us that doing the right thing means engaging in some form of conflict or confrontation. We must ask "to what extent do educators enable or empower practitioners to challenge the status quo?" It is not easy to maintain *and live up to* the moral commitment of the *praxis*-stance. In Australia, at least, to say out loud that one aspires to do the right thing or act rightly at all times is to invite a kind of cynical response – it is to risk being seen as moralistic rather than moral (which is precisely beside the point, since being moralistic is to judge other people by one's own moral rules, as a species of technical action or *poiēsis* rather than morally-committed action or *praxis*).

3. TO WHAT EXTENT DO THE CONDITIONS OF PRACTICE ENABLE, CONSTRAIN OR DISABLE PRAXIS?

Our discussion of practice architectures indicates how *praxis* and the possibility of *praxis* is shaped discursively, socially and materially. We have also suggested that the contemporary conditions of schooling can be less than nurturing for education and *praxis*. Increasingly complex and standardised administrative and economic systems regulate and constrain teaching and learning for teachers and students, threatening the integrity of experiencing educational practice as *praxis* – right conduct that avoids doing harm and injustice to those involved in and affected by education. Under such conditions, we have suggested, *praxis* as morally-committed action, oriented and informed by traditions, is threatened.

Judyth Sachs (2003) writes of "the activist professional" in teaching. She envisages a teaching profession in which teachers are actively involved as educators not only with respect to their students, but also in relation to their own learning as professionals and as a profession, and in relation to improving their collective practice in the communities of practice in the settings and situations in which they work. We agree with her view. We believe, moreover, that taking this view of the profession implies five specific challenges for education and for educators: challenges including (1) the re-moralisation of practice, (2) the re-invigoration of professionals, (3) the revitalisation of professional associations, (4) the renewal of educational institutions, and (5) a recovery and revitalisation of educational traditions. These, we believe, are challenges that everyone concerned with education today has a responsibility to confront, though some more than others, and education professionals more than most.

3.1 Re-moralisation of practice
Throughout this volume, contributors have argued that education is *moral action* – and that it requires *praxis*. In our view, education today is more constrained than ever before by regulations and system constraints that aim to make education 'teacher-proof', so desired learning outcomes for students will be brought about by teachers acting in accordance with systemic rules and policies. These rules and policies prescribe state-approved goals for schooling (note that here we distinguish 'education' from 'schooling', meaning by the latter the systematised institutional arrangements governing the actions of teachers and the learning of students). They prescribe approved curricula and syllabi intended to orient learning towards state-approved ends and student learning outcomes. They prescribe approved teaching methods and approaches (sometimes described in contemporary Anglo-American educational literature as 'pedagogy', but using the term in a narrowed sense by comparison with the older European meaning of the term as a field of knowledge and an intellectual discipline concerned with upbringing). They prescribe approved methods of assessment, testing and examination for determining whether approved outcomes have been achieved by students. They prescribe approved methods of monitoring and evaluation for determining whether schooling is being conducted in accordance with rules and policies about approved learning outcomes, teaching methods and methods of assessment.

In the maze of good advice constructed by these prescribed rules and policies for the conduct of schooling, the teacher's possibilities for action are constrained. Decisions about how to act in the interests of these particular students in this particular situation must be taken with an eye to what is prescribed. Arguably, these constraints threaten the possibility of education itself by constraining the professional practitioner to act on what the state regards as necessary for the good of the students and the society. Under such circumstances, from the perspective of the professional educator, we might say, practice is *'de-moralised'*.

Against these standardising tendencies, we believe, more room for discretionary action must be found, to encourage and support teachers in making moral decisions about what they believe will be in the best interests of these particular students and this particular community, *in their professional view* and on the basis of their locally-informed *practical deliberation* about locally-particular needs, circumstances and opportunities. Making this space for professional judgement and practical deliberation would support a *re-moralisation* of practice – encouraging teachers to act, to a greater extent, as educators rather than as operatives of the institutions and systems that regulate their work.

3.2 Re-invigoration of professional practitioners

It is one thing to ask for room for professional practitioners to move within the framework of regulated systems in the interests of the good for persons and the collective good for humankind. As we saw in Chapters Eight (Hardy) and Nine (Wilkinson), however, this requires creating opportunities for practitioners to develop their *praxis*, and opportunities for institutional leaders to model and support *praxis*. In Australia at least, contributors to this volume believe that this requires the development of more extended opportunities for teachers to engage in collective self-reflection and self-development, for example through practitioner research in the form of participatory action research.

Creating room for practitioners to move towards doing what is educationally right for particular students and communities in particular local settings also requires a new investment of trust in teachers to be and to act as what Lawrence Stenhouse (1975), following Eric Hoyle (1974), called 'extended professionals'. It means giving educators not only the intellectual, technical, practical and critical tools to do their work but also the professional autonomy and responsibility to act in the interests of students, their communities and their societies. This investment of trust would constitute a *re-invigoration of professional practitioners* that would recognise that they are professionals dedicated to the interests of their students and society, not just to their own self-interests or the interests of the institutions in which they work.

3.3 Revitalisation of professional associations

The challenge to create a body of professional practitioners committed to education is not just a challenge to produce these practitioners one by one, through initial and continuing professional education. It is also a challenge to produce conditions in the profession in which practitioners can learn from one another, and collectively establish educational, administrative and social practices which will support educational *praxis*. This is a challenge for professional associations in education which have sometimes intended to be supportive of practitioners in this way, but may instead have contributed to the bureaucratisation and standardisation of educational practice, for example by producing curricula or codes of conduct which relieve each educator of the opportunity and the responsibility to act in the interests of each student, their local community, and the society they serve. That is, sometimes professional associations have acted to regulate rather than to inform and orient practice – and to encourage *poiēsis* rather than *praxis*.

Contributors to this volume have argued that enabling *praxis* requires 'finding' (Russell & Grootenboer, Chapter Six) or recovering the moral imperatives of *praxis* from within the day-to-day operations of educational institutions, and then sustaining and supporting *praxis* in the work of education professionals. Professional associations could take a leading role in assisting educational practitioners in this task of recovery and support, helping educators to act not as the instruments of institutions and education systems, but as persons committed to the development and self-development of students and their communities who respond sensitively to local needs, opportunities and circumstances, not just in standardised ways.

We believe that for this to occur professional associations must meet the challenge of *revitalisation* so that they become vital to their members as sources of wisdom about how to act educationally, not solely or principally sources of technical advice and support about what or how to teach in any given field or area.

3.4 Renewal of educational institutions
In modern and post-modern times, educational institutions have increasingly been seen as providers of educational services, and students and their families have increasingly been encouraged to see themselves in the roles of client and customer *vis-à-vis* these institutions. On these views, educational service providers are increasingly seen as providing the means for students to acquire knowledge and skills that will confer employment opportunities and economic benefits. These benefits are among the benefits teaching and learning can confer, but, as we have seen, there are other social, civil and political values that education, properly speaking, can confer. In this volume, Adlong (Chapter Eleven) showed that educational institutions are not alone in conferring these values: community education in the case of some education for sustainability initiatives he discussed also confers these civic values and virtues.

We believe that there is a challenge to *renew the educational purposes and work of educational institutions* today, to ensure that their work expresses and realises the moral and civic virtues indispensable to education as well as the benefits schooling can confer. In Australia, federal and state governments have recently endorsed sets of values that aim to orientate educational institutions towards a values platform. It remains to be seen how such a platform will be enacted.

3.5 Recovery and revitalisation of educational traditions
If *praxis* is to thrive in educational institutions, in professional associations, and in the work of educational practitioners, then we believe that education today faces the challenge of *recovering and revitalising educational traditions*. These are the traditions of thought and theory that inform educational *praxis* not by providing knowledge that can be 'applied' in practice, but in the sense that they give educational practice its meaning and significance. The European traditions of *pedagogy* that continue today, have for centuries provided guidance to practitioners

by orienting them in the work of 'upbringing' of which formal education and schooling are a part. These traditions have increasingly come under challenge in modernity as a particular notion of 'scientific theory' aimed at application in the field of practice came to take hold (see Carr, 2006). This view of theory aims to supply practitioners with valid and reliable knowledge for producing desired effects, like desired learning or behavioural outcomes for students. As our critique of *technē* and *poiēsis* in this volume has shown, however, technical action can be useful in providing guidance for action where the ends and means are known, but they do not help us deal with "uncertain practical questions" (Reid, 1978; see note v, Chapter Two) in which the question is about what one should *do*, and to which an answer is given by *doing* something. What is always uncertain for *praxis* is what one should do *at all* in this situation, under these circumstances (including the action of not taking action in this case). In the case of *poiēsis*, by contrast, what is to be done is already known rather than uncertain, and the only questions that arise are whether it has yet been done, and whether it has been done well or badly. In *praxis*, ends and means are always in question (what and whether to act, and how to act). In *poiēsis*, the end is known and only the means to attain the end are in question (whether to act and what to do are known; only how well it will be done is uncertain). The tradition of pedagogy asks and aims to answer questions about *both* educational ends and means, not just questions about means (as if the ends of education were known and settled).

By contrast with the 'applied science' view of educational theory, the tradition of pedagogy aims to orient a teacher, or a person doing upbringing, towards the work of upbringing as work of a certain kind. It aims to help us understand the meaning and significance of education and upbringing in terms of the good for students and the good for humankind. While pedagogy may provide technical guidance on how to achieve particular kinds of outcomes, it begins from questions about the nature of individuals (the persons being educated or brought up) and how they should be regarded – for example, as persons to be respected, with rights to autonomy and with responsibilities to others. It begins, too, from questions about the nature of knowledge – for example, not solely as information that can be learned, but as grounded in the experience of people and communities of practice. And it begins from questions about the persons who do the educating or upbringing, and about their relationships with those they educate or bring up, and about the values and virtues they should model and express in their pedagogical work.

These traditions risk being eclipsed by the technical thought and action that have become so pervasive in our times. They involve questions of human, social and political values that escape the technical values of efficacy and efficiency. But they remain relevant for education today. For our times and our circumstances, it falls to us, as educators, to provide new ways of understanding and doing education that respond to the ways learners are today, in the culture and society of today, in relation to the kinds of knowledge and information available today, and the historical circumstances of the world today. Education, as we understand it, is a commitment to achieving, by teaching and learning, the good for each individual and for their community and society.

For these reasons, we believe, there is *a challenge to recover and revitalise the educational traditions of pedagogy* in our times, to orient and guide educators in our world and our times by orienting the ways we understand or might understand education, the world, knowledge, our students and our communities and societies. This task of revitalising the tradition of pedagogy falls principally to all educators, but more specifically to teacher educators, educational administrators, policy makers and educational researchers. Without this recovery and revitalisation, the meaning and significance of education itself is under threat. Indeed, we believe, what 'education' means today is, in the minds of many involved in education as well as outside it, decreasingly distinct from what is meant by 'learning' or 'teaching' or 'training' or 'socialisation' or even 'indoctrination'. In our view, if the meaning and significance of education are forgotten, then other precious things are also at risk, not least civility, democracy and the very possibility of a good for humankind.

How this good is achieved changes over time. New answers are always required to the questions: "what should we teach, how should we teach it, how should learning be assessed and how should all these processes be evaluated and changed in the light of their consequences?" Educators and educational administrators, at all levels, must create and defend freedom for *praxis* (as Brennan Kemmis, Chapter Ten, described it). They must create and defend the freedom for practitioners to deliberate as professionals about what to do in particular settings, the freedom to make moral and professional decisions, but always with an expectation that those decisions can be justified by reference to the people involved, the particular circumstances at that moment, and to the traditions that inform *educational* action.

4. HOW BEST CAN PRAXIS BE DEVELOPED IN INITIAL AND CONTINUING EDUCATION?

Although the concept of *praxis* was used by Aristotle in the third century BC (before Christ), we believe that the pattern and fabric of an educator's life in the twenty-first century should also embody *praxis*. Teacher educators must ensure that their work expresses and realises the moral and civic virtues that are indispensable to education. In her recent review of teacher learning that progresses from pre-service preparation through to the induction and professional development of teachers, Feiman-Nemser (2001) identified the "fragmentation" and "conceptual impoverishment" in programs for teacher learning that prevented a coherent continuum of development (p. 1049). We argue that the strategic and explicit development of a *praxis stance* should be a central task of initial and continuing teacher education. While the generation of a *praxis* stance begins in life experiences long before pre-service teachers enter university, the process of explicating, interrogating and cultivating a *praxis* stance for educators should become an essential aspect of pre-service teacher education and continue throughout the continuum of teacher learning. In this way, the continual development and deepening of a *praxis* stance, which is a vital component of enabling *praxis*, can become part of the "connective tissue" (Feiman-Nemser, 2001, p. 1049) that sustains professional learning.

Many of the cases in Section Two of this book adopted a *praxis* lens to interrogate existing practices and/or recent research studies concerned with enhancing professional practice. This process, undertaken from multiple perspectives, revealed insights and implications for the initial and continuing education of teachers and other professionals. One of the underlying themes to emerge from the chapters is that our identity and sense of agency, who we are, how we see ourselves and how others see us, affects the way we live our lives as educators. This is not a trivial insight, nor is it a novel one. Over the years, scholars have recognised the vital role that aspects of *praxis* such as agency, identity, integrity, reflective practice, courage, emotion, morality, beliefs and values play in the living of the life of a teacher (see, for example, Day & Leitch, 2001; Hansen, 2001; Hargreaves, 2001; Palmer, 1998; Richardson, 1996). While many teacher education programs are now recognising, and even privileging, one or some of these aspects, we believe that the concept of *praxis* draws together aspects of becoming and being an educator to form an overarching principle for initial and continuing education: the continual development of *praxis*.

As teacher educators and professional developers, we must consider how we create opportunities for *praxis*, and how we orient pre-service teachers and serving teachers towards learning from their own experience. It is a question to be put to our curricula, our pedagogies, and to our modes and practices of assessment. But there are many other questions. Based on the theoretical chapters and illustrative cases presented in this book, we are in a position to put forward a series of guiding questions that provide a frame of reference for all educators to more critically consider the underlying principles, and the impact, of the practice architectures that frame their programs.

By suggesting that we foreground the practice architecture that frames a particular teacher education program, we are asking: to what extent do these kinds of *sayings, doings* and *relatings* (the conditions) enable or constrain teacher learning in general and praxis development in particular? For example:

- What language and theoretical orientations do we choose to frame teacher learning and why are they privileged above others?
- Whose voices are being sought and listened to?
- What values and virtues do we express and model in our actions as educators?
- What objects and resources are privileged and why is this so?
- How and why are the program resources/readings/theoretical orientations selected?
- In what ways do programs explicitly discuss the nature and purpose of education from multiple perspectives?
- To what extent do programs provide opportunities for building and extending the capacity of practitioners to:

- interpret situations and make justified professional judgements;
- establish responsive and responsible relationships;
- exercise professional autonomy and responsibility;
- continue to reflect critically and collaboratively on lived experience in order to learn from it; and
- establish and foster meaningful relationships and expectations that develop a sense of belonging as they seek to live a certain kind of life?

Enabling *praxis in and through* education and teacher education requires creating conditions for people to *live* educationally, not by applying rules but by *being* 'philosophical' about what they are doing. Our teacher educational curricula may provide theoretical resources for such a way of living, but more is required. Our courses must also provide opportunities for pre-service teachers or teachers participating in continuing professional development activities to *act* and to *reflect* on their action, to *learn from experience* and *to live a certain kind of life as a professional practitioner* – a life that embodies praxis.

5. TO WHAT EXTENT CAN PRAXIS BE SAFEGUARDED AND PRESERVED?

In his (1995) book *Philosophy as a Way of Life*, the French historian of Hellenistic and Roman philosophy Pierre Hadot suggested that the aim of the philosopher was to live properly and well. Philosophers seek wisdom (etymologically, *philo-sophia* is the love of wisdom) so that they can live a 'philosophical' life. Hadot (1995) refers to the ancient distinction between three parts of philosophy – dialectic or logic, physics, and ethics. In considering how *praxis* can be safeguarded and preserved, however, we must give up a certain way of thinking about the so-called 'gap' between theory and practice. In ancient times, philosophical or theoretical discourse, *in itself* or *for its own sake*, was not the point. What *was* and we suggest still is the point is *how we live* – living 'philosophically'. As Hadot says, "…philosophy itself – that is, the philosophical way of life – is no longer a theory divided into these parts, but a unitary act, which consists in *living* logic, physics, and ethics. In this case, we no longer study logical theory – that is, the theory of speaking and thinking well – we simply think and speak well. We no longer engage in theory about the physical world, but we contemplate the cosmos. We no longer theorize about moral action, but we act in a correct and just way (pp.267; emphasis in original).

We see in these ideas something this volume has been striving towards. Guided by Hadot, 'enabling praxis' means not theorising about saying (logic), doing (physics) and relating (ethics), but actually saying, doing and relating in ways that are wise and prudent, and informed by theoretical knowledge made available in traditions of thought and traditions of living – a way of life. As Hadot suggests, the 'philosophical' life is not just a matter of theory; it is a matter of practice. We think it is the same for educators – a matter of *living* a 'logic' in particular ways of thinking and speaking, *living* a 'physics' in particular kinds of action in the world, and *living* an 'ethics' in particular ways of relating to others. It is this unitary practice or *praxis* to which our pedagogical efforts are – or should be – directed as educators and teacher educators.

By way of summary, we offer a characterisation of a teacher named Beth to underscore the inherent themes presented in this chapter. This illustrative portrayal describes the conditions under which praxis can be enabled and embodied – the living of 'a certain kind of life' – a life where praxis has been foregrounded in initial teacher education, and safeguarded, preserved and sometimes constrained in continuing professional education.

Embodying praxis: a characterisation

It is nearing the end of the school year. We enter a classroom that is alive. Immediately we notice that the students are actively engaged in work that requires them to interpret and analyse authentic inquiry-based tasks, to make decisions, and produce new texts that demonstrate understanding. The students are so engaged, they do not even acknowledge that we have entered their learning space – they are now used to visitors who come and go to assist, observe or participate in their activities. It is a natural aspect of their learning community where collaborative work is commonplace.

Beth, their teacher, is not where convention would put her – at the front of the class. Long ago, Beth had learned to let go of many traditional roles such as teaching from the front because traditions like this no longer resonate with her beliefs about effective pedagogy and her sense of *praxis* that had been developing since her pre-service days. But becoming a *praxis*-oriented teacher had not been an easy process.

When Beth arrived at university, she held many personal beliefs about teaching that had been influenced by thirteen years of experience and observation as a student in school classrooms. Her years at university had presented Beth with many experiences that shook her established beliefs. Never before had she considered the question 'in whose interests' when thinking about education and its impact on students. During her professional school-based experiences (practicums), she put new ideas about pedagogy into practice with varying degrees of success. She experienced many contradictions while learning to teach that included a misalignment between university and school-based ideals and practices, contradictory beliefs, a lack of support from teachers in schools who were meant to support her, and established classroom norms that produced barriers when she attempted to implement innovative ideas and practices.

What made the difference for Beth in her initial teacher education were the repeated opportunities to: interrogate her lived experiences, collectively reflect on and critique her experiences, and develop personal theories with her peers and receive support to learn from her experiences so that she could reframe her personal stance. In addition, her initial teacher education program had continually provided opportunities for her to make professional judgements and later collectively share and justify those judgements with her peers and teacher educators. In fact, almost all of her assessment items required Beth to undertake this process to some extent.

Now a teacher with seven years of experience in the classroom, Beth can appreciate how her teacher education program prepared her for being an autonomous and responsible professional who needs constantly to be aware of the character and consequences of her actions. While she often felt frustrated that she was not simply given 'the correct answers', by now Beth has come to understand that her university experience nurtured a sense of open-mindedness and responsibility. Adopting this personal stance has given her a sense of being empowered to deliberate and to act as a professional educator, and an enduring commitment to acting in a reasoned way. It is now second nature for Beth to think about whether or not her actions are justified and morally defensible - they avoid harm and injustice. These are values that she now tries to instil in her students and the community of learners that she strives to create and of which she aims to be an active member.

Beth's first school had been in an area where a majority of students came from low socio-economic status families. As a beginning teacher, she had been part of a community of teachers who participated in continuing professional conversations about their practice. The teachers supported each other to remain attuned to the needs of their students, especially on days when the conditions in the school proved challenging. Justice, equity and values were part of their everyday discourse. The principal encouraged all staff to attend professional learning seminars run by teachers and outside providers. In addition, the principal gained funding for a whole-school action research project that focused on equity, technology and critical literacies.

Since arriving in her new school, however, Beth has had to contend with a number of conflicts and confrontations. Her current school does not seem to encourage or implement innovative practices. There are few regular opportunities to meet other teachers to discuss ideas. Since the beginning of the year, some staff have been overtly cynical about Beth's practices and beliefs although others have shown a silent but publically unsupportive respect for what she is trying to achieve. Two teachers that Beth admires because of their obvious rapport with students and their professional commitment towards learning have briefly talked to her about her approach and encouraged her to "keep trying".

There are a number of routine, school-wide practices in place that are contrary to what Beth believes about effective pedagogy and to her sense of *praxis*. The students in her own classroom initially confronted Beth with negative attitudes as she slowly tried to implement practices with which the students were unfamiliar. Her students had developed a set of shared understandings about what learning should be like: teacher-directed lessons and 'teaching from the front', for example. They were operating on the basis of a rather different understanding of what constituted learning than the one Beth held. Her students seemed resistant to, or at the very least inexperienced with, learning collaboratively through inquiry-based tasks of the kind Beth had developed, and been successful with, over the years.

Clearly, there is a disparity between Beth's perception of what constitutes the 'good' for all students, and the sayings, doings and relatings that not only constitute the practice architecture in her new school but also affect the learning culture and expectations of the students in her class.

When faced with adversity or a challenge like the one Beth confronts, human beings are pressed to act. Rarely can they choose not to act or to ignore the position in which they find themselves. If we had entered Beth's classroom at the beginning of the year, we would have witnessed a very different classroom – a classroom in which there was a contest over the way things would or could be done. One of the first things Beth did was to negotiate a new 'didactic contract' (Brousseau, 1986 cited in Clarke, 1997) that clearly articulated a shared set of understandings and obligations about what constitutes learning and success. What we are observing now, by contrast, is a classroom alive with energy, enthusiasm and active learning. It is a community of practice which these students have joined, moving from the "legitimate peripheral participation" (Lave and Wenger, 1991) of the newcomer to the confident participation of the "old timer".

What can safeguard and preserve the *praxis* of teachers like Beth and other educators? In Beth's teacher preparation program, and in her first years of teaching, she experienced freedom to develop *praxis*. Space was made for her to undertake practical deliberation and make professional judgements in all facets of her learning – including judgements that were not always as wise as they might have been, she readily acknowledges. Learning from experience, and by making mistakes through her beginning years as a classroom teacher, Beth developed a sense of professional autonomy and responsibility to act in the interests of students, their communities and their societies. She now understands that the educators she encountered at university and the principal in her first school had invested trust in her ability which, in turn, invigorated her sense of identity as a professional practitioner.

When Beth found herself faced with contradictions and confrontations in her current school, it took resilience, a consistent will and a determined commitment on her part to live the 'certain kind of life' of an educator and not give in to the dominant culture of the school. Now, with her circle of friends in her current school, she is being re-invigorated not only in her continuing development as a teacher, but also in terms of collective and collaborative leadership. There were a number of ways she sought revitalisation.

She was proactive in seeking support by making connections both outside and inside the school. The professional association for teachers that she was a member of had an excellent website that connected her to other teachers and allowed her to both access and share resources. Professional associations become vital to teachers like Beth not only as sources of support and wisdom about how to act educationally but also to affirm and deepen their praxis stance.

Beth was also proactive in making contact with her local university to inquire about academic partners who might be interested in collaborative research. She encouraged the two teachers she respected to join her, and they were pleased to do so. She was proactive, too, in monitoring the policy initiatives of government education authorities, and always tried to find ways she could incorporate emerging ideas into the practices she was developing – though sometimes in ways that changed aspects of what the state might have expected. Beth was 'living philosophically'.

Our aim in closing this chapter with a characterisation of educational *praxis* was to highlight the salient ideas that we believe contribute to answering the questions we asked in Chapter One and to illustrate how a teacher might be 'living philosophically'. One crucial assumption underpins this illustrative case – that an educator, at all levels of education, has developed a *praxis* stance – an explicit understanding of where one stands in terms of one's willingness and commitment to act morally, to do no harm and to avoid injustice. In short, what safeguards and preserves education is *doing* education and not just schooling. What safeguards and preserves *praxis* is *living* it, not just alone but in solidarity with others. Not just in discrete acts or decisions but in collective consciousness that acts make histories.

NOTES

[1] By contrast, Louis Althusser, the French Marxist scholar, defined practice from a stark and uncompromising observer perspective:

By *practice* in general I shall mean any process of *transformation* of determinate given raw material into a determinate *product*, a transformation effected by a determinate human labour, using determinate means (of 'production'). In any practice thus conceived, the *determinant* moment (or element) is neither the raw material nor the product, but the practice in the narrow sense: the moment of the *labour of transformation* itself, which sets to work, in a specific structure, men [sic], means and a technical method of utilizing the means. This general definition of practice covers the possibility of particularity: there are different practices which are really distinct, even though they belong organically to the same complex totality. Thus, 'social practice', the complex unity of the practices existing in a determinate society, contains a large number of distinct practices. This complex unity of 'social practice' is structured ..., in such a way that in the last resort the determinant practice in it is the practice of transformation of a given nature (raw material) into useful *products* by the activity of living men working through the *methodically organized* employment of determinate *means of production* within the framework of determinate relations of production (1963, ¶22).

[2] In noting that practices are 'collectively established', we are consciously pointing towards Alasdair MacIntyre's (1983, p.175) complex but comprehensive definition of practices:

By a 'practice' I ... mean any coherent and complex form of socially established cooperative human activity through which goods internal to that form of activity are realised in the course of trying to achieve those standards of excellence which are appropriate to, and partially definitive of, that form of activity, with the result that human powers to achieve excellence, and conceptions of the ends and goods involved, are systematically extended.

[3] See Shotter, 1997, on Wittgenstein's 1953 notion of "knowing how to go on" as the criterion of understanding. In Wittgenstein's and Shotter's views, the criterion of understanding is not having 'matching' ideas, but being able to respond appropriately to take the next steps in the action of continuing a conversation, or playing a game, or continuing the stream of activities that make up a project or task.

REFERENCES

Althusser, L. (1965). On the materialist dialectic, in Louis Althusser, For Marx. Retrieved from Louis Althusser Archive: http://www.marxists.org/reference/archive/althusser/1963/unevenness.htm, August 3, 2007.

Aristotle (2003). *Ethics*, trans. [1953] J.A.K. Thompson, revised with notes and appendices [1976] Hugh Tredennick, with an introduction [1976, 2003] Jonathon Barnes, and preface [2003] A.C. Grayling. London: The Folio Society.

Carr, W. (2006). Education without theory. *British Journal of Educational Studies*, *54* (2), 136-159.

Clarke, D. (1997). *Constructive assessment in mathematics: Practical steps for classroom teachers*. Berkeley, CA: Key Curriculum Press.

Day, C. & Leitch, R. (2001). Teachers' and teacher educators' lives: The role of emotion. *Teaching and Teacher Education*, *17*(4), 403-415.

Dewey, J. (1897). *My pedagogic creed*. Initially published as a pamphlet and reprinted in 1929 by The Progressive Education Association. Washington, D.C.

Dewey, J. (1916). *Democracy and education*. New York: Macmillan.

Dunne, J. (1993). *Back to the rough ground: 'Phronēsis' and 'technē' in modern philosophy and Aristotle*. Notre Dame, IND: University of Notre Dame Press.

Feiman-Nemser, S. (2001). From preparation to practice: Designing a continuum to strengthen and sustain teaching. *Teachers College Record*, *103*(6), 1013-1055

Gadamer, H.G. (1967). Theory, technology, practice: The task of the science of man, *Social Research*, *44*, .529-561.

Gadamer, H.G. (1980). Practical philosophy as a model for the human sciences, *Research in Phenomenology*, *9*, 74-85.

Giddens, A. (1976). *New rules of sociological method*. London: Hutchinson.

Hadot, P. (1995). *Philosophy as a way of life*, ed. and intro. Arnold I. Davidson, trans. Michael Chase. Oxford: Blackwell.

Hansen, D. T. (2001). Teaching as a moral activity. In V. Richardson (Ed.), *Handbook of research on teaching* (pp. 826-857). Washington D.C: American Educational Research Association.

Hargreaves, A. (2001). Emotional geographies of teaching. *Teachers College Record*, *103*(6), 1056-1080.

Horkheimer, M. (1972). Traditional and critical theory, in Max Horkheimer *Critical Theory*. New York: The Seabury Press.

Hoyle, E. (1974) Educational innovation and the role of the teacher. *New Forum*, *14*, 42-44.

Lave, J. and Wenger, E. (1991). *Situated learning: Legitimate peripheral participation*. Cambridge: Cambridge University Press.

MacIntyre, A. (1983). *After virtue*, 2nd edition. London: Duckworth.

Marx, K. (1999). *The eighteenth brumaire of Louis Napoleon*, trans. Saul K. Padover. Marx/ Engels Internet Archive. http://www.marxists.org/archive/marx/works/1852/18th-brumaire/ch01.htm Retrieved July 28, 2007.

Palmer, P. J. (1998). *The courage to teach: Exploring the inner landscape of a teacher's life*. San Francisco, CA: Jossey Bass.

Richardson, V. (1996). The role of attitudes and beliefs in learning to teach. In J. Sikula, T. J. Buttery, & E. Guyton (Eds.), *Handbook of research on teacher education* (pp. 102-119). New York: Association of Teacher Educators.

Sachs, J. (2003). *The activist teaching profession*. Buckingham: Open University press.

Schatzki, T. (2002). *The site of the social: A philosophical account of the constitution of social life and change*. University Park, Pennsylvania: University of Pennsylvania Press.

Shotter, J. (1997). Wittgenstein in practice: From 'the way of theory' to 'a social poetics'. In C.W. Tolman, F. Cherry, R. van Hezewijk, and I. Lubek (Eds.) *Problems of theoretical psychology*. York, Ontario: Captus Press, 1997.

Stenhouse, L. (1975). *Introduction to curriculum research and development*. London: Heinemann Education.

Wittgenstein, L. (1953). *Philosophical investigations*, trans. G E M Anscombe. Oxford: Blackwell.

Vygotsky, L. (1978). *Mind and society*. Cambridge, MA: Harvard University Press.

AFFILIATIONS

Stephen Kemmis
School of Education
Charles Sturt University, Wagga Wagga, Australia

Tracey J. Smith
School of Education
Charles Sturt University, Wagga Wagga, Australia

STEPHEN KEMMIS

14. EPILOGUE

A radical proposal

In this volume, contributors have enunciated a view of *praxis* as right conduct, situated in practices and practice architectures. They have enunciated a view of *educational praxis* as that kind of *praxis* that aims at the development and self-development of each individual as a person through teaching and learning, and at the development and self-development of the communities and societies in which they live. The process of education, which is realised through *educational praxis*, aims to achieve the good for each person and the good for humankind. Contributors to this volume envisage forms of education that do not merely help teachers and students to understand or to discourse about the good, but to actually *do* what is good. We envisage forms of education that enable teachers and students to live a good life, not just prepare them for it. As suggested in Chapter Thirteen, like the ancient philosophers studied by Pierre Hadot (1995), we envisage forms of education that enable people to think and speak well, to act constructively and well, and to relate to others well, in ways that avoid doing harm or contributing to injustice.

To adopt such a view of education, *in practice*, might, if taken seriously, require some radical changes in education and teacher education, not to mention educational administration and policy making, and even the ways educational institutions are constructed and funded. This Chapter suggests some of the ways in which education might need to be done differently if it is to be *education for praxis* – education for living rightly, and education that contributes to the good for humankind.

TEACHERS

Teachers doing *educational praxis* are committed to developing students' knowledge, capacities and values about living well. Educational *praxis* is not just a matter of providing them with knowledge about living well, or giving them opportunities to write or speak about living well, but a matter of actually enabling them to live well. This means helping students to think and speak well inside and outside the classroom (or wherever the learning takes place), to act well inside and outside the classroom, and to relate to others well inside and outside the classroom. Such an education is not just a *preparation* for living well *at some time in the*

Kemmis, Stephen and Smith, Tracey J. (2008) Enabling praxis: Challenges for education.287-295

future, but a matter of *enabling students to live well now* by helping them in their development as persons and as members of their communities and society

Teachers living this kind of *educational praxis*, moreover, are committed to demonstrating and modelling how to live well – by thinking and speaking well, by acting constructively and well, and by relating to others well in terms of recognising and respecting others and by ensuring that they do not cause harm or maintain social practices or structures that bring about the injustices of oppression or domination (Young, 1990). In matters of truth, they aim more to be reasoned than to be right. In matters of acting in and on the world, they aim more for sustainability than for satisfaction. In matters of living in society, they aim more to be with and among people, and to care for people, than to be above or against people or to beat them in any game.

Teachers adopting this view of *educational praxis* see it as their primary task not just to 'teach' what living well *means*, but to create conditions under which their students can *develop* 'right' ways of living in the here and now, in the classroom and beyond it. Their work is the work of *enabling their students' praxis* in right living inside and outside the classroom – ways of thinking and speaking and listening (and reading and writing) well, ways of acting constructively and well, and ways of relating well to others. Such teachers' work is not just a matter of theoretical or philosophical discourse, though this discourse has a place in developing the capacity to act and live well, it is also and more importantly a matter of acting and living well in the classroom and in lives lived beyond the classroom (or wherever learning takes place). This is Pierre Hadot's (1995) distinction, noted in Chapter Thirteen, between *theoretical* or *philosophical discourse* and *living 'philosophically'*. Living 'philosophically' is living rightly as this is understood by a person who aims, by their personal conduct and as a member of a community of people similarly committed to doing what is good for each and the good of all. Teachers adopting this view of *educational praxis* develop the *praxis* of their students, not just their students' capacities to *discourse about* what is right. They develop a *praxis stance* in their students not just as a preparedness or readiness for *praxis*, but as a basis for their students to *live* and practise *praxis* in the situations in which they find themselves in the world here and now, inside and outside the classroom.

STUDENTS

Of course education – an education – is a developmental process. *Enabling praxis* and *developing a praxis stance* are steps towards *praxis* for students. For the teacher, educational action must always *be praxis* – all of the teacher's actions that are directed towards constituting an education for each student and all students must be *praxis*. At any moment, *enabling praxis* for students, does not mean that all of their actions must be *praxis* immediately, but their actions should be oriented towards *praxis*. Students have to learn, by experience and from their own experience, what *praxis* requires in any situation. They must learn that what *praxis* requires will be different in different situations. It is not always easy or self-evident what it means to think and speak well, to act constructively and well, or to relate to others well. Learning these things requires life experience: it requires learning that rules of thumb can guide one towards right conduct, but that right conduct can be difficult to achieve in difficult circumstances, where it is uncertain what it is right to think or say, what it is right to do, or how one should relate rightly to others. *Enabling praxis* requires *helping students to reflect on the conduct, character and consequences of their thinking, their actions, and their ways of relating to others.* Enabling *praxis* requires teaching students to be 'philosophical' about what they think and say, what they do, and how they relate to others.

Enabling praxis will mean one thing with very young children, something else with children in the middle years of childhood, something else again in late childhood and early adulthood, and yet something else in the case of adult learners. Capacities for thought, action and relationships develop and change through these stages, building on what has gone before. But the teacher who aims not only to *prepare students for praxis* but to *enable praxis in the here and now* must create opportunities for students to *act* and to *search for and find what is right* – good for themselves and their own development, good for their families and communities, and good for humankind. This in turn requires learning and developing knowledge and understandings, skills and capacities, and ways of relating to others that *aim* to be constructive and rewarding, on the one hand, but also *in fact* avoid causing destruction, suffering, harm or injustice. It requires creating circumstances where students can learn, *from their own and from others' experience*, what is *unsustainable* in thought and speech, what is *unsustainable* in action in the material world, and what is *unsustainable* in relationships with others. Throughout a life, people who want to gain wisdom learn these things, from their own and others' experience, in different ways, and in consequence of different life circumstances. It is the educator's task to find ways to make it possible for people at different ages and stages to learn these things by examining their own experience.

The educator must therefore develop *learning architectures* and *practice architectures* (see Chapter Three) that *enable praxis* by creating opportunities for students to learn from experience – their own and others'.

SUBJECT MATTER

Established conventions of schools and schooling, established conventions of curricula and syllabi, established conventions of teaching and learning in educational institutions, established conventions of assessment and examinations, and established conventions of administering and evaluating teaching and learning are conventions that are today as much or more steered by notions of efficiency (and cost-efficiency) as they are steered by their efficacy, particularly if, by 'efficacy' we mean achieving *educational outcomes* rather than just *learning outcomes*. Educational outcomes are by their nature uncertain, diverse and varied, grounded in the different life experiences of individual people and the different stories and histories of families, groups, communities and societies. Except in the most general sense of the good for each person and the good for humankind, there are no firm and fixed educational outcomes. What an *educated person* will do in any situation will depend on their capacities to respond to circumstances, their capacities to act wisely and prudently. The educated person doesn't always 'get it right', but does act rightly more often than not.

By contrast, there are altogether too many *learning outcomes* towards which schools and other educational institutions orient their work. Given long, crammed lists of things that states want students to learn, teachers risk being transformed into technicians whose task it is to charm or challenge students to attain. Taken one by one, the topics and objectives in these lists of learning outcomes might be appropriate and wise. It is not certain, however, that teaching these topics and pursuing these objectives will *enable praxis* in students, if teachers' work is driven principally by the obligation (to educational authorities) to have students learn just what is on these lists. On the contrary, too close an adherence to what is on the lists may take teachers' attention away from the learners in front of them and fix it instead on the administrators and managers 'behind' them. It risks distracting teachers from the circumstances, crises, capacities, opportunities and interests of *these* particular learners and *this* community, and instead fix their attention on the requirements of an educational bureaucracy and an educational system which is, in the end, indifferent to the *particular* needs, interests and circumstances of these students and their community. For such reasons, teachers may feel torn between obligations and duties to an employer and to the students and community (or trade or profession) they also serve.

What teachers experience in such cases is the tension between schooling and education, and it translates into the tension between acting as an operative of the system and acting as a moral agent, the tension between *poiēsis* and *praxis*.

The task of the educator is always to construct conditions under which people can learn. It is not people in general who are to be taught, however. It is particular people in this classroom or this on-line forum or the particular readers of this textbook. The more the teaching addresses an abstracted and general population – like all the fourth-graders in a state – the less it will recognise the particular needs, interests and circumstances of particular students or learners. Not people in general but these particular people and the particular communities in which they live are the addressees of the educator's educational *praxis*. The educator acts *with* and *for* these others, not *on* or *over* them. They are not 'raw material' to be moulded into pre-given shapes and lives, but co-participants in a shared social life, in which we have shared fates. The educator always encounters them as persons worthy of the recognition and respect due to the Other. They are the other 'half' of – and partners in – the dialogue or conversation the educator enters with them. They and their communities are the others with whom the educator shares time, space and the resources of the planet. And, yes, I do include here that irritating boy in the back row, that girl silently texting on the mobile phone, that one staring out the window with something else on their mind, the bully, the one who makes outrageous racial slurs against those refugee students, and those refugee students themselves, who have brought such different life experiences into this shared learning space.

There is not just harmony in the world; there are also conflicts of point of view, of values, of culture. There is not just agreement and mutual understanding; there are also disagreements. People are not always in intersubjective agreement, nor is intersubjective agreement always easily reached; people interpret themselves, their lives and their communities differently. There is not always consensus about what should be done – and there are always conflicting self-interests that provoke the enduring question "whose interests does this serve?" These conflicts, misunderstandings, diverse viewpoints, misinterpretations, disagreements and conflicting interests are precisely the states of affairs that call forth *praxis* and *educational praxis* from the educator, rather than *poiēsis*. These are the very states of affairs that call for education (and for educators). They are the states of affairs that call for something more than the kinds of teaching or training or learning or socialisation that bind people to blind rules, taken-for-granted norms, and established conventions. Precisely because they are uncertain practical problems, the educator responds to such states of affairs not by following dogmas, rules or doctrines, but as a person with the unique task of the educator: the task of exploring, interpreting and conversing about differences and difficulties so that people can learn things *for themselves*, so that they too can *be* reasonable. So they can live *philosophically* by themselves and for others: so they can think and speak well, so they can act constructively and well, and so they can relate well to others, against suffering, harm and injustices of domination and oppression.

Acting philosophically is a hard task for a teacher, let alone for a student in many overcrowded and under-resourced school classrooms, in the face of crammed curricula and state or national testing and examination schemes that press students and their teachers toward standardised outcomes using standardised, state-endorsed teaching and learning strategies. Yet, despite the difficulties, there is something profoundly liberating in the knowledge that this is in fact the educator's task – to join with others in the task of *living philosophically*, to introduce their students to what it means to live philosophically, and to enable them to live philosophically here and now, where the learning is taking place, as well as beyond the learning setting. There is something liberating for the educator – and increasingly for the student, too – in the knowledge that *this* is the overarching task and that this task stands above the achievement of this or that particular learning outcome chosen from among all the *educationally-possible* learning outcomes that teachers might strive towards and that students might seek to attain. What is liberating is that an educator with the commitment to living philosophically in dialogue and conversation with others knows that there is a profound purpose to education that puts the immediacy of curricula, assessments, the management of classrooms and educational institutions *into perspective*. This knowledge permits educators to have priorities, and to see journeys of life and sustainable futures beyond the immediate tasks imposed by curricula and assessments and the expectations of education authorities.

If *life* and living philosophically is what education aims at, then the learning architectures that enable teachers and students to live well *in* education need to find room for life – time and space for learning that engages life rather than 'deferring' it (imagining that it will only be much later in life that students will use or apply their learning). Learning architectures for living philosophically need to give students the chance to encounter and engage life, and where possible enable *praxis* in response to the problems and issues life throws up for us. Educators interested in creating such learning architectures might thus be thinking about how to design kinds of encounters with life that offer students opportunities to engage constructively with worthwhile life problems.

I will offer no recipes for the design and enactment of such opportunities – they are the things educators need to design and enact for themselves, in relation to the needs and interests of their students, the needs and interests of their communities, and the educational opportunities that history and the world around us offer up to us as requiring our response. These architectures are things educators must design as vehicles to demonstrate *praxis* – their own *praxis* and, increasingly, the *praxis* of their students. Such architectures will call forth *praxis* from students if they pose uncertain practical problems for them, problems that require them to *do* something in response. The best kinds of problems are ones that require students to do something significant – morally, practically, socially or environmentally – not just problems whose answer is to do what one is told to do. Powerful learning architectures are theatres for *praxis*.

Learning architectures that enable students to encounter and engage significant issues and concerns, and respond to irrationality, unproductiveness, suffering and injustice can be constructed from what is to hand. The formal curriculum might contain useful information, helpful topics, helpful exercises or good advice about how to assess what has been learned. It is not necessary to throw them away; indeed, the formal curriculum offers students important knowledge, skills and values that make it possible to engage with significant issues (like the ability to read, or analyse texts, or calculate statistics, or use scientific instruments, to give some obvious examples). The educator who aims to enable students to live philosophically seeks opportunities for students to encounter and engage life and the world. I would imagine that a teacher who wanted to be this kind of educator would seek opportunities for her students to encounter the world by being outdoors and engaging with problems like the unsustainable use of resources. I would imagine that a *praxis-oriented teacher* would want to find opportunities for students to debate issues of current concern in the community or world politics. I would imagine that such teachers, as educators, would want to find opportunities for students to make a difference in the world by such means as helping to plant indigenous vegetation to restore a degraded landscape in the community in the interests of maintaining biodiversity; helping out at a home for senior citizens to ease loneliness or suffering; helping to secure supplies of clean potable water for a village (locally or somewhere else in the world) to improve health in the village; by reducing waste of resources and energy to improve the sustainability of the earth's resources and to make a contribution to intergenerational justice; by imagining and developing innovative solutions to technical and material problems to improve the quality of goods and services for people and communities; by finding enterprising ways to contribute to local lives and economies though participating in community and economic development in ways that will help communities to survive and thrive.

The progressivism of the early twentieth century (see, for example, Dewey, 1916) and the 'New Basics' and 'productive pedagogies' movements in Australia in the early twenty-first century (see, for example, State of Queensland, 2004) are among the many educational traditions that encourage such activities, aiming to secure active student engagement in learning, worthwhile learning, intellectual quality and recognition of cultural and social differences. Similarly, there are initiatives in 'place-based' education and in education for sustainability that aim to help students understand the relationship between the local and the global, the relationship between the personal and the political, and the place of each individual in the cosmos and the living world. These traditions offer resources for the design of learning architectures that enable students to enter the life of communities that aim to 'live philosophically'.

MILIEUX: A RADICAL PROPOSAL

These are not Utopian aspirations. We live in particular, local milieux in a world in which the structures and contents of scientific and other discourses, social structures and practices, and material and economic arrangements are bedevilled by irrationality, injustice, harm and suffering, and unproductive and unsustainable arrangements. Global warming is just one example of the consequences of the structures and practices that have shaped how people have lived in the last two hundred years or so. The practice architectures in and through which we live our lives are discursively-, socially- and materially-economically-shaped in ways that may lead us into unsustainable ways of being. To live otherwise, we must avoid or eliminate, as far as possible, character, conduct or consequences that are untoward, distorted, destructive or unsustainable because they are

- irrational (discursively unsustainable),

- unjust (causing or supporting domination or oppression), alienating or excluding (morally- and socially-unsustainable),

- unproductive (materially-economically unsustainable), or

- the unjustifiable causes of suffering or dissatisfaction for particular persons or groups.

These different faces of unsustainability are 'built into' some of the practice architectures that shape our lives, enabling and constraining our possibilities for *praxis*. The structures and practices of schooling, for example, sometimes include ways of thinking and saying that are irrational, ways of doing that are unproductive or harmful, or ways of relating that cause or maintain suffering, exclusion or injustice. The student who suffers bullying in a school, the student whose life experience is not recognised by a sexist curriculum, the student who is indoctrinated into irrational beliefs, the student whose life opportunities are

293

diminished by forms of teaching that serve the interests of particular groups at the expense of others' interests – all endure consequences wrought by practice architectures that are flawed and in need of reconstruction. This task of reconstruction is part of the task of the educator as a *professional* educator (as a member of what Judyth Sachs (2003) calls "the activist teaching profession"), through her or his lived *educational praxis*. The educator cannot be a 'social engineer' or a 'do-gooder' or someone who hopes to cure social ills through indoctrination or forced socialisation of students. The educator refuses these labels and methods. The educator instead works *educationally* by 'living philosophically' – engaging students in rational, reasoned discussion that provides justifications for knowledge, engaging students in forms of action that are constructive and avoid harm or waste, and relating to students – and having them relate to one another – in ways that avoid suffering and the harms of exclusion or injustice. By so doing, the educator 'lives a certain kind of life' – a life that is in a way distinct from other forms of life. It is distinguished by its commitment to the development and self-development of each individual and the development and self-development of the communities and societies in which they live and work.

By thus standing apart, by living philosophically, the educator aims to help others do what he himself or she herself models: self-reflection as a basis for learning from experience, adopting a *praxis stance*, learning to be open-eyed and open-minded, leaning to respond more wisely and prudently to people and circumstances, learning to correct one's ways of doing things in the light of their observed consequences, and learning to observe and reflect in order to *discover* what the consequences are. By modelling these virtues, the educator aims to develop *students'* capacities to live philosophically, to develop a *praxis* stance that will give them a way of living in the world, and acting against irrationality, harm, waste, suffering and injustice.

The educator lives in this way as the ancient philosophers did, and for the same reason: to model a way of being and living that is rationally, socially and materially sustainable and thus to bring into the world a way of living that might also inform the life of polities, communities, states and nations. It is to do one's best to *live* a sustainable life in the conviction that, by doing so, she or he also engages with others in ways that foster sustainable ways of being in the communities and societies in which one lives. To live this way is to make what is today a radical choice: the choice to refuse irrationality, harm, suffering, exclusion and injustice even though these flaws have been woven by people and by history into the fabric of the lives we lead in the cultural-discursive, social-political and material-economic structures and practices that shape our contemporary world.

It might not be apparent to the person who begins a course in teacher education that the choice to be a teacher might include the choice to live 'a certain kind of life' – the philosophical life. The contributors to this volume believe that the choice to be a teacher *is* a moral choice – if that teacher aims to be an educator rather than a technician. We believe that the choice to be an educator involves making a commitment to *educational praxis*. Teacher education and the continuing professional development of teachers, therefore, involves developing a *praxis stance* in pre-service teachers, and reinvigorating the moral and educational commitments of serving teachers. On this view, the central task of the educator and the teacher educator, not only in and for students in the classroom but also for people and citizens in the world at large, is *enabling praxis*. At its core, this is our radical proposal.

REFERENCES

Dewey, J. (1916). *Democracy and education*. New York: Macmillan.
Hadot, P. (1995). *Philosophy as a way of life*, ed. and intro. Arnold I. Davidson, trans. Michael Chase. Oxford: Blackwell.
Sachs, J. (2003). *The activist teaching profession*. Maidenhead, BK: Open University Press.
State of Queensland (Department of Education and the Arts) (2004). *The New Basics Research Report*. Brisbane, Queensland: Department of Education and the Arts. Available (in seven parts) via http://education.qld.gov.au/corporate/newbasics/html/research/research.html; retrieved August 28, 2007.
Young, I.M. (1990). *Justice and the politics of difference*. Princeton, NJ: Princeton University Press.

AFFILIATIONS

Stephen Kemmis
School of Education
Charles Sturt University, Wagga Wagga, Australia

CONTRIBUTORS

Stephen Kemmis
Stephen Kemmis is Professor of Education in the School of Education, Charles Sturt University, Wagga Wagga. He has written extensively on critical participatory action research and the nature and study of practice. Among his publications are *Becoming Critical: Education, Knowledge and Action Research* (with Wilfred Carr; Falmer, London, 1986) and the chapter "Participatory Action Research: Communicative action and the public sphere" (with Robin McTaggart; in Norman Denzin and Yvonna Lincoln, eds., *The Sage Handbook of Qualitative Research*, 3rd edn., Thousand Oaks, California, 2005).

Jan Ax
Jan Ax is lecturer in educational studies at the University of Amsterdam in the Netherlands. He published and did research in educational policy and school organisation, especially in the domain of secondary education and senior vocational education. His teaching subjects are instruction and curriculum, educational research methods, educational policy and school organisation.

Matts Mattsson
Matts Mattsson has a Ph D in Social Work and lectures in Special Pedagogy at the Stockholm Institute of Education, Sweden. His doctoral thesis was part of an action-research project carried out in a local community in the northern part of Sweden: *Hard times - A study of the Swedish Model on a local level* (1996). Other books deal with Community Work, Research and Development, and Special Education. The latest publication is Mattsson & Kemmis (2007), 'Praxis-related research: Serving two masters?' In *Pedagogy, Culture & Society*, 15:2.

Petra Ponte
Petra Ponte was awarded an MA with distinction in Special Education in 1984 from Amsterdam University (The Netherlands), with educational innovation and educational psychology as subsidiary subjects. She has published in the fields of special education, pupil guidance in schools for primary and secondary education, and – more recently – cross-cultural collaboration, teachers' professionalism and action research by teachers. She combined her research post at ICLON, Leiden University (Graduate School of Teaching) with a Professorship at Fontys University of Applied Sciences. She is an active participant in international networks and was recently visiting scholar at the University of Sydney and visiting professor at Charles Sturt University, both in Australia.

Karin Rönnerman
Karin Rönnerman is Associate Professor at the Department of Education, Göteborg University, Sweden. Her research interest is within the field of school development and teacher professional development. She has written books and articles about action research carried out in collaboration between groups of teachers and researchers.

Tracey J. Smith
Tracey Smith spent many years as a classroom teacher before becoming a lecturer at Charles Sturt University, Wagga Wagga in 1999. Recently she completed her PhD that explored the use of narrative practices in a pre-service teacher education program. Professionally, her interests lie in researching teacher education practices and teacher learning and the relationship between teaching, learning and assessment in primary mathematics classrooms. Tracey has written journal articles and book chapters related to classroom-based assessment practices, the teacher-as-researcher in a mathematics classroom and enhancing students' numeracy development.

Christine Edwards-Groves
Christine Edwards-Groves (PhD) is a lecturer (literacy) in the School of Education at Charles Sturt University, Wagga Wagga. Christine's main research interest is in the field of explicit teaching, professional development and classroom interaction. She has published a variety of texts, including *On Task: Focused Literacy Learning* (2003), *Connecting Students to Learning through Explicit Teaching* (2001) and *Building an Inclusive Classroom through Explicit Pedagogy* (2003).

Deana Gray
Deana Gray teaches at the Lutheran Primary School, Wagga Wagga, NSW, Australia, where she is also the school's Literacy Coordinator. She has been a primary school teacher for a number of years, including several years in a special support setting for children with autism. While this book was in the initial stages of writing, she was a Lecturer in the School of Education, Charles Sturt University, Wagga Wagga campus. During this period, she completed her Bachelor of Education (Honours) degree, researching student teachers' responses to self-reflection activities distributed through the School of Education's Bachelor of Education (Primary) course. She continues her own self-reflective practice as a classroom teacher researching her own teaching.

Peter Grootenboer
Peter Grootenboer is a senior lecturer in Mathematics Education at Charles Sturt University. Before moving into the tertiary sector he spent twelve years as a classroom teacher in Australia and New Zealand. Peter's research interests are largely in the effective dimension of learning, particularly in mathematics education. His research experience is diverse, having published in mathematics education, educational leadership and teacher education.

Helen Russell
Helen Russell is a lecturer of Information Technology in the School of Education, Charles Sturt University, Wagga Wagga. Prior to tertiary teaching, Helen spent many years as a classroom teacher in various primary and secondary schools. She completed a PhD in 2005 in which she investigated the lived experiences of laterlife computer learners. Helen has since published a number of papers relating to the ontological and existential benefits of laterlife learning. Other research projects have focused on the learning experiences of teachers and students as beginning users of information and communication technologies.

Ian Hardy
Ian Hardy is lecturer in Education at the School of Education, Charles Sturt University, Wagga Wagga campus. His research interests are in the areas of educational policy, teacher professional development and educational reform. Recent publications have focused on the context of teachers' professional development in Australia, with an emphasis upon the state of Queensland, and academics' perceptions of the value of tertiary teaching qualifications in an Australian university.

Jane Wilkinson
Jane Wilkinson spent a number of years as a classroom teacher, consultant and Deputy Principal before becoming a lecturer at Charles Sturt University in 2002. Recently she has completed her PhD exploring how dominant media representations of ethnically and socioeconomically diverse women leaders were taken up, challenged and/or interrogated by a group of senior women academics in Australian universities. Professionally, Jane's interests include educational leadership, issues of social justice and equity in schooling and the intersection of the media upon education as a field. Jane has written a number of articles on women's leadership in the fields of education and agriculture.

Roslin Brennan Kemmis
Ros Brennan Kemmis is a senior lecturer in Vocational Education and Training at CSU. She has a career in education that crosses over into the early childhood, primary and secondary sectors. Her research interests lie in online delivery, Indigenous staff and student participation in VET and the area of VET pedagogy. She has written a variety of articles and research reports based on these interests. She is a member of the Research in Vocational Education and Training (RIVET) Community of Scholars. She also has responsibility for a variety of subjects within the VET teacher preparation courses at CSU and is particularly interested in the intersection between VET sector qualifications and compliance arrangements and the ethos and traditions of University study.

William Adlong
William Adlong has completed a Masters in Social Ecology and is currently conducting an action research PhD project emphasising informal and collaborative

learning in building a response to climate change. He has worked for years with academics in researching their teaching, and with colleagues he has been exploring a collaborative reflection academic staff development model, as reported in some conference papers. This has led to his receiving a citation for outstanding contributions to student learning from the national Carrick Institute for Learning and Teaching in Higher Education. William is chair of the Environmental Management Advisory Committee on the Wagga campus of Charles Sturt University and he has also taken active roles in local civic and environmental groups.

INDEX

A

action research, 6, 11, 25, 31, 66, 67, 71,
77, 78, 82, 83, 91, 106, 127, 131, 132,
144, 146, 159, 166, 219, 235, 238,
239, 251, 252, 253, 259, 260, 261,
275, 282, 297, 298, 299
actions
irreversibility, 21, 47, 58
agency, 5, 7, 11, 12, 38, 51, 75, 173, 185,
187, 188, 189, 190, 209, 232, 236,
250, 251, 264, 265, 266, 273, 279
apprenticeships, 197, 205
Aristotle, ix, 9, 15, 16, 17, 18, 19, 21, 22,
33, 34, 35, 37, 38, 39, 40, 61, 78, 227,
228, 234, 237, 246, 249, 250, 253,
254, 255, 257, 260, 271, 278, 285

B

Beck, Ulrich, 219, 230, 232, 233, 234,
236, 237, 238
Bildung, 259

C

capital, 167, 172, 175, 177, 179, 181,
182, 183, 184, 185, 187, 190, 197,
254
Carr, Wilfred, 80, 81, 82, 210, 215, 219,
226, 229, 235, 237, 238, 259, 260,
277, 285, 297
climate change, 12, 217, 218, 219, 220,
221, 222, 223, 224, 225, 226, 230,
231, 237, 239, 300
collaborative reflection, 90, 266, 300
communicative action, 57, 61, 101, 217,
229, 230, 232, 233, 236, 238, 252
communicative space, 12, 90, 100, 105,
135, 217, 234, 235, 236
communities of practice, 30, 54, 55, 57,
85, 274, 277

conflict, 41, 48, 51, 203, 252, 253, 254,
272, 273
connectedness, 7, 8, 80, 91, 105, 152,
267

D

Dewey, John, 30, 79, 80, 82, 83, 85, 88,
106, 250, 270, 285, 293, 295
discourse, 23, 34, 41, 44, 50, 65, 78, 82,
87, 101, 102, 103, 128, 129, 130, 138,
145, 146, 147, 157, 176, 185, 186,
202, 211, 231, 236, 238, 260, 280,
282, 287, 288
Discourse, 147, 192
dispositions
critical, vii, 5, 8, 10, 21, 22, 23, 26,
28, 30, 31, 34, 39, 40, 41, 43, 45,
46, 47, 59, 60, 61, 65, 66, 69, 72,
74, 78, 81, 82, 83, 86, 88, 89, 90,
91, 92, 94, 95, 96, 100, 101, 102,
103, 105, 127, 128, 129, 133, 142,
144, 145, 146, 158, 162, 169, 174,
176, 182, 184, 185, 187, 188, 190,
191, 207, 209, 210, 212, 218, 219,
220, 229, 235, 238, 239, 249, 252,
255, 259, 267, 269, 275, 282, 285,
297
shaping of, 40
Dunne, Joseph, 5, 6, 10, 13, 20, 26, 27,
32, 33, 34, 230, 270, 285

E

economic rationality, 236
education for sustainability, 219, 220,
240, 265, 276, 293
educational practice, 3, 5, 6, 28, 58, 60,
94, 105, 139, 235, 243, 244, 254, 263,
268, 273, 275, 276

Q

Lightning Source UK Ltd.
Milton Keynes UK
UKOW031829211111

182440UK00005B/73/A